Lukas Junker

Equity Carveouts, Agency Costs, and Firm Value

GABLER EDITION WISSENSCHAFT

Entrepreneurship

Herausgegeben von
Professor Dr. Malte Brettel, RWTH Aachen,
Professor Dr. Lambert T. Koch, Universität Wuppertal,
Professor Dr. Tobias Kollmann, Universität Kiel,
Professor Dr. Peter Witt, Wissenschaftliche Hochschule für Unternehmensführung (WHU), Vallendar

„Entrepreneurship" ist ein noch relativ junger Forschungszweig, der jedoch in Wissenschaft und Praxis stetig an Bedeutung gewinnt. Denn Unternehmensgründungen und deren Promotoren nehmen für die wirtschaftliche Entwicklung einen zentralen Stellenwert ein, so dass es nur folgerichtig ist, dem auch in Forschung und Lehre Rechnung zu tragen.

Die Schriftenreihe bietet ein Forum für wissenschaftliche Beiträge zur Entrepreneurship-Thematik. Ziel ist der Transfer von aktuellen Forschungsergebnissen und deren Diskussion aus der Wissenschaft in die Unternehmenspraxis.

Lukas Junker

Equity Carveouts, Agency Costs, and Firm Value

With a foreword by Prof. Dr. Malte Brettel

Deutscher Universitäts-Verlag

Bibliografische Information Der Deutschen Bibliothek
Die Deutsche Bibliothek verzeichnet diese Publikation in der Deutschen Nationalbibliografie; detaillierte bibliografische Daten sind im Internet über <http://dnb.ddb.de> abrufbar.

Dissertation Rheinisch-Westfälische Technische Hochschule Aachen, 2005

1. Auflage September 2005

Lektorat: Brigitte Siegel / Nicole Schweitzer

Der Deutsche Universitäts-Verlag ist ein Unternehmen von Springer Science+Business Media.
www.duv.de

Umschlaggestaltung: Regine Zimmer, Dipl.-Designerin, Frankfurt/Main

Gedruckt auf säurefreiem und chlorfrei gebleichtem Papier

ISBN-13:978-3-8350-0092-6 e-ISBN-13:978-3-322-82117-1
DOI: 10.1007/978-3-322-82117-1

Foreword

Equity carveouts (ECOs) as an instrument of financing and reorganization have increased in popularity: In 1999/2000, more than 40% of German IPO volume is accounted for by equity carveouts. Prominent examples are the carveout of Infineon (Siemens) and of T-Online (Deutsche Telekom). However, activity has decreased since the boom year 2000, and in 2002 and 2003 not a single ECO has taken place. In 2004, the planned ECO of Hapag-Lloyd was cancelled, and Deutsche Telekom even bought back T-Online. Thus, in practice there is no clear verdict on ECOs as instruments of financing and reorganization. The academic literature has been occupied with the subject for 15 to 20 years, but with heterogeneous results: Some contributions lack stringent theoretical foundations, coupled with effective empirical analysis, others limit their scope to the short-term effect of ECOs. Consequently, the overall effect of ECOs on firm valuation still remains unclear.

The present thesis by Lukas Junker attempts to answer exactly this question. It analyzes the effects of ECOs on firm valuation (holding company as well as subsidiary). Thus, the thesis closes an important gap in current research – after the waning of IPO activity since 2001, a complete assessment of the activity until 2000 also from a long-term perspective is now possible for the first time – which is of great practical interest due to the significant share of ECOs in IPO activity, as well as of great theoretical interest due to the dual role of ECOs as instrument of both financing and reorganization.

With his thesis, Lukas Junker makes an exceptionally valuable research contribution. It treats a current and practically relevant subject at the right time. Not only is it based on a stringent and even innovative theoretical foundation, but also on unique empirical analysis. Thus, the present thesis clearly exceeds what is commonly asked from a doctoral dissertation: It not only makes a novel theoretical contribution, by creating a consistent reference framework, but it also links it to an exceptional empirical analysis, which is thoroughly discussed and compared and contrasted with existing research.

The present thesis draws its special value for the reader from the author's ability to work both theoretically and to illustrate the theory practically. Researchers can profit from the most complete work on ECOs yet published based on a Germans sample. Practitioners can draw concrete implications from the well-explained and well-founded results. And student could not find a better overview of equity carveouts.

I wish that this thesis wins the broad readership that it deserves.

Professor Dr. Malte Brettel

Acknowledgements

This dissertation would not have been possible without the help of many people, to whom I wish to extend my gratitude.

First, I am greatly indebted to Professor Dr. Malte Brettel, my thesis advisor. He has helped form my thinking in fundamental ways, and I would have not have completed this dissertation without his help and ideas. I also owe much gratitude to Professor Dr. Rüdiger von Nitzsch, my second thesis advisor, for helpful comments that have substantially improved the dissertation.

I would like to thank McKinsey & Company, Inc. for financial support during my leave of absence.

I would like to thank fellow doctoral students for stimulating discussions, especially Daniel Zipser and Jan Henrik Soll. Earlier drafts of this dissertation were presented at the FGF/KfW seminar in Frankfurt and at RWTH Aachen. The feedback from participants at these events has been very helpful.

Finally, but very importantly, I would like to thank my parents for endowing me with the requisite education to successfully complete such an endeavour, and for always supporting me in everything I did. I would like to thank my partner Susanne Weber for providing me with the love and care that made this year a pleasant experience.

Lukas Junker

Content Overview

Table of Contents

List of Tables

List of Figures

List of Abbreviations

AIC	Akaike information criterion
AktG	Aktiengesetz
APT	Arbitrage pricing theory
AR	Abnormal return
ARCH	Autoregressive conditional heteroskedasticity
BHAR	Buy-and-hold abnormal return
BIC	Schwarz (Bayesian) information criterion
BörsG	Börsengesetz
BörsO	Börsenordnung
Capex	Capital expenditures
CAPM	Capital asset pricing model
CAR	Cumulative abnormal return
CEO	Chief executive officer
CGPE	Cumulative GARCH prediction error
CSPE	Cumulative standardized prediction error
CTAR	Calendar-time abnormal return
CUSUM	Cumulative sum of squares
EBITDA	Earnings before interest, taxes, depreciation, and amortization
ECO	Equity carve-out
EGLS	Estimated generalized least squares
EREIT	Equity Real Estate Investment Trust
GARCH	Generalized autoregressive conditional heteroskedasticity
GLS	Generalized least squares
GMM	Generalized Method of Moments

GPE	GARCH prediction error
HGB	Handelsgesetzbuch
IBES	Institutional broker estimate system
IPO	Initial public offering
JGLS	Joint generalized least squares
KonTraG	Gesetz zur Kontrolle und Transparenz im Unternehmensbereich
LM	Lagrange multiplier
LR	Likelihood ratio
M&A	Mergers&acquisitions
MTB	Market-to-book ratio
MV	Market value
NPV	Net present value
n.s.	Not significant
OLS	Ordinary least squares
ROA	Return on assets
SEO	Seasoned equity offering
SPE	Standardized prediction error
Sub	Subsidiary
SUR	Seemingly unrelated regression
TransPubG	Gesetz zur weiteren Reform des Aktien- und Bilanzrechts, zu Transparenz und Publizität
WLS	Weighted least squares
WpHG	Gesetz über den Wertpapierhandel

1 Introduction

1.1 Problem statement

Equity carve-outs (ECOs), the initial public offering of shares in a subsidiary of a group of companies, are an instrument of financing and reorganization that has continually gained in importance in Germany until 2000 (Kaserer/Ahlers (2000)). During 1999/2000, ECOs represented 40% of IPO volume on German capital markets, including such prominent examples as Infineon/Siemens, or T-Online/Deutsche Telekom. Recently, however, public opinion on ECOs has cooled: Parallel to the decline of the German IPO market, no ECOs have taken place in 2002 and 2003. The planned reacquisition of T-Online by Deutsche Telekom, the cancellation of the planned ECO of Hapag-Lloyd by TUI, and the persistent difficulties in the Postbank ECO by Deutsche Post have sparked a further re-evaluation of ECOs and related financial transactions.

In the academic literature, research on ECOs is connected to the broader discussion on the benefits and costs of diversification. For a long time, focused business strategies were deemed superior in the U.S. academic literature, and strongly advocated in prominent articles oriented towards practitioners (e.g. Prahalad/Hamel (1990)), based on empirical evidence of a conglomerate discount (e.g. Berger/Ofek (1995)). Recently, however, a re-evaluation has set in, triggered in part by new empirical evidence negating the existence of a diversification discount (e.g. Campa/Kedia (2002), Villalonga (2004)), and theoretical models coming to a more balanced evaluation of the costs and benefits of internal capital markets (e.g. Stein (1997), Stein (2002)). In the context of the New Institutional Economics movement, this debate falls into the general discussion of the relative benefits of markets and hierarchies. The study of groups of companies (Konzerne) as hybrid forms of organization, namely as hierarchies incorporating internal markets, has recently garnered lively interest (e.g. Bolton/Scharfstein (1998)). Within this field, ECOs can be interpreted as an instrument to introduce further market elements into hierarchies. More specifically, the strengthening of external capital market control leads to a reconfiguration of incentives within the group of companies involved. Consequently, ECOs can be assumed to affect agency costs and thus firm value. However, due to the dual character of ECOs, encompassing both financing and reorganization aspects, and in view of the current controversial discussion of the benefits and drawbacks of internal capital markets, the direction of this effect is not a priori clear.

Against the backdrop of the dual re-evaluation in both public opinion and academia, the present study analyzes the short-term and long-term capital market reaction to ECOs on the German capital market, based on a sample of 55 observations from the 1984-2003 period. An ample literature on ECOs has developed since the first U.S. study (Schipper/Smith (1986)), and the first German study (Pellens (1993)), concentrating mostly on the short-term capital market reaction in an event study setting. However, while the literature has borrowed from various theoretical frameworks, such as signaling (e.g. Slovin/Sushka/Ferraro (1997)), and most importantly agency theory (e.g. Allen/McConnell (1998)), hypothesis development has remained somewhat ad hoc. Also, recent innovations in empirical methodology have not been consistently applied, creating doubts on the robustness of the results to methodological alternatives. Indications on the long-term effects of ECOs on firm value exist (Vijh (1999), Brettel/Junker/Pinker (2004)), but results are inconsistent. The overall effect of ECOs on firm value thus remains unclear.

In order to respond to these gaps, hypothesis development in the present study is guided by principal-agent theory as unifying framework. Since the seminal study by Jensen/Meckling (1976), agency theory has gained a status as near orthodoxy in corporate finance, notwithstanding the recent gain in influence of behavioral approaches (e.g. Barberis/Thaler (2003) for a review)). The conflict of interest between shareholders (principal) and management (agent) is interpreted as the core problem of corporate governance (e.g. Shleifer/Vishny (1997)). In numerous empirical papers, the efficiency of alternative organizational forms and financing arrangements is evaluated by analyzing their effect on agency costs (e.g. Amihud/Lev (1981) on diversifying mergers for an early example). In the present study, the effects of ECOs on firm value are thus couched in terms of their impact on agency costs.

In order to assess the short-term capital market reaction to ECOs, more recent empirical methods incorporating cross-sectional dependence and time-varying volatility are used.

ECOs from the 1998-2000 peak years are included in the long-term analysis for the first time, so that a more complete assessment of the long-term effects of ECOs can be achieved. On this basis, the present study attempts more definite answers on the relationship between ECOs and firm value.

In the remainder of this introduction, a definition of ECOs is provided, and the special interest in ECOs is explained more thoroughly. Then, the literature on ECOs is reviewed in more detail, and the gaps in existing research briefly touched upon above are explained.

The objective of the present study is presented in more detail, limitations are discussed, and the approach is outlined.

1.2 Definitions

1.2.1 Group of Companies

As has been briefly discussed in the problem statement, ECOs are subsidiary IPOs. In order for a legal entity to be classified as a subsidiary under German corporate law (§290 HGB), it must form a part of a group of companies (Konzern) under common control (§18 AktG). The present study will thus be extensively concerned with the analysis of groups of companies.[1]

Before offering a detailed definition of an ECO, it is therefore be expedient to touch on the subject of groups of companies (Konzern). Thanks to the availability of thorough reviews of the German law on groups of companies, its economic implications (Pellens (1994), Schenk (1997a), Rau-Bredow (1999)) and its specific implications for ECOs in prior dissertations (Nick (1994), Hennigs (1995)), this section is relatively brief.

The salient characteristics of German groups of companies have been studied from three main perspectives: legal, accounting, and economic.[2]

From a *legal* perspective (e.g. Emmerich/Habersack (2003), a standard textbook for legal scholars), a group of companies as defined in German corporation law emerges from the management of a controlling and one or more dependent companies under common leadership (§18 AktG). Dependent companies are defined as separate legal entities on which another company (controlling company) can exert (directly or indirectly) a controlling influence (§17 I AktG). A controlling influence is assumed if a company is majority-owned by another company (§17 II AktG). On this basis, two fundamentally different forms of groups of companies need to be distinguished: the contractual group of companies (Vertragskonzern, based on a control contract in the sense of §§291ff. AktG), and

[1] The importance of groups of companies as economic phenomenon is underlined by the study of Görling (1993), who found that nearly three quarters of all German corporations were part of groups of companies in 1992, while among listed German corporations even more than 95% were part of groups of companies. Görling's results are broadly confirmed by Pellens (1994) and Mellewigt (1995). A comprehensive German textbook on groups of companies is Theisen (2000); of further interest is Albach (2001a); a literature survey is provided in Mellewigt/Matiaske (2000)

the factual group of companies (faktischer Konzern, not based on a control contract, but where a common leadership supported by a controlling influence is in place, §§311ff. AktG).

From an *accounting* perspective a group of companies is interpreted as a structure that has to submit consolidated financial statements (Konzernabschluss).[3] The German-GAAP rules (§290 I HGB) make reference to the legal definition of groups of companies from corporate law (§18 AktG). Under IAS (rule 27.12), a group of companies is defined differently based on the control concept. The existence of a group of companies, which leads to the requirement to report consolidated IAS statements, is assumed if one company can exert control over another company. Control is assumed either in the case of majority ownership, or if other factors, such as e.g. board majority, suggest a controlling influence (e.g. Busse von Colbe et al. (2003)).

From an *economic* perspective, a group of companies is commonly defined as a collection of separate legal entities which form a durable single economic unit (Schenk (1997a), Mellewigt/Matiaske (2000)).[4] In contrast to a single company, the constituent entities act as (potentially) independent parties on the relevant product and factor markets. Elements of market coordination are thus integrated into groups companies. Consequently, groups of companies can be interpreted as a hybrid form between the polar extremes of market and hierarchy (e.g., Nick (1994), Theisen (2000)).

The somewhat preliminary nature of above definition is explained by the relative neglect of groups of companies in economic research (e.g. Rau-Bredow (1999), Mellewigt/Matiaske (2000)), and the corresponding pre-eminence of legal and accounting approaches.

Notwithstanding its relative imprecision, for the purposes of the present study, the economic perspective is clearly the most relevant. For the analysis of ECOs, it is only of secondary importance if the group of companies in question is a contractual or a factual group of companies; or which accounting treatment is applied to the subsidiary in the consolidated financial statements.

---

[2] A fourth perspective, which is disregarded here, is the tax perspective, e.g. consolidated tax filing status (Organschaft)

[3] Standard accounting textbooks (Konzernrechnungslegung) are Schildbach (2001), Baetge/Kirsch/Thiele (2002), Busse von Colbe et al. (2003)

[4] The terms collection of separate legal entities ("rechtliche Vielfalt") and single economic unit ("wirtschaftliche Einheit") were coined by Pohmer (1964)

In the present study, the general definition of groups of companies is further narrowed down in order to include only such groups of companies where the controlling company is an exchange-listed corporation. This requirement is not justified guided by theoretical considerations, but constitutes a prerequisite for the empirical part of the study, which makes use of capital market data.

Based on the economic perspective, the concepts of separate legal entities and single economic unit is operationalized in the following simplified way, leading to the subsequent working definition of group of companies that is used throughout the present study:

> A group of companies is defined as a collection of at least two separate legal entities that form a single economic unit in the sense that one entity (the parent) holds a majority stake in the other entity (the subsidiary), where the parent is an exchange-listed corporation

1.2.2 ECO

The key characteristics of an ECO are well described in the definition provided by Copeland/Weston (1992), p. 679:

> "An equity carve-out involves the sale of a portion of the firm via an equity offering to outsiders. In other words, new shares of equity are sold to outsiders, which give them the ownership of a portion of the previously existing firm. A new legal entity is created. The equity holders in the new entity need not be the same as the equity holders in the original seller. "

An alternative, but qualitatively similar, definition is provided by Schipper/Smith (1986), p. 154:

> "An equity carve-out is the initial public offering of some of the stock of a wholly-owned subsidiary. A subsidiary offering resembles a primary offering of seasoned stock or convertible debt claims on an entire firm's assets in that cash is received from the public sale of securities."

In order to reach a more precise understanding, the different elements of the definitions of Copeland/Weston (1992) and Schipper/Smith (1986) are analyzed in more detail in the following and modifications made to the definitions are discussed:

- *"A new legal entity is created"*: As a prerequisite for an ECO, the respective corporate segment to be sold must be a separate legal entity in the form of a corporation (Aktiengesellschaft). If the segment has not been a legal entity before, a new legal entity has to be created first. Parent and subsidiary form a group of companies.

- *"a wholly owned subsidiary"*: The entity in question must be wholly owned by the parent. For the purposes of the present study and in accordance with the definition of groups of companies defined above, this condition is relaxed. The subsidiary in question must be controlled by the parent.[5] Commonly, control is understood as majority ownership (e.g. Kaserer/Ahlers (2000)). Thus, the sale of a minority stake by financial investors does not qualify as an ECO.

- *"the sale of a portion of the firm"*: In a typical ECO, the parent retains a controlling stake post-transaction (e.g. Schipper/Smith (1986), Pellens (1993), Slovin/Sushka/Ferraro (1995), Vijh (1999)). Consequently, the subsidiary typically remains part of the group of companies in the sense of §18 AktG after the transaction. However, a divestment of the entire ownership interest qualifies as an ECO as well.

- *"via an equity offering to outsiders"/ "initial public offering of stock"*: A public sale of securities implies the listing on a stock exchange. Legally, initial listings on German stock exchanges are primarily regulated in §§36-49 BörsG and §§49-58 BörsO (Hennigs (1995)). In order to qualify for an exchange listing, the respective corporation must fulfill certain admission criteria that differ by market segment.[6]

  In the present study, equity offerings are more broadly defined to include also offerings of shares to outsiders where outsiders have already owned a limited fraction of shares prior to the transaction. In accordance with Kaserer/Ahlers (2000), the maximum threshold for prior outside ownership (free-float) is set at 4%.

Based on the above discussion, the following working definition is adopted throughout the present study:

> An ECO involves the sale of equity in a subsidiary by a group of companies to outside investors via a public offering of shares involving an exchange listing of the subsidiary. If the segment in question is not a separate legal entity, a new corporation has to be created prior to the transaction. The parent must be the majority owner of the subsidiary prior to the ECO. However, it is permissible that up to 4% of shares are free-float, or up to 49% of shares are held by other investors prior to the ECO

[5] This convention is also commonly adopted in the more recent literature, e.g. Vijh (1999)

[6] A detailed discussion of these admission criteria, e.g. minimum size, is contained in Hennigs (1995), Section 2.1

While ECOs can differ in various parameters, such as the fraction of ownership sold, the market segment used, or the investor groups targeted, one of the most salient characteristics is the form of placement. Two fundamentally different types of placement need to be distinguished (e.g. Kaserer/Ahlers (2000), Langenbach (2001)): Primary placements and secondary placements.

In a primary placement, the subsidiary engages in a capital increase (§182 AktG). New shares are created and sold to the public. The parent company does not make use of its subscription right or the subscription right is excluded (§186 AktG). The proceeds from the offering flow exclusively to the subsidiary.

In a secondary placement, the parent company offers its shares in the subsidiary to the public. No new shares are created. The proceeds from the offering flow exclusively to the parent company. The share capital of the subsidiary does not change.

While pure secondary placements are rather uncommon (Kaserer/Ahlers (2000)), mixtures of primary and secondary placement are regularly observed. A more thorough discussion of the characteristics of primary and secondary placements is contained in Langenbach (2001, p. 185))

1.3 Motivation: The special interest in ECOs

1.3.1 Dual character of ECOs as means of financing and reorganization

ECOs are particularly intriguing class of transactions from a theoretical standpoint. In order illustrate the unique economic implications of ECOs, it is useful to compare ECOs to similar transactions: SEOs (secondary equity offerings) and spin-offs.[7] The following discussion focuses on economic differences, legal differences in German corporate law are discussed in e.g. Fleischer (2001).

SEOs and ECOs: In an SEO, the exchange-listed parent, increases its capital (§182 AktG) and engages in the sale of new shares. SEOs are similar to ECOs in the form of secondary placements – both transactions result in a cash inflow at the parent – but they differ in the type of shares offered. In an SEO, shares of the parent are offered, while in an ECO, shares of a subsidiary are offered (Schipper/Smith (1986) provide a more detailed discussion of further differentiating features). A key difference is that an SEO in general does not have any immediate consequences for the organization structure of the group of companies, while an ECO increases the independence of the subsidiary.

Spin-offs and ECOs: Similar to ECOs, spin-offs require that the activities to be spun off are first grouped in a separate legal entity (e.g. Habbel (2001), Schultze (1998), Schenk (1997b), Bühner (1998)). Then, shares in the subsidiary are distributed to the shareholders of the parent company as a tax-free dividend, pro-rata to the ownership stakes they hold in the parent company.[8] Thus, the shareholders in the parent and the subsidiary are initially identical. However, a spin-off is usually linked to an IPO of the subsidiary, so that the subsidiary shares distributed to the parent shareholders can be freely traded (Cusatis/Miles/Woolridge (1993)). Two key features delineate a spin-off from an ECO. First, contrary to an ECO, a spin-off leads to a complete separation of parent and subsidiary; post-transaction the former subsidiary is no longer part of the group of companies, as is the case in an ECO where the parent company retains control. Second, contrary to an ECO, a spin-off does not generate any immediate proceeds from the sale of shares, since shares are distributed as a tax-free dividend. Finally, while spin-offs are a frequently used class of transactions in the U.S. (e.g. Schipper/Smith (1983)), they are of little significance in Germany in the sense that only very few such transactions have been recorded (Bühner (1998); Schulze (1998), Kaserer/Ahlers (2000)).[9]

From the above discussion (summarized in Figure 1) it emerges that ECOs, stated in non-technical terms, fall in-between SEOs and spin-offs An SEO is a pure financing transaction that usually does not involve a reorganization. A spin-off involves a reorganization, but no financing. An ECO, in contrast, combines both elements.

Following Nick (1994), ECOs can thus be interpreted as having a dual character, combining financing and reorganization.[10]

---

[7] Löffler (2001) discusses additional types of transactions, e.g. split-ups. A thorough comparison of different transaction types is also found in Schultze (1998)

[8] (Schipper/Smith (1986) and Slovin/Sushka/Ferraro (1995) for a more detailed discussion; see Schultze (1998) for the legal treatment of spin-offs under German law; a more thorough comparison of ECOs and spin-offs is contained in Frank/Harden (2001))

[9] For a European perspective, see Bühner/Digmayer (2003)

[10] For a similar interpretation of ECOs, see Powers (2003)

Figure 1: Dual character of ECOs

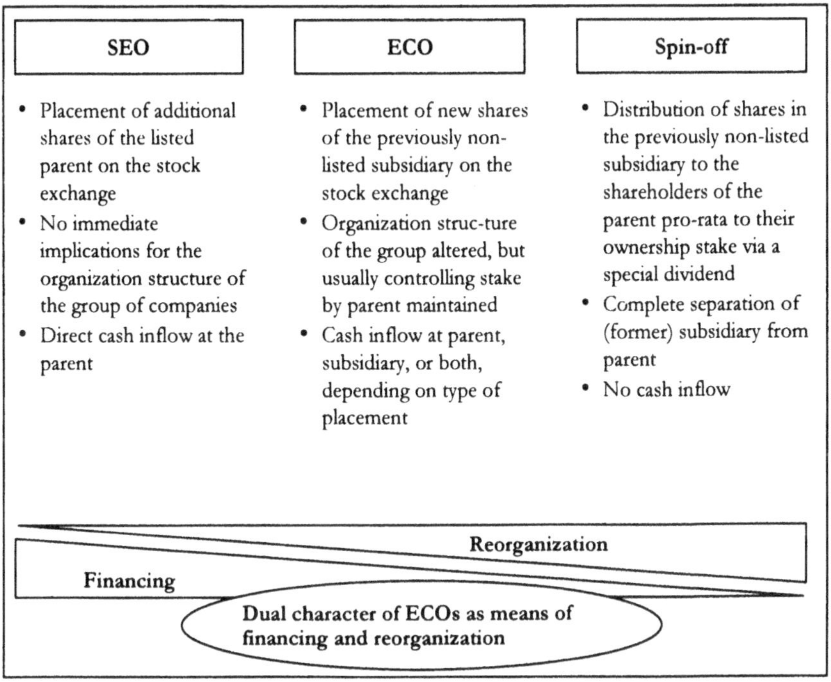

This dual character unique to ECOs has two important consequences:

- In analytical terms, ECOs constitute a more complex transaction than SEOs or spin-offs; ECOs are undertaken based on a mixture of both financing and reorganization motives. In analyzing their consequences, both elements must thus be disentangled

- As has been established in the literature, the capital market reacts differently to transactions associated with financing and reorganization. While SEOs are related to a negative short-term and long-term capital market reaction (for a recent review, see Ritter (2003)). While the results of the literature on SEOs and spin-offs can thus be While the results of the literature on SEOs and spin-offs can thus be drawn on in the analysis of ECOs, the net consequences of ECOs are not a priori clear.[11]

In conclusion, the dual character of ECOs renders these transactions both a particularly intriguing and complex subject of study.

1.3.2 Empirical significance of ECOs on the German capital market

Are ECOs an empirically significant phenomenon on the German capital market? In order to illustrate the empirical significance, the frequency of ECOs on German stock exchanges is shown in Figure 2.

The ECO of Kolbenschmidt from Metallgesellschaft in 1984 has been widely identified as the first German ECO (e.g. Pellens (1993)). In total, 55 ECOs by exchange-listed parents have taken place on German stock exchanges between 1984 and 2003. ECO activity is heavily concentrated in 1999 and 2000. No ECOs have taken place in 2002 and 2003. This pattern closely mirrors the development of IPO activity in Germany (e.g. Arbeitskreis Finanzen der Schmalenbach-Gesellschaft (2003)).

Compared to the U.S. the absolute number of transactions in Germany is small. Vijh (1999) has identified 721 ECOs on U.S. capital markets for his sample period 1981-1995. However, ECOs are an important phenomenon on German capital markets in relative terms: The 23 ECOs in 1999 and 2000 have raised EUR 7.9 bn, or 40% of the total IPO volume on German capital markets.[12]

In conclusion, ECOs are a significant phenomenon on the German capital market and thus merit attention. Over and above that, the time pattern of ECO activity suggests that a particularly opportune point in time for the study of ECOs has been reached: Analyzing ECO activity between 1984-2001 from a distance of three years where no such transac-

---

[11] These results are remarkably solid across different geographies and time periods. Core articles of the U.S. empirical SEO literature are Asquith/Mullins (1986), Masulis/Korwar (1986), Mikkelson/Partch (1986), Schipper/Smith (1986), Kalay/Shimrat (1987), Spiess/Affleck-Graves (1995), Loughran/Ritter (1997), Teoh/Welch/Wong (1998b), Eckbo/Masulis/Norli (2000), and Denis/Sarin (2001). Recent German studies are Padberg (1996) and Stehle/Ehrhardt/Przyborowski (2000). Core articles of the U.S. empirical spin-off literature are Schipper/Smith (1983), Miles/Rosenfeld (1983), Hite/Owers (1983), Copeland/Lemgruber/Mayers (1987), Woo/Willard/Daellenbach (1992), Cusatis/Miles/Woolridge (1993), Allen et al. (1995), Seward/Walsh (1996), and Desai/Jain (1999). Other types of divestiture transactions such as sell-offs also lead to positive announcement period returns, e.g. Montgomery/Thomas/Kamath (1984), John/Ofek (1995), Lang/Poulsen/Stulz (1995)

[12] More detailed descriptive statistics and detailed information on sample selection and data sources follows in the empirical part, Section 4.2

tions have taken place, it has become possible for the first time to develop a more definite evaluation of the longer-term effects of ECO activity during that period.[13]

Figure 2: Frequency of ECOs

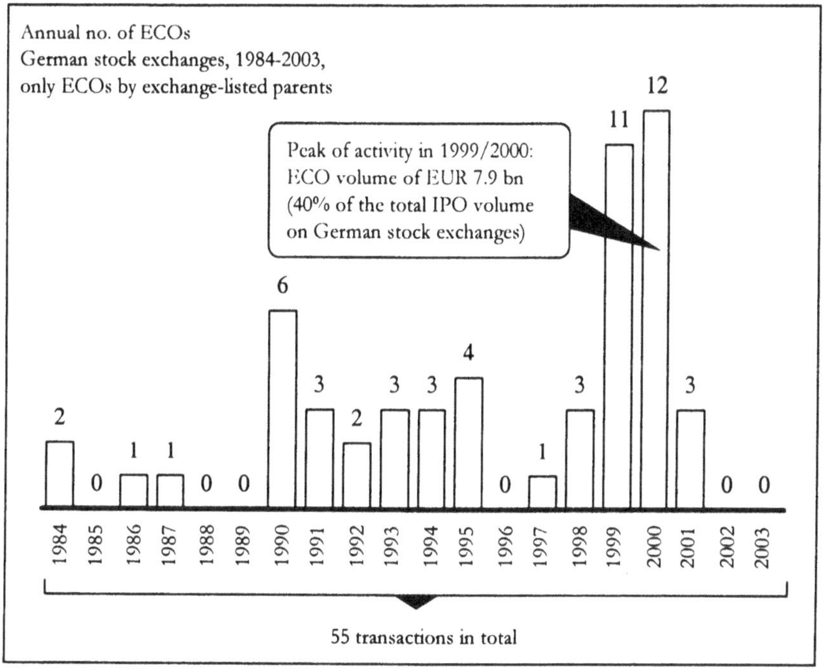

1.4 Existing ECO research

1.4.1 U.S. ECO literature

The U.S. ECO literature is largely empirical: the study of mainly the short-term capital market reaction and underlying changes in operating performance and other variables such as ownership structure are the dominant theme. Formal theoretical treatments are few.

---

13 The fluctuations of IPO volume over time and the repeated occurrence of 'hot issue periods' with increased activity are a well-researched phenomenon, e.g. Ibbotson/Jaffe (1975); or Lowry/Schwert

The earliest article of the U.S. ECO literature is Schipper/Smith (1986). The authors compare ECOs to SEOs in an event study framework. They find a positive announcement date excess return for ECOs (in contrast to a negative effect for SEOs) in the order of 2%. While from a methodological point of view, progress beyond the traditional event study framework has been limited, this result has been repeatedly confirmed in the later literature (e.g. Allen/McConnell (1998), Vijh (2002)). Schipper/Smith (1986) hypothesize that the positive announcement effect is explained by an increase in public disclosure, the opportunity for more effective incentive-based contracts, and the potential benefits from restructuring management of assets.

Klein/Rosenfeld/Beranek (1991), in another early article on ECOs, stress the nature of ECOs as temporary arrangements. They find that the majority of ECOs is followed either by a complete divestiture or a reacquisition by the parent. They interpret ECO as preparatory transactions for a later sell-off of the subsidiary, which is first "showcased" on the capital market. However, they do not find statistically significant differences in the announcement effect depending on the occurrence and type of the second event, which is potentially due to their small sample size.

Most of the subsequent literature on ECOs concentrates on explaining the positive announcement effect identified by Schipper/Smith (1986). Two broad groups of explanations have been developed: the signaling hypothesis and the efficiency gains hypothesis.

The *signaling hypothesis* is due to Nanda (1991), one of the few substantive non-empirical contributions to the ECO literature. The author develops an extension to the well-known Myers/Majluf (1984) adverse selection model. In Nanda's (1991) framework, a group of companies prefers to issue subsidiary equity instead of parent equity (i.e. engage in an ECO instead of an SEO) if it has private information that the subsidiary is overvalued relative to the parent. While the announcement of an ECO thus signals overvaluation of the subsidiary, it also signals undervaluation of the parent. Since parent assets are typically larger than subsidiary assets, the correction of the parent undervaluation caused by the signal outweighs the negative effect of the subsidiary's overvaluation. Consequently, ECOs lead to a positive announcement effect.

The predictions of Nanda's (1991) model have been empirically tested by Slovin/Sushka/Ferraro (1995). These authors argue that the hypothetical overvaluation of the subsidiary and the undervaluation of the parent signaled by the ECO should affect

(2002) and Lowry (2003) for more recent treatments

rival firms of parent and subsidiary in the same industry, assuming misevaluation is not purely firm-specific. Analyzing announcement date excess returns to rival firms, the authors find a negative announcement effect for the subsidiary's rivals, but they do not find a significant announcement effect for the parent's rivals. The evidence on parent's rivals is thus contradictory to Nanda's model (if the ECO signals undervaluation of the parent's industry, the rival firms should exhibit a positive announcement effect), while the evidence on the subsidiary's rivals is inconclusive: The effect on the subsidiary's rival firms could be interpreted as both consistent with Nanda's model (an ECO signals overvaluation of the subsidiary, and assuming that this overvaluation is not purely firm specific, of the subsidiary's industry), and with efficiency gains (an ECO leads to efficiency improvements, and thus negatively affects competitors in the same industry).

The *efficiency gains hypothesis* has been developed ad hoc. It predicts that the efficiency of operations, using various performance measures such as stock returns, Tobin's Q or accounting profits, improves thanks to ECOs.

A core article examining efficiency gains due to ECOs is Allen/McConnell (1998), who interpret ECOs as asset sales intended to finance other activities. The authors presume that managers have a preference for increasing the discretionary capital under their control and that ECOs will therefore only take place when the firm is capital constrained and funds are required to undertake additional activities preferred by managers.[14] Consistent with their hypothesis, Allen/McConnell (1998) find empirical evidence that highly-leveraged firms are particularly likely to undertake ECOs. Furthermore, in their analysis of different subsamples based on the use of ECO proceeds, they find a positive announcement effect only for ECOs where proceeds are used to repay debt or pay a dividend to shareholders. ECOs where proceeds are retained and used for investment purposes do not lead to positive announcement period abnormal returns in their sample.

Hulburt/Miles/Woolridge (2002), Vijh (2002) and Powers (2003), in the most comprehensive contributions to date, explicitly test the efficiency gains and the signaling hypothesis against each other.

Hulburt/Miles/Woolridge (2002) replicate Slovin/Sushka/Ferraro's (1995) tests of the signaling hypothesis but find negative announcement period returns to both parent and subsidiary rivals. The authors interpret this evidence as contradictory to Nanda's (1991) model, which predicts positive returns to parent rivals due to the signaling of parent undervaluation given by the ECO announcement. The authors then examine various accounting data and find that for both parent and subsidiary, level of operations (measured by e.g. sales growth) and efficiency of operations (measured by e.g. return on assets) increase post-ECO on an industry-adjusted basis. The authors interpret this as evidence of efficiency gains generated by ECOs.

Vijh (2002) applies a novel methodology to test the signaling hypothesis, which focuses on the relative size of parent and subsidiary. While Nanda's (1991) model predicts that the positive announcement effect of an ECO is the greater, the larger the relative size of the parent, Vijh (2002) finds empirical evidence to the contrary. Consequently, Vijh (2002) concentrates on different variants of the efficiency gains hypothesis in his further analyses. In a multivariate regression framework, Vijh (2002) finds that the announcement effect is positively related to refocusing, the mention of financing or investment motives for the ECO, the mention of disclosure motives for the ECO (e.g. reducing perceived undervaluation because of a lack of transparency of the diversified group of companies pre-ECO), the issuance of both primary and secondary shares, and the occurrence of a full divestiture of the subsidiary after the ECO. Vijh's (2002) evidence of a positive capital market reaction to both financing motives (repayment of debt) and investment is somewhat contradictory to Allen/McConnell (1998). Vijh (2002) interprets his evidence as indicating that ECOs are efficiently used to simultaneously meet financing needs of the parent and investment needs of the subsidiary.

Powers (2003) is the most recent empirical contribution testing efficiency gains and signaling hypotheses. Powers (2003) finds negative abnormal post-ECO returns and negative abnormal operating performance of the subsidiary. Furthermore, he detects a negative relationship between the percentage of shares sold in the ECO and the subsequent performance of the subsidiary (measured in terms of accounting returns and stock market returns). He thus concludes that, consistent with Nanda's (1991) model, ECOs are indeed undertaken when management has private information that the subsidiary is overvalued. The decline in operating performance found by Powers (2003), while robust to different types of industry adjustment, directly contradicts opposite evidence documented in Hulburt/Miles/Woolridge (2002), calculated using similar methodology. The significant negative long-term abnormal returns contradict evidence by Vijh (1999), discussed below,

---

[14] This presumption is based on Jensen's (1986) often cited article on the agency costs of free cash flow

which is based on a significantly larger sample. The stark contrast of Powers' (2003) results to the existing literature suggest his conclusions have to be interpreted carefully.

Summarizing above review, the empirical evidence clearly leans towards the efficiency gains hypothesis, while the signaling hypothesis receives relatively weak support. In light of this evidence, the ad-hoc development of the efficiency gains hypothesis appears somewhat unfortunate.

Finally, two core articles of the ECO literature not focusing on the short-term announcement effect are Allen (1998), who in a rare example of case study research in corporate finance presents a detailed case study of a manufacturer of biomedical, recycling, and environmental monitoring equipment that established a satellite structure via a total of 11 ECOs of wholly-owned subsidiaries, and Vijh (1999) on long-term returns after ECOs.

Vijh (1999) is the first and to date most extensive study of long-term returns after ECOs. Using a number of different benchmarks, he does not find significant underperformance for neither parent nor subsidiary over a three-year period following the ECO. Despite large sample sizes, his results are largely insignificant or non-robust to changes in methodology. Vijh (1999) conjectures that the superior performance of ECOs compared to IPOs and SEOs (which exhibit long-term underperformance) could be explained by the benefits of increased focus of the parent and the monitoring position that the parents continues to hold in the subsidiary. However, he is unable to find statistically significant empirical support for these hypotheses. Vijh (1999) thus concludes that the lack of underperformance of ECOs may thus be simply due to an efficient market reaction to the announcement. However, given the insignificance of results, long-term abnormal returns after ECOs essentially remain unclear.

To conclude the above literature review, Table 1 establishes stylized facts on U.S. ECOs.[15]

---

[15] The above review has ignored the rich treatments in practitioners' journals, mostly very favorable to ECOs building on the ideas of the core competence movement, e.g. Anslinger et al. (1997), Anslinger/Klepper/Subramaniam (1999), Anslinger/Bonini/Patsalos-Fox (2000), Annema/Fallon/Goedhart (2001, 2002), Frank (2001)

Table 1: Stylized facts on U.S. ECOs

Subject area	Stylized facts
Characteristics of firms undertaking ECOs	• High leverage • Poor performance
Announcement date excess stock returns to parent firms	• In the order of 2%

Alternative determinants of announcement effect	• Efficiency gains hypothesis supported. Announcement effect positively related to:
	  • divestment of non-core business (parent and subsidiary not in same industry)
	  • issuance of both primary and secondary shares
	  • increase in disclosure on the subsidiary following the ECO
	• Role of alternative uses of the funds raised via the ECO (payout vs. investment) in generating efficiency gains is somewhat unclear
	• Signaling hypothesis not supported
	  • Both the subsidiary's and the parent's rivals exhibit a weak negative announcement effect
	  • The announcement effect of the ECO parent is positively related to the relative size of the subsidiary

Development of parent and subsidiary post-ECO	• No evidence for abnormal stock returns • Unclear development of operating performance • Subsequent full divestiture of subsidiary anticipated by capital market and leading to higher announcement returns

1.4.2 German ECO literature

The German literature on ECOs mainly consists of PhD theses and a limited number of articles.[16]

German work on ECOs from the first half of the 1990s is Pellens (1993), Nick (1994), Hennigs (1995), and Hasselmann (1997). Pellens (1993) and Hasselmann (1997) empirically analyze the short-term and long-term capital market reaction to ECOs, but fail to come to robust conclusions due to the small sample size of 11. The PhD theses by Nick (1994) and Hennigs (1995) are theoretical treatments of the advantages and disadvantages of ECOs. While Nick (1994) adopts a neo-institutionalist perspective and examines whether ECOs increase economic efficiency, Hennigs' (1995) work neglects efficiency or shareholder value considerations and evaluates ECOs mainly from the perspective of parent company management. Given the lack of either empirical analysis or formal models in both theses, the conclusions reached are difficult to evaluate.

The first article with solid empirical results on German ECOs is Kaserer/Ahlers (2000). The authors examine the capital market reaction to ECOs in a classical event study framework reminiscent of Schipper/Smith (1986), and find a positive and a significant positive announcement effect. Kaserer/Ahlers (2000) further examine the relationship between the announcement effect and the type of placement, and find a significantly more positive announcement effect for pure primary placements.

Additional PhD theses by Löffler (2001) and Langenbach (2001) confirm above empirical results on the short-term announcement effect and further extend the empirical work on German ECOs based on larger sample sizes.

Löffler (2001) jointly analyzes sell-offs and ECOs as methods of divestiture. Using univariate and multivariate regression analyses, Löffler (2001) tests variants of the efficiency gains hypothesis and finds that the announcement effect is positively related to a reduction in diversification via the divestiture. In addition, the influence of further variables, such as ownership structure, on the announcement effect is examined. However, the relevance of Löffler's (2001) results for the ECO literature is limited due to the characteristics of her sample: The sample is heavily tilted towards sell-offs (144 cases) and contains only very few ECOs (21 cases). Furthermore, it is at least doubtful that a joint analysis of ECOs and sell-offs in a common sample is analytically permissible given the different characteristics of the two types of transactions.

Langenbach (2001), in an extensive theoretical treatment, compares the effectiveness of internal control mechanisms (pre-ECO), with particular reference to the role of management accounting, to external control mechanisms (post-ECO). In the empirical part of his thesis, he confirms the positive announcement effect of German ECOs. Interestingly, he finds negative long-term abnormal returns of the subsidiary in the subsequent years.

---

[16] The flourishing legal ECO literature, on such questions as e.g. subscription rights for parent shareholders, is not considered here. Recent examples are Bohnel (1999), Busch/Groß (2000), Fleischer (2001), Lutter (2001), Trapp/Schick (2001), Wackerbarth (2002)

Figure 3: Abnormal stock returns surrounding ECO announcements

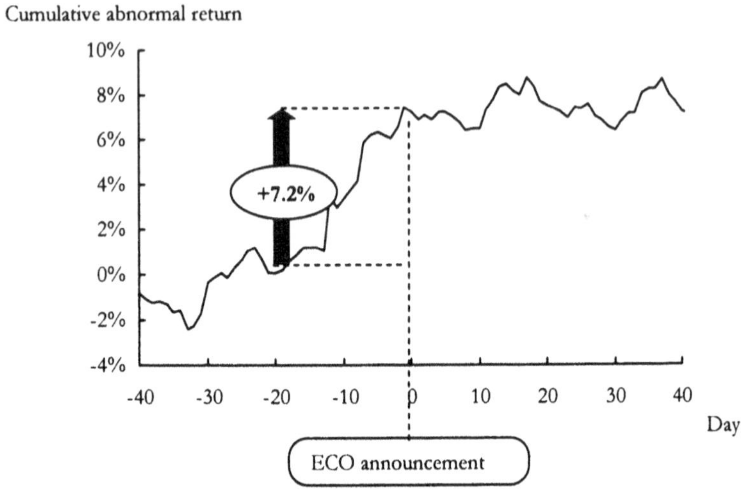

Source: adapted from Brettel/Junker/Pinker (2004)
Cumulative average abnormal return surrcounding announcement day, based on market model residuals.
Sample of 50 ECOs on German exchanges, 1984-2000

The influence of ownership concentration in the parent on the announcement effect of German ECOs is empirically examined by Elsas/Löffler (2003). The authors hypothesize that a higher degree of ownership concentration in the parent pre-ECO signifies tighter control of parent management. Consequently, the authors further argue, the potential efficiency gains from ECOs are smaller. The authors find empirical support for their hypothesis in that the announcement effect is negatively related to the degree of parent ownership concentration and several other proxies for blockholder control pre-ECO. In further analyses, Elsas/Löffler (2003) also find a positive relation between the announcement effect and refocusing. They do not find evidence for a special monitoring role of banks.

In the most extensive empirical study on German ECOs to date, Brettel/Junker/Pinker (2004) examine the short-term and long-term capital market reaction. The positive short-term announcement effect found in previous studies is confirmed. Extending the event window to 20 days, assuming gradual information dissemination, the authors find an economically highly significant announcement effect of 7.2% (Figure 3). A significant long-term abnormal return cannot be found. This result is robust to different methodologies.

The two most recent contributions on German ECOs are Wagner (2004) and Fucks (2004). Wagner (2004), based on a sample of ECO announcement (including withdrawn transactions), analyzes the determinants of the short-term capital market reaction. He finds that those ECOs that lead to a reduction in volume of the internal capital market lead to more positive announcement returns. An influence of market timing on the capital market reaction is not found. Fucks (2004) analyzes the determinants of the ownership stake sold by the parent and the relative proportion of primary and secondary shares offered. He finds that the amount sold increases with financing needs of the subsidiary, but decreases with dispersion of parent ownership. Similarly to Wagner (2004), an influence of market timing cannot be detected: The ownership fraction sold cannot be explained by capital market conditions.

Table 2: Stylized facts on German ECOs

Subject area	Stylized facts
Characteristics of firms undertaking ECOs	• N/A
Announcement date excess stock returns to parent firms	• In the order of 1.5%; higher excess returns when extending the event window

Alternative determinants of announcement effect	• Efficiency gains hypothesis supported. Announcement effect positively related to:
	  • divestment of non-core business (parent and subsidiary not in same industry)
	  • issuance of both primary shares
	  • dispersed ownership structure of parent pre-ECO
	• No influence of market timing on announcement returns

Development of parent and subsidiary post-ECO	• No evidence for abnormal stock returns • Unclear development of operating performance • Role of second events unclear

Finally, in articles oriented toward practitioners, Hornung/Wullenkord (2001) retrace the ECO of MG Metals Trading by Metallgesellschaft on the London Stock Exchange, and

Arbeitskreis Finanzierung der Schmalenbach-Gesellschaft (2003) gives procedural recommendations on the structuring of ECOs.[17]

To summarize, Table 2 establishes stylized facts on German ECOs. While the German literature on ECOs in general has suffered from limited sample sizes, a comparison of U.S. and German results reveals far-reaching similarities: ECOs are associated with positive announcement returns in both geographies. The positive announcement return is primarily related to efficiency gains. However, hypothesis development in the German literature has remained similarly ad hoc as in the U.S. literature. Finally, the long-term returns after ECOs and the role of second events are unclear for both geographies.

1.4.3 Gaps in existing research

While the above review was mainly aimed at establishing stylized facts on ECOs, based on the literature, it has also touched on gaps in existing research. Research on ECOs is a flourishing area of the U.S. finance literature, and the German literature, where effective empirical research has historically been impeded by small sample sizes, is catching up in terms of empirical contributions. However, despite the substantial progress made, three key deficiencies of the present literature can be identified:

1. The analysis of the determinants of the capital market reaction has not been based on a ***unified theoretical framework***, guiding hypothesis development. With the exception of the signaling hypothesis (which is based on solid formal modeling, but which has largely been empirically falsified as far as ECOs are concerned), hypothesis development has been mostly unsystematic and driven by the empirical data.

2. While the short-term capital market reaction to ECOs has been extensively researched and documented in an event study framework, more ***recent methodological developments*** in empirical finance, such as e.g. the stochastic modeling of volatility have not been applied in the analysis of the capital market reaction.

3. In contrast to the relatively well-documented short-term reaction to the ECO announcement, ***the long-term returns*** after ECOs remain unclear. Also, the relationship between short-term and long-term effects has not been researched.

[17] Further practitioner articles are Schmitz (1997) and Volk (2000)

Consequently, a definite answer to the effects of ECOs on firm value, the net effect of short-term and long-term reaction, is still outstanding. Do ECOs on average *sustainably* create value and why? Are there recognizable patterns in the capital market reaction, with initial overoptimism followed by particularly pronounced long-term corrections? And if at least some ECOs lead to long-term value creation, what are their defining characteristics? These questions remain unanswered for Germany as well as the U.S.

In the following, the three core gaps in existing research identified above are discussed in more detail.

The lack of a *unified theoretical framework* underlying the analysis of ECOs is especially apparent in US empirical work using multivariate regression analyses to explain the ECO announcement effect: As insinuated in the review of articles testing the efficiency gains hypothesis, some work leaves the impression that hypotheses have not been developed ex ante, but instead have been reverse-engineered, based on empirically observed patterns in the data (e.g. Vijh (2002)). A fitting example from the German literature is Wagner (2004), who borrows hypotheses from such diverse theoretical areas as signaling, agency theory, and market timing in his work. Furthermore, the common 20-page journal article format favors the concentration on a single aspect, e.g. a discussion of one value lever, instead of a broad analysis of potential determinants of value creation (e.g. Allen/McConnell (1998)). The German PhD dissertations on ECOs, on the other hand, while providing thorough and thoughtful theoretical treatments, generally put little emphasis on generating testable empirical predictions (e.g. Nick (1994)). The efficiency gains hypothesis, the dominant explanation for the short-term positive capital market reaction to ECOs in the literature, has thus not been rigorously developed, or even clearly defined.[18]

More *recent methodological developments* in empirical corporate finance or econometrics have not been applied in the empirical analysis of ECOs. Methodological progress has been limited since the original Schipper/Smith (1986) event study, as already pointed out in above review. While the short-term capital market reaction has been extensively researched, it is unclear whether it is fully robust to methodological variations. Recent improvements to event study methodology include the simultaneous estimation of the

---

[18] This point is further illustrated by the lack of a common terminology: Vijh (2002) uses the term "divestiture gains hypothesis", and defines five subhypotheses, one of which (the "financing strategy hypothesis") predicts substantially the same as Allen/McConnell's (1998) "managerial discretion hypothesis". Powers (2003) prefers the term "efficiency rationale".

Figure 4: Potential patterns of stock market reaction to ECOs

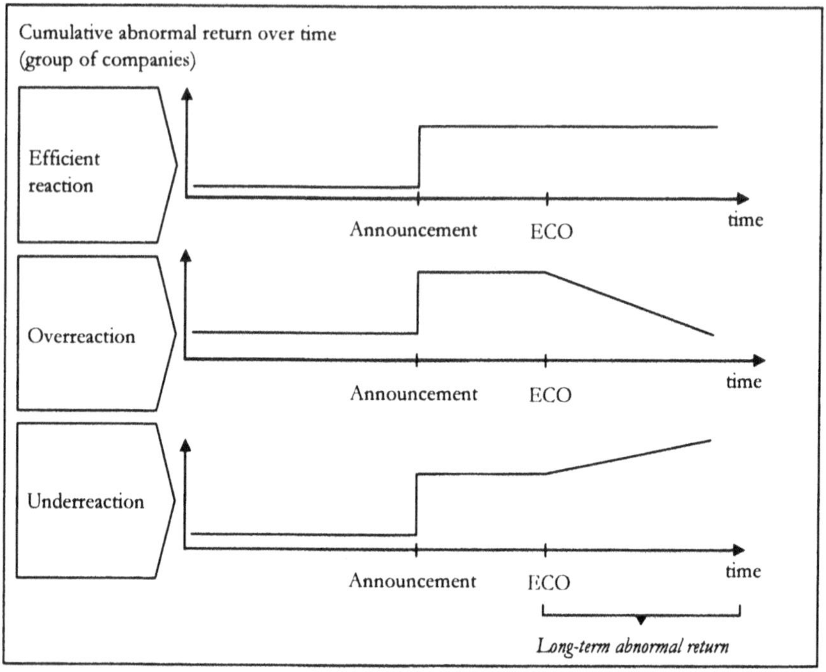

equation system applying seemingly unrelated regression (SUR) in order to take into account cross-sectional dependence, and the modeling of volatility as an autoregressive process (GARCH).

The *long-term returns* after ECOs are unclear. Neither Vijh (1999) nor Powers (2003), despite their large sample sizes, or Brettel/Junker/Pinker (2004), can find evidence of either over- or underperformance. Assuming capital market efficiency, we must assume, as Vijh (1999) does, that the capital market in his positive short-term reaction, correctly anticipates future efficiency gains. However, a conclusion that ECOs sustainably create value over the long-term based on such an assumption alone would be clearly premature.

Given the pattern of capital market reaction observed for similar transactions, a pattern of underreaction or overreaction is equally possible (Figure 4). [19]

1.5 Objective

1.5.1 Core research questions

The overriding objective of this study is to reach a definite evaluation of the effects of ECOs on firm value on the German capital market and their determinants. In order to reach an answer to this question, this study aims to systematically close the gaps in existing research discussed in the previous section. Specifically,

1. Hypotheses about the effects of ECOs on firm value and core value levers are developed using *agency theory* as unifying theoretical framework. Hypothesized effects of ECOs on firm value are framed in terms of reductions/increases of agency costs. Hypothesis development is guided by a two-dimensional framework, incorporating as the two dimensions the determinants of agency costs and the agency relationships affected by ECOs. Neighboring areas of finance, namely the diversification/internal capital markets, asymmetric information, executive compensation, and blockholder control literatures, respectively, are drawn on.
2. The short-term capital market reaction to German ECOs is reassessed applying recent methodological developments.
3. Long-term returns to German ECOs are examined using the largest sample available to date, i.e., including the 1999-2000 peak years for the first time. Recent methodological advances in the long-term returns literature and simulation techniques are applied in order to ensure robustness of the results. Hypotheses on the determinants of short-term and long-term returns are then empirically tested via multivariate regression analysis.

1.5.2 Limitations

Before outlining the organization of this study in more detail, it is expedient to briefly discuss what this study does not aim to do. The approach sketched above has four main limitations:

---

[19] See Fama (1998) for an extensive discussion of the empirical research documenting underreaction and

- *Verbal development of hypotheses.* This study will not develop an equation-based formal model of ECOs (for examples of formal models on related transactions see e.g. Zingales (1995b), Maug (2001) concerning IPOs, or Aron (1991) on spin-offs). The dual character of ECOs would require to incorporate both financing and organizational effects, and makes formal modeling especially complex. The ECO literature has not yet reached a stage that is sufficiently mature to allow for such a model.
- *Potential biases in econometric analysis.* An empirical study of value creation due to ECOs suffers from econometric problems common to corporate finance research in general (e.g. Börsch-Supan/Köke (2002)). Sample selection potentially creates an endogeneity bias, i.e. it is possible that ECOs are undertaken precisely by those groups of companies for whom these transactions are value-enhancing, but that ECOs are not value-enhancing in general. Control variables will thus be used to reduce potential unobserved heterogeneity and reduce endogeneity bias. Furthermore, variables are subject to measurement error. Existing data (capital market data, financial statements, auxiliary data on e.g. ownership structure) must function as imperfect proxies for unobservable variables (e.g. agency costs). Where possible, a variety of proxies will thus be used in order to evaluate the robustness of results.
- *Sample size.* While the present study is based on the largest sample in the German ECO literature (55 observations), the sample is still relatively small. While this could be seen as a caveat to the analysis compared to the large-sample U.S. studies, the smaller sample size offers the opportunity to use detailed data prohibitively costly to collect for large samples (Elsas/Löffler (2003)). Where possible, potential biases due to small sample size will be corrected for, using the appropriate econometric methods, such as bootstrapping.
- *Sharp theoretical focus.* Rival theories, e.g. Nanda's (1991) adverse selection argument, or behavioral considerations, are a priori excluded as potential determinants of value creation, due to the exclusive focus on agency theory. Building on the results of previous work – primarily Slovin/Sushka/Ferraro (1995) and Vijh (2002), who refute the signaling hypothesis, and also the recent work by Wagner (2004) and Fucks (2004), who find no support for market timing – the present study assumes that efficiency gains are the sole source of (potential) value creation from ECOs.

---

overreaction to different types of transactions such as mergers or stock splits

While this is certainly a limitation, the author believes that a rigorous treatment on the basis of one stringent theory better contributes to the advancement of the ECO literature.

1.6 Outline

In Section 2, theoretical foundations are laid by demonstrating the importance of an underlying theory of the firm for corporate finance research, and by establishing agency theory as the pre-eminent such underpinning. The development of agency theory is sketched insofar relevant for corporate finance. In applying agency theory to ECOs, a two-dimensional framework for estimating agency cost changes associated with ECOs is developed, and the elements of the two dimensions, determinants of agency costs, and principal-agent-relationships affected by ECOs, are derived.

In Section 3, four value levers associated with agency cost changes due to ECOs are defined guided by the two-dimensional framework. Then, detailed and testable hypotheses are developed for each of the four levers focus and investment efficiency, information asymmetries and disclosure, incentive compensation, and ownership concentration.

In Section 4, the data are presented. Then, empirical methods for the analysis of abnormal returns are reviewed. Results concerning short-term abnormal returns, long-term abnormal returns, and the determinants of short-term and long-term abnormal returns are presented. A discussion of the results and implications for research and practice finishes the section. Finally, Section 5 concludes.

2 Theoretical Foundations

2.1 Section outline

The present study develops hypotheses about the short-term and long-term effects of ECOs on firm value based on positive agency theory. The subsequent sections serve five purposes: Establish the need for a theory of the firm as foundation for corporate finance (Section 2.2), and discuss agency theory as pre-eminent such foundation (Section 2.3); demonstrate how agency theory can be applied to empirical corporate finance (Section 2.4), and finally introduce a two-dimensional agency framework for the analysis of ECOs as a guide to hypothesis development (Section 2.5).

2.2 Theoretical foundations of corporate finance

2.2.1 Need for a theory of the firm

Much in the same way as neoclassical economics, the emergent finance research from the 1950s and 1960s, concentrating on such topics as portfolio selection and capital asset pricing, and applying novel microeconomic methods, essentially treated the firm as a production function (Jensen/Smith (1984)).

Jensen/Meckling (1976) is one of the earliest and most influential works from corporate finance that took object with the traditional neoclassical approach (p. 308):

> "While the literature in economics is replete with references to the 'theory of the firm', the material generally subsumed under that heading is not actually a theory of the firm but rather a theory of markets in which firms are important actors. The firm is a 'black box' operated so as to meet the relevant marginal conditions with respect to inputs and outputs, thereby maximizing profit, or, more accurately, present value."

Since then, demands for a theory of the firm as a foundation for corporate finance research have been repeatedly made.[20] Williamson (1988), in his survey on corporate governance and corporate finance, underlines the importance of the study of institutions for corporate finance (p. 587):

> "Financial economics, like general equilibrium theory more generally, is essentially non-institutional [...]. The substantial accomplishments of this research tradition not-

---

[20] Ross (1987) is one of the few articles that articulates an opposing view, stressing the importance of "friendly competition" between economics and finance

withstanding, there is growing agreement that institutions matter in ways not hitherto acknowledged or even imagined."

Later, Jensen (1993) in his presidential address to the American Finance Association stresses how the takeover battles of the 1980s have put organizational conflicts into the focus of public attention and corporate finance research, but concludes that (p. 872)

> "... we have to understand even better than we do now the factors leading to organizational failures (and successes): we have to break open the black box called the firm, and this means understanding how organizations and the people in them work. In short, we're facing the problem of developing a viable theory of organizations."

In a recent survey article on the theoretical foundations of corporate finance, Zingales (2000) again asserts a close relationship between corporate finance and underlying theories of the firm (p. 1624):

> "Corporate finance is the study of the way *firms* are financed. Theory of the firm, thus, has a tremendous impact on the way we think about corporate finance, the way we do empirical research, the policy implications we derive, and the topics we choose to study. Even the most practical applications of this discipline, like the way we value firms, are unconsciously slaves to some underlying theory of the firm."

Today, it is thus largely uncontroversial among financial economists that a theory of the firm is a necessary foundation for corporate finance research.

2.2.2 New Institutional Economics

2.2.2.1 Origins of New Institutional Economics

The rise of importance of the theory of organizations for corporate finance mirrors, or more precisely, originates from, a similar development in general economics. Neoclassical economics was primarily a theory of markets, populated by firms acting as rational decision makers (Demsetz (1988)).[21] The considerable success of market economies fostered an academic climate where other forms of economic organizations than markets were seen as arising only to compensate for market failures (Milgrom/Roberts (1988a)). As a response to the perceived deficiencies of neoclassical economics, attempts were made to incorporate more realistic assumptions into microeconomic models (Hutchison (1984)).

---

[21] In an interesting historic explanation, Demsetz (1988) traces the focus on markets and the price system back to the 18th century and Adam Smith's famous "invisible hand": the development of classical economics was fuelled by the political debate about the optimal scope of government in the economy,

The departure from the view of the firm as a single rational decision maker required the analysis of how firms function and how they emerge. As a response, *New Institutional Economics* emerged in the late 1960s (for a review of its origins, see Williamson (1985)).[22]

New Institutional Economics is the study of institutions, how they arise, and what purposes they serve, its fundamental message being that institutions matter for economic performance (for a thorough review, see Furubotn/Richter (1997), Klein (2000) and the references contained therein). While New Institutional Economics can be traced back to the early work of Coase (1937), its development into a self-conscious academic movement is largely due to Williamson, who also first used the term "New Institutional Economics" in his (1975) book. The 1984 and 1985 symposia of the Journal of Institutional and Theoretical Economics further contributed to the development of the discipline.

2.2.2.2 *The contractual view of the firm*

New Institutional Economics serves as a label for a number of theoretical approaches that are rather different in terms of their focus and spirit, and which often have little more in common than their shared interest in the study of institutions. However, all the different approaches have a common ground: the contractual view of the firm (Williamson (1999)).

Within the contractual view of the firm, a corporation is defined as a nexus of contracts between individuals that brings their heterogeneous objectives into equilibrium. This contractual view of the firm was introduced by Alchian/Demsetz (1972), and further developed in Jensen/Meckling (1976) and Fama (1980).[23]

In their seminal (1972) paper on team production, Alchian/Demsetz define the firm as (p. 794)

> "a contractual structure with 1) joint input production, 2) several input owners, 3) one party who is common to all the contracts of the joint inputs, 4) who has rights to renegotiate any input's contract independently of contracts with other input owners, 5) who holds the residual claim, and 6) who has the right to sell his central contractual residual status."

---

and how a well-functioning price system can lead to an efficient allocation of resources without central coordination

22 While the interest in the firm as an institution is a relatively new phenomenon for economics, its has been a primary issue in organizational behavior and sociology for much longer. However, Milgrom/Roberts (1988) criticize the "underdeveloped state of formal theorizing" in these disciplines

23 Behrens (1985) reviews the definitions from a legal perspective

Thus, instead of multilateral contracts as would be the case in a market setting, the relationships between agents within a corporation are largely governed by unilateral contracts with the legal entity that serves as the contracting nexus (Jensen (1983)).

Jensen/Meckling (1976) generalize the Alchian/Demsetz definition to incorporate all contracts a firm entertains, and to include other organizations apart from the capitalist firm Alchian/Demsetz had in mind (p. 310):

> "We believe the emphasis that Alchian and Demsetz place on joint input production is too narrow and therefore misleading. Contractual relations are the essence of the firm, not only with employees, but with suppliers, creditors, and so on. The problem of agency costs and monitoring exists for all of these contracts, independent of whether there is joint production in their sense.[...] It is important to recognize that most organizations are simply legal fictions which serve as a nexus for a set of contracting relationships among individuals."

In a further refinement, Fama (1980), while subscribing to the "set of contracts" perspective, separates the manager (3 and 4 in Alchian/Demsetz (1972)) from the residual risk bearer (5 and 6) (p. 289):

> "In the classical theory, [...] the entrepreneur is taken to be both manager and residual risk bearer. [...] As a consequence, this literature fails to explain the large modern corporation in which control of the firm is in the hands of the managers who are more or less separate from the firm's security holders. [We] set aside the typical presumption that a corporation has owners in any meaningful sense."

2.2.2.3 Subdisciplines of New Institutional Economics

Three main subdisciplines are commonly identified with the heading of New Institutional Economics (e.g. Williamson (1990)): Property rights, transaction cost economics, and agency theory.

While Williamson (2000) concedes that, "awaiting a unified theory, we should be accepting of pluralism" (p. 595), he makes a helpful, attempt at a hierarchical classification of the three approaches based on the object of analysis (see Figure 5).

Property rights essentially refers to the study of the institutional environment and its ramifications for the functioning of the institutions of governance. The starting point of the property rights literature is the seminal work by Coase (1960), who demonstrates that in the absence of transaction costs, e.g. given costless court ordering, the distribution of property rights is irrelevant.

Figure 5: Subdisciplines of New Institutional Economics

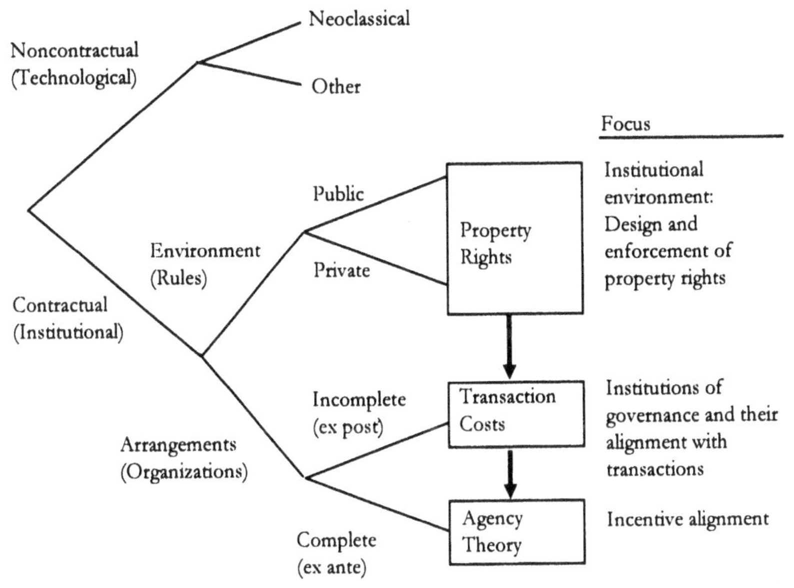

Source: Adapted from Williamson (1990, 2000)

Transaction cost economics studies the governance of contractual relations. The canonical problem of the transaction cost literature has been formulated by Coase (1937): vertical integration. Transaction cost economics, analyzing the ex post stage of contract, studies how transactions differ and how governance structures need to be designed correspondingly (e.g. Klein/Crawford/Alchian (1978), Grossman/Hart (1986)). Central to transaction cost economics is the question of firm or market, which are evaluated as alternative governance mechanisms (Williamson (1975, 1985, 1999)).

Agency theory, in turn, studies how incentives can be aligned ex ante, given a certain governance structure, and how changes in governance structures affect incentives. Agency theory developed following the pioneering work of Berle/Means (1932), who first analyzed the potential conflicts of interest from the separation of ownership (in the hands of dispersed shareholders, the principals) and control (in the hands of employed managers, the agents) in the modern US corporation.[24]

2.2.2.4 *Agency theory as foundation of corporate finance*

Williamson's (2000) hierarchical classification of the subdisciplines of New Institutional Economics implies that agency theory is most suited to serve as theoretical foundation for typical corporate finance questions: How does capital structure affect the incentives of managers? In what way does diversification affect managers' incentives and what effect does this have on the investment behavior of firms? Does the existence of large block-holders change management incentives?

Demsetz (1988) makes a similar point: agency theory studies questions of internal firm organization that cannot be answered based on transaction cost considerations. For example, Alchian/Demsetz (1972) derived the optimal organization of team production based on differences in shirking opportunities, i.e. on what where essentially agency cost arguments.

While admittedly, Williamson's (2000) hierarchical classification is not exceedingly rigorous, and even Williamson himself (1988) presents agency theory and transaction cost economics as alternative approaches for analysis of similar problems in his application of transaction cost economics to project financing, applications of transaction cost economics in the corporate finance literature are extremely rare.[25]

Agency theory, in contrast, has proven to be very well suited in: It has become the standard language of corporate finance researchers, and the prevailing view of the firm in corporate finance today (Zingales (2000)) is based on the seminal article by Jensen/Meckling (1976), appropriately entitled "Theory of the firm: managerial behavior, agency costs, and capital structure". The large body of corporate finance research de-

---

[24] From historical interest is the evaluation of Marshall's (1928) approach to agency, discussed in Stiglitz (2000), p. 1467: "Marshall, too, intuitively recognized the principal-agent problem – managers' interests and shareholders' interests did not coincide. On the other hand, Marshall's resolution of this quandary, that managers seemed to be 'well-behaved' in spite of a seeming absence of explicit incentives, attributed the success of the British corporation in no small measure to a combination of British breeding and upbringing."

[25] Bolton/Scharfstein (1998) postulate the need for a unified theory that integrates approaches to vertical/lateral integration based on transaction cost economics and to the separation of ownership and control based on agency theory; lucid comments on the interrelation between transaction cost economics and agency theory are also provided by Holmström/Roberts (1998)

veloped since the mid-1970s is thus deeply rooted in agency theory (Eisenhardt (1989) contains a survey of empirical applications of agency theory).

The overriding influence and near-status as new orthodoxy of agency theory is also proven in recent survey articles on the foundations of corporate finance: While Shleifer/Vishny (1997) is exclusively based on agency theory, in the Zingales (2000) survey article, four of the five approaches to a theory of the firm discussed have their roots in agency theory. Another recent survey article on financial contracting by Hart (2001) is firmly rooted in New Institutional Economics as well. Demsetz (1997) even calls the rise of agency theory a "quiet revolution" in economics.[26]

Other approaches to organization theory, such as the Resource-Based View originating from strategic management research (e.g. Wernerfelt (1984)), while highly popular among practitioners (e.g. Prahalad/Hamel (1990)), have failed to exert much influence in corporate finance. Williamson (1999), although not impartial for obvious reasons, is outright dismissive of the Resource-Based View owing to "obscure and often tautological definitions of key terms; and failures of operationalization" (p. 1093) and the lack of a clear efficiency criterion. Only very isolated attempts at operationalizing the Resource-Based View in a corporate finance context have been made, with a notable exception being Rajan/Zingales (1999), who describe the firm as web of specific investments built around a critical resource.

2.3 Agency theory and its implications

2.3.1 The core question of agency theory

On the basis of the contractual view of the firm, agency theory studies the contract between a principal and an agent, who provides a service on behalf of a principal (Jensen/Meckling (1976)). The agency relationship, "is one of the oldest and commonest codified modes of social interaction." (Ross (1973), p. 134). Given the impossibility of complete contracts, the principal has to delegate some decision-making authority to the agent.

The actions of the agent cannot be fully observed by the principal. This gives the agent discretion to act in his own interest. Consequently, assuming that the principal's and

[26] On the other hand, he contends that the "focus on agency relationships has also led to neglect of some useful neoclassical theorizing" (p. 428)

agent's interests are not identical, and that both principal and agent maximize their personal utility, the agent's actions can deviate from the principal's interests, leading to agency costs (Ross (1973)).

Agency theory studies optimal contractual arrangements that minimize agency costs, depending on parameters of the contracting environment, such as organizational form.

2.3.2 Development of agency theory and its subdisciplines

2.3.2.1 The two subdisciplines of agency theory

Two distinct strands of literature studying contracts between principals and agents have developed (Jensen (1983)):

- Principal-Agent Theory
- Positive Agency Theory

The common core of the two strands is that both are based on the fundamental tautology that utility-maximizing agents minimize the agency costs in any contracting relationship (Jensen (1983)), and both focus on determining the most efficient contract governing a principal-agent relationship (Eisenhardt (1989)). However, the two subdisciplines differ substantially: Principal-agent theory focuses on the employer-worker relationship and is concerned with the formal modeling of optimal compensation contracts, extending the simple one-period, one-agent, one-task agency problem to complex multi-period, multi-agent, multi-task, multi-layer constellations, and analyzing the impact of risk preferences, information asymmetry, and uncertainty (Levinthal (1988)). Positive agency theory, in contrast, focuses on the shareholder/manager relationship and is concerned with explaining the organizational forms and contracts that we empirically observe (Jensen (1983)).

The two subdisciplines are reviewed and contrasted in the following.

2.3.2.2 Principal-agent theory

As discussed, Principal-Agent Theory is concerned with the development of optimal incentive arrangements that minimize agency costs by providing optimal incentives to the agent, modeling the effects of preferences, uncertainty and information (Holmström/Tirole (1989)). The classical tradeoff is between effective, i.e. high-powered, incentives for the agent, and efficient risk sharing, i.e. minimal risk exposure of risk-averse agents (Prendergast (2002)). Pioneering work that has shaped the discipline includes Spence/Zeckhauser (1971), Ross (1973), Mirrlees (1976), Holmström (1979), Lazear/Rosen (1981), Grossman/Hart (1983), and Holmström/Milgrom (1987).[27]

Spence/Zeckhauser (1971), identified by Jensen (1983) as the first work in Principal-Agent Theory, model the effects of the "adverse incentive problem", namely the moral hazard problem, caused by the nonobservability of the behavior of the policyholder, on the design of optimal insurance contracts. Ross in his (1973) article coined the term "principal-agent problem" and studies under what properties of the principal's and agent's utility functions an optimal payout function (incentive scheme) for the agent can be devised. Additional work on moral hazard models includes Mirrlees (1976), who models optimal payout functions given different levels of information asymmetry and risk aversion, and depending on the functioning of the labor market, as well as Holmström (1979), who develops the informativeness principle. The informativeness principle states that the payout function for the agent should be based on a sufficient statistic of the agent's behavior, which means that all data incrementally informative of the agent's behavior should be included in the performance measure. Later work extends the original papers: For example, Lazear/Rosen (1981) find that tournaments that compare agents by rank can be an efficient way of incentivizing risk-averse agents, since performance rank is insensitive to common uncertainties; Grossman/Hart (1983) model the principal-agent problem when the agent's risk preferences are independent of action; and Holmström/Milgrom (1987) develop a multi-period agency model where the agent can choose his effort over time, conditional on how well he has done up to that point in time.

Principal-Agent Theory has been criticized for its lack of empirical orientation, and the low explanatory power of its normative predictions for actual contracting practices observed in reality, due to the extremely stylized nature of its mathematical models (Jensen (1983), Eisenhardt (1989); in the German literature: e.g. Gedenk (1998)).

[27] An excellent non-technical introduction to Principal-Agent Theory with extensive bibliographic notes can be found in Furubotn/Richter (1997), Chapters, 5.9, 5.10; further of interest are the surveys by Levinthal (1988), Eisenhardt (1989) and more recently Sappington (1991), Gibbons (1998), Prendergast (1999) with an emphasis on compensation; and Hunt (1986) and Lambert (2001) with an emphasis on accounting. Holmström/Tirole (1989) provide an excellent more general overview of theories of the firm

2.3.2.3 *Positive Agency Theory*

Positive Agency Theory is considerably less formal and has a much stronger empirical orientation than Principal-Agent Theory. Positive Agency Theory focuses on the relative efficiency of different organizational forms in terms of mitigating agency problems, and analyzes the effects of the contracting environment and the monitoring/bonding technology on the forms of contracts and organizations that we observe (Jensen (1983)). For example, positive agency theory studies the effect of different forms of financing (debt, equity), understood as different forms of principal-agent contracts, on firm value.

In the center of interest of Positive Agency Theory is the relationship between shareholders and management of a corporation (Eisenhardt (1989)), namely the original Berle/Means separation of ownership and control issue. The development of positive agency theory is due to a relatively small number of authors and works (especially Jensen/Meckling (1976),[28] Fama (1980), Fama/Jensen (1983a, 1983b, 1985)). Applications on corporate finance topics, both theoretical and empirical, are abundant (see the surveys by Jensen (1983), Harris/Raviv (1991), Myers (2001) on capital structure, and Shleifer/Vishny (1997) on corporate governance).

Given its special relevance to the present study, it is expedient to review the core work of positive agency theory in more detail.

Jensen/Meckling (1976) is the first application of agency theory to corporate finance, and has shaped the approach and terminology of the discipline. The authors interpret the relationship between an owner-manager (agent) and outside financiers (principals) as an agency relationship. Agency costs arise from the conflict of interest between agent and principals and are defined as the sum of three components:

- *Monitoring costs*: Costs expended by the principal in order to monitor the agent's actions. An example for a monitoring mechanism are security analysts.
- *Bonding costs*: Costs expended by the agent in order to commit not to act against the principal's interests. An example for a bonding mechanism is financial disclosure.

---

[28] Also recognized by Williamson (1988) as the "entering wedge" out of which agency theory developed

- *Residual loss*: Remaining divergence of interest between principal and agent given optimal levels of monitoring and bonding expenditures.[29]

The authors identify two different types of agency costs of outside financing, the agency costs of equity and the agency costs of debt. On this basis, the authors develop an agency theory of capital structure: The optimal capital structure jointly minimizes the agency costs of debt and equity:[30]

- *Agency costs of equity*: The manager derives utility not only from returns to equity, but also from perquisite consumption. In the case where the manager owns 100 percent of the firm, he bears the full cost of perquisite consumption in the form of a decrease in firm value. However, when outside equity financing has been raised, part of the decline in firm value will be borne by outside shareholders. The manager thus has an incentive to overconsume perquisites. This misalignment of incentives leads to the agency costs of equity, which are an increasing function of the ownership stake held by outside shareholders.

- *Agency costs of debt*: While the agency costs of equity could be avoided by using debt financing instead, outside debt also creates agency costs. In a highly levered firm, the manager's equity can be interpreted as a call option on the firm, with its strike price equal to the face value of debt (Black/Scholes (1973)), and its value increasing in the volatility of the underlying. This leads to the so-called asset substitution effect: The manager has an incentive to invest in risky projects in order to increase option value. "If they turn out well, he captures most of the gains, if they turn out badly, the creditors bear most of the costs." (Jensen/Meckling (1976), p. 333). This misalignment of incentives leads to the agency costs of debt, which are an increasing function of leverage.

Optimal capital structure is then derived as the tradeoff between the agency costs of equity and debt. In an efficient capital market, outside financiers will rationally anticipate

[29] The relative extent of monitoring and bonding costs and the residual loss are determined in a simple optimization problem: The model assumes decreasing returns to monitoring and bonding activities, and such costs are expended up to the optimal point where the marginal returns from additional monitoring or bonding are equal to the incremental gain in firm value. The three components of agency costs can thus be interpreted as substitutes, with their relative weight being determined by their relative effectiveness.

[30] In deriving the agency costs of equity and debt, Jensen/Meckling (1976) use as starting point of their analysis a zero-agency costs entrepreneurial firm where the owner-manager owns 100 percent of the capital.

the agency costs of debt and equity, and firm value is reduced correspondingly. The magnitude of agency costs depends on the characteristics of the contracting environment, such as monitoring costs (e.g. cost of measuring the manager's performance), the managerial labor market and the market for corporate control.[31]

Building on the core of positive agency theory developed in Jensen/Meckling (1976), the series of articles by Fama (1980) and Fama/Jensen (1983a, 1983b, 1985), is mainly concerned with demonstrating how the modern corporation can be an efficient form of organization despite the agency problems arising from the separation of ownership and control. In all articles, the authors adopt a natural selection perspective on economic organization: "The form of organization that survives in an activity is the one that delivers the product demanded by customers at the lowest price while covering costs" (Fama/Jensen (1983b), p. 327). Given its prevalence, the modern corporation must thus be an efficient form of organization.[32]

Fama (1980) develops two propositions on the separation of decision making and risk bearing, and the role of the managerial labor market:

- The separation of decision making (by the professional manager), and risk bearing (by the equity holders) in the modern corporation is efficient
- The resulting agency costs are limited by the disciplining force of the managerial labor market that penalizes non-value maximizing managerial behavior

The separation of decision making and risk bearing is efficient because the security holders can diversify their risk in the capital markets, while the manager cannot diversify the risk of his human capital, and will thus be risk averse. However, due to the diversification of their portfolios, the security holders can only take a limited interest in personally overseeing the activities of any one firm in their portfolio, which in turn implies a large degree of separation of ownership an control.

The consequent agency problem is mitigated by the disciplining role of the managerial labor market and the board of directors: The outside managerial labor market exerts a direct pressure to compensate managers for their performance, so that non-value maxi-

---

[31] Jensen/Meckling (1976) hypothesize that agency costs increase with firm size since monitoring becomes inherently more difficult in larger organizations. The optimal scale of the firm is determined as the tradeoff between the marginal reduction in firm value due to agency costs from additional outside financing, and the marginal benefits from managerial diversification

[32] This argument was first developed by Alchian (1950)

mizing behavior will lead to a reduction in future compensation; the board of directors, as a "market-induced institution" acts as internal monitor, that endogenously arises from managerial competition.[33] Non-value maximizing behavior will thus result in an ex post wage revision process, which resolves ex ante managerial incentive problems.

Fama/Jensen (1983a), building on Fama's (1980) line of thought, argue that the benefits of optimal risk bearing and management specialization in a corporation are likely to outweigh the costs of controlling for agency problems, particularly in circumstances where organizations involve complex hierarchies and large amounts of capital:

- The almost complete separation allows for efficient risk bearing: risk can be spread across a large number of diversified investors (shareholders) who can individually decide how much risk they want to bear and for how long; consequently, diversified investors charge less for risk bearing than managers who are generally more risk averse due to their lack of diversification[34]
- The separation of ownership and control allows for specialization of management, given that managerial skills are not necessarily tied to wealth or the willingness to bear risk
- In order to mitigate agency problems, decision control systems, such as the board of directors, can be created. The costs of these mechanisms have to be weighed against the benefits of optimal risk bearing and management specialization

Fama/Jensen (1983b) show that effective control procedures in complex organizations where risk bearing is separated from decision making, also require a separate decision control function.[35] Separation of risk bearing and decision control is efficient since in the

---

[33] Fama makes a rather subtle argument here: Lower-level managers, whose value on the managerial labor market is judged by the success of the whole firm, put pressure on higher-level managers to engage in value-maximizing behavior; the board of directors is thus understood as a mechanism of managerial self-control arising from managerial competition. Interestingly, from a German perspective, this implies that codetermination, or the presence of employee representatives on the board, can be an efficient form of organization. Fama acknowledges the possibility of managerial collusion, but stresses the mitigating role of outside directors

[34] While corporations allocate residual claims (the stochastic net cash flows that remain after contractual obligations to all other parties have been fulfilled) to dispersed shareholders, limited partnerships, in contrast, generally restrict residual claims to important decision makers: Consequently, decision makers have to be chosen not only according to their managerial skill, but also depending on their wealth and willingness to bear risk, and optimal risk diversification is not achieved

[35] Fama/Jensen (1983b) present a four-step decision process (initiation, ratification, implementation, monitoring), where two steps are combined under the term decision management (initiation,

case of a large number of residual claimants, delegation of decision control decreases costs. The authors mention three mechanisms that undertake a function of decision control: the stock market, by sending visible signals on the consequences of decisions; the market for corporate control, by making inefficient managers subject to hostile takeovers; and finally and most importantly, the board of directors, whose outside members have an incentive to act in the residual claimants' interest in order to build their reputation as decision control experts on the market for corporate directors.

Finally, Fama/Jensen (1985) establish shareholder value maximization as optimal investment decision rule for corporations. In a perfectly competitive capital market, with costless trading and rational pricing, a corporation's shareholders will evaluate all decisions according to their contribution to the current market value of their residual claims.[36] Given agency costs, however, market value is only be maximized up to the point where the incremental increase in market value is offset by the incremental increase in cost for decision control systems mitigating agency problems.

Taken together, the series of articles by Fama/Jensen thus provides a relatively complete rationalization of the key features of modern corporations using agency arguments. Building on these foundations, numerous extensions have been made to positive agency theory, focusing mainly on the role of alternative mechanisms for controlling agency costs, e.g. product market competition (e.g. Hart (1983)), hostile takeovers (e.g. Morck/Shleifer/Vishny (1989)), large institutional investors (e.g. Shleifer/Vishny (1986)), or large creditors (Diamond (1989)). Most of the theory is reviewed in the broad survey by Shleifer/Vishny (1997).

2.4 Application of agency theory to empirical corporate finance

2.4.1 The classic corporate finance approach to agency theory

Ideally, absolute agency costs could be directly measured, and the efficiency of different organizational forms could thus be directly compared. However, such an approach is of course infeasible. While a considerable empirical literature exists that tests the predictions

implementation), and the remaining two steps under the term decision control (ratification, monitoring).

[36] This argument was already formalized earlier by Fama (1978): In a perfectly competitive capital market, the investor's consumption stream is only constrained by current wealth, i.e. the market value of current and future resources.

of agency theory against actual observed contracting practices, such approaches have limitations due to the nonobservability of central parameters such as risk aversion or disutility from effort (Prendergast (2002)). Attempts at directly measuring agency costs of different organizational forms have thus hardly been made (Ang/Cole/Lin (2000) and Habib/Ljungqvist (in Press) are two rare exceptions). [37] Progress in this direction has been limited since the original statement in Jensen/Meckling (1976), who admitted that the exact empirical shape of the functions determining the agency costs of debt and equity in their model is unknown.

The corporate finance literature based on agency theory therefore in general does not focus on absolute agency costs, but evaluates the relative agency costs of different organizational forms or organizational features, by analyzing the changes in agency costs resulting from financial transactions associated with a change of organizational form (Shleifer/Vishny (1997)). In this context, agency costs are approximated based on such measures as Tobin's Q and equity value (Shleifer/Vishny (1997)).

For example, event studies, the "most common empirical methodology of corporate governance and finance" (Shleifer/Vishny (1997)) have been used to evaluate the efficiency a multitude of different types of transactions, ranging from stock splits (Fama et al. (1969), the first event study in finance) to diversifying mergers (e.g. Amihud/Lev (1981)), by calculating announcement date excess equity returns. [38] Positive announcement date abnormal returns to spin-offs, for example, are generally interpreted as evidence of a decrease in agency costs thanks to the breakup of a diversified organization (e.g. Desai/Jain (1999)).

Event studies are based on the presumption that the total economic of an event can be measured via the short-term capital market reaction. Under the condition of an informationally efficient capital market, all information pertaining to the event is immediately impounded into the stock price (e.g. Fama (1970)), and capital market participants have rational expectations. Thus, an abnormal behavior of stock returns after the announcement

[37] This approach has not been met without criticism: Gomes/Livdan (in press) contend that the empirical predictions of agency-based models are "usually very hard to quantify" due to the lack of a measure of absolute agency costs, and as a consequence, direct empirical support is often limited, or mainly comes from the failure of competing theories

[38] A rare exception of an article that explicitly considers both the effects on stockholders and bondholders is Mansi/Reeb (2002), who study the consequences of diversification

of the event is not to be expected, and the long-term behavior of stock returns can be disregarded (e.g. Fama (1998)).

2.4.2 Critique

The validity of the approach outlined above rests on two assumptions:

1. Equity is the only incomplete contract, and shareholder value maximization is therefore socially optimal
2. On efficient markets, shareholder value is determined by agency costs

In the following, the realism of these assumptions will be discussed in more detail.

The assumption that *equity is the only incomplete contract* is a direct consequence of the definition of the firm adopted in agency theory. The firm is a nexus of contracts. All contracts are complete, with the exception of equity: shareholders put up capital in return for the promise of an uncertain future return. Shareholders, as the residual claimants, thus bear the entire risk (Fama (1980)). "All the other members of the nexus would be indifferent to the choice made by equity holders because they are contractually protected against any negative consequence" (Zingales (2000), p. 1632).

It follows that the effect of management's decisions will directly and entirely show up in the market value of equity, and maximization of shareholder value is tantamount to economic efficiency (Becht/Bolton/Röell (2003)). Consequently, as Shleifer/Vishny (1997, p. 746) put it, "if the stock price falls when managers announce a particular action, then this action must serve the interests of managers rather than those of the shareholders." Therefore, within an agency framework, the consequences of corporate actions can be evaluated by analyzing the stock market response alone. Other factors, such as the effect on compensation or bond prices can be ignored since these contracts are assumed to be complete.

The assumption of *efficient markets* implies that agency problems are the sole source of potential inefficiency, and rules out alternative explanations for differences in shareholder value. This result follows from the core of neoclassical theory: input and output markets are perfectly competitive, firms produce homogenous goods, based on a homogenous technology (e.g. Mas-Collel/Whinston/Green (1995), or any other standard microeconomics textbook).[39] The corporate finance literature, firmly rooted in neoclassical economic theory, implicitly assumes the efficiency of markets, i.e. efficient product, labor and capital markets (Zingales (2000)), and concentrates on analyzing the effects of a single source of inefficiency, namely agency costs.

For example, the presumption of perfect competition on product markets eliminates market power as an explanation for revaluations after takeovers. While transactions such as takeovers can naturally affect firm value in a way totally unrelated to agency costs, but still consistent with market efficiency, e.g. by altering the production function, or simply by increasing scale, these considerations are generally not the focus of corporate finance.[40]

Taken together, the shareholder value principle and the presumption of market efficiency allow to interpret abnormal stock returns caused by various corporate transactions as direct evidence of changes in agency costs (Shleifer/Vishny (1997a)). In conclusion, these two assumptions jointly constitute the prerequisite for the validity of the classic corporate finance application of agency theory.

The realism of the two assumptions has been repeatedly criticized:

- There are other incomplete contracts apart from equity, and shareholder value maximization therefore need not be socially optimal
- Markets are not efficient, and therefore other drivers of shareholder value are potentially more important than agency costs

The broader political discussion aside, shareholder value maximization has also been criticized from a theoretical perspective (for a review see Becht/Bolton/Röell (2003), also see Walsh/Seward (1990), incorporating perspectives from organization theory).[41] Beginning with Jensen/Meckling's (1976) asset substitution problem and Myer's (1977) debt overhang problem, there is a large number of articles commenting on stockholder-bondholder conflicts and the consequences that decisions favoring stockholders can have on

---

[39] An instructive review of the disciplining role of labor, product, and capital markets is contained in Holmström/Tirole (1989), Sections 4.1-4.4; for the underlying assumptions of neoclassical theory see also Jensen/Meckling (1976) and more generally Schenk (1997), Chapter 3, Section 1

[40] Exemplifying this approach is for example the review by Jensen/Ruback (1983) on the market for corporate control: while operational synergies are cited as potential value driver, the article concentrates on the elimination of inefficient managerial behavior as explanation for the valuation effects of takeovers.

[41] For recent German perspectives on the shareholder value principle see Jürgens/Naumann/Rupp (2000), Kürsten (2000), Albach (2001b), Coenenberg (2003), and Fiss/Zajac (2004)

bondholders.[42] Zingales (2000) contends that equity is by far not the only incomplete contract: For example, workers (beyond their explicit contract specifying a certain amount of current compensation in return for certain services) invest in firm-specific human capital in return for the uncertain promise of above-market future compensation. This investment constitutes an implicit contract whose value can be affected by management decisions.[43] Consequently, shareholder value maximization is not necessarily socially optimal in more realistic complex incomplete-contracting settings.

The realism of the market efficiency assumption is equally questionable. While for corporate finance, particularly capital market efficiency is a central assumption, there has been an ongoing and controversial discussion on the subject (core review articles are Fama (1970), Fama (1991), befittingly entitled "Efficient Capital Markets" and "Efficient Capital Markets II"; as well as Roll (1977), Jensen (1978), Fama (1998), Malkiel (2003) and Shiller (2003)). If capital markets are not efficient, shareholder value can be driven by e.g. psychological biases in investor behavior (e.g. Barberis/Shleifer/Vishny (1998) for a behavioral asset pricing model). If the assumption of capital market efficiency is relaxed, short-term abnormal returns found in event studies can thus no longer be assumed to measure the total economic impact of the event, since the capital market expectations driving short-term abnormal returns need not be rational. This argument is the basis for the sprawling literature on long-term abnormal returns after corporate events (e.g. Ritter's (1991) seminal work on long-term underperformance of IPOs): If capital markets are not fully efficient, the long-term behavior of stock prices need not be random.

Despite the criticism, however, shareholder value maximization and the presumption of market efficiency still overwhelmingly dominate corporate finance. One reason is the lack of tractable alternative models. On a more theoretical level, the pre-eminence of agency explanations over other explanations for firm value is justified by the presumption that in the absence of agency problems, any operational effects, such as e.g. merger synergies, can be perfectly replicated by a set of contracts between the companies involved. Exemplifying this evaluation are Shleifer/Vishny (1997, p. 738), who strongly assert that "the

---

[42] Parrino/Weisbach (1999) in one the very few empirical analyses on stockholder-bondholder conflicts come to the conclusion that the effect of such conflicts on firm value is generally small; on theoretical grounds, this is explained by Diamond (1989), who asserts that managers will abstain from asset substitution in order to build firm reputation as dependable borrower. Group formation as a remedy to stockholder-bondholder conflicts is modeled by Rau-Bredow (2001)

[43] From a property rights perspective it has been argued, however, that shareholder value maximization can still be efficient given that shareholders have the least protected contract (e.g. Williamson (1985)).

agency problem is serious: the opportunities for managers to abscond with financiers' funds, or to squander them on pet projects are plentiful and well-documented".

In light of the dominant position, this study therefore adopts the classic corporate finance approach to agency theory. However, the assumption of capital market efficiency is relaxed insofar as long-term stock returns are included in the analysis.

2.5 A two-dimensional agency framework for the analysis of ECOs

2.5.1 Efficiency criterion and framework dimensions

The above section has sketched the common application of agency theory as underpinning of corporate finance research: it focuses on the relative change in agency costs, as proxied for by the change in equity value. In the present study, effects of ECOs on firm value will thus be couched in terms of changes in incentive alignment and subsequent reductions or increases in agency costs.

Reiterating the implications of Positive Agency Theory for empirical corporate finance methodology, ECOs are analyzed as follows in the present study:

- *Equity is the only incomplete contract*: Potential changes in agency costs caused by ECOs are measured based on the change in shareholder value
- *Efficient markets*: Changes in shareholder value after ECOs are interpreted as evidence for a change in agency costs due to the transaction

This methodology results in an intuitive efficiency criterion:

ECOs constitute an efficient form of restructuring if they are associated with a reduction in agency costs, proxied for by the change in equity value related to the transaction.

In this context, the change in equity value refers to the difference between equity value of the groups of companies prior to the ECO and the value of the portfolio of parent and subsidiary after the ECO.[44] Both a short-term event study perspective and a long-term perspective are adopted in measuring the change in equity value. However, in light of the above discussion on capital market efficiency, the final yardstick for determining ECO value creation are not the capital market expectations leading to the short-term reaction, but the actual long-term behavior of stock returns.

---

[44] Detailed definitions are provided in Section 4.3.1

In order to guide the development of hypotheses on the change in agency costs, a prior understanding of two questions is required:

- What are general determinants of agency costs?
- What agency relationships are affected by an ECO?

These questions are discussed in the following two sections, and results are synthesized to form a two-dimensional agency framework for the analysis of ECOs. The development of such a framework is especially important in light of the "ex-post rationalization" approach relatively common in the earlier corporate finance literature: Valuation effects of a certain transaction are first empirically measured, and ex post rationalized as evidence for a reduction/increase in agency costs. Exemplifying this approach is e.g. Schipper/Smith (1986) on ECOs. The more recent literature derives hypotheses on the basis of specific predictions on the development of agency costs ex ante, often supported by a formal model, and then tests these hypotheses empirically. This approach is exemplified by e.g. Rajan/Servaes/Zingales (2000) on internal capital markets.[45]

In order to guide development of hypotheses on the impact of ECOs on agency costs, an understanding of the generic determinants of agency costs identified in the theoretical literature is therefore needed. The following sections derive the determinants of agency costs on the basis of a semi-formal analysis, combining elements from Positive Agency Theory and Principal-Agent Theory.

2.5.2 First dimension: determinants of agency costs

2.5.2.1 Determinants of agency costs in Positive Agency Theory

In Positive Agency Theory, agency costs arising in the shareholder/manager relationship are the main focus. Interest divergence between agent and principal (shareholders and managers) and monitoring/bonding technology have been modeled as core determinants of agency costs in the literature.

[45] Ironically, Miller (1999) remarks that the general consistency of the real-world data with the predictions of the model in corporate finance articles is hardly surprising, since the authors would otherwise not have submitted their work for publication

Jensen/Meckling (1976), on which the following section is based, determine agency costs as the difference between firm value in the case of a manager-owned firm without outside financing (i.e. no separation of ownership and control) and firm value in the case of separation and control, where external shareholders are interpreted as principal and the manager as agent. In this context, interest divergence is approximated by the extent of outside equity ownership.

Figure 6: Firm value and private benefits in the absence of monitoring

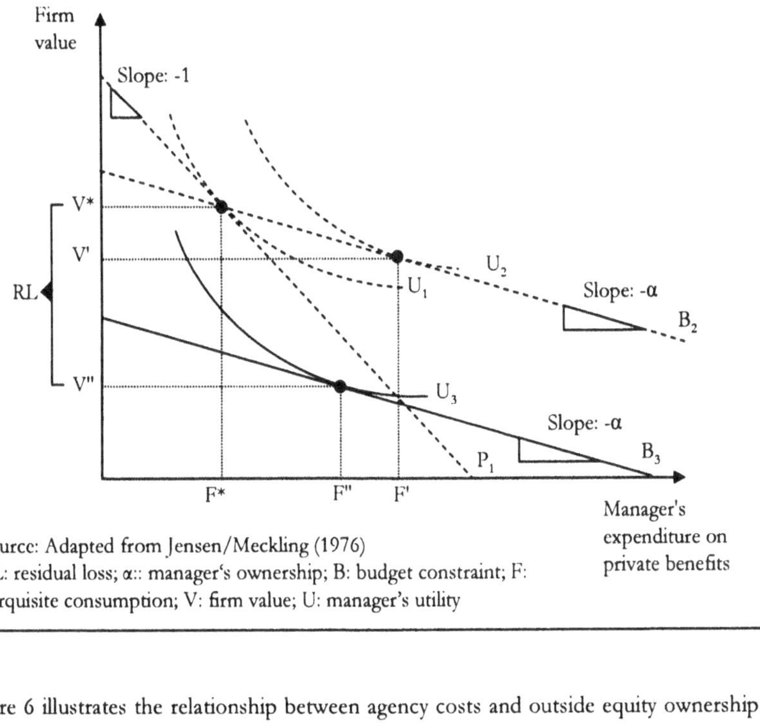

Source: Adapted from Jensen/Meckling (1976)
RL: residual loss; α:: manager's ownership; B: budget constraint; F: perquisite consumption; V: firm value; U: manager's utility

Figure 6 illustrates the relationship between agency costs and outside equity ownership.[46] The manager (agent) faces a trade-off between increasing firm value (V) and expending

[46] The discussion below exclusively focuses on the agency costs of equity. While ECOs are associated with a change in capital structure that potentially also affects the agency costs of debt, the agency costs of equity clearly bear higher relevance to the subject of study. Furthermore, wealth transfer (from bondholders to shareholders) arguments are generally rejected in the previous ECO literature, e.g. Schipper/Smith (1986)

resources on perquisite consumption, i.e. private benefits (F). This trade-off results in a budget constraint[47] (B_1). The manager's utility derived from firm value and private benefits, is represented by the manager's indifference curves (U_1, U_2, U_3).

In the case of a manager-owned firm, the budget constraint has a slope of -1 (B_1): an increase in private benefits leads to a corresponding reduction in firm value by the same amount. The owner-manager maximizes his utility by choosing optimal levels of firm value and private benefits (V*, F*).[48] This is the zero-agency cost base case.

Figure 7: Firm value and private benefits under monitoring

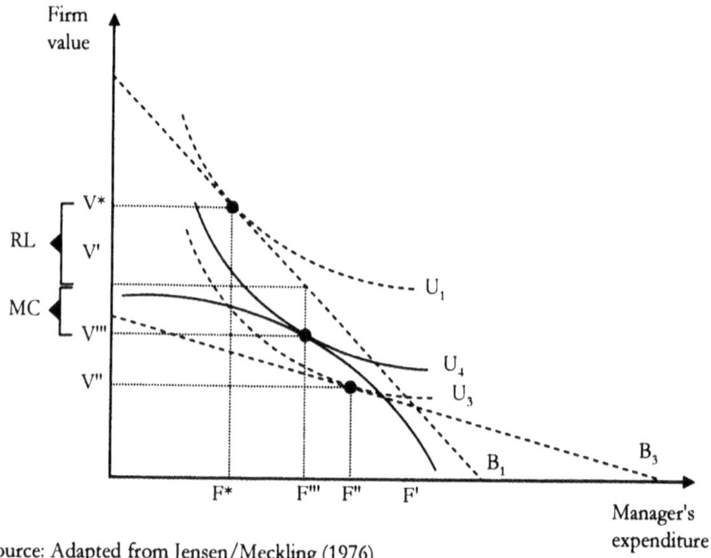

Source: Adapted from Jensen/Meckling (1976)
RL: residual loss; MC: monitoring costs; B: budget constraint; F: perquisite consumption; V: firm value; U: manager's utility

47 The budget constraint is determined by firm size and investment; here, an arbitrary firm size is picked and held constant

48 It is assumed that private benefits and firm value are not perfect substitutes, i.e. that a manager always chooses a positive level of private benefits

Assuming outside financing is needed in order to fund a positive NPV investment project, the owner-manager sells a fractional equity ownership of 1-α to external shareholders (with himself retaining α). As a consequence, the budget constraint flattens (B_2), and the manager increases expenditures for private benefits to F', while firm value declines to V'. However, on an efficient capital market, fractional ownership cannot be sold on the basis of V*, due to the external shareholders' anticipating the manager's expenditures on private benefits. The budget constraint faced by the manager thus not only flattens, it also shifts downwards (B_3). Consequently, in optimum, firm value is V", private benefits are F", and the manager derives a (lower) utility of U_3. Agency costs are given by the difference between V* and V". In terms of the components of agency costs discussed previously (Section 2.3.2.3), these agency costs are entirely residual loss (RL).

The above discussion has ignored the possibility of monitoring or bonding activities that can be undertaken to limit expenditures on private benefits. Figure 7 extends the discussion to include monitoring activities. The manager's indifference curves and budget constraints (U_1/B_1, U_3/B_3) are as in the previous figure. The introduction of monitoring activities leads to a new curvilinear budget constraint (B_4). By incurring monitoring costs (MC), shareholders can curtail the manager's expenditures on private benefits. It is assumed that monitoring activities exhibit decreasing returns to scale, hence the curvilinear shape. The previous optimal point (V", F", U_3) changes to (V'", F'", U_4).

Total agency costs are given as the sum of residual loss (RL) and monitoring costs (M), and are smaller compared to the previous case without monitoring costs. As discussed in Jensen/Meckling (1976), bonding activities can be interpreted as equivalent to monitoring activities, and their relative amount will be determined by the marginal returns to each activity. The relative effectiveness of monitoring and bonding is determined by the respective monitoring/bonding technology used.[49]

Summarizing, the above discussion has derived two general determinants of agency costs:

- Extent of interest divergence
- Monitoring/bonding technology

---

[49] Jensen/Meckling (1976) discuss the effectiveness of security analysts as monitoring technology and of annual reports as bonding technology, Fama (1980) discusses the managerial labor market, and Fama/Jensen (1983b) discuss decision control systems in general (refer back to the review in Section2.3.2.3)

2.5.2.2 *Determinants of agency costs in Principal-Agent Theory*

In Principal-Agent Theory, agency costs arising in the employer/worker relationship are the main focus. The literature is concerned with analyzing optimal compensation arrangements that minimize agency costs. Accordingly, agency costs depend on the characteristics of the principal's and agent's utility functions. The information environment and risk aversion have been modeled as core determinants of agency costs.

Within a simple one-agent, one-period, one-task principal-agent model (e.g. Ross (1973)), the utility of the (risk-neutral) principal is given by output (x) less the wage (z) paid to the agent. The principal chooses an incentive scheme that maximizes his utility (Equation (1)), taking into account utility-maximizing behavior by the (risk-averse) agent (Equation (3)) and respecting the agent's participation constraint (Equation (2)). The principal's problem is thus given by the following equations, where the function f(x | a) is the probability distribution of output (x), conditional on the agent's action (a), and U_{min} represent the agent's reservation utility over all states (s) of the world (e.g. Ross (1973), Holmström (1979)):

(1) $$max \int [x - z(x)] f(x \mid a^*) dx, \quad s.t.$$

(2) $$\int U[s(x)] f(x \mid a) dx - c(a^*) \geq U_{min}$$

(3) $$a^* = \underset{a}{arg\,max} \int U[z(x)] f(x \mid a) dx - C(a)$$

As seen from Equation (3), the agent chooses an optimal action (a*), that maximizes the sum of his utility (U) from compensation (z) less his disutility from effort (C).[50] Compensation is dependent on output (x), where output in turn depends on the action chosen by the agent.

Since the above model is too general in order to serve as a useful benchmark for empirical work (Gibbons (1998), Prendergast (1999), Lambert (2001)), it is generally operationalized using simplifying assumptions[51]. A frequently-used operationalization of the above general equations is the LEN-model (Holmström/Milgrom (1987, 1991), Spremann (1987)). LEN stands for linear sharing rule, exponential utility, and normally distributed output.

---

[50] This separability is generally assumed in order to facilitate mathematical exposition (e.g. Haubrich (1994))

[51] Grossman/Hart (1983) provide a solution algorithm for the general model

The crucial advantage of the LEN-model is that, making certain assumptions, the optimal sharing rule is linear (see Holmström/Milgrom (1987) for a mathematical proof; Wagenhofer/Ewert (1993) for extensions).[52] The LEN-model makes the following three assumptions:

- Incentive compensation (z) linearly increasing in the agent's efforts (a), where z_0 is a fixed wage and z_1 is the variable component

(4) $$z(a) = z_0 + z_1 x$$

- Exponential utility with constant absolute risk aversion[53] (r) and convex disutility from effort (C)

(5) $$C(a) = a^2$$

- Normally distributed output.

(6) $$x \sim N(a, \sigma^2)$$

The agent's utility function is thus given by the following equation:

(7) $$U(z,a) = 1 - e^{-r(z-a^2)}$$

The first-best solution to the optimization problem would arise under two alternative conditions: if the principal could perfectly observe the agent's actions and could thus impose the optimal action on the agent, incentive compensation (z_1) would be zero (Mirrlees (1974)); or alternatively, if the agent were not risk averse, incentive compensation (z_1) would be one, i.e. the agent would essentially buy the firm from the principal (Shavell (1979)). Under the second-best solution, the optimal incentive scheme is derived trading off the motivational effect of incentives against the costs of exposing the agent to risk. Agency costs are given as the difference between the first-best and the second best-solution (Holmström (1979)). Mathematically, agency costs (AC) depend on the agent's risk aversion and the variance of output (for a complete derivation of the result, see Spremann (1987)):

---

[52] This assumption is of course a simplification of reality; in fact, non-linear sharing rules are frequently observed, e.g. bonuses that are paid when a specific performance threshold is reached (e.g. Prendergast (1999) for a review)

[53] Constant absolute risk aversion has the advantage that risk aversion is independent from agent wealth

$$AC(r,\sigma)=\frac{r\sigma^2}{2+4r\sigma^2} \tag{8}$$

From Equation (8), it can be immediately seen that agency costs are an increasing function of the agent's risk aversion and an increasing function of output variance. Stated differently, the costs of incentivizing an agent increase with risk aversion and the information environment.

Output variance, in the simple LEN-model, is a proxy for the information environment: The principal infers the agent's (unobservable) action from (observable) output; however, the greater the variance of output, the greater the principal's uncertainty about the action the agent has taken. More technically, output is thus interpreted as a noisy signal of the agent's effort. Agency costs depend on the quality of the signal. Intuitively, a very precise signal increases the probability that a low effort level (or an undesirable action) by the agent will be detected (Demougin/Fluet (2001)). Signal quality can be measured in different ways. The likelihood ratio (Holmström (1979)) measures the probability that the action taken by the agent is correctly inferred from the signal. Further conditions for the ranking of different signals have been developed by Kim (1995). If multiple signals are available, Holmström's (1979) informativeness principle prescribes that incentive pay is to be based on all measures incrementally informative of the agent's actions. Banker/Datar (1989) examine under what conditions a linear aggregation of multiple signals is efficient. While in the above simplified case, it is assumed that the principal observes output, later work has modeled more complex information environments. For example, the output of an agent that has to fulfill multiple complex tasks may itself not be observable (Holmström/Milgrom (1991); Baker (1992)). Generally speaking, agency costs thus depend on the properties of the information environment.

In summary, the above section has derived two general determinants of agency costs:

- Risk aversion
- Information environment

2.5.2.3 Synthesis

Interestingly, the Positive Agency and Principal-Agent literature take opposite vantage points: Instead of beginning with an owner-manager and examining the effects of an increasing separation of ownership and control as in Jensen/Meckling (1976), a complete separation of ownership and control, representative of an employment relationship where the employee receives a fixed wage, is assumed as starting point in Principal-Agent Theory and incentive compensation is introduced in order to mitigate the consequences (Levinthal (1988)). Table 3 summarizes the salient differences between positive agency theory and principal-agent literature.

Table 3: Comparison of Positive Agency Theory and Principal-Agent Theory

	Positive Agency Theory	Principal-Agent Theory
Starting point	Owner-manager seeking outside financing	Employment relationship
Risk tolerance	Risk-neutral principal Risk-neutral agent	Risk-neutral principal Risk-averse agent
Wealth constraints	Yes	No
Cause of agency problem	Wealth-constrained owner-manager needs outside financing in order to fund investment project	Risk-averse agent desires fixed wage irrespective of the outcome of his work
Interest divergence between agent and principal	Given outside equity financing, manager (agent) prefers higher level perquisite consumption than outside shareholders	Given a fixed wage, agent prefers lower levels of effort (disutility from effort)
Observability	Outside financiers do not observe perquisite consumption, only firm value	Principal does not observe agent effort, only outcome
Role of monitoring	By engaging in costly monitoring activities, outside financiers can curtail perquisite consumption	By engaging in costly monitoring, the principal can receive a (noisy) signal about agent effort
Optimal solution to agency problem	Trade-off increased firm size (with corresponding increase in firm value thanks to additional positive NPV investment projects) against overconsumption of perquisites caused by additional outside financing	Trade-off high-powered incentives for agent to increase output against the cost of such incentives caused by the agent's risk aversion
Core determinants of agency costs	Extent of interest divergence Monitoring/bonding technology	Agent's risk aversion Information environment

While Table 3 clearly shows the stark differences in spirit between Positive Agency Theory and Principal-Agent Theory, it also underlines the common ground between the two subdisciplines. Some differences deserve further highlighting: In Positive Agency Theory, the extent of incentives (managerial equity ownership) is not limited by risk aversion, but by wealth constraints. Consequently, in Jensen/Meckling (1976), risk aversion does not play a role. Furthermore, while Jensen/Meckling (1976) and the Positive Agency Theory literature focus on the *cost* of alternative bonding/monitoring technologies, the Principal-Agent literature discusses the implications of monitoring mainly in terms of characteristics of the information environment, e.g. the precision of signals about the agent's effort.[54] Finally, while the source of interest divergence in principal-agent theory is the disutility from effort, in positive agency theory, it is represented by the consumption of private benefits.

In the present study, only those determinants of agency costs are selected that can be reasonably assumed to depend on organizational form, i.e. which can be affected by ECOs. Generally, for the analysis of ECOs, the perspective of positive agency theory bears a greater relevance: Shavell's (1979) result for the case of a risk-neutral agent (it would be efficient to sell the firm to the risk-neutral agent) seems outright impossible to implement. Further, the realism of the disutility from effort parameter for top managers has been repeatedly criticized in the literature (e.g. Gedenk/Albers (1994), Gedenk (1998), Prendergast (1999)). Finally, it is unlikely that the risk tolerance of the agents involved will change as a consequence of the ECO. This eliminates risk tolerance as a determinant of agency cost changes due to ECOs.

The following three determinants of agency costs are thus used as a guide for hypothesis development:[55]

- *Interest divergence*: The fundamental source of interest divergence in the modern corporation is the separation of ownership and control (Jensen/Meckling (1976)). The (exogenous) variable "interest divergence" is unusual in terms of the Principal-Agent literature. However, in the spirit of the Positive Agency Theory literature, proxies for interest divergence such as preference for empire building (Jensen (1986), entrenchment (Shleifer/Vishny (1989)), short-termism (Narayanan (1985)), or herding (Scharfstein/Stein (1990)) appear more reasonable than the much-criticized "disutility from effort".

  Foremost instruments used to reduce interest divergence are stock ownership by the agent, or incentive compensation (e.g. Baker/Jensen/Murphy (1988)), which ties the utility of the manager to shareholder value. However, wealth constraints

[54] One of the rare exceptions is Demougin/Fluet (2001), who include an explicit cost of monitoring in their model and analyze the trade-off between higher-powered incentives and more intense monitoring

[55] Similar dimensions have been identified in Schultze (1998) and Ebers/Gotsch (2001)

of managers and limits on what are levels of compensation reckoned to be politically acceptable preclude that interest divergence is fully resolved by incentive compensation (Murphy (1999)).

Consequently, a non-remediable degree of interest divergence remains, the extent of which depends on organizational form insofar as organizational features can change the nature of incentives (e.g. De Motta (2002) for a discussion in an internal capital markets context).

- *Information environment*: The information environment determines how difficult it is for the principal to observe the agent's actions. There is generally no functional relationship between the agent's actions and outcome, since outcome is also determined by exogenous shocks, as operationalized in the LEN-model in the previous section. Therefore, the agent's actions cannot be fully inferred from the (observable) outcome (e.g. Holmström (1979)).

  The information environment depends, among other factors, on organizational form: For example, the bundling of cash flows in diversified firms reduces the impact of exogenous shocks on outcomes, assuming that these shocks are not perfectly correlated across business segments, and thus facilitates estimating the agent's (manager's) effort (Nanda/Narayanan (1999)). Also, the creation of subsidiary stock can facilitate the provision of incentive-based compensation by providing an additional signal of agent effort (e.g. Aron (1991) for a formal treatment)

- *Monitoring/bonding technology*: Given a certain initial interest divergence and information environment, the actual severity of the agency problem is *ceteris paribus* determined by the effectiveness and efficiency of the monitoring/bonding technology. While the information environment can be interpreted as a measure of the initial noisiness of the signal of the agent's action, monitoring/bonding technology refers to the cost of obtaining the signal, or of increasing the precision or credibility of the signals, or of obtaining additional signals of the agent's actions.

  Building on the foundations laid by Positive Agency Theory, monitoring/bonding technology has more recently been analyzed in the flourishing area of corporate governance research (for excellent reviews see Shleifer/Vishny (1997), Becht/Bolton/Röell (2003), Denis/McConnell (2003); further see the series of articles by LaPorta et al. (1997, 1998, 2000a, 2000b, 2002), LaPorta/Lopez de Silanes/Shleifer (1999), and Shleifer/Wolfenzon (2002) on international comparisons of governance systems; for recent German perspectives, see Prigge (1998), Helmis (2002), Jürgens/Rupp (2002), Schmidt (2003)). From an agency theory perspective, corporate governance research discusses the effectiveness and efficiency of different monitoring/bonding technologies in curtailing agency costs, often in an international context of comparative corporate governance. Mechanisms commonly covered in the literature (e.g. Walsh/Seward (1990), Jensen (1993) for influential classifications) are external mechanisms (large shareholders (Shleifer/Vishny (1986)), creditors (Stiglitz (1985)), product markets (Hart (1983)), the market for corporate control (Grossman/Hart (1980a, 1981)), managerial labor markets (Fama (1980)), the institutional environment (La Porta et al. (1997)), accounting rules (Bushman/Smith (2001)), and internal mechanisms (the board (Morck/Shleifer/Vishny (1989)), internal capital markets (e.g. Stein (1997)).

Monitoring/bonding technology directly depends on organizational form insofar as different organizational forms make use of different monitoring technologies: For example, a diversified firm substitutes an internal capital market that finances the divisions' projects for the external capital market (e.g. Gertner/Scharfstein/Stein (1994)).

While the above discussion has underlined that all three general determinants of agency costs are dependent on organizational form, treatments of agency costs in the ECO literature have generally focused on monitoring/bonding technology (Löffler (2001), Langenbach (2001)). Löffler (2001) discusses the following external and internal control mechanisms: external capital market, legal and regulatory environment, factor markets, product markets, and the board of directors. Langenbach (2002) considers the external capital market, the product market, the managerial labor market and, notably, internal management accounting.[56]

As stated, this study will take a more general approach and explicitly consider changes in agency costs due to all three determinants.

[56] An empirical investigation of the effectiveness of internal management accounting as a control mechanism for subsidiaries is Littkemann (2001)

2.5.3 *Second dimension: agency relationships affected by ECOs*

2.5.3.1 *Organizational hierarchies as cascades of agency relationships*

The second dimension of the two-dimensional agency framework for the analysis of ECOs consists of the principal-agent relationships affected by ECOs. Before identifying these, a more general discussion of principal-agent relationships in hierarchies is in order.

In the spirit of Ross (1973), agency relationships are a universal mode of social interaction. While Positive Agency Theory focuses on the shareholders/manager relationship, and Principal-Agent Theory focuses on the employer/worker relationship, these perspectives are thus too narrow in order to capture the complexities of modern corporations (Bolton/Scharfstein (1998))

For example, conflicts of interest leading to agency problems can also be found between:

- Shareholders and supervisory board members
- Supervisory board members and executive board members
- Executive board members and division/functional managers
- Division/functional managers and department heads

Above (non-exhaustive) list illustrates the multi-tiered nature of large organizations. The core of Positive Agency Theory thus has to be complemented in order to further the understanding of groups of companies.

Holmström/Tirole (1989), in the tradition of the Principal-Agent literature, have taken exception with the prevalent model using a simple technical argument (p. 106):

> "The two-tier capitalist-management model creates the potentially misleading impression that the internal hierarchy (below management) can be summarized in reduced form by an exogenous random production function. [...] The mistake is in assuming that the manager's action can be described by a maximization over his expected utility given his sharing rule, when in fact it will be determined by the outcome of a non-cooperative game, where the expectation of the worker's action plays a central role."

In addition, Holmström/Tirole (1989) object against the common "grand contracting" assumption, i.e. that the principal can design a so-called grand contract with all agents (management, workers), and that recontracting between the agents is prohibited.

Later, Bolton/Scharfstein (1998) demand that (p. 97):

"the firm should be understood as being comprised of (at least) two tiers of agency relationships: one between investors and corporate headquarters and the other between corporate headquarters and the divisions."

However, both Holmström/Tirole (1989), and Bolton/Scharfstein (1998) nearly a decade later, come to the conclusion that research on multi-layer agency relationships unfortunately has been relatively scarce. While the Principal-Agent literature has applied agency theory to the analysis of the inner workings of hierarchies,[57] there is only a very limited number of formal analyses on that explicitly take into account multi-layer agency problems. The most notable earlier multi-layer agency models are Tirole (1986), Holmström/Milgrom (1990), and McAfee/McMillan (1995). Tirole (1986), for example, analyzes a two-tier organization with an owner, a supervisor, and a worker. In designing the optimal incentive scheme for the supervisor and the worker, the owner must take into account the possibility of collusion between the supervisor and the worker. The optimal contract differs from the case where this possibility is not taken into account.

The above discussion thus clarifies the need for taking into account agency problems at all levels in evaluating the efficiency of organizational forms. Figure 8 provides a stylized illustration how the hierarchical layers of a group of companies can be understood as a cascade of agency relationships.

2.5.3.2 Groups of companies as two-layer agency structures

While the preceding section has demonstrated how agency theory can be adapted to the analysis of hierarchies with multiple levels, the study of groups of companies requires further refinements to theory in order to fully capture real-world complexities. While the fundamental agency problem of the separation of ownership and control equally applies to groups of companies and single corporations, groups of companies cannot be merely interpreted as particularly complex forms of multi-level hierarchies.

The working definition of groups of companies developed in Section 1.2.1 highlights two core characteristics inherent in the groups of companies that are subject of study: groups of companies can be interpreted as hybrid forms between markets and hierarchies; and

[57] For example, Gjesdal (1982) has developed a model for optimal hierarchical design based on information and communication costs; Calvo/Wellisz (1978) have developed a model of optimal firm size based on the costs and effectiveness of supervision; the tournament literature (e.g. Lazear/Rosen (1981)) has analyzed how hierarchies can foster competition among agents; and Waldman (1984) has modeled the internal labor market within a hierarchy, focusing on optimal promotion policies

Figure 8: Groups of companies as cascades of agency relationships

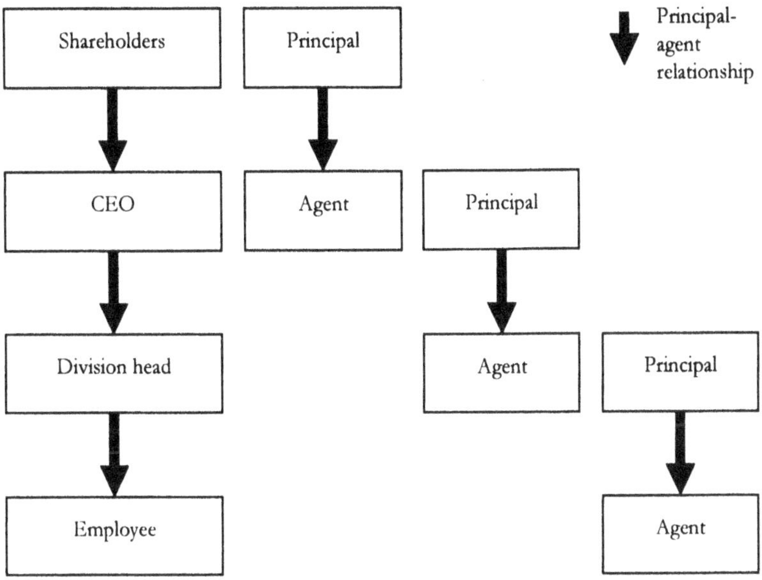

Source: Adapted from Coenenberg (2003)

only the parent, which is an exchange-listed corporation, accesses the external capital market.

These two distinct properties that differentiate groups of companies from single corporations are also relevant in the framework of agency theory.[58]

1. *Internal capital markets*: The parent company allocates resources across organizational units on the internal capital market, where organizational units compete. The properties of internal capital markets and their efficiency compared to the external capital market have recently spawned a rich literature, mostly originating from Meyer/Milgrom/Roberts (1992) and from Gertner/Scharfstein/Stein (1994). Most of this literature is based on agency theory (a detailed review follows in Sec-

[58] For a more general and thorough discussion of the specifics of groups of companies in an agency framework, see Schenk (1997a), Rau-Bredow (1999)

tion 3.3.3) and models the agency costs of the internal capital market and compares these to agency costs of external financing.

2. *Exchange-listed parent*: By definition, the groups of companies that are subject of the present study have a parent company that has the legal form of corporation (Aktiengesellschaft) and that is exchange-listed, while the organizational unit in question is not exchange-listed prior to the ECO. Parent management thus has an agency relationship to external shareholders. Furthermore, it is assumed that only the parent raises external financing.

Throughout the present study, the two characteristics described above are captured within a simple stylized model of a group of companies (Figure 9). For simplicity and tractability reasons, agency relationships between e.g. division managers and workers are not explicitly considered.[59] The intuition behind this simplification is based on the definition of the firm as nexus of *explicit* contracts discussed above (Section 2.2.2.2), which considers all contracts as complete, with the exception of the shareholders' residual claim. The analysis will thus exclusively focus on two agency relationships:

- The agency relationship between parent shareholders and parent management
- The agency relationship between parent management and division management

This model is tantamount to the assumption that the group of companies in question is an M-form organization (Chandler (1966), Williamson (1975)) with two levels. The parent company, which is an exchange-listed corporation, controls several divisions. These divisions in turn, can be separate legal entities, or simply distinct organizational units of the parent. While this stylized structure apparently implies a significant departure from the legal reality of complex multi-level structures, it provides a basis for economic analysis.

A possible objection to the stylized model is that assuming an M-form organization throughout is a non-permissible overgeneralization.

[59] Further agency relationships not considered are e.g. the relationship between management and supervisory board (subscribing to the assumption that the supervisory board is not subject to incentive problems, as laid out in Fama/Jensen (1983a)); and the agency relationship between the management of subsidiaries and potential external financiers that can exist in pyramidal structures where external financing is raised at multiple levels of the group (Rau-Bredow (1999))

Figure 9: Types of agency relationships in groups of companies

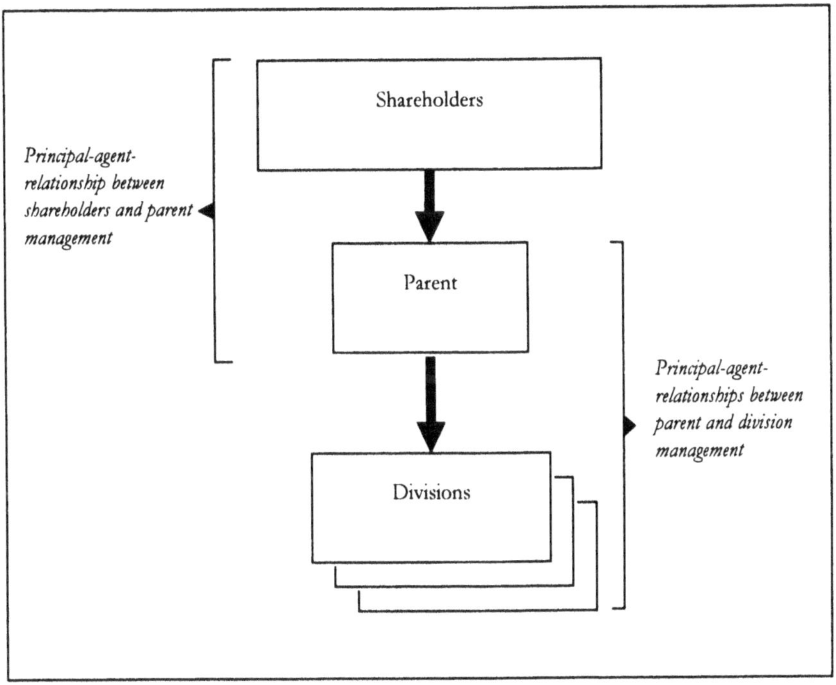

There are three central counterarguments:

- The M-form organization is a prerequisite for the separation of an organizational unit via an ECO; the author is not aware of instances where functional areas have been separated. This point is supported by Nick (1994), who also provides an extensive review of the literature on organizational forms.
- The assumption of M-form organization merely serves as stylized assumption that allows to capture internal competition for capital; the assumption could be relaxed without qualitatively changing the results of the analysis. Furthermore, the M-form organization is implicitly assumed in throughout the internal capital markets literature (e.g. Stein (2003)).[60]

[60] For the same reason a further detailing of the model in the spirit of the German literature focusing on the classification and definition of different organizational forms ("Stammhauskonzern", "Management-

- According to Holmström/Tirole (1989), p. 126, there is no "agency related work modeling these organizational forms" (and the author is unaware of any later such work). From the perspective of agency theory, the differences and implications of these organizational forms are thus not well understood.

Summarizing above section, the implications multi-layer agency relationships have to be taken into account in analyzing the efficiency of organizational forms. In the analysis of groups of companies, the implications of the internal capital market and the pyramidal structure need to be modeled. Throughout the present study, a simple stylized two-tier model is applied in order to capture these specifics.

2.5.3.3 *ECOs as special case of two-layer agency structures*

On a very general level, agency theory is uniquely suited to be used for the analysis of ECOs since it can easily incorporate the dual character of ECOs as means of financing and reorganization. As Williamson (1988) writes in his comparative survey on transaction cost economics and agency theory (p. 576):

> "[I] argue that rather than regard debt and equity as 'financial instrument', they are better regarded as different governance structures"

In analyzing the consequences of ECOs on agency costs, it is thus possible to capture both the financing and reorganization properties.

On a more specific level, the stylized two-tier agency model for the analysis of groups of companies developed in the previous section can be easily extended in order to capture the principal-agent relationships affected by ECOs.

Figure 10 illustrates the changes to the agency relationships of a stylized group of companies effected by an ECO. Pre-transaction, there are two agency relationships, as discussed in the previous section: between the shareholders of the parent company and parent management, and between parent management and division/subsidiary management. Post-transaction, a third agency relationship emerges between the shareholders of the subsidiary and subsidiary management.

Holding", "Finanzholding" etc.; e.g., Klemm (1990)) is not attempted. The stylized model is meant to act as a blueprint that can accustom all such forms

Figure 10: Changes to agency relationships in groups of companies related to ECOs

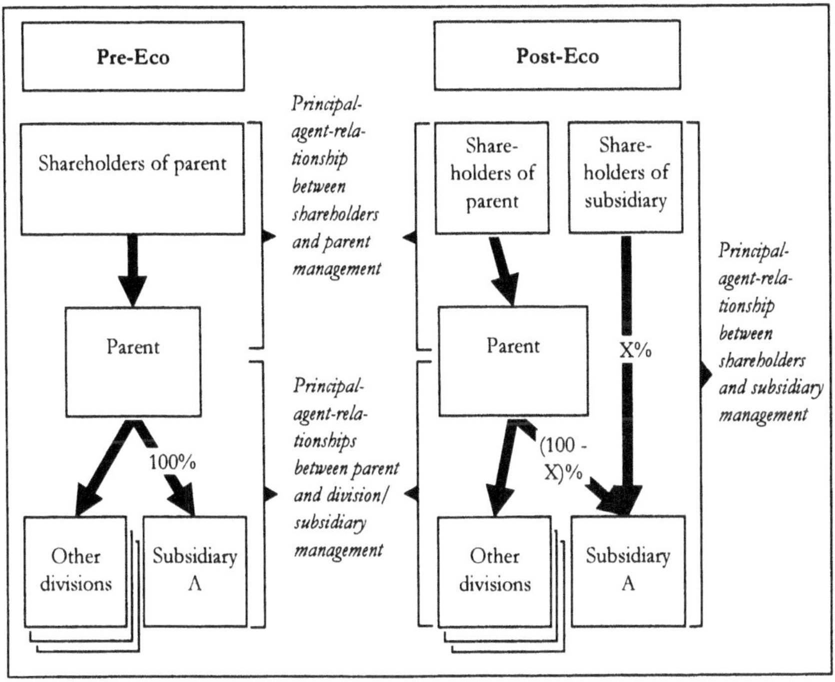

Applying the efficiency criterion for ECOs developed in Section 2.5.1, ECOs thus constitute an efficient form of restructuring if the change in agency costs from the following three relationships is negative:

- The potential change to the agency cost of the agency relationship between parent shareholders and parent management effected by the transaction
- The potential change to the agency cost of the agency relationship between parent management and division/subsidiary management effected by the transaction
- The potential agency costs from the agency relationship between subsidiary shareholders and subsidiary management

2.5.4 *Two-dimensional agency framework for the analysis ECOs*

Analytically, the three determinants of agency costs discussed in the previous section, and the three different agency relationships identified in the stylized two-tier model of the group of companies discussed above, can be synthesized into a two-dimensional agency framework for the analysis of ECOs (Figure 11). A comprehensive evaluation of ECOs from an agency perspective thus has to examine each of the 9 (3 x 3) framework compartments: Using the efficiency criterion developed in Section 2.5.1, the efficiency of an ECO as a form of restructuring is determined as the change in total agency costs summed over the nine compartments.

Figure 11: Two-dimensional agency framework for the analysis of ECOs

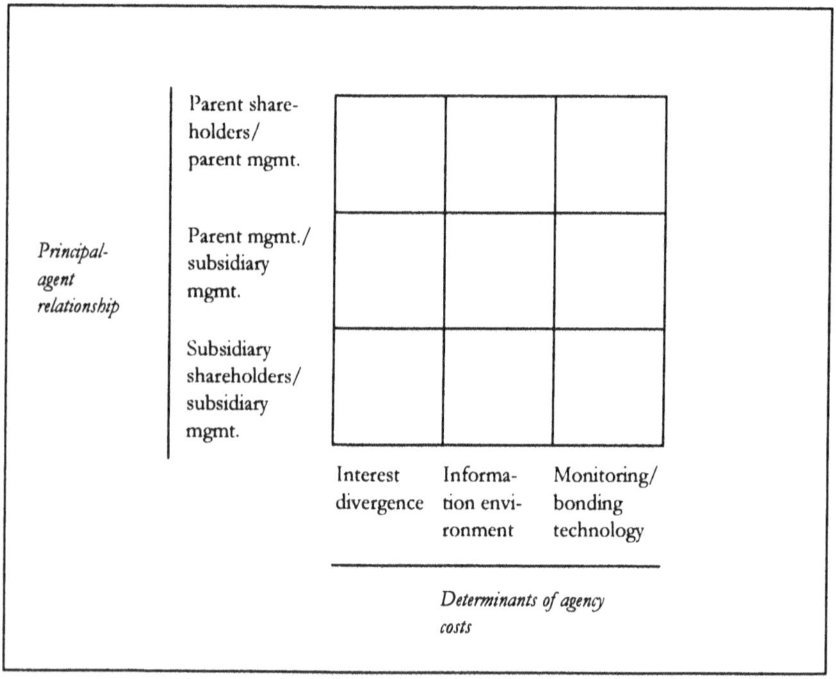

3 Hypothesis development

3.1 Section outline

On the basis of the two-dimensional agency framework introduced previously, Section 3.2 identifies initial hypotheses on the development of agency costs and groups these into four value levers: focus and investment efficiency, information asymmetries and disclosure, incentive compensation, and ownership concentration. Sections 3.3, 3.4, 3.5, and 3.6 discuss each lever in turn and develop testable empirical predictions on the change in agency costs.

3.2 Development of value levers

3.2.1 Potential effects of ECOs on agency costs

In the previous section, a two-dimensional agency framework for the analysis of ECOs has been developed. This agency framework is designed as a guide for hypothesis development. As discussed, ECOs constitute an efficient class of transactions if on average a reduction in agency costs is achieved in sum of the 3x3 framework compartments.

In the following, potential effects of ECOs on agency costs resulting from an analysis of each of the 3x3 framework compartments are discussed (Figure 12 and Figure 13). While a detailed discussion is relegated to the subsequent sections, the following points deserve highlighting:

- Agency costs in the parent shareholders/parent management relationship are potentially reduced in two ways. First, depending on the use of the proceeds, an ECO can reduce the volume of the internal capital market, or free cash flow in the sense of Jensen (1986), and can thus reduce the scope of overinvestment owing to managerial empire building activities (Allen/McConnell (1998)). Thus, interest divergence declines. Second, the increased disclosure in the subsidiary also increases transparency of the group of companies by reducing complexity and thus facilitates valuation of parent stock (Zuckerman (2000), Krishnaswami/Subramaniam (2001), Gilson et al. (2001), Vijh (2002)).

Figure 12: Potential reduction of agency costs due to ECOs

Principal-agent relationship	Interest divergence	Information environment	Monitoring/b. technology
Parent shareholders/ parent mgmt.	**Decrease in overinvestment** due to reduced volume of the internal capital market (Jensen (1986), Allen/McConnell (1998))	**Increase in transparency** of the parent due to the separation from the subsidiary (Zuckerman (2000), Krishnaswami/ Subramaniam (2001), Vijh (2002))	
Parent mgmt./ subsidiary mgmt.	Improved investment efficiency due to **reduced cross-subsidization and** influence activities (Milgrom (1988), Rajan/Servaes/ Zingales (2000))		**Improved monitoring incentives** for the parent in its new role as external **blockholder** (Shleifer/Vishny (1986))
Subsidiary shareholders/ subsidiary mgmt.	Reduction of interest divergence thanks to introduction of **stock-based compensation** for subsidiary management (Schipper/ Smith (1986), Keating (1997))	**Improved disclosure** thanks to separate susbsidiary annual report (Glosten/Milgrom (1985), Gilson et al. (2001))	

Determinants of agency costs

Figure 13: Potential increase in agency costs due to ECOs

Principal-agent relationship	Interest divergence	Information environment	Monitoring/b. technology
Parent shareholders/ parent mgmt.	**Increased overinvestment** based on capital inflow from ECO (Allen/McConnell (1998))		
Parent mgmt./ subsidiary mgmt.	**Continuation of cross-subsidization** if subsidiary largely remains part of group of companies		**Collusion** of parent and subsidiary management at the expense of minority shareholders (Pagano/Röell (1998), Burkart/ Panunzi (2004)
Subsidiary shareholders/ subsidiary mgmt.	**Excessive compensation** due to managerial influence on own pay (Bebchuk/ Fried/Walker (2002))	Increased information asymmetries due to **complementarity of public and private information** (Kim/Verrecchia (1994))	**Expropriation of minority shareholders** by the parent as dominant blockholder (Johnson et al. (2000))

Determinants of agency costs

In contrast, a potential increase of agency costs in the parent shareholders/parent management relationship can originate from exacerbated overinvestment due to the capital inflow generated by the ECO.

- Agency costs in the parent management/subsidiary management relationship are potentially reduced thanks to improved investment efficiency. The potential distortions on an internal capital market, e.g. cross-subsidization (Rajan/Servaes/Zingales (2000)) or influence activities (Milgrom (1988), Meyer/Milgrom/Roberts (1992)), can be mitigated, as empirical evidence from the spin-off literature indicates (Gertner/Powers/Scharfstein (2002), Ahn/Denis (2003), Burch/Nanda (2003)). In addition, parent management takes on a new role as a blockholder in the subsidiary and undertakes monitoring activities over different channels than before, e.g. the supervisory board (e.g. Shleifer/Vishny (1986)).

  However, it is unclear if these effects materialize: If the subsidiary remains largely part of the group of companies, cross-subsidization can persist or even increase. Also, the parent's role as a blockholder need not be beneficial under all circumstances: The literature recognizes the danger of collusion of parent and subsidiary management at the expense of minority shareholders (Pagano/Röell (1998), Burkart/Panunzi (2004)).

- Agency costs in the subsidiary shareholder/subsidiary management relationship are a new phenomenon after the ECO. The extent of these costs is potentially positively affected by the possibility of introducing stock-based incentive compensation for subsidiary management (Schipper/Smith (1986), Keating (1997)), but negatively affected by the danger of excessive compensation owing to managerial influence on its own pay (Bebchuk/Fried (2003)). An additional beneficial effect comes from increased disclosure on the subsidiary, reducing information asymmetries (Glosten/Milgrom (1985), Gilson et al. (2001)); but again, a potential countervailing effect is present, namely a potential increase in information asymmetries due to the complementarity of private and public information (Kim/Verrecchia (1994)). Furthermore, the agency costs from this relationship are determined by the potential expropriation of minority shareholders by the parent as dominant blockholder (Johnson et al. (2000)).

Interestingly, the only two compartments where no immediate effect can be expected is the monitoring/bonding technology in the parent shareholder/parent management relationship and the information environment in the parent management/subsidiary management relationship. Both can reasonably be assumed not to change.

The presence of both potential negative and positive effects shows that the net impact of ECOs on agency costs is not a priori clear from a theoretical standpoint. Further, the variety of different potential effects testifies to the complexity of ECOs as a class of transactions caused by their dual character as financing and reorganization instrument.

3.2.2 Aggregation of framework compartments into four value levers

The above section has derived hypothetical effects of ECOs by analyzing each of the nine framework compartments in turn, and underlined the complexity of determining the net impact of ECOs on agency costs.

In the following, related compartments of the matrix are grouped along the determinants of agency costs for the sake of hypothesis development. While the development of detailed hypotheses compartment by compartment would be perfectly feasible, such aggregation not only provides additional structure to hypothesis development, but is also advisable on theoretical grounds: Agrawal/Knoeber (1996) stress that the alternative mechanisms to control agency costs are interdependent in such a way, that greater use of one mechanism can be optimally related to less use of an alternative mechanism. Thus, greater use of one mechanism need not be unequivocally positively related to firm performance. Walsh/Seward (1990) similarly contend that internal and external mechanisms are simultaneously determined. Thus, while a certain class of transactions might lead to a decrease in total agency costs due to e.g. an improvement in the information environment, the changes in agency costs in the individual principal-agent relationships affected need not all point in the same direction.

In order to capture this simultaneity, and in keeping with the literature, four aggregate value levers are thus defined: Focus and investment efficiency, incentive compensation (together covering the interest divergence dimension), information asymmetries and disclosure (covering the information environment dimension) and ownership concentration (covering the monitoring/bonding technology dimension), as illustrated in Figure 14.

Figure 14: Value levers in the two-dimensional agency framework

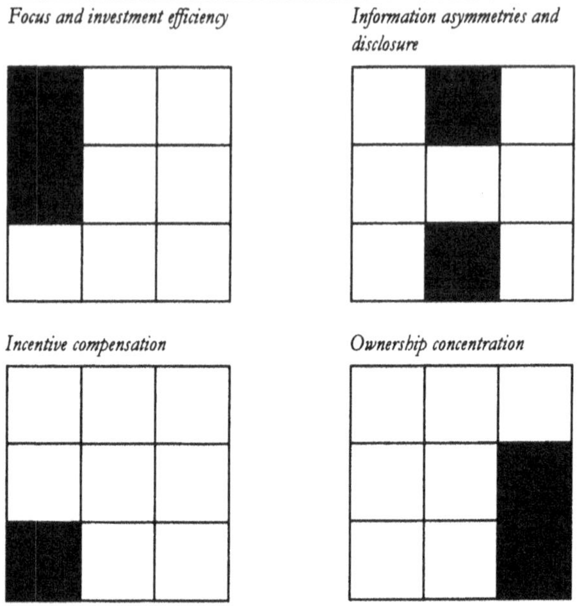

Black compartments indicate areas hypothesized to be affected by ECOs

Before detailed and empirically testable predictions are developed, the four levers are presented in some more detail below:

- *Focus and investment efficiency*: Via the ECO, the degree of diversification of the group of companies is reduced; the group of companies focuses its activities on fewer business segments (Schipper/Smith (1986); Vijh (1999)). From an agency perspective, investment efficiency has been discussed as the key driver for the effects of focus on firm value (Montgomery (1994), Gertner/Scharfstein/Stein (1994), Martin/Sayrak (2003), Stein (2003); also see the detailed literature review in Section 3.3.2.1). Before the ECO, the subsidiary's investment projects are financed on the internal capital market of the group of companies, where different divisions/subsidiaries compete for resources. As discussed in Section 2.5.3.2, internal capital markets are a key feature of groups of companies. After the ECO, the subsidiary can access the external capital market directly. Also, depending on the form of placement, the ECO potentially reduces the size of the internal capital market in the remaining group of companies (Kaserer/Ahlers (2000), Vijh (2002)). Does the substitution of the internal capital market with the external capital market improve investment efficiency at the subsidiary, and does it improve investment efficiency at the remaining group of companies?

- *Information asymmetries and disclosure*: Following an ECO, the financial disclosure on the subsidiary increases. The increase in disclosure constitutes a change to the information environment. An improved availability of information to external investors can reduce agency costs (Gilson et al. (2001) and Krishnaswami/Subramaniam (2001) for similar studies on spin-offs). On the other hand, the available information can be distorted, e.g. due to transfer pricing arrangements between parent and subsidiary (Langenbach (2001)). Furthermore, the increase in financial disclosure affects potential information asymmetries between different shareholder groups (informed and uninformed investors, e.g. Glosten/Milgrom (1985)). The literature discusses controversially whether information asymmetries are reduced (e.g. due to a more informative price system (Habib/Johnsen/Naik (1997)) or increased (e.g. due to the complementarity of private and public information (Kim/Verrecchia (1994)). Can potential value creation from ECOs thus be explained by a net reduction in information asymmetry?

- *Incentive compensation*: The creation of listed subsidiary stock via the ECO allows for the introduction of stock-based incentive compensation for subsidiary management (Schipper/Smith (1986)). Incentive compensation alters the utility function of the manager and thus reduces initial interest divergence to shareholders (e.g. Baker/Jensen/Murphy (1988); Jensen/Murphy (1990), Baker (1992); for an excellent literature review see Murphy (1999)). The introduction of incentive compensation in the subsidiary can thus reduce agency costs (see Aron (1991) for a formal model; Vijh (2002) for empirical evidence; Seward/Walsh (1996) for a similar study on spin-offs). On the other hand, incentive compensation can be an instrument of entrenched managers to increase their private benefits (Bebchuk/Fried/Walker (2002), Bebchuk/Fried (2003)). Is the introduction of incentive compensation after ECOs thus a source of value creation?

- *Ownership concentration*: Via the ECO, the parent reduces its ownership in the subsidiary, but usually retains a controlling stake (e.g. Vijh (1999)). This controlling stake can create agency costs from the potential collusion between parent management and subsidiary management, at the expense of the (external) minority shareholders in the subsidiary (e.g. Shleifer/Vishny (1997), Becht/Bolton/Röell (2003)). Furthermore, the planned complete divestiture of the subsidiary by the parent subsequent to the ECO has been shown to have a positive effect on announcement returns (Klein/Rosenfeld/Beranek (1991), Vijh (2002)). On the other hand, the existence of a controlling shareholder can reduce agency costs since a controlling shareholder has stronger incentives to monitor (subsidiary) management (for a review of the literature on blockholders, see Shleifer/Vishny (1997); Becht/Boehmer (2003) for a review of ownership and control in a German context). Does the extent of remaining parent influence after the ECO thus play a role in value creation?

3.3 Lever 1: Focus and investment efficiency

3.3.1 Treatment in the ECO literature

In the literature, value creation from ECOs has regularly been attributed to increased focus of the remaining group of companies. ECOs are interpreted as a form of divestiture of non-core businesses (Schipper/Smith (1986), Vijh (1999), Hulburt/Miles/Woolridge (2002), Vijh (2002); in the German literature: Löffler (2001)). Questions relating to firm value and diversification are of particular relevance to the analysis of ECOs, since ECOs by definition are undertaken by at least to some extent diversified groups of companies.

Within the ECO literature, hypotheses on the effects of refocusing have usually been drawn from previous empirical work, which has found value increases related to different form of divestitures (asset sales: John/Ofek (1995); spin-offs: Daley/Mehrotra/Sivakumar (1997), Desai/Jain (1999)); or higher stock returns associated with focus: (Comment/Jarrell (1995)).

In order to achieve a solid theoretical grounding, this study develops hypotheses on the role of focus in ECOs based on a broader discussion of the effects of diversification on corporate value in general: After discussing different theoretical perspectives on diversification, the empirical evidence on diversification, investment efficiency, and firm value is reviewed, and the empirical predictions of agency theory for the relation of diversification and firm value are analyzed in more detail. After laying these foundations, specific hypotheses on the role of focus and investment efficiency in ECOs are derived.

3.3.2 *Focus and corporate valuation*

3.3.2.1 *Theoretical perspectives*

Can diversification be consistent with maximization of corporate value on theoretical grounds?[61] While the emphasis in the literature has been on empirical work (see the following section), there have been considerable theoretical efforts.

The early literature, written in the aftermath of the conglomerate merger wave of the 1960s (e.g. Matsusaka (1993), Servaes (1996), Hubbard/Palia (1999) for reviews), identified the coinsurance effect of diversification: If cash flows of different business segments are not perfectly correlated, diversification decreases risk and thus allows for higher debt capacity. Assuming that higher leverage can create value, e.g. thanks to tax shields, diversification can be value-maximizing (Lewellen (1971)). While conceptually appealing, Lewellen's argument was not borne out by the data: Diversified firms have not been found to be more leveraged on average than focused firms (e.g. Lang/Stulz (1994)).

The more recent literature has identified three explanations for diversification, following Montgomery (1994) and Martin/Sayrak (2003):[62]

- The market power explanation
- The resource-based explanation
- The agency explanation

The ***market power explanation*** posits that diversification can increase market power and is thus positively related to value (Montgomery (1994)). Examples for ways in which diversification can increase market power are deep pockets, where profits from one market are used to support predatory pricing in another market (Bolton/Scharfstein (1990)); mutual forbearance, where competitors meeting on multiple markets recognize their interde-

---

[61] In accordance with the corporate finance literature, this study ignores operational synergies as an explanation for diversification. As Rajan/Servaes/Zingales (2000) underline "In a world where all contracts could be written at no cost, two separate companies could achieve no less and no more than two divisions of the same company" (p. 49)

[62] Other miscellaneous explanations exist: Matsusaka (2001) interprets diversification as a search process where firms search for a match for their firm-specific capabilities across industries; Bernardo/Chowdry (2002) interpret diversification in a real-options framework where focused firms derive additional value compared to diversified firms from their yet unexhausted option to diversify; Matsusaka/Nanda (2002) derive the value of diversification from the transaction costs of external capital market financing that is shown to be less frequent for diversified firms

pendence and compete less vigorously (e.g. Scott (1982), Bernheim/Whinston (1990)); and reciprocal buying, where interrelationships among large diversified firms foreclose markets to smaller competitors (see Tirole (1995) for a review of diversification and market power from the perspective of industrial organization).

The *resource-based explanation* interprets diversification as an answer to overcapacity in the core business, which cannot be sold at market prices (Wernerfelt/Montgomery (1988)). Diversification is thus a profitable way of employing underused resources, leading to economies of scope (Teece (1980, 1982), Panzar/Willig (1981)). According to Burch/Nanda/Narayanan (2002), diversification should be less frequent in high-growth industries since underutilization of resources is less likely. Apart from industry conditions, the efficient level of diversification depends on the specificity of resources and the productivity in the core business (Schoar (2002)): Under the traditional neoclassical assumption of decreasing returns to scale, firms shift finite organizational capabilities to a more productive activity when returns decrease in the primary activity. Consequently, firms that are less productive in their core business, and firms with less industry-specific skills, but more firm specific skills (e.g. financial planning) will be more diversified in equilibrium (Maksimovic/Phillips (2002)). Gomes/Livdan (2004) additionally find that in a neoclassical framework, diversification is more frequent when the primary activity is large (due to decreasing returns to scale) and when the secondary activity has low fixed costs. While diversification can thus be interpreted as "efficient response to productivity differentials" (Gomes/Livdan (2004)), the resource-based explanation is both consistent with a positive and a negative relation between diversification and firm value (Montgomery (1994)), since those firms are most likely to diversify that have a below-average productivity in their primary activity.

The *agency explanation* views diversification as an inefficient strategy pursued by self-interested managers attempting to increase private benefits. The agency explanation thus assumes a negative relation between diversification and firm value. Different forms of self-interest have been discussed in the literature: Managers pursue diversification in order to increase resources under their control (Jensen (1986), Stulz (1990)), namely by undertaking human-capital specific investment leading to entrenchment (Shleifer/Vishny (1989)), or by choosing investments that limit their personal exposure to risk (Amihud/Lev (1981)); to improve career prospects as running a complex organization improves external perception of inability (Gibbons/Murphy (1992)). Further inefficiencies potentially result from self-interested behavior of division managers on the internal capital market of the diversified firm (e.g. Meyer/Milgrom/Roberts (1992)), or from inefficient cross-subsidization of divisions (e.g. Scharfstein/Stein (2000), Rajan/Servaes/Zingales (2000)).

While controversy persists on the motives of diversification (Villalonga (2003b)), the agency explanation has been favored in the recent discussion (Montgomery (1994)), not least because its predictions most closely match the general enthusiasm for focused strategies in the business press and the management literature (Martin/Sayrak (2003))[63]. In keeping with the overriding theoretical stance of this study, the following section exclusively considers the agency explanation for diversification.

3.3.2.2 Empirical evidence

The *agency explanation* reviewed above predicts a negative relationship between diversification and corporate valuation. Does the empirical evidence support this proposition? The business press and standard textbooks come to the unanimous conclusion that diversification destroys value, as exemplified in Comment/Jarrell (1995, p. 67):[64]

> "Managers are now advised to eschew diversification and to shrink the far-flung enterprises that resulted from diversification strategies. In their public statements, managers are apt to say that they want to concentrate on a core business, and they are likely to rationalize mergers and growth strategies, as well as divestitures and restructuring, as reflecting a strategy of specialization. [...] In addition, judging from their public statements, top managers have come to view focus as a policy objective in and of itself."

However, the academic discussion is much more controversial, and since the initial negative verdict on diversification in the early empirical studies (Lang/Stulz (1994), Berger/Ofek (1995)), the literature has developed considerably. Most importantly, it has repeatedly been underlined that evidence for lower valuations of diversified firms cannot be directly interpreted as evidence that diversification destroys value (Lamont/Polk (2001); Khanna/Tice (2002); Graham/Lemmon/Wolf (2002), Villalonga (2004b)). Villalonga (2003) differentiates between three hypotheses on the relation between diversification and firm value:[65]

---

[63] Montgomery (1994) makes a proposal for reconciling the resource-based and agency explanations: Observed diversification patterns conform to the resource-based explanation; however, actual diversification does not stop at the optimal level, but exceeds the optimal level due to agency problems

[64] Martin/Sayrak (2003) provide further examples

[65] This framework is similar to Fama (1970), who coined the strong-, semi-strong-, and weak-form hypotheses of capital market efficiency

- The strong-form hypothesis of the diversification discount: Diversified firms trade at a discount relative to what those firms would be worth if they had not diversified
- The semi-strong-form hypothesis of the diversification discount: Diversified firms trade at a discount relative to what those firms would be worth if they were split up
- The weak-form hypothesis of the diversification discount: diversified forms trade at a discount relative to single-segment firms in the same industries

A valuation differential between diversified and focused forms is thus not interpreted as evidence of value destruction; instead, endogenous selection can explain such a result, e.g. diversification is particularly likely for firms that had already been valued at a discount before they diversified (Lang/Stulz (1994))

The empirical literature mirrors this development: the earlier work provides evidence on the existence of a weak-form discount. Diversified firms have lower Tobin's Qs on average than focused firms (Wernerfelt/Montgomery (1988), Lang/Stulz (1994)). Furthermore, diversified firms trade at a discount relative to focused firms in the same industry, as measured by a sum-of-the-parts valuation of the diversified firms' segments (Berger/Ofek (1995)). There is a strong negative relationship between managerial stock ownership – interpreted as a measure of interest alignment between management and shareholders – and the degree of diversification (Denis/Denis/Sarin (1997)). In addition, transactions that reduce the degree of diversification lead to positive announcement returns (spin-offs, e.g. Daley/Mehrotra/Sivakumar (1997), Desai/Jain (1999); asset sales: John/Ofek (1995); corporate refocusing programs: Berger/Ofek (1999)), and focused firms have higher stock returns (Comment/Jarrell (1995)). Markides (1995) finds that profitability improves after refocusing programs.

More recent work tests the semi-strong- and strong-form hypotheses, and finds mixed results. Lamont/Polk (2001) find that part of the diversification discount is due to higher expected returns for diversified firms. Graham/Lemmon/Wolf (2002) find that part of the diversification discount is explained by the acquisition of discounted target firms. Whited (2001) finds that the difference in Tobin's Q between diversified and focused firms is explained by measurement error. Villalonga (2004b), using an econometric method correcting for sample selection bias, does not find evidence for a diversification discount. Mansi/Reeb (2002) find that the debt of diversified firms is valued at a premium compared to focused firms, and that overall firm value does not significantly differ between diversified and focused firms. Campa/Kedia (2002), using Heckman's two-stage method to correct for sample selection error, even find a relatively robust diversification premium.

In conclusion, the evidence on the strong-form diversification discount is inconclusive. Adding to the complexity is that the results are hardly robust to the data, time period, and geography. Martin/Sayrak (2003) contend that the validity of results is severely impeded by data limitations, such as inconsistency in segment reporting and industry definitions. Empirically, Berger/Hann (2003) find evidence of a diversification discount also under the new SFAS 131 segment reporting rules introduced in 1998, but Villalonga (2004a), using establishment level data, which is of a finer granularity than the usual segment reporting data used in empirical studies on diversification, finds a diversification premium. Servaes (1996), in his historical analysis on diversification, finds a diversification discount for the 1970s, but no discount for the 1960s. International evidence on the value of diversification is equally mixed: Lins/Servaes (1999) find a diversification discount in Japan and the U.K., but not in Germany; Lins/Servaes (2002) find a discount in seven emerging markets; and Fauver/Houston/Naranjo (2003) in a broad international analysis, find discounts or premiums depending on the state of capital market development in the respective country.

Robert H. Gertner, in a recent research roundtable (Villalonga (2003)), befittingly concludes (p. 13):

> "The diversification discount, like many controversial academic issues, has taken a life of its own. And like many other controversial academic issues, the more we study it, the less clear it becomes."

Despite the inconclusive results of the more recent empirical work, which largely fail to establish clear evidence for either of the three theoretical perspectives reviewed, the following section, in accordance with the general stance of the present study, is again exclusively based on the agency explanation.[66]

[66] Above review has largely ignored German contributions on the topic of diversification (e.g. Funk (1999), Hinterhuber et al. (2000)). Researchers have very strongly criticized the lack of theoretical foundations in German work (Mellewigt/Matiaske (2000)).

3.3.3 Inefficient investment and agency costs

3.3.3.1 Forms of inefficient investment in diversified firms

The agency explanation of corporate diversification interprets corporate diversification as an inefficient strategy followed by self-interested managers, and identifies several potential investment inefficiencies as the agency costs of diversification. Thus, the agency explanation commonly frames agency costs in terms of costs arising from inefficient investment related to internal capital markets;[67] such as e.g. Burch/Nanda/Narayanan (2002), or Scharfstein/Stein (2000), who write (p. 2537):

> "While it may be clear to most observers that diversification can destroy value, it is much less clear exactly how it does so. One general theme in the literature is that the conglomerate form of organization somehow exacerbates the investment inefficiencies that arise from managerial agency problems."

The emphasis on investment is of particular relevance in terms of the stylized two-layer model of groups of companies used in the present study (Section 2.5.3.2): as discussed, the existence of an internal capital market is assumed by definition. Agency theory can provide testable predictions relating to the efficiency of such internal capital markets, and the likely consequences of a reduction in size and scope (as results from an ECO) of such internal capital markets on investment efficiency.[68]

Stein (2003) provides an instructive classification that incorporates agency problems on two levels: First, diversification can lead to distorted across-firm allocations of capital, e.g. self-interested managers raise too much capital in order to pursue diversification strategies (Jensen (1986)). Second, diversification can lead to distorted within-firm allocation of capital, e.g. weak divisions are inefficiently subsidized (Rajan/Servaes/Zingales (2000)). In the following, the agency theory on across- and within-firm investment efficiency is reviewed insofar relevant to ECOs.[69]

---

[67] Alternative explanations, such as the relationship between diversification and incentive compensation (e.g. Aron (1991)), or the relationship between diversification and information asymmetry (e.g. Bens/Monahan (2004)) are discussed in later sections

[68] Adopting a different approach based on organization theory, Menne (2000) examines the relation between organizational structure and investment from a behavioral perspective, with a special focus on bounded rationality

[69] Given the weak empirical support in the context of ECOs (see Section 1.4.1) and the recent general skepticism towards the signaling literature (Zingales (2000)), adverse selection models in the spirit of Nanda (1991), e.g. Myers/Majluf (1984), Myers (1984), Greenwald/Stiglitz/Weiss (1984), or the earlier signaling models of Ross (1977) and Leland/Pyle (1977), will not be considered as an explanation for

3.3.3.2 *Inefficient across-firm allocations*

Stein (2003) identifies four possible sources of distortion in across-firm allocations due to agency problems: empire-building, reputational and career concerns, inertia, and overconfidence.

The *empire-building* hypothesis assumes that managers have a taste for running large firms, instead of merely profitable firms. Consequently, they will essentially invest all internally available funds on investment projects, whether positive-NPV or not (Jensen (1986, 1993)). Jensen (1986) writes (p. 324):

> "Managers have incentives to cause their firms to grow beyond the optimal size. Growth increases managers' power by increasing the resources under their control. [...] Conflicts of interest between shareholders and managers over payout policies are especially severe when the organization generates substantial free cash flow. The problem is how to motivate managers to disgorge the cash rather than investing it at below the cost of capital or wasting it on organization inefficiencies."

However, the conflict of interest between managers and shareholders does not lead to overinvestment in all states of the world. A second problem is that managers lack credibility when internal resources are insufficient and additional financing is needed, as described by Stulz (1990), p. 5:

> "The informational asymmetry between managers and shareholders leads to inefficient investment when cash flow is low because management cannot credibly convince shareholders that cash flow is insufficient to take advantage of all positive NPV opportunities. Management always tells shareholders that the firm cannot take advantage of all its positive NPV opportunities. Consequently, shareholders never believe management's assertion that cash flow is too low, because management always benefits from increasing investment."

Thus, in terms of investment efficiency, there is a tradeoff between overinvestment (caused by empire-building) and underinvestment (caused by a lack of internal resources). Overinvestment can be constrained by limiting managerial discretion over internally available funds, i.e. by increasing leverage, so that managers are forced to pay out funds in order to service the debt (Jensen (1986)), but increased leverage at the same time increases the danger of underinvestment. Formal models of the tradeoff between over- and underinvestment and the optimal amount of leverage are provided by Stulz (1990), Harris/Raviv (1990), Hart/Moore (1995), Li/Li (1996), and Zwiebel (1996).

---

distortions in across-firm allocations. Dybvig/Zender (1991) and Persons (1994) controversially discuss if managers are likely to act in the interest of current shareholders at the expense of future shareholders

In the context of diversification, the empire-building hypothesis predicts that managers will engage in diversifying acquisitions or projects in order to increase firm size (Jensen (1993)), e.g. when growth opportunities in the core activity have been exhausted. In order to extend and preserve an empire, two types of investment are especially attractive: Investments that reduce the danger of the empire going out of business, namely investments in unrelated activities that decrease cash flow volatility and thus reduce the manager's personal risk exposure (Amihud/Lev (1981)); and investments that require manager-specific human capital and thus strengthen the chance of the manager to entrench himself in his job (Shleifer/Vishny (1989))

Diversified firms can thus be assumed to have a more severe overinvestment problem. At the same time, diversification also has a positive effect insofar as it reduces cash flow volatility and thus facilitates adjusting leverage to the optimal level, simultaneously making over- and underinvestment less likely (Stulz (1990)).

Reputational and career concerns can elicit inefficient behavior patterns by managers. In order to boost their labor market value, managers can diversify in order to acquire a reputation for being able to run complex organizations (Gibbons/Murphy (1992).[70] Furthermore, managers can be tempted to boost short-term performance at the expense of long-term shareholder value, typically by generating short-term profitability increases by cutting non-observable expenses such as maintenance (e.g. Narayanan (1985), Stein (1988, 1989)); or, conversely, if the act of investing is observable, by overinvesting in order to build a reputation for an ability to identify good investment projects (Bebchuk/Stole (1993)). Such behavior is favored by the relative intransparency of diversified firms versus focused firms (see Section 3.4.3). Another possible consequence of career concerns is herding, where managers copy decisions of other managers, in the hope that the labor market infers that the managers is more likely to be smart if his investment decision is the same as that of other agents (Scharfstein/Stein (1990)).

Finally, across firm allocations can be distorted by managerial *inertia*, where managers prefer a "quiet life", and thus delay the shutdown of unprofitable investments, but at the

---

by attempting to sell equity which they perceive as overvalued

[70] Aggarwal/Samwick (2003a) argue that incentives can prevent managers from diversifying when the deterioration in firm performance from diversification and the corresponding loss in incentive compensation more than compensate managerial private benefits from diversification; Goel/Nanda/Narayanan (2004) provide a different perspective on career concerns and conglomerates, arguing that in the presence of differential informativeness of divisional cash flows of managerial ability, career concerns affect the allocation of capital and intangible resources

same time are also reluctant to initiate new investments (Bertrand/Mullainathan (2003)), or by shirking pure and simple, where managers forego profitable investment opportunities to avoid additional oversight responsibilities (Aggarwal/Samwick (2003c)); and by *overconfidence*, where managers are overoptimistic about investment projects (e.g. Weinstein (1980)), and thus overinvest, but at the same time are reluctant to raise external financing when they constantly perceive the firm as undervalued (Heaton (2002)).

Empirical evidence of agency-related distortions of across-firm allocations is abundant. Investment is not only correlated to investment opportunities, but also to cash, i.e. the amount of internal resources available (for a survey see Hubbard (1998))[71]. This can be interpreted as evidence of empire-building: managers invest all available resources, irrespective of the quality of investment opportunities. In a related piece of evidence, acquirers generally overpay in unrelated acquisitions, as shown by the negative announcement effect (Roll (1986), Morck/Shleifer/Vishny (1990)), which again can be interpreted as evidence of empire-building. Similarly, unexpected cash windfalls not related to business activity (e.g. from legal settlements) are not paid out to shareholders, but reinvested (Blanchard/Lopez de Silanes/Vishny (1994)). Together, these pieces of evidence form a solid support for the empire-building hypothesis. Furthermore, firms have abnormally strong operating performance before IPOs or SEOs, which can be interpreted as evidence for short-termism (Hansen/Crutchley (1990), Loughran/Ritter (1997)).

Summarizing the evidence, agency related problems of investment inefficiency that distort capital allocation across firms do exist. Problems with empire-building and reputational or career concerns, leading to overinvestment, can be assumed to be particularly severe ex post in diversified firms. Such problems could explain a potential diversification discount. A clear relationship between managerial inertia or overconfidence and diversification does not exist.

---

[71] Starting with Fazzari/Hubbard/Petersen (1988), a broad literature on financing constraints and investment has developed; if investment is not only correlated to measures investment opportunities, but also to measures of internally available resources, it is concluded that a firm is financially constrained, i.e. it cannot raise as much external financing as needed. Empirically, the difficulty is that measures of internal resources (cash) are at the same time measures for investment opportunities, since cash is dependent on past profitability, and future investment opportunities also depend on past profitability. Thus, finding an investment-cash correlation is insufficient for concluding that the firm is financially constrained and investment is inefficient. See the debate between Kaplan/Zingales (1997, 2001) and Fazzari/Hubbard/Petersen (2000); Alti's (2003) formal model; and further empirical work by Lang/Ofek/Stulz (1996), Lamont (1997), Houston/James/Marcus (1997), and Shin/Stulz (1998)

3.3.3.3 Inefficient within-firm allocations on internal capital markets

Within the groups of companies subject of this study (refer back to the stylized model in Section 2.5.3.2), divisions do not access the external capital market directly. Instead, they compete for resources on the internal capital market. The emerging internal capital markets literature compares the efficiency of investment on internal capital markets with the efficiency of external capital markets. What are possible distortions of investment allocations caused by internal capital markets? Stein (2003) defines an ad hoc efficiency criterion (p. 67):

> "Loosely speaking, a collection of assets should optimally reside under the roof of a single firm to the extent that the firm's internal capital market can do a more efficient job of allocating capital to these assets than would the external capital market, if the assets were located in distinct firms."

Stein (2003) identifies two defining characteristics of internal capital markets: First, finance is centralized, i.e. headquarters (the parent company) is the only provider of finance to the divisions. Second, headquarters has unconditional control rights, i.e. it can take resources away from one division to reallocate them to another division.

Several attempts have been made to model internal capital markets (Gertner/Scharfstein/Stein (1994), Stein (1997), Rajan/Servaes/Zingales (2000), Scharfstein/Stein (2000), Gautier/Heider (2002), De Motta (2002), Stein (2002), Inderst/Müller (2003)). Commonly the models make an assessment of the efficiency of internal capital markets based on a comparison to external capital markets. Typically, the case where two projects are financed separately is compared to the case where the two projects (divisions) are jointly financed via an institution called headquarters (e.g. Stein (1997)). Agency problems then arise in the relationship between headquarters and division managers.

While the models differ in their emphasis and operationalization, some recurring themes emerge: The relaxing of financing constraints and efficient reallocation of capital across divisions thanks to an informational advantage are identified as core benefits of internal capital markets:

- Internal capital markets lead to the *relaxing of financing constraints*. In the presence of financial constraints, a parent company (or headquarters, as it is mostly called in the literature) can raise more financing than a collection of standalone focused firms (Stein (1997), Rajan/Servaes/Zingales (2000), De Motta (2002), Gautier/Heider (2002), Stein (2002), Inderst/Müller (2003)). Suppose that project managers and headquarters have ex ante private information about project outcomes with certainty, but the external capital market can only observe an uncertain success probability ex ante. If projects now seek financing on a stand-alone basis, the external capital market will not provide capital if the estimated success probability is too low: The external capital market will not believe project managers when they reveal their private information about a favorable project outcome, since empire building managers will always promise favorable outcomes in order to obtain more resources. Now suppose that a parent company has 10 projects, each with a 50% success probability. While under certain numerical assumptions, the external capital market would not provide financing to any of the projects standalone, it will provide financing for 5 out of 10 projects to the parent company, relying on the parent company to use its private information to channel the capital provided to the 5 "right" projects in the second step.[72] The relaxing of financing constraints is assumed to increase firm value, since it allows implementing otherwise unfunded positive-NPV projects and thus alleviates underinvestment.

- The parent company can engage in an *efficient reallocation* of capital to divisions thanks to its *informational advantage*. As described above, internal capital markets can allow the parent company to raise additional funds, which are then channeled to the most productive divisions (Stein (1997), Rajan/Servaes/Zingales (2000), Stein (2002), Gautier/Heider (2002), De Motta (2002)). The informational advantage of the parent company is modeled in different ways: Formalizing the traditional argument by Alchian (1969), namely that the parent company has greater monitoring incentives, Gertner/Scharfstein/Stein (1994) and Stein (2002) model the informational advantage of the parent company versus the external capital market. De Motta (2002) and Stein (2002) identify increased incentives for division managers to increase effort or engage in information production on an internal capital market, assuming that the parent company's investment decisions are more sensitive to effort or that such information can be better communicated to the parent company than to the external capital market.

On the negative side, self-financing, socialist reallocation due to rent-seeking, diminished entrepreneurial incentives, and agency problems at the parent company are identified as the costs of internal capital markets:

---

[72] A more advanced numerical example is provided in Stein (1997), a formal model using an optimal

- As discussed above, internal capital markets models commonly assume that the relaxing of financing constraints is a benefit of internal capital markets, since it reduces underinvestment. However, the relaxing of financing constraints can also lead to overinvestment, caused by *self-financing* (Inderst/Müller (2003)): if cash flows are pooled, the probability increases that the firm has internal resources available that allow to self-finance projects without returning to the capital market. Under the usual empire building assumption, this can be value-destroying

- The flip-side of efficient reallocation by the parent company is inefficient *socialist reallocation* (Rajan/Servaes/Zingales (2000), Scharfstein/Stein (2000)). Rajan/Servaes/Zingales (2000) model socialist reallocations, transferring resources from strong divisions to weak divisions, as an instrument to decrease the diversity of divisions and thus curtail power struggles and non-cooperative behavior. Scharfstein/Stein (2000) model socialist reallocations as compensation to managers of weak divisions that have firm-specific human capital to make such managers stay with the company. The latter model is closely related to the concept of influence costs (Milgrom (1988), Milgrom/Roberts (1988b), Meyer/Milgrom/Roberts (1992)), where employees engage in non-productive rent-seeking activities.

- The *reduction in entrepreneurial incentives* in internal capital markets is modeled by De Motta (2002), Gautier/Heider (2002) and Stein (2002). While Stein (1997) assumes largely passive agents, the latter models analyze the effect that reallocations can have on incentives. Following Gautier/Heider (2002) and Stein (2002), managers of weak divisions have less incentives to exert effort when they anticipate that the resources they generate can be transferred to other divisions; conversely, managers of strong divisions will exert less effort as well, since they can free-ride on the transfers they anticipate to receive. De Motta (2002) contends that division managers have less incentives to increase profitability when the parent company gives less weight to current profitability in its investment decisions compared to the external capital market, because it can better infer inherent division productivity.

- Finally, internal capital markets introduce another layer of agency relationships, which can cause additional agency costs. The only model that explicitly takes into account the effect of *agency costs at the parent level* is Scharfstein/Stein (2000). In this model, parent management prefers to distort capital allocations to divisions rather

contracting approach is provided in Inderst/Müller (2003)

than paying cash incentives to division managers, since this is less costly in terms of private benefits at parent level.

Summarizing the above arguments, a clear prediction of the efficiency of internal capital markets compared to external markets does not emerge. As Stein (2003) concludes, the efficiency of internal capital markets thus ultimately remains an empirical question.

While often-times general work on the valuation of diversified firms, e.g. the evidence on the diversification discount discussed in Section 3.3.2.2, is interpreted as evidence for the efficiency of internal capital markets, there exists some empirical work that is more directly related to questions of investment efficiency.

Lamont (1997) studies the effect of an oil price shock on the investment of the non-oil divisions of diversified oil companies. In the absence of financial constraints, non-oil division investment should only be dependent on their investment opportunities, which are by definition not affected by the exogenous shock. However, Lamont (1997) finds that non-oil investment significantly declined in responses to the oil price decrease, which he interprets as evidence for cross-subsidization on the internal capital market. Given that the non-oil division had average investment levels but below industry-average performance pre-shock, the decline is interpreted as correction of overinvestment due to inefficient socialist capital allocation. Shin/Stulz (1998) find further evidence for reallocation on the internal capital market: divisional investment is correlated to other divisions' cash flows.

Rajan/Servaes/Zingales (2000), testing their formal model, analyze the direction of transfers between divisions. Using Tobin's Q as a measure of investment opportunities, they find evidence of transfers from divisions with good opportunities to divisions with weaker opportunities. Consistent with the predictions of the model, such inefficient socialist allocations are more likely as measures of diversity increase.

Further articles using variants of Lamont's (1997) natural experiment methodology find evidence of efficient winner-picking reallocation (Khanna/Tice (2001) in their analysis of the investment of diversified retailers in response to the market entry by Wal-Mart); and evidence of a negative relation between exogenous increases in diversity of investment opportunities and firm value (Lamont/Polk (2002)).

In the most sophisticated such analysis to date, Billett/Mauer (2003) further examine the efficiency of transfers in internal capital markets. Responding to the criticism of measurement error in Tobin's Q (e.g. Whited (2001)), the commonly used measure for investment opportunities, Billett/Mauer (2003) construct a novel measure of investment efficiency based on segment ROA and financial constraints.[73] Based on this measure, Billett/Mauer (2003) find that some efficient (i.e. from low ROA to high ROA) transfers to financially constrained segments do take place and increase excess value. However, inefficient subsidies to constrained segments are much more prevalent.[74]

Recently, several authors have analyzed the change in investment efficiency after spin-offs (Burch/Nanda (2003), Gertner/Powers/Scharfstein (2003), Ahn/Denis (2004)) and asset sell-offs (Dittmar/Shivdasani (2003)). Consistently, they find an improvement in investment efficiency post-transaction, related to a reduction in diversity (Burch/Nanda (2003)), which limits the extent of socialist reallocation (Ahn/Denis (2004)).

Summarizing the above evidence, internal capital markets appear to foster investment distortions. Although predictions from formal models go in both directions, and some empirical evidence for efficient reallocation does exist, the literature mostly indicates inefficient reallocation in diversified firms.

3.3.4 Focus, investment efficiency, and ECOs

The above two sections have been focused on the agency costs of diversification: The empirical evidence indicates that diversification is related to across-firm investment distortions resulting from overinvestment and reputational and career concerns, and to within-firm investment distortions resulting from socialist capital allocation on the internal capital market. Irrespective of the ongoing controversial discussion about the potential existence of a diversification discount, it can thus be concluded that focus is positively related to investment efficiency.

The effect of ECOs on investment efficiency is relatively complex, because it is related to both focus and internal resources of the group of companies. The role of focus is unambiguous: The diversity of investment opportunities of the group of companies is reduced

---

[73] The measure is calculated as follows: Segments are split in segments paying and receiving subsidies on the basis of capital expenditures and after-tax cash flow, and the relative efficiency of transfers is calculated based on relative segment ROA and a size- and earnings-adjusted fitted Q. Furthermore, the likelihood of a segment facing financing constraints is assessed via a logit model of dividend policy estimated based on focused firms; assuming that dividends are a clear sign that no financial constraints exist (e.g. Fazzari/Hubbard/Petersen (2000)).

[74] Interestingly, such subsidies can also increase excess value. This counterintuitive evidence is consistent with Rajan/Servaes/Zingales (2000) where ex post inefficient transfers are made in order to decrease diversity and prevent even greater investment distortions

thanks to the ECO. The stronger the reduction in the diversity of investment opportunities, the less likely are continued inefficient capital reallocations post-ECO. Therefore, the effect of ECOs on firm value is positively related to a reduction in the diversity of investment opportunities via the ECO.

The role of internal resources of the group of companies is more complex. Assuming pre-ECO overinvestment, a reduction in internal resources is positively related to firm value. The development of internal resources and its association with investment efficiency can be measured in three ways.

First, change in internal resources depends on the use of the ECO proceeds. ECOs lead to an inflow of capital. Depending on the use of the ECO proceeds, the size of the internal capital market of the group of companies can both be reduced or increased. Assuming a direct payout of the funds raised to shareholders or debtholders, internal resources of the group of companies are decreased through the ECO and overinvestment is made less likely (for similar argument see Allen/McConnell (1998), Kaserer/Ahlers (2001)). However, assuming that the funds raised are retained, the internal resources of the group of companies increase, and the scope for overinvestment is widened. This differentiates ECOs from spin-offs, and compromises the applicability to ECOs of the results of spin-off literature on investment efficiency.

Second, the change in internal resources, and thus the effect of ECOs on investment efficiency is related to the degree of separation between parent and subsidiary achieved after the ECO. If the parent retains control in the subsidiary, continued inefficient capital reallocations are possible.

Third, the consequences of a change in internal resources, and hence the effect of ECOs on investment efficiency is related to the degree of inefficiency pre-ECO. The scope for improvement is the greater, the more overinvestment there is pre-ECO.

Taking together the three arguments above, the overall effect of ECOs on investment efficiency is thus ambiguous. Also, it is not trivial to disentangle the ceteris paribus effects of the four potential determinants in order to formulate testable hypotheses. Under some simplifying assumptions, the following effects of ECOs on investment efficiency can be expected.

- As discussed, an increase in focus is unambiguously positively related to investment efficiency.

- Since in general not all ECO proceeds are paid out, ECOs on average lead to an inflow of capital. It is particularly likely that the funds raised are not used for positive-NPV investment opportunities but lead to overinvestment, where the group of companies already overinvested pre-ECO. Thus, the effect of ECOs on firm value is expected to be negatively related to the presence of pre-ECO overinvestment. In the long-term, the effect of ECOs on firm value is also expected to be negatively related to persistent overinvestment. However, a payout of ECO proceeds to shareholders or debtholders effectively curbs the scope for overinvestment post-ECO. Thus, the effect of ECOs on firm value is expected to be positively related to a payout of ECO proceeds.
- When there is pre-ECO overinvestment, a reduction in internal resources can be expected to be especially valuable.
- Finally, an effective separation of parent and subsidiary is expected to be valuable especially in those cases where there is pre-ECO overinvestment. If the parent retains control in the subsidiary, the size of the internal capital market is not effectively reduced. This is potentially most harmful in those cases where internal resources are used in order to sustain inefficient overinvestment. Thus, the effect of ECOs on firm value is expected to be positively related to the creation of effective impediments against continued inefficient reallocations post-ECO via a separation of parent and subsidiary.

The above arguments lead to the following hypotheses:[75]

H1A: The effect of ECOs on firm value is positively related to a reduction in divisional investment opportunities post-ECO

H1B: The effect of ECOs on firm value is negatively related to the presence of overinvestment

H1C: The effect of ECOs on firm value is positively related to a payout to shareholders/debtholders of the proceeds from the ECO

H1D: The effect of ECOs on firm value is positively related to the creation of effective impediments against continued inefficient reallocations post-ECO via a separation of parent and subsidiary

[75] Hypotheses are operationalized in the empirical part, Section 4.3.4.4

Figure 15 illustrates how these hypotheses are related to the two-dimensional agency framework for the analysis of ECOs.

Figure 15: Focus and investment efficiency hypotheses in the two-dimensional framework

FOCUS AND INVESTMENT EFFICIENCY

The effect of ECOs on firm value is ...

Principal-agent relationship	Interest divergence	Information environment	Monitoring/b. technology
Parent shareholders/ parent mgmt.	**H1B**: ... negatively related to the presence of over-investment **H1C**: ... positively related to a payout to shareholders/debtholders of the proceeds from the ECO		
Parent mgmt./ subsidiary mgmt.	**H1A**: ... positively related to a reduction in divisional investment opportunities post-ECO **H1D**: ... positively related to the creation of effective impediments against continued inefficient reallocations post-ECO via a separation of parent and subsidiary		
Subsidiary shareholders/ subsidiary mgmt.			

Determinants of agency costs

3.4 Lever 2: Information asymmetries and disclosure

3.4.1 Treatment in the ECO literature

In the literature, value creation from ECOs has regularly been attributed to a reduction in information asymmetries between management and investors, or between different groups of investors, resulting from improved disclosure (e.g. Schipper/Smith (1986), Allen (1998), Langenbach (2001), Vijh (2002)). Articles in practitioners' journals equally often mention transparency motivations for ECOs (e.g. Anslinger et al. (1997)).

An ECO precommits the subsidiary to supply audited financial reports, which purportedly improves the investor understanding of the group of companies (Schipper/Smith (1986)). Empirically, the breakup of conglomerate stock into separate pure-play stocks leads to an increase in analyst coverage and a reduction of forecast errors in analysts' earnings estimates (spin-offs: Krishnaswami/Subramaniam (1999); ECOs, spin-offs and tracking stocks: Gilson et al. (2001)). Generally, analysts forecast earnings of focused firms more accurately than those of diversified conglomerates (Zuckerman (2000)).[76]

The only study directly relating information asymmetry to value creation from ECOs is Fu (2002). On the basis of transaction-level data, Fu (2002) estimates a measure of the probability of information-based trading pre- and post-ECO, which is indicative of information asymmetries between different investor groups. He finds a decrease in information-based trading after the ECO. The decrease in information-based trading is positively related to the announcement return.

Hypothesis development in the existing ECO literature has largely been ad hoc, e.g. based on managerial reports of a reduction in information asymmetries as a motivation for the ECO (e.g. Schipper/Smith (1986), Langenbach (2001)). This study develops theoretical foundations based on a general discussion of the role of information asymmetries in corporate valuation, and a review of empirical evidence of the role of disclosure from the accounting literature. After laying these foundations, specific hypotheses on the role of information asymmetries and disclosure in ECOs are derived.

---

[76] Baldwin (1984) finds that the introduction of mandatory segment reporting in 1970 significantly improved accuracy of the mean earnings forecast for diversified firms. In a similar study, Swaminathan (1991) finds that the introduction of segment reporting also reduces the dispersion of individual forecasts. On a more general note, Elton/Gruber/Gultekin (1985) find that analyst forecast error is not determined by market-wide measures of uncertainty, but depends on firm-specific factors

3.4.2 *Information asymmetries and corporate valuation*

3.4.2.1 *Theoretical perspectives*

Under the neoclassical assumptions of perfect information, information cannot play a role in corporate valuation, and changes in the disclosure of financial data cannot happen, since by definition market participants are perfectly informed (e.g. Watts/Zimmermann (1990), p. 132):

> "Information is costless and there are no transaction costs in the Modigliani and Miller (1958) and capital asset pricing model frameworks. Hence, if accounting methods do no affect taxes they do not affect firm value. In that situation, there is no basis for predicting and explaining accounting choice. Accounting is irrelevant."

A large body of work in market microstructure theory since the mid-1970s has been occupied with relaxing the assumption of perfect information and modeling how information is impounded into prices (for a review from an accounting perspective, see Verrecchia (2001)).[77] Seminal work in this area includes Grossman (1976, 1978), who principally developed the concept of the rational-expectations equilibrium and applied it to financial markets,[78] where traders condition and update their expectations on market prices, and Grossman/Stiglitz (1980), who analytically showed the impossibility of informationally efficient stock markets.[79] Later work has modeled more complex environments, where e.g. investors have heterogeneous private information, interpret public information heterogeneously, or do not process information efficiently.

In the context of corporate valuation, two types of information asymmetries are relevant:

- Information asymmetries between different investor groups
- Information asymmetries between management and investors

Information asymmetries between different investor groups are commonly modeled by assuming that there are three types of market participants: informed investors (possessing private information about firm prospects), uninformed investors, and a market maker (e.g.

---

[77] Lintner (1969), modeling the effect of diverse investor beliefs, is a predecessor of the later work

[78] The general concept of rational expectations was developed earlier in the context of macroeconomic investment models, e.g. Lucas/Prescott (1971)

[79] Their argument is as follows: if all information is contained in prices, it is sufficient to condition expectations on prices, and the acquisition of additional information is superfluous. Thus, if the

Grossman/Stiglitz (1980), Kyle (1985) for prominent examples of this approach). In this context, the existence of information asymmetries has two effects: a positive bid-ask spread, and reduced liquidity.

In the presence of asymmetric information, the market maker increases the bid-ask spread (Copeland/Galai (1983), Glosten/Milgrom (1985)): In Glosten/Milgrom (1985), the market maker must charge a positive bid-ask spread even in the absence of transaction costs and wealth limitations in order to compensate the cost of adverse selection. In the presence of informed investors, a sell order could indicate that informed investors have private information that firm performance is about to deteriorate. The market maker thus faces a potential demand imbalance (all informed investors are selling), and a risk of a falling stock price. This risk is compensated by the spread: the market maker buys the stock at the (lower) bid-price, and sells at the (higher) ask price. The bid-ask spread is thus a measure of the extent of information asymmetries. Given the bid-ask spread, uninformed investors can achieve only a lower return ex post (Amihud/Mendelson (1986)). Consequently, they ex ante expect a higher return in order to invest in the firm.

The effect of information asymmetries on liquidity is modeled by Diamond/Verrecchia (1991) and Merton (1987). In the Diamond/Verrecchia (1991) model, the presence of informed investors leads to the illiquidity of a stock because the informed investors want to prevent that their private information is revealed through their trading behavior.[80] Illiquidity in turn increases the risk that the stock will not be traded at a fair price, and thus deters institutional investors who anticipate trading large volumes from investing in the stock. In Merton's (1987) model, information asymmetries lead to illiquidity in a different way: Each investor is aware of only a limited number of stocks in which he can invest. For so-called "neglected stocks", i.e. stocks that are not known to most investors, less information is produced by market participants. Prices of these stocks thus do not reflect all available information. This increases the risk that the stock is not be traded at a fair price. Thus, firms with a smaller investor base have a higher expected return.[81]

---

acquisition of information is costly, investors will not acquire information in equilibrium. However, if no information is acquired, no information can be contained in prices.

[80] The argument goes as follows: If an informed investor has private information that the performance of a firm is about to deteriorate, and he sells a large volume of stock in the firm, the stock price will fall correspondingly; the information will be impounded into the stock price and is thus revealed to other market participants

[81] Merton (1987) can thus also be interpreted as a theoretical underpinning for the small-firm effect empirically found by Fama/French (1992, 1995, 1996a)

Consequently, information asymmetries between different investor groups increase a firm's cost of capital, due to a larger bid-ask spread and lower liquidity.

Information asymmetries between management and investors are commonly modeled within the classic agency framework, and in the context of estimation risk.

Within the classic agency framework, agency costs arise from the nonobservability of the agent's actions by the principal. As discussed in Section 2.5.2, information asymmetry between agent and principal is one of the key determinants of agency costs: if the principal could perfectly observe the agent's actions, there are obviously no agency costs, and agency costs increase with output uncertainty (e.g. Holmström/Milgrom (1987) for an exposition based on the LEN-model). The existence of information asymmetry between management and investors leads to agency costs and thus increases a firm's cost of capital (e.g. Bens/Monahan (2003) for a recent discussion).

The effect of estimation risk on the cost of capital is modeled by Barry/Brown (1985). Investors are assumed to determine their expected return based on parameters they estimate from available information on the firm in question. If only little information is available, there is a greater risk that the parameter estimates are wrong, and investors demand a higher return as compensation for this additional source of risk (Coles/Loewenstein/Suay (1995) and Clarkson/Guedes/Thompson (1996) discuss the measurement and diversification of estimation risk).

3.4.2.2 Empirical evidence

Empirical research on information asymmetries and corporate valuation requires measures of both information asymmetries and the cost of capital. This is not trivial, because neither is directly observable (Hail (2002)).

Information asymmetries have been estimated in different ways. The market microstructure literature focuses on measures such as the bid-ask-spread and liquidity. The corporate finance literature focuses on such proxies as accounting disclosure ratings and properties of analyst forecasts.

In order to measure cost of capital, researchers have relied on the Capital Asset Pricing Model (Sharpe (1964), Lintner (1965), Mossin (1966)), the dominant practitioners' approach in corporate finance,[82] and newer approaches from the accounting literature that determine an implied cost of capital from analysts' forecasts.[83]

Empirical results on the relationship between cost of capital and information asymmetries, where disclosure is used as a proxy for information, are provided by the accounting literature. The extensive "value-relevance" research, building on the pioneering earnings announcements studies by Ball/Brown (1968) and Beaver (1968), has established that accounting data contain information that affects stock prices, i.e. accounting data are value relevant (Healy/Palepu (2001)).[84] Against the backdrop of this result, the accounting literature has examined the influence of disclosure on the cost of capital. Botosan (1997, 2000) and Hail (2002) find that firms with superior disclosure ratings have a lower implied cost of capital. Healy/Hutton/Palepu (1999) find that firms with sustained improvements in disclosure ratings have contemporaneous positive abnormal stock returns.[85]

Consistent with theoretical predictions, empirical results thus show that high-quality disclosure reduces the cost of capital: By disclosing information, information asymmetries between management and investors and information asymmetries between different investor groups can be effectively reduced.

---

[82] Graham/Harvey's (2001) field research shows that the CAPM is used by more than 70% of US corporations; in contrast, Hupe/Ritter (1997) find that only 45% of German corporations apply a risk adjustment to their hurdle rate. Under the CAPM-approach, cost of capital is expected from historical realized returns. Due to the low correlation between realized returns and expected returns (Elton (1999)), this procedure is problematic. Fama/French (1996b) criticize the continued application of the CAPM in light of its unsatisfactory performance in empirical tests

[83] The implied cost of capital is calculated using a variant of the dividend-discount model. Market consensus estimates of future cash flows are identified based on analyst forecasts. Then, the dividend discount model is solved for the discount rate that equalizes cash flow forecasts and current market valuation. This discount rate constitutes the cost of capital (Ohlson (1995, 2001), Gebhardt/Lee/Swaminathan (2001), Gode/Mohanram (2003); a review is provided by Kothari (2001))

[84] The value-relevance literature is reviewed in Holthausen/Watts (2001); capital markets research in accounting is reviewed in Kothari (2001); the change in value relevance of accounting data over the past forty years is analyzed in Collins/Maydew/Weiss (1997)

[85] An alternative approach is adopted by Bloomfield/Wilks (2000), who study the effects of disclosure not based on empirical capital market and accounting data, but based on a laboratory experiment in which they replicate a financial market. Despite the stark difference in methodology, they come to similar results, name that disclosure lowers the cost of capital and increases market liquidity

3.4.3 Disclosure and agency costs

3.4.3.1 Role and types of disclosure

The previous section has established that disclosure of information by firms reduces the cost of capital. However, the empirical studies reviewed mostly take disclosure as an exogenous variable, while being silent about the determinants and motivation of disclosure. To what extent can firms reduce information asymmetries by voluntarily disclosing information, and what determines the degree of disclosure and remaining information asymmetries? Within agency theory, disclosure can be interpreted as a mechanism that improves the information environment, constrains self-interested behavior by management, and thus reduces agency costs. But under the assumption that they are self-interested, why then should managers be willing to disclose information?

In order to discuss these questions, the following section reviews in more detail the different types and roles of disclosure.

Holthausen/Verrecchia (1990) define information as data that influences investor expectations about the value of an asset. An important element of the information environment is disclosure of financial information by the company (Merton (1987), Lang/Lundholm (1996)). Choi (1973) offers the following definition of disclosure (p. 283):

> "The term financial disclosure is defined here as the publication of any economic information relating to a business enterprise, quantitative or otherwise, which facilitates the making of investment decisions. Economic information, in turn, is any datum that reduces the uncertainty about the outcomes of future economic events"

The role of disclosure has been extensively discussed in the accounting literature (for recent surveys see Verrecchia (2001), Healy/Palepu (2001). Healy/Palepu (2001) highlight the important role of disclosure in ensuring efficiency of a market economy (p. 407):[86]

> "Information and incentive problems impede the efficient allocation of resources in a capital market economy. Disclosure and the institutions created to facilitate credible disclosure between managers and investors play an important role in mitigating these problems."

[86] Kunkel (1982) discusses how disclosure can lead to Pareto improvements by leading to a more efficient allocation of resources across time and firms throughout the economy; Diamond (1985) discusses how public disclosure can lead to Pareto improvements by eliminating incentives to engage in the costly acquisition of private information

In the absence of market imperfections, firms would produce the optimal level of disclosure automatically, equalizing the marginal costs of disclosure and the marginal benefits (Healy/Palepu (2001)).

The benefits of disclosure consist of a reduction in the information asymmetries discussed above: adverse selection problems between different investor groups and between management and investors are reduced. More technically, Diamond/Verrecchia (1991) define the quality of disclosure as the precision of a Bayesian investor's beliefs about security value after receiving the disclosure, where a higher quality disclosure produces a more compact posterior distribution of beliefs. Interpreting disclosure as a measure of information asymmetries, as discussed above, theory thus predicts a negative relation between increased disclosure and the cost of capital (Verrecchia (1999), Leuz/Verrecchia (2000), Healy/Palepu (2001), Hail (2002)), i.e. when disclosure improves, the cost of capital declines.[87] This assumption is also underlying the empirical work discussed previously.

The costs of disclosure consist of potential disadvantages in product-market competition through disclosure of information to competitors, and a potential exacerbation of information asymmetries. The negative consequences of disclosure in product market competition are discussed in e.g. Wagenhofer (1990), who develops a model where disclosure can be costly in that positive information induces market entry by competitors. Hayes/Lundholm (1996) develop a model where it is value-maximizing to shift earnings between different segments of a diversified firm so that all segments report similar earnings, and segment reporting thus provides no information to competitors. Kim/Verrecchia (1994) present a model where disclosure increases information asymmetries, namely when public information is complementary to private information and disclosure thus exacerbates the informational advantage of informed investors. In Baiman/Verrecchia's (1996) highly stylized model, increased disclosure can reduce productivity when it renders stock price relatively less informative of managerial effort and thus increases residual agency problems when managers react by reducing their effort (further literature on the costs of disclosure is referenced in Healy/Hutton/Palepu (1999)).

Integrating the different approaches from the preceding literature, Verrecchia (2001) provides a formal model where the reduction in the information asymmetry component of the cost of capital, is traded off against reduced profits from disclosure of proprietary information to competitors in a Cournot duopoly.

However, in the presence of agency problems, managers do not necessarily choose the optimal level of disclosure, or reveal information truthfully. It is therefore necessary to distinguish between two different types of disclosure (Healy/Palepu (2001)):

- Mandatory disclosure
- Voluntary disclosure

The following two sections analyze the two types in more detail.

3.4.3.2 Mandatory disclosure and the institutional environment

Mandatory disclosure is determined by the institutional environment, i.e. corporate law and accounting standards (Ball/Kothari/Robin (2000); Bushman/Smith (2001)). While a comparative review of different accounting standards is clearly beyond the scope of the present paper (see e.g. Holthausen/Watts (2001) and the references contained therein), it is useful to briefly touch on the general influence of the German institutional environment on disclosure.

In their analysis of the role of accounting in the German financial system, Leuz/Wüstemann (2004) characterize the German financial system as one of relationship-based contracting, as opposed to the Anglo-Saxon arm's length system.[88] While in an arm's length system, mandatory disclosure plays a crucial role, enabling investors to monitor their financial claims and exercise their rights, it plays a lesser role in a relationship-based system. Under such a system, information asymmetries are to a greater extent resolved via private channels rather than public disclosure (Ball/Kothari/Robin (2000)). Thus, the core contracting parties such as large shareholders and key creditors are well informed, while outside investors face a lack of transparency. An example for such a private channel is information revealed by management to the supervisory board (where key parties are represented) under §90 AktG, but not necessarily to all shareholders (Leuz/Wüstemann (2004)).

---

[87] This analysis ignores second-order effects, e.g. changes to the incentives to investors to become privately informed when they anticipate public disclosure (as discussed in the economics literature on noisy rational expectations equilibria, e.g. Verrecchia (1982))

[88] For a typology of financial systems, see Berglöf (1997), Schmidt/Tyrell (1997), Allen/Gale (2000), and Schmidt/Tyrell (2004)

Despite the trend toward the adoption of international accounting standards following recent legal changes (e.g. Leuz/Verrecchia (2000)), Germany regularly ranks in the bottom third in international disclosure rankings (LaPorta et al. (1998), LaPorta/Lopez de Silanes/Shleifer (2003)).

Empirical evidence on the institutional environment generally suggests that accounting data under the German financial system is somewhat less informative than under the Anglo-Saxon system (Leuz/Wüstemann (2004)). However, the results are decidedly mixed: While Joos/Lang (1994) and Harris/Lang/Möller (1994) do not find evidence for difference in the value relevance of German HGB earnings to US GAAP/IAS earnings, Alford et al. (1993) and Ali/Hwang (2000) find superior value relevance of US GAAP/IAS earnings. In an extensive cross-country international comparison, Bhattacharaya/Daouk/Welker (2003) find that the cost of equity is higher in countries with high earnings opacity, measured by the occurrence of earnings aggressiveness, loss avoidance and earnings smoothing; with Germany ranking average on the earnings opacity score. Ball/Kothari/Robin (2000) equally find that earnings management is more prevalent in Germany than in the Anglo-Saxon countries (US, UK, Australia, Canada), and accounting earnings are less timely, measured by their lag to economic value creation. In a further international comparison, Leuz/Nanda/Wysocki (2003) equally provide evidence for a greater prevalence of income smoothing in Germany. In one of the very few empirical studies that directly compare German HGB to US GAAP/IAS standards, Leuz/Verrecchia (2000) find that the adoption of international accounting standards by German firms decreases the bid-ask spread and increases trading volume, i.e. the information asymmetry component of the cost of capital.[89]

3.4.3.3 *Voluntary disclosure and managerial incentives*

While accounting standards stipulate mandatory disclosure, management has discretion over voluntary disclosure. In light of the German institutional environment discussed above, voluntary disclosure is of special importance. Recent research has stressed the role of voluntary disclosure: Accounting standards necessarily leave discretion, so that disclosure quality is effectively not determined by accounting standards, but by management's reporting incentives (Ball/Robin/Wu (2003)).

---

[89] Consistently, the reduction of the cost of capital through improved disclosure is indicated as motivation for the switch of accounting regime by 50% of managers of DAX100 companies in survey evidence

In positive accounting theory (Watts/Zimmermann (1978, 1990)), management's reporting incentives and accounting choices are commonly discussed based on agency theory. Lambert (2001) underlines that "agency theory has been one of the most important theoretical paradigms in accounting during the last 20 years" (p. 3). In their review of positive accounting theory, Fields/Lys/Vincent (2001) interpret the role of accounting as that of a governance mechanism designed to mitigate agency costs: Higher disclosure quality increases the precision of publicly available information about management's investment and operating decisions; hence, commitments to disclose potentially reduce management's scope for inefficient investment (Bens/Monahan (2003))[90]. Within a nexus of contracts view of the firm, managers have incentives to choose among different accounting methods so that their private benefits are maximized, since a large number of contracts is based on accounting data (e.g. debt covenants: Smith/Warner (1979); management compensation: Healy (1985)). Evans/Sridhar (1996) explain that despite agency problems, some managerial discretion over accounting choice must remain, because the elimination of all managerial flexibility could result in a distortion of real activity, which would be more costly than a distortion of accounting numbers.

Agency problems and imperfect accounting regulation thus imply that information might not be disclosed up to the optimal level, or not be disclosed truthfully.[91] From a theoretical standpoint, full and truthful revelation can be induced, but at a cost. In Grossman/Hart (1980a), information is fully revealed because otherwise it will be inferred that the concealed information is most unfavorable, so complete revelation is privately optimal. Myerson's (1979) revelation principle indicates that any mechanism that involves untruthful reporting by the agent can at least be duplicated by an equilibrium mechanism where truthful reporting is induced. However, the revelation comes at a cost: The principal must commit to underutilize the revealed information, e.g. when the revealed infor-

---

(Pellens/Tomaszwewski (1999)). An empirical comparison between IAS and US GAAP, based on evidence from the Neuer Markt, is provided in Leuz (2003)

90 Kanodia/Lee (1998) provide a formal model of how disclosure, used as periodic performance report, can alleviate the overinvestment problem

91 Importantly, while agency problems and differential information are incorporated, all models discussed assume rational investors. In rare contrast, a recent example for a model concerned with the effects of bounded rationality is Hirshleifer/Teoh (2003). The authors model the effect of limited information processing capacity on valuation: If a multisegment firm has segments of different growth ("hidden gems" and "skeletons-in-the-closet"), but an investor with limited information processing capacity ignores segment reporting, and instead builds his expectations of future firm growth based on an extrapolation of the growth rate of the entire firm, growth will be underestimated, since the increasing weight of the high-growth segments over time will not enter into the calculation.

mation is negative, he must have ex ante committed not to reduce the agent's compensation accordingly.

Due to these costs, voluntary disclosure is not necessarily complete nor credible (Healy/Palepu (2001), Verrecchia (2001)). In practice, full voluntary disclosure does not take place (e.g. the formal models by Verrecchia (1983), Dye (1986)), and voluntary disclosure does not have the same credibility as mandatory disclosure (Verrecchia (2001) shows this in a communication game in a duopolistic setting, based on the original work by Crawford/Sobel (1982)).

Empirical evidence on voluntary disclosure indicates that higher voluntary disclosure quality reduces the cost of capital, similarly to more stringent mandatory disclosure, despite the completeness and credibility issues discussed. Gelb/Zarowin (2002) and Lundholm/Myers (2002) show that firms with high disclosure ratings have a high contemporaneous earnings-stock price association, i.e. their earnings are more value-relevant. Welker (1995) finds that firms with low disclosure rankings have higher bid-ask spreads.[92] As discussed, a direct link between voluntary disclosure and the cost of capital is established by Botosan (1997), Healy/Hutton/Palepu (1999), and Hail (2002).[93] Healy/Hutton/Palepu (1999) find positive abnormal stock returns for firms with sustained increases in disclosure ratings. They also find a decrease in the dispersion of analyst forecasts, which they interpret as evidence for a reduction in the information asymmetry component of the cost of capital. Botosan (1997) and Hail (2002), both directly relate disclosure ratings to the implied cost of capital. Based on a regression framework, they find that a superior disclosure rating decreases the cost of capital. Focusing on the US manufacturing sector, Botosan (1997) finds that superior disclosure is negatively related to cost of capital for firms with low analyst following, i.e. for firms where information from other sources is unavailable. Focusing on Swiss firms, Hail (2002) finds that superior voluntary disclosure can have an economically highly significant effect of around -2% on the cost of capital in a relationship-based financial system similar to the German system.

Concerning the costs of disclosure in terms of competitive disadvantages, Harris (1998) shows that business units in the least competitive industries are most likely to be reported as industry segments, which is consistent with value maximization. Indicative of the

---

92 Using managerial ownership as a proxy for interest alignment between shareholders and management, Warfield/Wild/Wild (1995) find that the informativeness of earnings is positively related to managerial ownership

managerial incentives to choose voluntary disclosures in order to maximize private benefits, Lang/Lundholm (1993) find that disclosure ratings improve in the six months prior to equity and debt offerings, which they interpret as evidence of managers' attempting to increase corporate valuation. Aboody/Kasznik (2000) find that news announcements are timed to stock options awards, which they interpret as evidence of managers' attempting to increase stock-based compensation. Bushee/Noe (2000) find considerable fluctuations in disclosure ratings over time, evidence that can be understood as indication of self-interested managers adjusting upwards and downwards the level of voluntary disclosures.

3.4.4 *Information asymmetries, disclosure, and ECOs*

The above section has discussed the detrimental consequences of information asymmetries on corporate valuation and the mitigating role of disclosure. Empirical evidence has been shown to be largely supportive of the negative relation between voluntary disclosure and cost of capital, and evidence broadly indicative of a somewhat lower informativeness of German HGB accounts compared to international accounting standards has been discussed.

ECOs can thus be expected to create value if the level of disclosure is increased and information asymmetries reduced correspondingly. More specifically,

- Information asymmetries among investors could be reduced by ECOs thanks to improving the availability of public as opposed to private information through increased public disclosure. The consequent resolution of the adverse selection problem should decrease the bid-ask-spread and increase liquidity
- Information asymmetries between investors and management could be reduced by ECOs either by increasing mandatory disclosure or improving managerial reporting incentives, thus leading to a reduction in residual agency problems and estimation risk

A prerequisite for both effects to materialize is that ECOs either increase mandatory disclosure or improve managerial incentives for voluntary disclosure. Assuming that voluntary disclosure is imperfect in light of agency problems, and that ECOs do not create an immediate incentive for improving voluntary disclosure, it can be hypothesized that a

[93] Sengupta (1998) shows that voluntary disclosure also decreases the cost of debt

potential decrease in information asymmetries is accounted for principally by an increase in mandatory disclosure.

An increase in mandatory disclosure follows from legal disclosure requirements (Publizitätspflicht): After the ECO, the subsidiary is required to submit its own set of audited financial statements, in accordance with §242 and §264 HGB. Prior to the ECO, information on the subsidiary, depending on its prior legal status, is usually only publicly available in the segment reporting section of the consolidated financial statements of the group of companies.

In Germany, mandatory segment reporting has only been introduced in 1998, when the law on corporate control and transparency (KonTraG) amended §297 I HGB by a sentence stipulating that the appendix to the consolidated financial statements of exchange-listed parent corporations must include segment reports (Krawitz (1997), Ordelheide/Stubenrath (1998), Claussen (1999)).[94] Before 1998, only segment sales had to be reported (Haller/Park (1994a, 1994b)). Currently, segment reporting is regulated under the DRSC 3, the standard established by the German accounting standards committee (Strobel (1999), Böcking/Beneke (1999), Mujkanovic (2000), Hacker (2002)).[95] Alternatively, segment reports can be submitted under SFAS 131 or IAS 14 (for a comparison of the different standards, see Hahn (2000), Alvarez (2002), Nardmann (2002), Hacker (2003)).

Notwithstanding the prior availability of segment reporting on the ECO, the increase in disclosure from the separate set of audited financial statements on the subsidiary is non-controversial. While Bens/Monahan (2003) find that multisegment firms with favorable disclosure ratings do not trade at a discount compared to focused firms, and the incremental information content of segment reports is widely acknowledged (e.g. Swaminathan (1991), Givoly/Hayn/D'Souza (1999) and the literature reviewed therein), practical implementation has been equally widely criticized (for German perspectives, see Bernards (1995) taking object with vague segment definition; Haller/Permanschlager (2002) evaluating FAS 131; and Alvarez/Fink (2003) and Feldkämper (2003) empirically analyzing

[94] The 2002 law on the reform of corporate and accounting law, transparency and disclosure (TransPubG; Gesetz zur weiteren Reform des Aktien- und Bilanzrechts, zu Transparenz und Publizität) stipulates segment reports also for non-exchange-listed parents, when some part of the group of companies is exchange listed (e.g. Knorr/Wittich (2002))

[95] The DRSC's role as a standard setter with advisory function is established in §342 HGB, see Schildbach (1999) and Scheffler (1999) for general information on its structure and competences

segment reports under DRS 3). Berger/Hann (2003), in the most extensive empirical analysis of segment reports to date, find that the introduction of SFAS 131 as new segment reporting standard under US GAAP in 1998, significantly reduced analyst forecast errors. At the same time, they must admit that segment definition is extremely vague: In their sample, the proportion of multisegment firms increases from 22% under SFAS 14 (the previous standard in effect from 1976 to 1997) to 40% under SFAS 131. Furthermore, they contend that "managers have strong incentives to manipulate internal segment information used in performance evaluation" (p. 165). Krishnaswami/Subramaniam (1999) equally stress the potential for managerial manipulation of segment reports. Also, some types of information, such as capital structure, cannot be credibly disclosed in segment reports (Gilson et al. (2001)).

Unrelated to disclosure and segment reporting, it can also be hypothesized that information asymmetries are mitigated via ECOs thanks to greater informativeness of the price system: uninformed investors can condition their expectations on a further set of stock prices (Habib/Johnsen/Naik (1997)).[96]

In conclusion, it can be solidly assumed that ECOs lead to an increase in mandatory disclosure thanks to a separate set of audited financial statements. The increase in disclosure is likely to reduce information asymmetries between investors: The relative weight of publicly disclosed information versus private information decreases. Likewise, the increase in disclosure is likely to reduce information asymmetries between investors and management. Consequently, thanks to improved transparency, agency costs in the parent shareholder/parent management and subsidiary shareholder/subsidiary management relationships decline.[97]

The magnitude of this effect is dependent on the extent of pre-ECO information asymmetries. In the present study it is hypothesized that more severe pre-ECO information asymmetries are positively related to the potential reduction in agency costs via an ECO,

---

[96] Habib/Johnsen/Naik (1997) formally derive this conclusion based on a Grossman/Stiglitz (1980) type model, where a more informative price system reduces the demanded liquidity premium

[97] A countervailing argument has recently been developed by Hadlock/Ryngaert/Thomas (2001), Thomas (2002), and Clarke/Fee/Thomas (2004): These authors hypothesize that information asymmetries surrounding multisegment firms are actually less pronounced, despite lower disclosure. Assuming that investors' prediction errors are not perfectly correlated across segments, the uncertainty about total firm value can be lower than for stand-alone firms. While information asymmetries concerning divisional performance are thus more pronounced, they are assumed to partially cancel out. This effect is called the "information diversification hypothesis" (Thomas (2002)). Empirical evidence is to some extent supportive of this prediction.

i.e. when pre-ECO information asymmetries are severe due to inferior voluntary disclosure, the increase in mandatory disclosure thanks to the ECO is assumed to be especially valuable. Interestingly, this hypothesis, while based on an entirely different rationale, is also consistent with developed in adverse selection models (such as most prominently Myers/Majluf (1984), and Nanda (1991) with application to ECOs). In these models, the announcement of an equity issue sends a negative signal, which is the stronger, the greater the extent of pre-announcement information asymmetries. In the case of ECOs, according to Nanda's (1991) model, the announcement signals undervaluation of the parent relative to the subsidiary, and given the greater size of the parent, is thus hypothesized to trigger a positive announcement effect. Thus, more severe the pre-ECO information asymmetries, creating higher adverse selection costs, should lead to a stronger positive announcement effect.

Summarizing, in terms of the two-dimensional agency framework for the analysis of ECOs, ECOs thus improve the information environment in the parent shareholder-parent management and the subsidiary shareholder-subsidiary management relationships.

More precisely, the above arguments lead to the following hypotheses:[98]

H2A: The effect of ECOs on firm value is positively related to the extent of information asymmetries among investors and between investors and management prior to the transaction

H2B: The effect of ECOs on firm value is positively related to the reduction in information asymmetries among investors and between investors and management after the transaction

Figure 16 illustrates how these hypotheses are related to the two-dimensional agency framework for the analysis of ECOs.

[98] Hypotheses are operationalized in the empirical part, Section 4.3.4.4

Figure 16: Information asymmetries and disclosure hypotheses in the two-dimensional framework

INFORMATION ASYMMETRIES AND DISCLOSURE

The effect of ECOs on firm value is ...

Principal-agent relationship		Interest divergence	Information environment	Monitoring/b. technology
	Parent shareholders/ parent mgmt.		**H2A**: ... positively related to the extent of information asymmetries among investors and between investors and management prior to the transaction	
	Parent mgmt./ subsidiary mgmt.			
	Subsidiary shareholders/ subsidiary mgmt.		**H2B**: ... positively related to the reduction in information asymmetries among investors and between investors and management after the transaction	

Determinants of agency costs

3.5 Lever 3: Incentive compensation

3.5.1 Treatment in the ECO literature

In the literature, value creation from ECOs has also been attributed to improved incentive compensation for former divisional managers by tying compensation to the newly-established subsidiary stock price (Schipper/Smith (1986), Allen (1998), Vijh (2002)).

Schipper/Smith (1986) cite evidence that the incentive contracts of subsidiary managers are usually revised following the ECO in order to incorporate subsidiary share price as a measure of performance. In a German context, Langenbach (2001) cites moderate evidence that an improvement in the attractiveness of management positions of the subsidiary, allowing to attract high-quality human capital, can be a motivation for an ECO.

The existing ECO literature has thus largely relied on managerial reports indicating improved incentive alignment as a motive for ECOs, while ignoring the controversies surrounding stock-based incentives in the general economic discussion (e.g. Bebchuk/Walker (2003)). This study develops more solid theoretical foundations based on a survey of recent perspectives on compensation and incentives from the economics and management literature. Hypotheses are then derived on the role of incentive compensation in ECOs.

3.5.2 Incentive compensation and corporate valuation

3.5.2.1 Theoretical perspectives

The increase in executive compensation during the 1990s[99] has both fueled an intense public debate, as well as a controversial academic discussion, with participants from different disciplines such as economics, finance, accounting, management, and organization (Murphy (1999)). The academic literature is rife with examples of pay practices perceived as excessive; for the purposes of the present study, one such example shall suffice (Conyon/Murphy (2000), p. 640):

> "Indeed, Disney's Michael Eisner, dubbed by pay-critic Graef Crystal (1991) as the 'Prince of Pay', exercised options worth £348 million in December 1997, thus single-handedly out-earning the aggregate pay cheques of the top 500 CEOs in the United Kingdom"

---

[99] Murphy (1999) provides evidence that top management compensation has increased more strongly than average workers' compensation in the US; Schwalbach (1999) provides similar evidence for Germany

In the economics literature, incentive compensation has long been a topic of interest (e.g. Taussig/Barker (1925); Roberts (1959)). Empirical studies from such diverse areas as retail department stores (Banker/Lee/Potter (1996)), sports (Fernie/Metcalf (1996)) and agriculture (Foster/Rosenzweig (1994)), as well as laboratory experiments (e.g. Tosi/Katz/Gomez-Mejia (1997)) have clearly established that workers respond favorably to monetary incentives.[100]

In the literature, incentive compensation has been discussed based on two competing perspectives:

- Agency theory
- Managerial power

These two perspectives are discussed in the following section.[101]

Agency theory has clearly become the dominant paradigm underlying economic analysis of incentive compensation (Gibbons (1998), Murphy (1999), Aggarwal/Samwick (1999), Prendergast (1999), Bertrand/Mullainathan (2001)). The influence of agency theory even extends to neighboring disciplines, such as the management literature (e.g. Bloom/Milkovich (1998)) or organization theory (e.g. Barkema/Pennings (1998)).

Adopting the agency perspective, outcome-based incentives are used to align the interest of principal (shareholder) and agent (manager) when the agent's actions are unobservable by the principal (refer back to Section 2.5.2.2). The optimal compensation contract maximizes the risk neutral shareholders' objective, subject to an incentive compatibility constraint (the manager maximizes his utility) and a participation constraint, i.e., compensation must exceed the manager's reservation utility (Mirrlees (1976), Holmström (1979), Grossman/Hart (1983)).[102] At the most basic level, agency theory predicts that executive

[100] In accordance with the general economics literature, sociological perspectives, which contend that explicit incentives can be harmful in that they reduce intrinsic motivation, are ignored in the present study (Prendergast (1999))

[101] A thorough review of executive compensation, including a large descriptive part on actual contracting practices, is provided by Murphy (1999); earlier reviews are Finkelstein/Hambrick (1988) and Gomez-Mejia/Wiseman (1997). Reviews on the provision of incentives in organizations are Gibbons (1998) and Prendergast (1999). A review from an accounting research perspective is included in Bushman/Smith (2001). Useful introductory articles are Abowd/Kaplan (1999), Hall/Murphy (2003); and Schwalbach (1999) for a German perspective

[102] This discussion only considers the agency cost of equity. Agency conflicts arising in other contracting relationships are ignored. For a discussion of the interrelationship between managerial compensation and the agency costs of debt, refer to John/John (1993)

compensation is positively related to performance (Ross (1973)). Findings that executive compensation is most strongly associated to firm size (e.g. Baker/Jensen/Murphy (1988), Tosi et al. (2000)),[103] have repeatedly led agency theorists to make strong demands in favor of the introduction of compensation systems with stronger pay-performance sensitivity, preferably stock-based (e.g. Jensen/Murphy (1990b)).[104] Murphy (1995) writes:

> "In practice, effective pay-for-performance contracts combine below-market base salaries with high potential payoffs based on stock-price appreciation (including dividends). Annual and long-term bonus plans based on accounting profits rather than stock-price performance are reduced or eliminated, and are replaced by increased grants of stock options and restricted stock. "

Similar to Murphy (1995), agency theorists generally assume the superiority of stock-based incentives over other forms of incentive compensation because of their robustness against distortion, as Holmström/Tirole (1993) conclude from a formal model (p. 707):

> "Stock prices are uniquely suited for compensation purposes, not so much because they are accurate, but because they are accurate, third-party assessments. This is, we believe, why stock prices have come to play such a central role in managerial incentives [...]."

Within agency theory, stock price-based incentives, such as stock options, are thus understood as part of an optimal incentive arrangement that mitigates agency problems (Hall/Murphy (2003)). Recently, managerial equity ownership has also been interpreted as a form of incentive compensation, where managers are penalized for weak performance by a decrease in value of their equity holdings (Hall/Liebman (1998), Core/Guay/Larcker (2003)).

Over the past couple of years, a competing perspective has come into focus: the ***managerial power*** approach (Bertrand/Mullainathan (2000, 2001), Bebchuk/Fried/Walker (2002), Bebchuk/Fried (2003)).[105] This perspective can be traced back to organization theory, where the role of power in organizational behavior has long been recognized (see Finkel-

---

[103] German empirical evidence for a positive pay-firm size relationship is included in Schmid (1997), Schwalbach/Grasshoff (1997), Elston/Goldberg (2003);.

[104] Rationalizations of the positive pay-size relationship exist: Efficiency-wage theory (Shapiro/Stiglitz (1984)) assumes that above market wages in large organizations act as a disciplining device: employee shirking is more of a problem in large organizations where monitoring is more difficult; if shirking is detected and employees are fired, they will be unlikely to find another job with equally high pay, thus they will not shirk. In a different explanation taken from human capital theory, Brenner/Schwalbach (2001) show that firm size largely proxies for managerial talent based on German and UK data

stein (1992) for a review). Finkelstein/Hambrick (1989) argue that the balance of power between the board and the CEO is a major determinant of CEO compensation; Tosi/Gomez-Mejia (1989) hypothesize that the CEO and other actors under his or her command can be more influential than the principals (shareholders) in certain settings; and Lambert/Larcker/Weigelt (1993) model managerial power as alternative hypothesis to agency theory.

The managerial power approach thus interprets compensation as a part of the agency problem itself (Bebchuk/Fried (2003)): It is assumed that managers have substantial power over their own pay, which they use in order to earn above market pay levels, and limit their compensation risk. Contrary to standard agency theory, which assumes that the board of directors acts in the shareholders' interests (Fama (1980)), the managerial power view presumes that boards do not effectively control the CEO (Bebchuk/Fried/Walker (2002)).[106] The market for corporate control and the managerial labor market are equally considered insufficient in ensuring efficient compensation contracts. According to the managerial power view, the use of stock-based incentive compensation thus does not reflect incentive alignment but managerial attempts to provide compensation in the least transparent way in order to limit "outrage costs", e.g. damage to reputation from public criticism at excessive compensation levels (Bebchuk/Fried (2003)). Thus, pay levels are constrained not by principals controlling their agents, or by market forces, but by outside political pressure. Since good firm performance eases such pressures, a correlation of good firm performance with high pay levels is therefore not in itself a confirmation of agency theory (Betrand/Mullainathan (2001)): It can barely signify that the parties involved are willing to acquiesce to higher pay levels given superior firm performance, even if such performance is not genuinely related to managerial effort.

The managerial power approach has been especially popular with German academics, who in line with the general public have criticized the introduction of stock option plans

[105]The term "managerial power approach" is due to Bebchuk/Fried/Walker (2002); Bertrand/Mullainathan (2000, 2001) use the term "skimming"

[106] Interestingly, an early predecessor to this view is Steinitzer (1908): "Fazit: Der Aufsichtsrat ist – soweit er funktionell überhaupt etwas ist – ein die Verwaltung in seinem eigenen Interesse beeinflussendes Organ. Weiter nichts. Die Rechtsauffassung eines zwischen den Gesamtaktionären und dem Aufsichtsrat bestehenden 'Mandats'verhältnisses ist durchaus unsinnig – wenn nicht beide ziemlich identisch sind. Gerade da, wo sich die Mehrheit der Aktien in den Händen kleinerer, zersplitterter, regierungsunfähiger Aktionäre befindet, wo also das Schutzbedürfnis am größten ist, vertritt der Aufsichtsrat am wenigsten 'die' Aktionäre." (p. 150)

as rent-seeking behavior by self-serving managers (Bernhardt/Witt (1997), Wenger/Knoll (1999)).[107]

Agency theorists, in contrast, fervently criticize the managerial power approach. The salient counterarguments against the managerial power view as sole explanation for observed compensation patterns are reviewed in Murphy (2002) and Hall/Murphy (2003): The central argument is that the explosion in the use of stock-based incentives has been accompanied not by an increase, but by a stark decrease in managerial power, as witnessed by the increased proliferation of independent boards and compensation committees, and the tightened disclosure rules for compensation. Murphy (2002) also criticizes that the concept of "outrage costs", while being too simplistic in the first place, is also vague to such a degree that it is not empirically testable.

3.5.2.2 Empirical evidence

The controversial theoretical discussion just reviewed has been unfolding against the backdrop of ample empirical work on compensation. However, a core difficulty in empirical work on executive compensation is the definition of unequivocal cause-and-effect relationships: Is it superior firm performance that leads to greater subsequent rewards in terms of above-average compensation, or is it above-average compensation that leads to subsequent superior firm performance (Demsetz/Villalonga (2001))? A cross-sectional comparison of the valuation of firms with different compensation systems thus will not answer the question; sophisticated structural equation models incorporating leads and lags would be necessary in order to identify causalities (Core/Guay/Larcker (2003)).

Not surprisingly though, empirical studies examining the relationship between managerial equity ownership (as a proxy for pay-performance sensitivity) and firm valuation come to mixed results (Demsetz/Lehn (1985), Morck/Shleifer/Vishny (1988), McConnell/Servaes (1990), Loderer/Martin (1997), Cho (1998), Himmelberg/Hubbard/Palia (1999), Demsetz/Villalonga (2001)).[108] When the endogeneity of managerial ownership is taken into account, a significant relationship between firm valuation and managerial equity owner-

---

[107] While the prevalence of stock options and stock-based incentive plans in Germany has not reached US levels, they have become increasingly widespread in the 1990s. Lutter (1997) lists the earliest such programs in Germany

[108] The above discussion is centered on the tradeoff between incentive alignment and risk. Other potential negative implications from managerial equity ownership, namely management entrenchment (Shleifer/Vishny (1989)) are not considered. A thorough review of studies relating managerial equity ownership to firm performance is provided in Demsetz/Villalonga (2001), Appendix A

ship cannot be detected. This is no surprise insofar as agency theory does not predict that a higher pay-performance sensitivity is always preferable;[109] a strong pay-performance sensitivity can be too weak for some firms, and a weak pay-performance sensitivity can be too strong for some other firms, depending on such variables as risk aversion and uncertainty.

An alternative approach consists of relating changes in compensation systems to changes in firm value; i.e. the classic event study framework (Warner (1985)). Such a research design, while theoretically valid, in practice suffers from ambiguous announcement dates (Murphy (1999)). Also, there is evidence that the introduction of stock-option plans is deliberately timed by managers to precede announcements of favorable news (Yermack (1997)). Attempts at identifying relationships between certain compensation patterns and corporate valuation have thus been largely futile (Prendergast (2002)).[110]

Thus, in differentiating agency theory from the managerial power approach more detailed question need to be asked. Two different streams of empirical work can be broadly distinguished:

- Analyses of the pay-performance relation aimed at testing if it follows the pattern predicted by agency theory
- Analyses of contracting patterns aimed at testing if they reflect managerial power

Empirical analyses of the first question commonly use panel data: For a cross-section of firms, it is analyzed if longitudinal changes in executive compensation are positively related to changes in firm performance. Under this approach, the endogeneity problem faced by pure cross-sectional designs discussed above is overcome: The question asked is not if firms with higher pay-performance sensitivity have higher valuations, but more fundamentally, if longitudinally, a positive pay-performance sensitivity exists at all, as predicted by *agency theory*. using firm fixed effects in panel regressions, firm-specific influences on the level of compensation are neutralized. Studies applying this approach have confirmed a positive relationship for different components of compensation (cash compen-

---

109 In Jensen/Meckling (1976), the agency costs of equity are an increasing function of outside equity ownership; however, this result only holds in the case of a risk-neutral manager

110 In a novel attempt, Habib/Ljungqvist (in press) empirically estimate agency costs as a value shortfall from a stochastic frontier of maximum firm value. They find that the value shortfall is significantly related to a number of variables proxying for agency problems, and conclude that many firms operate under suboptimal incentive structures at any given point in time, but that boards adjust incentives dynamically to reduce the value shortfall over time

sation, stock-based incentives), different performance measures (stock performance, accounting measures of performance), different time periods, and different geographies (e.g. US, UK, Japan, Germany). Earlier studies found such a relationship focusing exclusively on cash compensation (Murphy (1985), Coughlan/Schmidt (1985)).[111] Later studies included stock and options (Jensen/Murphy (1990a), and the change in value from existing stock and option holdings (Hall/Liebman (1998)). For Germany, a positive relationship between performance and compensation is documented in Schwalbach/Grasshoff (1997), the first German empirical study on executive compensation, Schmid (1997), Schwalbach (1999), and Elston/Goldberg (2003). Incorporating all elements of compensation, in the US on average a $5-$10 change in CEO wealth per $1000 change in firm value has been found (Murphy (1999)). Hall/Liebman (1998) show that pay-performance sensitivity has sharply increased during the 1990s, along with the more widespread use of stock options. More than 95% of this sensitivity is due to stock-based incentives (Murphy (1999). While it has been contended that such a sensitivity is still too low in order to be consistent with agency theory, numerical simulations have shown that for a realistic set of parameter values,[112] the detected sensitivity can be consistent with standard agency models (Garen (1994), Haubrich (1994), Grasshoff/Schwalbach (1999)[113]). It has also been shown that the detected sensitivity leads to substantial swings in CEO wealth for common changes in firm performance (Hall/Liebman (1998)).

Empirical analyses of the second question seek to relate the level of and changes in compensation not to performance, but to measures of ***managerial power***. Researchers have analyzed if compensation patterns inconsistent with agency theory can be directly traced to deficiencies in corporate governance associated with managerial power.

Managerial power his usually understood as a function of the effectiveness of the board of directors as a monitor (see Finkelstein (1992) for a review of the determinants of managerial power). It has been found that variables commonly associated with the effectiveness of corporate boards as monitors (presence of an external blockholder, presence

---

[111] Tosi et al. (2000) meta-analyze 137 existing studies and equally find a clear pay-performance link. While these authors conclude that the explanatory power of changes in performance for changes in pay is very low, they admit that most of the studies included in their meta-analysis are based on cash-compensation only

[112] Ferrall/Shearer (1999) is an example for a maximum-likelihood approach of estimating agency model parameters, based on payroll data from a copper mine

[113] Grasshoff/Schwalbach (1999) also show that a low sensitivity can result from the assumption that alternative performance measures are costly to obtain

of institutional investors, small board size), are related to more pronounced pay-performance sensitivities and to lower absolute pay levels. In the management literature, empirical studies relating executive compensation to monitoring variables have long been common (McEachern (1975), Finkelstein/Hambrick (1989), Tosi/Gomez-Mejia (1989, 1994), Werner/Tosi (1995)).[114] Based on survey evidence using a 17-item construct of monitoring activities of CEO pay, Tosi/Gomez-Mejia (1989, 1994) find that the extent of monitoring activities that take place is positively related to the influence of external blockholders and directors. The authors also find that CEOs can exert significantly less influence on their own pay in firms with an external blockholder, based on survey responses from personnel officers.

Quantitative evidence indicates that executive compensation levels are higher when more directors have been appointed by the CEO (Lambert/Larcker/Weigelt (1993), Core/Holthausen/Larcker (1999)) and more directors are also members of other companies' boards (Core/Holthausen/Larcker (1999)), when the CEO is also Chairman (Cyert/Kang/Kumar (2002)), when there are no external blockholders (Lambert/Larcker/Weigelt (1993)) and when there are no independent institutional investors represented on the board (David/Kochhar/Levitas (1998)). For Germany, it has been found that ownership dispersion is related to higher pay levels (Schmid (1997), Elston/Goldberg (2003)), while bank influence reduces pay levels (Elston/Goldberg (2003)).

Further evidence in favor of the managerial power view concerns instances where executive compensation is raised in response to events that are clearly beyond management's control (Schwetzler (1999)): Blanchard/Lopez-de-Silanes/Shleifer (1994) report that a substantial fraction of cash windfalls received by firms after legal settlements are used for executive compensation. Bertrand/Mullainathan (2001) find that CEOs of companies

---

[114] While some studies in the management literature make explicit reference to agency theory, most studies cannot be considered an effective test of agency theory due to imprecise variable definition. Instead of analyzing pay-performance sensitivities by relating time-series changes in compensation to changes in performance, as is common in the economics literature, the studies from the management literature commonly approximate pay-performance sensitivity by the variable (bonus/total cash compensation). This definition suffers from substantial flaws: It ignores non-cash compensation, the main driver of pay-performance sensitivity; it is not a true measure of sensitivity, since fixed salary can also vary in response to performance changes, or bonuses can be of different variability in the cross-section; and it is subject to severe measurement error, since the labeling of compensation components ("bonus", "salary") in compensation surveys can be erroneous. Consequently, articles from the management literature, while published in reputable journals such as the Academy of Management Journal, do generally not figure at all in economics literature reviews such as Prendergast (2002)

without large blockholders have been found to be rewarded for "luck", i.e. changes in exogenous market factors, such as oil prices, exchange rates, or industry growth rates, while well-governed firms filter out luck in CEO compensation. Bertrand/Mullainathan (2000) find that a tightening of anti-takeover legislation, as has taken place in many US states in the early 1990s, leads to an increase in mean pay levels in firms without a large blockholder, while in firms with a large blockholder, it leads to an increase in the pay-performance sensitivity. They interpret this as evidence that managers in poorly-governed firms use their power to increase their own pay in response to the decreased takeover threat, while in well-governed firms, the market for corporate control is substituted by another disciplining mechanism, namely more intense incentive pay.

Empirical evidence for other elements of the managerial power view is more scarce. Evidence that firms deliberately use pay practices that make the total amount of compensation less transparent (such as e.g. pension plans) is largely anecdotal (Bebchuk/Fried/Walker (2002)).

Synthesizing the evidence on the two question, empirical work has convincingly demonstrated a clear link between pay and performance for different time periods, hierarchy levels, and geographies. While the influence of governance variables such as ownership dispersion on executive pay has been shown, and it is thus uncontroversial that agents under certain circumstances can influence their own pay, managerial power alone is therefore not an overall conclusive explanation of observed compensation patterns. [115]

The empirical evidence supportive of both classic agency theory and managerial power has led to attempts to reconcile the two perspectives: From a theoretical standpoint, classic agency theory and the managerial power approach are not mutually exclusive (Lambert/Larcker/Weigelt (1993)). Management researchers, such as Barkema/Gomez-Mejia (1998), have long adopted a more pragmatic empirical approach that includes both variables related to performance and variables related to managerial power and governance as determinants of compensation. However, from an economics viewpoint, agency theory

[115] Empirical evidence on managerial power is largely concentrated on US samples. While different results could be suspected for the German governance system, evidence by Kaplan (1994) indicates that similar patterns can be assumed for Germany. Kaplan (1994), in an empirical comparison of the relationship between firm performance and management turnover between the US and Germany, demonstrates that the same association between inferior performance and terminations obtains in both countries, thus rejecting allegations that in Germany managers can use their power to entrench themselves in their positions

clearly remains the dominant paradigm in explaining executive compensation, not least due to the largely pre-formal, anecdotal formulation of the managerial power approach.

In accordance with the general stance of the present study, the following section is thus be exclusively based on agency theory, in explaining in more detail how certain incentive arrangements can mitigate agency problems, while the managerial power approach is again taken up in hypothesis development.[116]

3.5.3 Incentive compensation and agency costs

3.5.3.1 Determinants of optimal incentive compensation

After the previous section has established the still-dominant position of agency theory in the study of executive compensation, this section examines in more detail what specifically determines incentive compensation in an agency framework.[117] As already stated, agency theory interprets incentive compensation as a mechanism to mitigate agency problems: The optimal compensation arrangement minimizes agency costs and maximizes firm value.

In order for the provision of incentives to be both effective and efficient, incentive provision has to incorporate the agency theory parameters such as risk aversion, effort disutility, and uncertainty (e.g. Core/Guay/Verrecchia (2003)). Agency theory has made a number of empirically testable predictions about the pay-performance sensitivity and optimal executive compensation design:

- Negative trade-off between risk and incentives: Assuming a risk-averse manager, the pay-performance sensitivity is decreasing in the informativeness of the performance measure with respect to the agent's actions (Holmström (1979)). If the performance measure available is noisy, the agent's actions cannot be precisely inferred from the performance measure. The agent thus bears the risk that a high effort level on his part will not translate into an equally favorable realization of the performance measure. Therefore, a risk averse agent will demand a risk premium.

---

[116]The discussion of ownership concentration as a governance variable is taken up in Section 3.6

[117] In line with the financial economics literature, the present study focuses on the efficient provision of incentives; although potentially important, issues concerning the practical implementation of incentive compensation, such as transaction costs, are ignored (Wenger/Knoll (1999), Schwetzler (1999) provide practical guidelines in a German context)

Incentive compensation is thus more costly under conditions of high uncertainty. Consequently, the pay-performance sensitivity is reduced under such conditions.

- Choice between multiple objective performance measures: The negative trade-off between risk and incentives implies that, when multiple performance measures (e.g. stock price and accounting profits) are available, those measures more informative of the agent's actions will have greater weight in the compensation contract (Holmström (1979), Lambert/Larcker (1987)). Lambert (1986) hypothesizes that a high firm growth rate is related to low degree of informativeness of accounting measures with respect to firm performance, and thus predicts a greater use of stock price as performance measure in early-stage firms.

- Relative Performance Evaluation (RPE): The negative trade-off between risk and incentives also implies that exogenous factors beyond the agent's control, such as the industry growth rate, should be filtered out, since such factors increase the agent's compensation risk without providing additional incentives (Holmström (1982)). Criticism of the standard implication has come from multiple angles: It can be inefficient to insulate managers from outside shocks, e.g. currency fluctuations, when such an insulation eliminates managerial incentives to undertake actions to reduce the firm's exposure to such forces (Baker/Jensen/Murphy (1988)). Furthermore, the much smaller probability that instruments based on relative performance, such as indexed options, lead to a payout for the executive, means that risk-averse undiversified executives assign much lower values to such instruments, and in turn must be compensated more highly, which makes relative performance evaluation a costly form of compensation (Hall/Murphy (2002)).

- Scope of managerial responsibility: Prendergast (2002) develops a formal model showing that incentive pay also depends on the scope of managerial responsibility. In an uncertain environment, the principal might wish to delegate more decision-making authority to the agent. Consequently, the agent has more influence on outcomes, and the agent's actions have a potentially higher marginal product. Thus, incentives have to be more intense. Therefore, a *positive* trade-off between risk and incentives can be optimal.

- Choice between subjective and objective performance measures: The role of subjective performance measures is formally analyzed in Baker (1992, 2000) and Baker/Gibbons/Murphy (1994). When an employee's contribution to the principal's objective (firm value) is not observable, some other performance measure informative of the agent's action has to be chosen (Baker/Gibbons/Murphy (1994)). The choice of this performance measure involves a trade-off between noise (i.e. the incremental informativeness of the measure with respect to the agent's actions) and the danger of distortion (Baker (2000)).[118] Distortion refers to activities the agent might undertake to deliberately distort the performance measure, e.g. influence activities in the sense of Milgrom (1988). While subjective performance measures are potentially less noisy, they can be more easily distorted than objective performance measures. Generally, accounting data as performance measure are considered to be more likely to suffer from deliberate managerial distortion than stock prices (Aron (1991) for examples; also see Schwetzler (1999), and refer back to Section 3.4.3.3). A related consideration with respect to objective performance measures is the "gaming" of performance measures (e.g. Prendergast (1999) for a review), particularly in the context of multitask environments (Holmström/Milgrom (1991)), where agents de-emphasize tasks not tied to incentives in favor of other tasks tied to incentives.

Summarizing the above, the optimal contract, i.e. the contract that minimizes agency costs, is based on a mix of performance measures, the relative weight of which is determined according to their relative noise and distortion risk. The total intensity of incentives is determined based on considerations of firm-specific risk and scope of managerial responsibility.

A large body of empirical work is concerned with examining the compliance of actual contracting patterns with the above propositions of agency theory:

- Negative trade-off between risk and incentives: While Garen (1994), based on a small sample, finds only weak evidence, Aggarwal/Samwick (1999), in the most extensive large-sample empirical study to date, confirm the presumed negative trade-off. Both CEOs and other top executives of firms with more volatile stock prices have less performance-based compensation. In a refinement of the analysis,

[118] Baker (2000) provides the following instructive example: A project manager is reassigned while his project is still ongoing. The project manager can be evaluated on two alternative performance measures: the final profitability of the project (after it has been finished), or a current estimate of expected profitability of the project. While the final profitability of the project is a noisy measure of the manager's effort (e.g. because final the profitability of the project also depends on the efforts of the manager's successor), it cannot be distorted. In contrast, current expected profitability is less noisy, since it gives a clear picture of expected project success at the current stage, but it is subject to distortion by the manager, who could e.g. hide negative information.

Jin (2002) separates market- from firm-specific risk and finds that, as predicted, the pay-performance sensitivity decreases with firm-specific risk, while it is ambiguously related to market risk.[119]

- Choice between multiple objective performance measures: In empirical studies comparing the use of accounting-based and stock-based performance measures for bonus contracts, Lambert/Larcker (1987), Sloan (1993), and Ittner/Larcker/Rajan (1997) find that a lower weight is placed on the more noisy performance measure. Lambert/Larcker (1987) also find a larger weight on stock price as performance measure in early-stage firms. However, Core/Guay/Verrecchia (2003) largely fail to find such evidence when analyzing total compensation: the relative weight of stock-based incentives increases with the variance of the stock price.
- Relative performance evaluation: Empirical tests of relative performance evaluation have led to mixed results. While there is some evidence that RPE is implemented in cash compensation, in that bonuses are negatively related to industry performance (weak evidence in Antle/Smith (1986), based on a small sample; stronger evidence in Gibbons/Murphy (1990), based on a large sample; mixed evidence depending on the measure of industry performance in Janakiraman/Lambert/Larcker (1993)), stock options that are indexed or otherwise tied to peer-group performance are virtually non-existing (Murphy (1999)). This result in clearly not consistent with agency theory. Consequently, empirical studies that include stock-based incentive compensation in the analysis fail to find evidence for RPE (Aggarwal/Samwick (1999)).
- Scope of managerial responsibility: A direct empirical test of Prendergast's (2002) model has not yet been made. However, Jin (2002) finds that the pay-performance sensitivity increases with CEO productivity (using such proxies as Tobin's Q, absolute amount invested, early-stage firm), controlling for firm-specific risk. Smith/Watts (1992), in their analysis of relation between the investment opportu-

---

[119] In an interesting insight from the management literature, Miller/Wiseman/Gomez-Mejia (2002) find a curvilinear relationship between risk and incentives: For very low risk levels, pay-performance sensitivity is also low, since input monitoring can be used instead of output-based incentive pay. Unfortunately however, their empirical study suffers from severe variable definition problems, as discussed above. In related evidence, Stroh et al. (1996) find that task programmability is negatively related to the use of variable pay.

nity set and managerial compensation, come to a similar conclusion. In the management literature, Finkelstein/Boyd (1998) using a LISREL model, find that among high-performing firms, there is a significant relation between the latitude managers have in making strategic choices (proxy for managers' marginal productivity) and compensation, while they fail to detect such a relationship in low-performing firms. The authors interpret this finding as evidence that high-performing firms, consistent with agency theory, incorporate managerial responsibility considerations in compensation design.

- Choice between subjective and objective performance measures: Hardly any empirical evidence is available on the choice between subjective and objective performance measures, owing to the paucity of information collection on evaluation of workers with poorly measured output (Prendergast (1999)). However, for top executives, objective performance measures, namely stock price, overwhelmingly dominate (Murphy (1999)). Some evidence is available on the negative properties of accounting data as performance measure. While usually classified as an objective performance measure, there is evidence that managers deliberately manipulate accounting data in order to influence compensation (Healy (1985) for evidence on opportunistic accrual accounting; Dechow/Sloan (1991) for evidence of opportunistic R&D spending).

In conclusion, supportive empirical evidence is strong enough so that it can confidently be asserted that observed contracting patterns do largely reflect predictions from agency theory, i.e., incentive compensation is effectively used in order to mitigate agency problems, although with some substantial exceptions (e.g. Abowd/Kaplan (1999) for a similar reading of the evidence).

3.5.3.2 Stock and options as alternative forms of incentive compensation

Up to this point, the theoretical predictions and the accompanying empirical evidence discussed so far contain relatively little concrete normative content useful for compensation systems design: While agency theory makes clear normative predictions about e.g. the relationship about relative noise in different performance measures and their use in incentive compensation, more practical questions are not touched upon. What is the optimal level of pay-performance sensitivity for a manager with average risk aversion in a firm of such-and such size? When stock price, as established, is used as performance measure, should compensation be in the form of cash bonuses tied to the stock price, stock grants, or stock options? Some recent critiques from a more practical viewpoint shed light on these questions.

Recent critiques of orthodox agency theory tests come from Murphy (1999), and Core/Guay/Larcker (2003). Murphy (1999) criticizes that underlying the informativeness principle is the implicit assumption that the principal knows what action he wants the agent to take. Only under such conditions, the optimal performance measure is the measure most informative of the agent's actions. However, under the more realistic assumption that the principal does not know which action is optimal, the optimal basis for the contract is not the incrementally most informative measure, but the principal's objective itself. The principal's objective being shareholder value generation, it can thus be argued that stock price is the correct performance measure, even if e.g. accounting profits are more informative of managerial effort. Baker (1992) has developed a theoretical model showing that incentive contracts not based on the principal's objective, but on some other performance measure correlated with the principal's objective, need not be optimal under all circumstances, since the alternative performance measure does not respond to the agent's actions in exactly the same way as the principal's objective.

Building on the results by e.g. Hall/Liebman (1998), who finds incentives stemming from changes in the value of stock and option holdings are 53 times stronger than incentives provided by variable cash compensation, Core/Guay/Verrecchia (2003) argue that optimal incentives are not primarily a question of flow compensation, but of the optimal level of managerial equity ownership: Managerial equity ownership is thus interpreted as an instrument to provide a constant incentive level to management. This point is ignored in most of the compensation literature that focuses on flow compensation, or even more narrowly on cash compensation. Adopting the broader perspective, annual option and equity grants are not primarily a means of flow compensation, but an instrument to adjust managerial incentive levels back to equilibrium, e.g. because managers have exercised options and thus reduced their exposure to the firm (Core/Guay (1999)). The validity of empirical work ignoring the value of managerial equity holdings is thus questionable.

Taken together, Murphy's (1999) and Core/Guay/Larcker's (2003) arguments underline the special importance of managerial stockholdings and stock options as incentives. As discussed, Murphy (1999) and Conyon/Murphy (2000) show that more than 95% of US and UK executives at large corporations own company stock or stock options or both.

The relative advantages and disadvantages of stock and stock options have been extensively discussed in the literature (e.g. Hall/Murphy (2003) and the references contained therein). The use of stock options has been surrounded by controversy, especially in Germany (e.g. Knoll (1998), Wenger/Knoll (1999), Wenger/Kaserer/Knoll (1999)), since some of their properties seem most conspicuously incompatible with agency theory. While a detailed evaluation is beyond the scope of this study, a brief highlighting of the key points of the discussion will thus be expedient:

- Stock options have been criticized as a comparatively costly form of compensation, since risk-averse undiversified managers have been shown to value stock options at only approximately half of their (rational) Black-Scholes value (Lambert/Larcker/Verrecchia (1991), Hall/Murphy (2002)).[120]
- Stock options have been criticized as especially prone to entrenchment problems, as witnessed by repeated repricing of options following stock market declines (Brenner/Sundaram/Yermack (2000), Chance/Kumar/Todd (2000))
- Stock options have been criticized as vulnerable to opportunistic timing by managers, as witnessed by stock option awards preceding announcements of favorable news (Yermack (1997), Aboody/Kasznik (2000)).

However, the use of stock options over alternative forms of compensation has also been rationalized on different grounds:

- If managers are allowed to rebalance their personal portfolio in order to decrease their exposure to firm risk, stock option value to managers will be close to their rational Black-Scholes value (Ofek/Yermack (2000))
- Repricing does not necessarily constitute evidence of managerial entrenchment; it can also reflect efficient recontracting: Stock options that are far out of the money no longer provide incentives to managers; it can thus be efficient to provide renewed incentives (Saly (1994); Acharya/John/Sundaram (2000))
- Wealth gains from opportunistic timing of option grants appear minuscule against the associated risks in terms of reputation loss and insider trading charges (Core/Guay/Larcker (2003))

---

[120] Dittmann/Maug (2003), based on numerical estimations of a principal-agent model, conclude that stock options are a more expensive form of compensation than restricted stock because of their payoff-structure

- Furthermore, the use of stock options has been advocated in the literature as an instrument to add convexity to managerial conversation: For risk averse managers, the linear pay-off structure of stock can create incentives to reduce firm risk, e.g. falsely reject risky positive-NPV projects (Smith/Stulz (1985); May (1995) for supportive empirical evidence). If the manager's effort choice is not independent from variance, the optimal compensation contract is convex (Hemmer/Kim/Verrecchia (1999)).

In conclusion, there is currently no consensus in the literature on the relative merits of different forms of incentive compensation. While stock options have been arduously criticized, their pervasive use has also been rationalized. At this point, it can only be concluded that both stock grants and stock options are both legitimate forms of incentive compensation that can be used in order to design efficient contracts on the basis of the predictions from agency theory.

3.5.3.3 Compensation of division managers

The previous sections have established that contracting practice largely follows the pattern predicted by agency theory, the still-dominant paradigm in the analysis of executive compensation, while the academic discussion on the relative merits of alternative forms of incentive compensation is still controversial. This discussion has implicitly focused on incentive compensation for top executives, possibly thanks to easier data availability (Fisher/Govindarajan (1992), Lambert/Larcker/Weigelt (1993)).

In the context of the present study, however, the compensation of division managers is of greater interest. Before the ECO, managers of the subsidiary, irrespective of it possible legal status as separate legal entity, can be interpreted as division managers: The potential gains from the introduction of stock-based incentive compensation for subsidiary managers post-ECO thus hinges on the efficiency of their compensation arrangements pre-transaction. Researchers have identified a number of special problems that impede effective incentive compensation for divisional managers.

Complicating compensation arrangements for divisional managers is the more limited choice of performance measures for divisional managers. Three alternative sets of objective performance measures are available: firm stock price, firm accounting measures, and divisional accounting measures (Keating (1997)).[121]

The above section has established that stock price is a preferable performance measure as it suffers least from potential distortion (also see Holmström/Tirole (1993)), and because it most accurately reflects the principal's objective. However, a divisional stock price is by definition not available, and firm stock price is potentially only an extremely noisy measure of divisional manager performance. Using firm stock price as a performance measure would mean that all divisional managers would receive the same pay regardless of their individual performance (Schwetzler (1999)). Essentially the same problem impedes the use of firm accounting measures as performance measures. Consequently, divisional accounting measures remain. While hypothetically a less noisy measure of divisional manager performance, they suffer most severely from the distortion problems discussed above.[122]

In groups of companies, the cascading of agency relationships compounds the problem of choice of performance measure: Each hierarchical layer has fewer incentives to structure effective contracts than the prior layer. Baker/Jensen/Murphy (1988) argue that a layering of agency problems in a divisional organization has increasingly severe consequence on incentive compensation as one moves down successive organizational levels (p. 613-614):

> "Managers in hierarchical organizations, from supervisors to CEOs and boards of directors, are not principals in the sense usually modeled in the principal-agent literature. [...] The absence of pay-for-performance compensation systems for managers implies that managers have few incentives to structure and enforce value-maximizing contracts with subordinates."

In conclusion, there is reason to assume that compensation arrangements with division managers are less efficient from an agency point of view than compensation arrangements with top executives.

---

[121] The interrelationship between the use of subjective performance measures in compensation and the capital budgeting process is analyzed in Wulf (2002)

[122] The analysis assumes that divisional managers have full responsibility for division value. The choice of optimal divisional accounting measures in settings with limited controllability (cost centers, revenue centers) is discussed in e.g. Antle/Demski (1988), Hofmann (2002)

Empirical work on division manager incentive compensation is relatively scarce due to data availability issues and mainly comes from management researchers, based on data from compensation surveys or field surveys.

Gerhart/Milkovich (1990) find that division manager compensation is positively related to firm accounting performance. Similarly, Fisher/Govindarajan (1992) find that profit center manager compensation is positively related to profit center size, human capital factors (e.g. tenure) and firm accounting performance. Werner/Tosi (1995), refining previous analyses and conducting an empirical test of Baker/Jensen/Murphy's (1988) hypothesis of cascading agency problems, find that a positive pay-performance sensitivity for middle- to upper-level managers exists only in firms that are controlled by external blockholders, while pay is unrelated to performance in other firms. Thus, effective monitoring at the top appears to have a positive influence on the effectiveness of compensation further down the hierarchy.

Unfortunately, Gerhart/Milkovich (1990), Fisher/Govindarajan (1992), and Werner/Tosi (1995) are relatively preliminary approaches to the complex subject of incentive compensation: Among the three alternative performance measures, only firm accounting performance is considered in all three studies; and non-cash compensation is ignored.

Lambert/Larcker/Weigelt (1993) extend the scope of analysis to include stock and options, and stock price as performance measure. Also, for lack of available data, they approximate division accounting performance by industry-wide average accounting performance. They find that compensation of plant managers, division heads, and group heads is positively related to unit size, firm stock price, and unit accounting returns.

In analyzing the relative weight of different performance measures, Bushman/Indjejikian/Smith (1995) show that the use of aggregate performance measures relative to more localized performance measures in division manager compensation is an increasing function of intrafirm interdependencies: Interdependencies between divisions that cannot be accounted for by e.g. transfer-pricing schemes, and which thus lead to distortion of division accounting measures, empirically imply a greater use of firm-level performance measures.

In an additional analysis on the choice of performance measures, Keating (1997) finds that overall, the use of a performance measures declines with their inherent noise, consistent with agency theory. For example, division accounting metrics are used when division earnings proxy well for division value (i.e. in stable, low-growth environments), but firm accounting metrics are used when divisions are interdependent, and firm stock price is used in high-growth environments, where accounting data are less informative of value.

Aggarwal/Samwick (2003b) confirm the negative trade-off between risk and incentives for division managers: Divisional executives' compensation is shown to be both sensitive to firm stock returns and divisional sales, with the sensitivity to each measure decreasing with its variance. Thus, when division data is more volatile, firm-level measures are increasingly used. Pay-performance sensitivity of division executives is lower than for top executives.

In summary, the empirical evidence shows that compensation arrangements for division managers follow predicted patterns: Division managers' compensation is sensitive to performance, and the choice between different performance measures is guided by their relative precision. However, the empirical evidence also shows that division manager compensation is to a considerable extent dependent on either firm level measures, or accounting measures, which is indicative of potential distortion and noise inherent in the performance measure.

As Keating (1997) puts it, firms face a trade-off between either

- Paying division managers more in order to compensate for a higher compensation risk imposed due to the use of an imprecise performance measure
- Commit more resources to performance measurement, e.g. to increase the precision of divisional accounting data
- Reduce pay-performance sensitivity in response to imprecision of available performance measures and thus reduce incentives to exert effort

All three alternatives result in costs, be it in terms of higher compensation, increased monitoring expenditures, or reduced productivity. In conclusion, it can be assumed that division managers' compensation arrangements in general are less efficient than top executives arrangements.

3.5.4 Incentive compensation and ECOs

The previous section has concluded that division managers' compensation arrangements are generally less efficient than top executives', and has traced this inefficiency to the unavailability of appropriate performance measures, which are both precise and robust to distortion attempts.

In an ECO, former division managers of a group of companies become top executives of a newly formed, exchange listed subsidiary. Holmström's (1979) informativeness principle states that any variable that is marginally informative about the agent's actions can be used to improve contracting efficiency. Assuming that the subsidiary share price is a variable which contains incremental information about the agent's (the former division manager's) actions, ECOs can thus improve contracting efficiency by allowing to tie the former division manager's compensation to the newly established subsidiary stock price.[123]

The subsidiary stock price can be assumed to provide a much cleaner signal of managerial performance than the stock price of the group of companies. Aron (1991) even argues that (p. 507)

> "If indeed the stock market value of a diversified corporation is a weak signal of the productivity of any division, then from an incentive perspective single-product firms would strictly dominate diversification."

In addition, the use of subsidiary stock price potentially eliminates influence costs in a diversified group of companies, resulting from divisional managers' attempts at influencing performance measures and compensation arrangements (Milgrom (1988), Milgrom/Roberts (1988)).

In terms of the two-dimensional agency framework, ECOs thus have the potential to decrease agency costs by reducing interest divergence between principal (subsidiary shareholders) and agent (subsidiary management). The reduction in interest divergence results from the availability of a more precise performance measures (subsidiary stock price), which is also less prone to distortion or influence activities. In practice, the reduction of interest divergence is documented by either managerial stock ownership in the subsidiary, or the introduction of a stock options program.

Incorporating arguments from the managerial power approach, such a reduction in interest divergence is dependent on the degree of influence of subsidiary top executives over their own pay setting process, with too much influence leading to potential costs from excessive compensation.

---

[123] The technical prerequisite for such an improvement of contracting efficiency is that performance measures available prior to the ECO, such as parent stock price or divisional profits, are not a sufficient statistic of the subsidiary manager's actions; an assumption that is obviously not overly restrictive

These arguments lead to the following hypotheses concerning incentive compensation and ECOs:[124]

H3A: The effect of ECOs on firm value is positively related to the introduction of a stock options program or managerial equity ownership

H3B: The effect of ECOs on firm value is negatively related to managerial influence over the pay setting process in the subsidiary

Figure 17 illustrates how these hypotheses are related to the two-dimensional agency framework for the analysis of ECOs.

---

[124] Hypotheses are operationalized in the empirical part, Section 4.3.4.4

Figure 17: Incentive compensation hypotheses in the two-dimensional framework

INCENTIVE COMPENSATION

The effect of ECOs on firm value is ...

Principal-agent relationship		Interest divergence	Information environment	Monitoring/b. technology
	Parent shareholders/ parent mgmt.			
	Parent mgmt./ subsidiary mgmt.			
	Subsidiary shareholders/ subsidiary mgmt.	**H3A**: ... positively related to the introduction of a stock options program or managerial equity ownership **H3B**: ... negatively related to managerial influence over the pay setting process in the subsidiary		

Determinants of agency costs

3.6 Lever 4: Ownership concentration

3.6.1 Treatment in the ECO literature

In the ECO literature, a potential influence of ownership concentration on value creation has been discussed from different angles.

The effect of ownership concentration in the subsidiary has been discussed by Schipper/Smith (1986), Vijh (1999), and Powers (2003). Schipper/Smith (1986), documenting that parents usually retain voting control of the subsidiary after the ECO, first recognized a potential negative effect of parent majority ownership in the subsidiary (p. 179):

> "The potential conflict of interest with minority stockholders may attenuate the benefits of the separate financing obtained from a carve-out. Any anticipated expropriation of subsidiary assets by the parent firm will have a negative effect on the price at which the subsidiary stock is sold."

Later, Vijh (1999) hypothesizes that concentrated parent ownership, to the contrary, should increase monitoring incentives and thus be positively associated to value creation from the

ECO. However, his empirical evidence is inconclusive. A limitation to the author's analysis is that he does not consider the evolution of parent ownership over the period following the ECO, but only measures the parent stake sold in the ECO.

Powers (2003) finds that the percentage ownership in the subsidiary relinquished by the parent in the ECO is positively related to liquidity constraints of the parent. Thus, this author implicitly recognizes the benefits of control accruing to the parent from maintaining ownership in the subsidiary. The author, again, does not consider the evolution of parent ownership after the ECO. The effect of ownership concentration in the parent is discussed in Elsas/Löffler (2003). The authors hypothesize that ownership concentration improves monitoring incentives of large blockholders and thus reduces agency problems. Consequently, interpreting ECOs as mechanism to reduce agency costs, there should be less to gain from ECOs when the parent has concentrated ownership. The authors confirm their hypothesis by documenting a negative association between ECO announcement excess returns and ownership concentration in the parent.

Related to the subject of ownership concentration is the subject of second events following ECOs (Klein/Rosenfeld/Beranek (1991), Vijh (2002)). Klein/Rosenfeld/Beranek (1991) interpret ECOs as the (temporary) first stage in a two-stage process that ultimately leads to a full divestiture of the subsidiary or to a reacquisition by the parent. Empirically, they find higher announcement period excess returns for ECOs that are subsequently followed by a full divestiture, but they results are not significant. This evidence is confirmed by Vijh (2002). A formal model of IPOs, as two-stage processes, which is applicable to ECOs in particular, is provided by Zingales (1995a).

In conclusion, the ECO literature has documented a positive relationship between the relinquishment of parent control through a full divestiture and ECO value creation, while the overall evidence on ownership concentration in the subsidiary and ECO value creation remains inconclusive.

3.6.2 Ownership concentration and corporate valuation

3.6.2.1 Theoretical perspectives

Following Berle/Means (1932), the notion of dispersed ownership is well established among economists: In the modern corporation, control is assumed to be in the hands of professional managers, while ownership is in the hands of dispersed, atomistic shareholders. This perspective is consistent with capital market theory, where ownership concentration creates a cost in the form of foregone risk-diversification (Stiglitz (1985), Barclay/Holderness (1991)), and it is also underlying the seminal agency theory paper by Jensen/Meckling (1976), who describe a conflict of interest between a manager and diffuse shareholders.

Consequently, ownership structure has long been neglected as a potential determinant of corporate valuation. Beginning with empirical observations in the late 1970s and early 1980s that the standard model of dispersed shareholders was found not to fit a reality where corporations with concentrated ownership were discovered to be much more widespread than originally thought (e.g. Short (1994) for an extensive review of the early evidence; Holderness/Sheehan (1988) for an early US-study; Thonet/Poensgen (1979) for a pioneering German study), first theoretical models of concentrated ownership were developed. Jensen/Warner (1988), in their introduction to the Journal of Financial Economics special issue, first establish ownership concentration as a mainstream research subject in financial economics.

Theoretical models on ownership concentration generally focus on how and why large share blocks emerge. Different situations are considered:

- The entrepreneur's IPO decision (Zingales (1995a), Pagano/Röell (1998): When is it preferable to sell shares to atomistic small investors, and when is it preferable to sell shares in blocks to large investors?

- The takeover decision (Grossman/Hart (1980b), Shleifer/Vishny (1986), Stulz (1988)): Is there an influence of ownership concentration on the frequency of takeover attempts and the probability of being taken over, and what impact does this have on firm value?

- Product-market alliances (Allen/Phillips (2000)): What role do large share blocks play for the functioning of product-market alliances (such as e.g. R&D partnerships)?

- Strategic investment decisions (Zwiebel (1995)): What ownership structures emerge when blockholders can form coalitions in controlling firms?

Independently of these stylized situations, other authors have modeled the exogenous determinants of ownership concentration:

- Market liquidity (Holmström/Tirole (1993), Maug (1998), Kahn/Winton (1998), Bolton/von Thadden (1998)): What is the impact of secondary market liquidity on the attractiveness of ownership concentration and the potential trading profits large block owners can achieve?

- Legal investor protection (La Porta et al. (1997, 1998, 2000a, 2000b), La Porta/Lopez de Silanes/Shleifer (1999), Shleifer/Wolfenzon (2002)): What is the impact of the legal environment, and especially shareholder and creditor rights, on the attractiveness of ownership concentration in international comparison?

Taken together, theoretical models have mostly focused on the identification of characteristics of the firm and the contracting environment that endogenously determine optimal ownership concentration, rather than attempting to identify relationships between (exogenous) ownership concentration and firm value. In identifying these determinants, such diverse theoretical frameworks as market microstructure theory (e.g. Maug (1998)), transaction cost theory (e.g. Allen/Phillips (2000)), and property rights theory (e.g. Zwiebel (1995)), and most notably agency theory (e.g. Shleifer/Vishny (1986)) have been borrowed from.

In keeping with the general stance of the present study, the following section takes an agency theory perspective and focuses on discussing the agency costs of different ownership patterns.

3.6.2.2 *Empirical evidence*

Empirical work on ownership concentration has concentrated on two fundamental questions: How prevalent is ownership concentration, and what impact does this particular monitoring technology have on corporate valuation (Holderness (2003) for a review)? Often, ownership concentration is discussed in the context of the monitoring role of large shareholders, so-called blockholders.

Descriptive evidence on ownership concentration in an international context is provided by La Porta/Lopez de Silanes/Shleifer (1999) and Faccio/Lang (2002), documenting that ownership is less concentrated in Anglo-Saxon countries, largely consistent with the original Berle/Means (1932) view, and more concentrated in Europe and Asia. Evidence on ownership concentration in Germany is provided by La Porta/Lopez de Silanes/Shleifer (1999), Gorton/Schmid (2000), Franks/Mayer (2001), Köke (2001), Wojcik (2002), Becht/Boehmer (2003), Goergen/Renneboog (2003), and Edwards/Weichenrieder (2004).[125] While the results slightly differ due to sample selection, sample period, methodology, and data source, the following facts emerge:

- Ownership among German listed corporations is very concentrated. Using data based on tightened disclosure rules introduced 1995, around 60% of listed corporations are majority controlled (Köke (2001), Becht/Boehmer (2003)),[126] and more than 80% have a shareholder with at least a 25% stake (Gorton/Schmid (2000), Franks/Mayer (2001))
- Ownership is clustered around the control thresholds 25%, 50%, 75% (Köke (2001), Becht/Boehmer (2003))
- The mean actual voting control of the largest shareholder, adjusted for actual annual general meeting attendance, is larger than 50% (Köke (2001), Edwards/Weichenrieder (2004))

---

[125] Becht/Boehmer (2003) also contains a review of the literature with further references

[126] The WpHG law, introduced 1995, requires disclosure of equity stakes >5%. Before, only disclosure of stakes >25% was required. The new disclosure rules are reviewed in Becht/Boehmer (2003) and in more detail in Becht/Boehmer (1999)

- Commonly, there is only one large shareholder present (La Porta/Lopez de Silanes/Shleifer (1999), Faccio/Lang (2000), Köke (2001), Becht/Boehmer (2003))
- Nonfinancial firms are the most important blockholder group, families are second (Faccio/Lang (2000), Gorton/Schmid (2000), Becht/Boehmer (2003))
- Ownership concentration has not significantly declined during neither 1994-1998 (Köke (2001)) nor during 1997-2001 (Wojcik (2002))
- Pyramids as a control vehicle are relatively widespread (La Porta/Lopez de Silanes/Shleifer (1999), Franks/Mayer (2001)). The mean deviation between cash flow rights and voting rights of the largest shareholder is around 0.8 (Faccio/Lang (2000), Edwards/Weichenrieder (2004)).[127] However, for more than 75% of firms, there is no deviation between cash flow rights and voting rights (Köke (2001))

Concerning the association between ownership concentration and performance, empirical research has consistently failed to produce clear evidence based on Anglo-Saxon datasets.[128]

Based on US data, Holderness/Sheehan (1988), McConnell/Servaes (1990), Mehran (1995), Agrawal/Knoeber (1996) and Demsetz/Villalonga (2001) fail to detect an association between ownership concentration and firm performance, using various variable definitions for performance (Tobin's Q, stock returns, accounting profits) and ownership concentration (e.g. Herfindahl index, largest shareholder's holdings). Singh/Davidson III (2003) find no evidence of an impact of block ownership on SG&A expenses or asset turnover. Based on UK data, Weir/Lang/McKnight (2002) equally find no evidence of an association between ownership concentration and firm performance.

The German evidence is somewhat mixed: Thonet/Poensgen (1979) find that widely-held firms where there is no shareholder with at least 25% have significantly higher return on equity and market-to-book ratio. Lehman/Weigand (2001) also find a negative association between large block ownership by a family or mixed blockholders and return on assets, but no association between large block ownership by a nonfinancial firm and return on assets. Edwards/Nibler (2000), in contrast, find a positive association between large block

[127] Cash flow rights are calculated as the product of ownership stakes at each level of the pyramid; voting rights are the actual proportion of votes cast by the largest shareholder at the annual general meeting

[128] Research on the ownership structure and performance relationship suffers from the same endogeneity problems as research on managerial ownership and firm valuation, as discussed in Section 3.5.2.2

ownership by a bank, a foreign owner, or a family (if less than 50%) and the market-to-book ratio, but no association between large block ownership by a nonfinancial firm or a family (if more than 50%) and the market-to-book ratio. Gorton/Schmid (2000) find a positive association between ownership concentration and the market-to-book ratio as well as return on equity, irrespective of owner type. Finally, Gedajlovic/Shapiro (1998) detect a U-shaped relationship between ownership concentration and firm profitability.

In the most comprehensive international study to date, Gugler/Mueller/Yurtoglu (2003) find no relationship between ownership concentration and marginal Q in common law countries (consistent with the US/UK evidence reviewed above), and a positive relationship between marginal Q and dispersed ownership in civil law countries. Overall, empirical studies on ownership concentration and performance thus fail to detect a connection for Anglo-Saxon samples, and come to contradictory results for Germany.

Short (1994) and Börsch-Supan/Köke (2002) discuss severe econometric deficiencies present in many studies: Dichotomous variables based on arbitrary thresholds are used for measuring ownership concentration (e.g. >20% ownership by largest shareholder interpreted as effective control); a linear relationship between ownership concentration and performance is assumed; control variables for firm size, industry, or firm life cycle are not included; and the identity of the largest shareholder is sometimes not controlled for. Some studies fail to control for reverse causality (performance determines ownership concentration, e.g. by attracting large investors) or unobserved heterogeneity (a third factor determines both performance and ownership concentration). More fundamentally, studies suffer from the endogeneity problem identified in Section 3.5.2.2, which also compromises studies on managerial equity ownership. If optimal ownership concentration is endogenously determined, no relationship to firm performance can be detected by definition in cross-sectional analyses.

In conclusion, empirical research has documented a large extent of ownership concentration, but has mostly failed to detect a clear relationship of ownership concentration with performance. Thus, more detailed analyses based on arguments from agency theory is needed in order to identify potential confounding effects. In agency theory, ownership concentration is discussed in conjunction with the agency costs created by the use of blockholders as monitoring/bonding technology.

3.6.3 *Blockholders and agency costs*

3.6.3.1 *Benefits of blockholders*

It is generally assumed in agency theory that control mechanisms such as the managerial labor market, the product market, or incentive compensation, cannot fully resolve the conflict of interest between management and shareholders originating from the separation of ownership and control (Demsetz/Lehn (1985)). Thus, a necessity for shareholders to engage in active monitoring remains.

While the increase in firm value achieved thanks to monitoring management accrues to all shareholders pro-rata, the costs of monitoring are entirely borne by the shareholder engaging in the activity. Monitoring thus creates a positive externality (Demsetz/Lehn (1985)). In a corporation with dispersed ownership, therefore, a free-rider problem ensues from the public-good character of monitoring activities (Grossman/Hart (1980b), p. 42):

> "A fundamental problem with this delegation [of power from many to few] is that no individual has a large enough incentive to devote resources to ensuring that the representatives are acting in the interest of the represented. Since the representatives serve the public good, the social benefit to monitoring their activities is far larger than the private benefit to any individual."

While theoretically, small shareholders could cooperate in order to share monitoring costs, in reality, there are substantial impediments to coalition forming (e.g. Mayers (1998)). Large shareholders, however, have enough private incentives to monitor management, since their pro-rata share in the resulting improvement in firm value will be correspondingly larger (Stiglitz (1985)). At the same time, large shareholders have enough control over firm decisions to impose their interest in value maximization on management (Shleifer/Vishny (1997)).

This beneficial monitoring effect of large shareholders is very widely recognized in the literature (e.g. Demsetz/Lehn (1985), Pagano/Röell (1998), Burkart/Gromb/Panunzi (1997), Burkart/Panunzi (2004)).

Some authors model monitoring activities of large shareholders in conjunction with the market for corporate control (Grossman/Hart (1980a), Shleifer/Vishny (1986)), showing conditions under which large outside investors will assemble share blocks in poorly performing firms in order to bring about performance improvements.

3.6.3.2 *Costs of blockholders*

While the monitoring effect of large shareholders is generally accepted, the literature has recently concentrated on the costs of large blockholders. Two different types of costs have been identified: the potential expropriation of minority shareholders, and a detrimental effect on management incentives (Shleifer/Vishny (1997) provide a review).

Expropriation of minority shareholders can take place because, as Shleifer/Vishny (1997) stress, large shareholders represent their own interests, which they can use in order to redistribute wealth in both efficient and inefficient ways. While large shareholders have an interest in maximizing firm value, they can also derive so-called private benefits of control (Grossman/Hart (1980b)). Burkart/Panunzi (2004) argue that small shareholders can be negatively affected in the process (p. 1):

> "Unlike small shareholders, large blockholders have an incentive to monitor managers, thereby mitigating the agency problem between managers and shareholders. In addition, large shareholders can use their influence to pursue their own goals, possibly at the expense of the small shareholders. Hence, the view that ownership concentration necessarily protects minority shareholders is too simplistic."

Edwards/Nibler (2000) and Edwards/Weichenrieder (2004) even interpret the conflict of interest between the controlling shareholder and minority shareholders, as opposed to the conflict between management and shareholders, as the key governance problem for large German corporations. Faccio/Lang/Young (2001) come to a similar conclusion for Europe as a whole. The various forms of expropriation of minority shareholders, or private benefits of control, are reviewed in Johnson et al. (2000), under the term of "tunneling":[129] They range from outright theft or fraud such as insider trading, to legal variants, such as below-market asset sales or transfer pricing arrangements with other firms owned by the large shareholder, or exorbitant directors' compensation. An instructive case study is Vincent/Harris/Burns (2003), discussing how minority shareholders of Ford Canada sued the board of directors for breach of fiduciary duty by accepting a disadvantageous transfer pricing agreement with the controlling shareholder Ford Motor US, leading to prolonged losses at Ford Canada.[130]

---

[129] The term was originally coined to characterize the expropriation of minority shareholders in the Czech Republic (removing assets through an underground tunnel)

[130] Recent evidence on expropriation in transition countries is provided by Bertrand/Mehta/Mullainathan (2002), Yurtoglu (2003), and Yeh/Ko/Su (2003)

In extracting private benefits, large shareholders can also potentially collude with management, at the expense of minority shareholders. Such collusion is formally modeled by Pagano/Röell (1998) and Burkart/Panunzi (2004).

While intuitively, expropriation of minority shareholders clearly appears to be detrimental, Grossman/Hart (1980b) have shown that a differential treatment of minority shareholders, i.e. the existence of a certain amount of private benefits for large shareholders, can be socially optimal: If a widely-held firm is poorly performing, but the dispersed shareholders are unable to improve performance through monitoring because of the above free-rider problem, a large investor could make a tender offer to acquire the firm and improve value. However, assuming that each shareholder's tender decision is not pivotal for the success of the tender offer as a whole, a shareholder will only tender if the price per share offered is at least as great as the expected price per share after takeover and performance improvements have taken place; otherwise, the shareholder will just hold on to his shares and profit from the performance improvement. Consequently, the potential acquirer cannot extract any surplus, and the market for corporate control cannot function. Thus, it is in the small shareholders' interest to allow a certain extent of private benefits, so that value-enhancing takeovers can take place.

An important determinant of the extent of expropriation of minority shareholders is modeled in Grossman/Hart (1988) and Harris/Raviv (1988): The deviation from the one-share one-vote rule. This deviation describes the divergence between cash-flow rights (dividend rights) and voting rights of the largest shareholder. Cash flow rights and voting rights can diverge due to such mechanisms as non-voting shares, shares with multiple votes, or pyramids. Generally, it is argued that expropriation incentives increase with the divergence between cash flow rights and voting rights: When a large shareholder has voting control but little cash flow rights, he can use his control to extract private benefits, while at the same time, he will bear little of the consequent decrease in firm value (Grossman/Hart (1988)). Conversely, the power of controlling shareholders to expropriate small shareholders is moderated by their financial incentives not to do so, one of which is cash flow ownership (La Porta et al. (2002)).[131]

A potentially *detrimental effect on managerial incentives* as a second cost of large shareholders has been identified by Burkart/Gromb/Panunzi (1997) and is further discussed in

Burkart/Panunzi (2004). Based on a formal model, Burkart/Gromb/Panunzi (1997) argue that monitoring by large shareholders reduces managerial initiative: Managerial discretion gives rise to managerial private benefits (e.g. empire building, as discussed in Section 3.3.3) and thus stimulates managerial effort. Monitoring constrains managerial discretion and therefore stifles managerial initiative. Since large shareholders do not take into account managerial private benefits in their maximization problem, they overmonitor in equilibrium from a social point of view, i.e., their monitoring activities increase firm value by less than they reduce managerial private benefits. A dispersed ownership structure acts as a commitment by shareholders not to interfere (Burkart/Panunzi (2004)).

3.6.3.3 Role of the institutional environment

Ownership concentration has been taken up as a core subject in the international debate on the relative merits of different governance systems (for reviews see Shleifer/Vishny (1997), Mayers (1998), Dennis/McConnell (2003), Becht/Bolton/Röell (2003), Gugler/Mueller/Yurtoglu (2004)). From a systemic perspective, Schmidt (2004) has stressed that the different elements of a governance system are complementary, and that ownership concentration as an element must therefore be interpreted differently within the German insider-system of governance than within the Anglo-Saxon outsider-system.

Following the work of La Porta et al. (1997, 1998) an extensive "law and finance" literature has begun to develop. This literature studies the influence of the legal environment on finance, e.g. the development of financial markets, dividend policies, investment, and also ownership structure (La Porta/Lopez de Silanes/Shleifer (1999)) in international comparison. The law and finance approach is in stark contrast with the now classical law and economics approach: The law and economics approach postulates that regulation is unnecessary because financial transactions take place between sophisticated market participants who fully anticipate potential expropriation and correspondingly penalize firms that fail to contractually bind themselves to fair treatment. The law and finance approach in contrast, assumes that elaborate contracts are not enforceable or prohibitively costly, and that the legal environment thus plays a central role, as argued in La Porta et al. (2000b), p. 5:

---

[131] A detailed analysis of the agency costs of different mechanisms to separate control from cash flow rights is provided in Bebchuk/Kraakman/Triantis (2000); a formal model of pyramids is Wolfenzon (1999)

"One of the principal remedies to agency problems is the law. [...] The very fact that this legal protection exists probably explains why becoming a minority shareholder is a viable investment strategy, as opposed to just being an outright giveaway of money to strangers who are under few if any obligations to give it back."

With respect to ownership concentration, a legal environment with little investor protection changes the balance between benefits and costs of large shareholders. Following La Porta et al. (1998), an important determinant of legal shareholder protection is the family of law: common law or civil law. The authors conclude that shareholder (as well as creditor) rights are generally stronger in (Anglo-Saxon) common law countries than in (continental European) civil law countries (see also Johnson et al. (2000)).[132] Therefore, potential returns to monitoring management are greater in civil law countries, and greater ownership concentration should be expected (e.g. La Porta/Lopez de Silanes/Shleifer (1999)). Also, investors buy larger share blocks in order to protect themselves against expropriation, and investment becomes less attractive for minority shareholders (La Porta et al. (1998), p.1145):

"When they are poorly protected, small investors might be willing to buy corporate shares only at such low prices that make it unattractive for corporations to issue new shares to the public."

3.6.3.4 Empirical evidence on the agency costs of blockholders

As already discussed in Section 3.6.2.1, the aggregate effect of large blockholders on firm performance is ambiguous. More detailed analyses, however, can highlight costs and benefits, and the influence of the institutional environment. Ultimately, it is an empirical question whether the benefits in terms of a reduction in agency costs thanks to improved monitoring by large shareholders outweigh the costs in terms of the extraction of private benefits from control by large shareholders (Franks/Mayer (2001)).

The ***benefits of large blockholders***, the potential reduction in agency costs thanks to improved monitoring, are commonly measured indirectly, by relating monitoring activities to the presence of large shareholders, or by analyzing the stock market response to the purchase of large share blocks in an event study framework.

Barclay/Holderness (1989, 1991) and Bethel/Porter Liebeskind/Opler (1998) document positive announcement period excess returns for US firms where large shareholder pur-

---

[132] A succinct summary of the effects of legal environment on financial development is provided in Shleifer/Wolfenzon (2002)

chase share blocks. They interpret this finding as evidence that minority shareholders in a firm benefit from block purchases.[133] Bethel/Porter Liebeskind/Opler (1998) also document industry-adjusted profitability improvements following the block purchase, consistent with effective monitoring by blockholders.

Franks/Mayer (2001) present similar evidence on announcement effects for a German sample. Furthermore, Franks/Mayer (2001) analyze the influence of large blockholders on the association between poor firm performance and management turnover. They hypothesize that effective blockholder monitoring should lead to a closer relationship between poor performance and management board turnover. However, the data fails to confirm the hypothesis. Dherment-Ferere/Köke/Renneboog (2001) apply a similar research design on a sample of Belgian, French, German, and UK firms, and equally fail to detect a relationship between blockholder presence and a closer relationship between poor performance and management board turnover.

The *costs of large blockholders*, primarily the potential expropriation of minority shareholders, are approximated in three different ways in the literature (e.g. Dyck/Zingales (2004)):

- *Block premiums* are the difference between the negotiated price of large share block purchases and the stock exchange price and provide a direct estimate of private benefits of control (e.g. Barclay/Holderness (1989))
- *Voting premiums* are the difference between the exchange price of voting shares and the exchange price of non-voting shares (e.g. Lease/McConnell/Mikkelson (1983)) and equally provide a direct estimate of private benefits of control
- *Dividend policy* can also be understood as a proxy for the costs of large blockholders. While under standard Modigliani-Miller assumptions, dividend policy is irrelevant, minority shareholders under threat of expropriation prefer dividends to retained earnings, because retained earnings can be subsequently diverted (e.g. Myers (2000)).[134] Comparatively low dividend payout ratios, or dividend payout ra-

[133] Two alternative hypotheses can be rejected: Announcement period excess returns do not reflect the impounding of superior information into the stock price (excess returns are also positive when the block is priced at a discount to the stock exchange price; and the stock exchange price never catches up to the block price when blocks are priced at a premium); and announcement period excess returns also do not reflect overpayment by the acquirer (announcement period excess returns to the acquiring blockholder are insignificantly different from zero)

[134] Numerous researchers have worked on the "dividend puzzle": While the signaling theory of dividends (e.g. Bhattacharaya (1979)) has long dominated, recently other approaches have been developed (e.g.

tios unrelated to investment opportunities, can therefore be interpreted as evidence for expropriation of minority shareholders (La Porta et al. (2000b), Gugler/Yurtoglu (2003))

Barclay/Holderness (1989) find an average *block premium* of around 20% over the exchange price in their sample of large US block purchases, which they interpret as evidence for substantial private benefits of control.[135] Franks/Mayer (2001) document a block premium of 14% for a German sample.

Lease/McConnell/Mikkelson (1983), De Angelo/De Angelo (1985), and Zingales (1995b) all document *voting premiums* based on US samples, but these premiums are on average very small, suggesting low private benefits of control in the US. In contrast, Zingales (1994) finds an average voting premium of 82% for the Milan Stock Exchange, interpreted as evidence for severe agency problems.

Concerning *dividend policy* Gugler/Yurtoglu (2003), based on a German sample, find that dividend payouts are negatively related to the deviation of cash flow from control rights of the largest shareholder. Also, dividend payouts have an inverted-U shape relationship to control rights by the largest shareholder. The authors interpret these results as indicating minority shareholder expropriation: while large shareholders with relatively low levels of control use their influence to extract higher dividends from management, expropriation motives dominate at higher levels of ownership. Faccio/Lang/Young (2001), based on a West European sample, also find that dividend payouts decrease with the deviation of cash flow and voting rights. In addition, they find that dividend payouts are generally lower in civil law countries than in common law countries. Interpreting the deviation of cash flow and voting rights and legal family as proxies for the expected severity of the conflict between controlling and minority shareholders, the pattern of results is thus consistent with theoretical predictions.[136]

Gomes (2000)). La Porta et al. (2000b), Faccio/Lang/Young (2001), and Gugler/Yurtoglu (2003) each provide brief reviews

[135] Smaller share blocks (<5%) generally trade at premiums (if transaction is buyer-initiated) or discounts (if transaction is seller-initiated) to the exchange price. Such blocks are too small to confer private benefits; their price is determined by market liquidity costs (Holthausen/Leftwich/Mayers (1987))

[136] The effects of a deviation of cash flow and voting rights are further examined by Claessens et al. (2002) for an East Asian sample. They find that a separation of cash flow and voting rights leads to a valuation discount relative to comparable firms, which increases with the degree of separation. This result is independent of blockholder type, and mechanism used. In an 27-country sample, La Porta et al. (2002) also find a positive relationship between Tobin's Q and the cash flow rights of the largest shareholder.

The *role of the institutional environment* is analyzed by relating variables descriptive of the contracting environment in the respective country to measures of costs of blockholders.

La Porta/Lopez de Silanes/Shleifer (1999), based on a sample including the 20 largest corporations each from 27 countries, find that ownership concentration is robustly negatively related to the extent of legal shareholder protection: concentration is lowest in Anglo-Saxon countries, where legal protection is strong, and the monitoring role of large shareholders is therefore important. La Porta et al. (2000b), based on a sample from 33 countries, find that dividend payout ratios are higher in countries with better shareholder protection. Also, in countries with better shareholder protection, companies with good investment opportunities pay lower dividends, while in countries with weaker shareholder protection, dividends are unrelated to investment opportunities. The authors interpret these findings as evidence for minority shareholder expropriation in countries with weak shareholder protection. Dyck/Zingales (2004), based on a sample from 39 countries, find that block premiums are significantly negatively related to investor protection. Also, block premiums are significantly positively related to ownership concentration, as predicted by the theory.

In summary, there is some evidence for a positive monitoring effect of large shareholders, and robust evidence for the costs of large shareholders (in terms of voting premiums, block premiums, and dividend policy). However, these costs crucially depend on the institutional environment.

While these results are instructive, they do not indicate the net effect of ownership concentration on firm value. If ownership structure was purely endogenously determined as discussed above, an optimal degree of ownership concentration should result in equilibrium as argued by Demsetz/Lehn (1985), and the costs and benefits of large shareholders should balance out. Given that this conclusion has appeared unsatisfactory in light of the contradictory evidence for Germany, researchers have continued to attempt estimates of the net effect of large shareholders.

The most convincing evidence to date for Germany is provided by Edwards/Weichenrieder (2004). These authors separately examine the effects of large shareholder cash flow rights and control rights on the market-to-book ratio for a German sample. Consistent with theory, they find that cash flow rights are unambiguously positively related to the market-to-book ratio, while control rights have a negative impact, especially when the controlling shareholder is a financial or non-financial firm (opposed to a family). They interpret this finding as evidence that (p. 24):

> "...such largest shareholders are in a particularly good position to divert profits from minority shareholders, perhaps by exploiting business relationship between themselves and the firm in which they hold the largest stake."

The effect of monitoring is approximated by comparing two artificial benchmark scenarios (scenario 1: zero cash flow and control rights of largest shareholder, neither monitoring nor expropriation; scenario 2: 100% cash flow and control rights of largest shareholder, full monitoring incentives, no expropriation). The authors find an increase in value from scenario 1 to scenario 2 when the large shareholder is a family, but no increase if the large shareholder is financial or non-financial firm, confirming above evidence that for such shareholders, the expropriation effect outweighs monitoring benefits.

Summarizing the extensive evidence, the relationship between ownership concentration and corporate valuation is ambiguous on theoretical grounds. Both costs and benefits of large blockholders exist. However, in an institutional environment with weak shareholder protection, expropriation of minority shareholders as a consequence of ownership concentration appears more likely. German evidence tentatively indicates that the costs of large shareholders outweigh monitoring benefits, when large shareholders are financial or non-financial firms.

3.6.4 Ownership concentration and ECOs

As documented in the ECO literature, the parent commonly retains voting control of the subsidiary after the transaction (e.g. Schipper/Smith (1986)). Thus, the above discussion on the benefits and costs of concentrated ownership is directly relevant to ECOs. In a theoretical model of the going-public decision, Zingales (1995a) shows that the costs of ownership concentration can have a direct negative effect on the valuation of the subsidiary (p. 179):

> "The potential conflict of interest with minority stockholders may attenuate the benefits of the separate financing obtained from a carve-out. Any anticipated expropriation of subsidiary assets by the parent firm will have a negative effect on the price at which the subsidiary stock is sold. Resources consumed in tightening control over carved-out subsidiary assets or in resolving subsequent minority interest conflicts will also reduce the benefits associated with equity carve-outs relative to parent equity offerings."

In addition, the German evidence has shown that the net costs of ownership concentration can be expected to be particularly high when the controlling shareholder is a non-financial firm, as is usual for parent firms in ECOs: Expropriation appears to be easier when the controlling shareholder controls other firms and can use such intransparent arrangements as favorable supply contracts in order to conceal the true extent of expropriation (Edwards/Weichenrieder (2004)).

A very limited body of empirical evidence on majority-controlled subsidiaries (Holderness/Sheehan (1988), Murali/Welch (1989), Graham/Lefanowicz (1999)) comes to mixed evidence, but the most recent and econometrically advanced study (Graham/Lefanowicz (1999)) shows clear evidence of negative valuation consequences.

While Holderness/Sheehan (1988), based on a US sample, do not find significant differences in investment and compensation policies between majority-controlled subsidiaries and a matching sample of widely-held firms, and similarly, Murali/Welch (1989), based on a UK sample, do not find significant differences in profitability between majority-controlled subsidiaries and their matching sample, Graham/Lefanowicz (1999) in contrast, do find significant valuation discounts for majority-controlled subsidiaries in the UK. In a seemingly unrelated regression framework, they infer valuation multiples for the non-traded majority interest in the subsidiary held by the parent, using the fact that part of the parent market value must be accounted for by the stake in the subsidiary. The inferred valuation multiples for the majority-stake are then compared to the actual valuation multiples of the exchange-traded minority interest in the subsidiary. The authors find that majority-stakes are valued at significantly higher multiples. They also find that majority-stakes are valued at comparable multiples to a matching sample of widely-held firms. Thus, the valuation differential between the majority- and minority-stakes in the subsidiaries is due to a discount for the minority stakes.

While suggestive of a negative effect of ownership concentration in the subsidiary on firm value in an ECO, the above arguments are not yet sufficient for such a conclusion following a rigorous line of thought: A rational controlling shareholder (parent company) would expropriate subsidiary shareholders to such an extent that the marginal returns to expropriation less the marginal cost in terms of the decline in subsidiary value equals zero. Thus, optimal ownership concentration would be endogenously determined, based on firm characteristics, and no relationship between subsidiary ownership concentration and firm value should be expected cross-sectionally. In addition, assuming that the parent company is widely-held, subsidiary shareholders could neutralize all expropriation attempts by also holding shares in the parent company (Holderness/Sheehan (1988)): Any losses from expropriation at the subsidiary level would be symmetrically related to gains at the parent level.

The relationship between ownership concentration in the subsidiary and firm value hinges on the role of parent management: Only under the assumption that value expropriated by the parent company is not simply channeled through to parent shareholders, but appropriated by parent management, does expropriation of the subsidiary shareholders decrease overall value of the group of companies. Otherwise, a decrease in subsidiary market value will be mirrored by a corresponding increase in parent market value.

While in Germany subsidiary management is legally independent according to §76 AktG, this independence is in fact eroded by the widespread nomination of parent management to subsidiary supervisory board seats (Goergen/Renneboog (2003)). While such representation can be used beneficially, e.g. in constraining excessive compensation of subsidiary management (Section 3.5.2.1), it is also possible that subsidiary and parent management collude in the extraction of private benefits at the expense of subsidiary shareholders, as formal models (Pagano/Röell (1998), Burkart/Panunzi (2004)) have illustrated.

Ultimately, it is an empirical question, which of the two effects, beneficial monitoring, or self-interested collusion, dominates. Under the assumption of collusion, ownership concentration has a negative effect on corporate valuation, which also neutralizes or outweighs the potential benefits from monitoring. Events that decrease ownership concentration, such as a full divestiture, decrease expropriation and are thus positively associated with corporate valuation.

Under the assumption of effective monitoring, ownership concentration increases firm value. In terms of the two-dimensional agency framework for the analysis of ECOs, control by large blockholders is an alternative monitoring/bonding technology, that affects the agency costs in both the parent management-subsidiary management, and in the subsidiary shareholder-subsidiary-management relationships.

Given the specific characteristics of the German institutional environment, and the empirical evidence leaning towards a negative relationship between ownership concentration and firm value under the German institutional environment, it can be tentatively assumed that the negative collusion effect dominates in the long term. However, in the short term, it can be assumed that minority shareholders in the ECO value ongoing monitoring by the parent management: Alternative control structures cannot be assumed to be in place immediately post-ECO, but to develop over time only. Similar arguments can be found in Klein/Rosenfeld/Beranek (1991), who interpret ECOs as two-stage strategies, where the initial ECO is regularly followed by second event: mostly, ECO parents retain control in the subsidiary initially, but relinquish control in a second event, e.g. a full divestiture of the subsidiary.

These arguments lead to the following hypotheses concerning ownership concentration and ECOs:[137]

H4A: The effect of ECOs on firm value is positively related to the fraction of ownership retained by the parent company in the subsidiary immediately post-ECO

H4B: The effect of ECOs on firm value is positively related to a subsequent relinquishment of parent control

Figure 18 illustrates how these hypotheses are related to the two-dimensional agency framework for the analysis of ECOs.

3.7 Summary of hypotheses

In Section 3.2.2, the 3x3 compartments of the two-dimensional agency framework were aggregated into four value levers. In the following, hypotheses concerning the relationship between ECOs and agency costs were proposed for each of the four levers.

As a summary, Figure 19 presents the hypotheses developed within the two-dimensional framework.

---

[137] Hypotheses are operationalized in the empirical part, in Section 4.3.4.4

Figure 18: Ownership concentration hypotheses and the two-dimensional framework

OWNERSHIP CONCENTRATION

The effect of ECOs on firm value is …

Principal-agent relationship	Interest divergence	Information environment	Monitoring/b. technology
Parent shareholders/ parent mgmt.			
Parent mgmt./ subsidiary mgmt.			**H4A**: … positively related to the fraction of ownership retained by the parent company in the subsidiary immediately post-ECO
Subsidiary shareholders/ subsidiary mgmt.			**H4B**: … positively related to a subsequent relinquishment of parent control

Determinants of agency costs

Figure 19: Summary of hypotheses within the two-dimensional framework

The effect of ECOs on firm value is …

Principal-agent relationship	Interest divergence	Information environment	Monitoring/b. technology
Parent shareholders/ parent mgmt.	**H1B**: … negatively related to the presence of overinvestment **H1C**: … positively related to a payout to shareholders/debtholders of the proceeds from the ECO	**H2A**: … positively related to the extent of information asymmetries among investors and between investors and management prior to the transaction	
Parent mgmt./ subsidiary mgmt.	**H1A**: … positively related to a reduction in divisional investment opportunities post-ECO **H1D**: … positively related to the creation of effective impediments against continued inefficient reallocations post-ECO vi a separation of parent and subsidiary		**H4A**: … positively related to the fraction of ownership retained by the parent company in the subsidiary immediately post-ECO
Subsidiary shareholders/ subsidiary mgmt.	**H3A**: … positively related to the introduction of a stock options program or managerial equity ownership **H3B**: … negatively related to managerial influence over the pay setting process in the subsidiary	**H2B**: … positively related to the reduction in information asymmetries among investors and between investors and management after the transaction	**H4B**: … positively related to a subsequent relinquishment of parent control

Determinants of agency costs

4 Empirical Evidence

4.1 Section Outline

In Section 4.2, the sample collection procedure and the data sources employed are described. Also, descriptive statistics concerning the sample are presented. Variables required to test the hypotheses developed in the theoretical part are defined. In Section 4.3, the empirical methods employed are described. First, the efficiency criterion for ECOs developed in Section 2.5.4 is operationalized. Then, methods for the detection of short-term as well as long-term abnormal returns are presented, and multivariate regression models for the identification of the determinants of abnormal returns are discussed. Finally, in Section 4.4, the empirical evidence on short-term abnormal returns, long-term abnormal returns, and their respective determinants is shown. A discussion of the results, deriving implications for research and practice in Section 0 concludes the empirical part.

4.2 Data

4.2.1 Sample collection procedure and data sources

The sample of German ECOs was identified based on the IPO database of Deutsches Aktieninstitut. The database contains a complete list of IPOs on all market segments of German stock exchanges since 1950. For each IPO listed in the database, press reports were analyzed to identify if it was an ECO. Press reports were obtained from the Handelsblatt and Reuters databases. In addition, previous literature on ECOs was surveyed in order to identify potential further transactions (Pellens (1993), Hennigs (1995), Kaserer/Ahlers (2001), Langenbach (2002), Elsas/Löffler (2003)).

This procedure identified 74 ECOs on German stock exchanges, beginning in 1984 with the Metallgesellschaft/Kolbenschmidt transaction. Applying the definition developed in Section 1.2.2, 19 transactions had to be eliminated because the parent company was unlisted, 4 transactions had to be eliminated because the parent company was not listed on a German exchange, and 4 transactions ("non-IPO ECOs") were added where the subsidiary was exchange-listed prior to the ECO, but the free-float did not exceed 4%. The final sample thus contains 55 observations. For the cross-sectional regression analysis, 2 observations had to be excluded because of missing financial statement data.

Table 4: Summary of sample size

	No.
IPOs on German stock exchanges, 01/01/1984 - 01/01/2004	658
Total ECOs	74
ECOs by unlisted parents	-19
ECOs by parents listed on foreign exchanges	-4
Non-IPO ECOs	4
Final ECO sample	55
Financial statements not available	2
Financial services providers	
ECO parents	4
ECO subsidiaries	3
Sample for cross-sectional regression	
ECO parents	49
ECO subsidiaries	50

In addition, 4 ECO parents and 3 ECO subsidiaries from the financial services industry had to be excluded.[138] Sample size is summarized in Table 4.

Auxiliary data for the final sample was collected from multiple data sources. Due to less stringent disclosure requirements in Germany compared to Anglo-Saxon environment, on issues such as ownership concentration, management compensation, or segment financial data, comprehensive databases are not available for all data items necessary for hypothesis tests, or not available for the whole observation period. Where multiple data sources were used for the same item, e.g. financial statement data, cross-checks were administered in order to ensure data comparability and integrity across sources.

Announcement dates were identified by searching press reports from the Handelsblatt and Reuters databases, backwards from the IPO date. The announcement date was identified as the first press mention of a planned transaction, originating from the parent company itself and not from market speculation. When such an announcement was found, press reports were searched for a further six months backwards in order to identify a potential earlier announcement.

---

[138] The exclusion of financial services providers is common in the literature (e.g. Vijh (2002), Elsas/Löffler (2003) for recent examples from the ECO literature), because operating ratios common for industrial companies are not meaningful for banks and insurers

ECO data, such as number of shares offered, proportion of primary and secondary shares, and offering volume, were obtained from IPO prospectuses, where available, or from Handelsregister listings via the Dumrath&Fassnacht database. Stock return data surrounding the announcement and following the ECO were collected from Datastream. Industry classification codes were obtained from Hoppenstedt Firmendatenbank. Financial statement data for the sample was collected from annual reports or IPO prospectuses, where available. Where not available, data was collected from Hoppenstedt Aktienführer, Datastream, or Worldscope, in that order. Industry average financial statement data, such as e.g. industry ROA was calculated from Datastream. Analyst coverage data was obtained from IBES, via Datastream. Data on incentive compensation was collected from IPO prospectuses, where available, or from Handelsregister listings, obtained from the Dumrath&Fassnacht database. Ownership data was collected from Hoppenstedt Aktienführer, and where available, from BaFin reports according to §21 WpHG.

The data sources employed are summarized in Table 5.

Table 5: Summary of data sources

Item	Data source
ECO data	IPO prospectuses, Handelsregister reports from Dumrath&Fassnacht
Stock returns	Datastream
Industry classification data	Hoppenstedt Firmendatenbank
Financial statement data	Annual reports; Hoppenstedt Aktienführer; Worldscope
Analyst coverage	IBES via Datastream
Stock option plans	IPO prospectuses, Handelsregister reports from Dumrath&Fassnacht
Ownership data	Hoppenstedt Aktienführer, BaFin §21 WpHg reports

4.2.2 *Sample descriptive statistics*

Descriptive statistics on ECO frequency and volume are given in Table 6. Panel A show the annual frequency of ECOs on German exchanges during the 1984 to 2003 period. As can be seen from Panel A, the sample is concentrated in 1999 and 2000. This pattern mirrors the general state of the German IPO market, as can be seen from Panel B, which shows the annual frequency of IPOs, excluding ECOs. With an average offering volume of EUR 345 million, ECOs are significantly larger transactions than IPOs (with an average offering volume of EUR 69 million). Panel C shows the annual ECO volume in percent of the total IPO volume. Over the sample period, ECOs account for 29.6% of total IPO volume.

Further descriptive statistics on ECO characteristics are provided in Table 6. Two thirds of the average ECO volume is accounted for by primary shares. Among the 55 ECOs in the sample, 21 are pure primary offerings, while 7 are pure secondary offerings, and 27 are mixed offerings (not reported in the table). The median listing day return is 4.4% percent. Thus, while ECOs are subject to the underpricing phenomenon[139] extensively

Table 6: Frequency and volume of ECOs and IPOs

ECOs and IPOs, German stock exchanges, 1984-2004				
Panel A: ECOs				
		Offering volume (EUR million)		
Year	No.	Total	Average	Median
1984	2	49	49	49
1985				
1986	1	51	51	51
1987	1	3	3	3
1988				
1989				
1990	6	220	37	23
1991	3	155	52	47
1992	2	263	132	132
1993	3	245	82	71
1994	3	200	67	44
1995	4	689	230	157
1996				
1997	1	238	238	238
1998	3	496	165	53
1999	11	4,573	416	113
2000	12	10,683	890	101
2001	3	1,039	346	324
2002				
2003				
Total	55	18,905	343.7	75.9

[139] Prominent explanations of IPO underpricing are e.g. dynamic information acquisition (Benveniste/Spindt (1989)), where privately informed investors are induced to disclose their private information in return for being compensated with an underpriced issue (empirical evidence in e.g. Ritter/Welch (2002)); corruption (e.g. Loughran/Ritter (2002) for empirical evidence on "hot" IPOs during the 1999-2000 period); the winner's curse argument (Rock (1986)); information cascades, where IPOs are underpriced in order to induce positive "bandwagon" effects (Welch (1992)); lawsuit avoidance (e.g. Hughes/Thakor (1992)); sequential issuing strategies (Allen/Faulhaber (1989), Grinblatt/Hwang (1989)), where an underpriced IPO prepares a later overpriced SEO (relatively weak empirical evidence in Daniel/Titman (1995), Michaely/Shaw (1994)); and finally the marketing role of IPOs (Demers/Lewellen (2003), Aggarwal/Krigman/Womack (2002))

Table 6 (continued)

Panel B: IPOs, excl. ECOs					Panel C
		Offering volume (EUR million)			ECO share in
Year	No.	Total	Average	Median	IPO volume
1984	21	806	38	11	6.1%
1985	13	922	71	22	0.0%
1986	28	2,491	89	35	2.0%
1987	18	868	48	31	3.8%
1988	15	416	28	21	0.0%
1989	28	1,211	43	25	0.0%
1990	28	1,333	48	30	14.0%
1991	16	1,268	79	45	22.5%
1992	7	392	56	36	24.8%
1993	8	224	28	30	54.6%
1994	12	543	45	28	17.5%
1995	16	2,640	165	41	26.0%
1996	14	12,684	906	28	0.0%
1997	35	2,202	63	27	15.4%
1998	76	3,061	40	22	3.5%
1999	164	5,800	35	31	44.6%
2000	130	6,196	48	42	63.4%
2001	21	2,022	96	14	30.5%
2002	8	636	80	9	0.0%
2003					
Total	658	45,081	69	31	29.6%

discussed in the IPO literature (e.g. Ritter (2003a) for a further recent review of different underpricing theories), the extent of underpricing appears to be somewhat less severe than the 7-8% usually reported in the German IPO literature (e.g. Stehle/Ehrhardt (1999)).

Concerning ownership structure, it can be seen that parent companies on average retain a controlling majority in the subsidiary post-ECO, with median ownership of 63.1%. While management owns an average of 6.7% in the subsidiary post-ECO (via direct shareholdings and stock option grants), the distribution of management ownership is very heterogeneous in the sample. Mostly, management ownership in the subsidiary is restricted to the 1999-2000 ECOs in the sample, as can also be inferred from the zero median.

Table 7: Characteristics of ECOs

1984-2003 sample averages	**Average**	**Median**
Proportion of primary shares	66.6%	80.0%
Listing day return	18.7%	4.4%
Parent ownership in subsidiary pre-ECO	84.2%	97.0%
Parent ownership in subsidiary post-ECO	56.2%	63.1%
Free-float post-ECO	36.2%	33.0%
Management ownership post-ECO	6.7%	0.0%

The industry distribution of the ECO sample is shown in Table 8. The industry sectors are the FTSE 2-digit industry codes, which are used in Datastream.[140] For the sake of comparison, the industry distribution of German corporations (June 2004), as obtained from Datastream (June 2004), is also indicated. Inspection of the table shows that the ECO sample is weighted towards the engineering and machinery and diversified industry sectors. Also, the software and services sector is well represented among the ECO subsidiaries. On the other hand, the household goods and services sector is underrepresented. Overall, the industry distribution can be interpreted as a mild case of industry clustering. The observed pattern reflects on the dual character of ECOs discussed in Section 1.3.1: ECOs are both a means of reorganizing diversified industrial corporations, and of financing growth in expanding industries, such as software.

Statistical issues relating to the observed clustering of ECOs in certain time periods and certain industry sectors are discussed in Sections 4.3.2.4.1 and 4.3.3.4.

[140] A comparison to other classification schemes, such as the North American Standard Industry Classification (SIC) Codes, or the European Nomenclature statistique des Activités économiques dans la Communauté Européenne (NACE) codes indicated that the FTSE-Codes provided the most plausible categorization; a discussion of the impact of different incorrect industry classifications on empirical finance research is contained in e.g. Kahle/Walkling (1996), Krishnan/Press (2003), Bhojraj/Lee/Oler (2003)

Table 8: Sample industry distribution

Industry Sector	ECO Parents		ECO Subsidiaries		All German exchange-listed corporations	
	No.	Percentage	No.	Percentage	No.	Percentage
4 Mining					2	0.2%
7 Oil & Gas					2	0.2%
11 Chemicals	5	9.1%	2	3.6%	29	2.9%
13 Construction & Materials	1	1.8%	3	5.5%	48	4.7%
15 Forestry & Paper	1	1.8%	1	1.8%	8	0.8%
18 Steel & Other Metals			1	1.8%	8	0.8%
21 Aerospace & Defense					1	0.1%
24 Diversified Industry	6	10.9%			26	2.6%
25 Electronic & Electric	4	7.3%	6	10.9%	40	4.0%
26 Engineering & Machinery	12	21.8%	10	18.2%	76	7.5%
31 Automobile & Parts	1	1.8%	1	1.8%	23	2.3%
34 Household Goods & Textiles			1	1.8%	84	8.3%
41 Beverages			1	1.8%	34	3.4%
43 Food Producers & Processers					19	1.9%
44 Healthcare			3	5.5%	33	3.3%
47 Personal Care & House					10	1.0%
48 Pharmaceuticals & Biotech	1	1.8%			25	2.5%
49 Tobacco					1	0.1%
52 Retailers, General	4	7.3%	2	3.6%	25	2.5%
53 Leisure & Hotels					21	2.1%
54 Media & Entertainment	2	3.6%			56	5.5%
58 Support Services	1	1.8%	1	1.8%	44	4.4%
59 Transport			3	5.5%	21	2.1%
63 Food & Drug Retailers					2	0.2%
67 Telecom Services	2	3.6%	1	1.8%	16	1.6%
72 Electricity			2	3.6%	11	1.1%
77 Other Utilities	2	3.6%			11	1.1%
81 Banks	3	5.5%	1	1.8%	29	2.9%
83 Insurance	1	1.8%	1	1.8%	19	1.9%
84 Life Insurance					4	0.4%
85 Investment Companies	1	1.8%			25	2.5%
86 Real Estate	1	1.8%	3	5.5%	36	3.6%
87 Specialty & Other Financial	3	5.5%	1	1.8%	38	3.8%
93 IT Hardware	1	1.8%	2	3.6%	17	1.7%
97 Software & Services	3	5.5%	9	16.4%	167	16.5%
	55		55		1011	

Data on profitability, investment, capital structure, and valuation of sample companies is provided in Table 9. Definitions on the different operating ratios are provided at the bottom of the table. In order to provide an indication of the relative operating performance of sample firms, industry-adjusted values are also provided, as is common in the literature.[141] Industry-adjusted values are calculated as follows: For each sample firm, the 3-digit FTSE classification code is identified. Then, all German exchange-listed corporations in the same 3-digit industry sector are identified. If there are fewer than 5 corporations in the industry sector, the respective 2-digit sector is used. Then, an equal-weighted average operating ratio for all corporations in the industry sector is calculated. Finally, the calculated industry-average operating ratio is subtracted from the operating ratio of the respective sample firm. Discussions of methods for detection of abnormal operating performance are contained in Barber/Lyon (1996) and Lie (2001). Examples for similar approaches are e.g. Smith (1990), Healy/Palepu/Ruback (1992), or Jain/Kini (1994). In order to prevent potential distortions in operating ratios from changes in the scope of consolidation, all operating ratios are calculated for the fiscal year preceding the ECO. As is common in the literature on operating performance, the following discussion is largely based on sample medians instead of sample averages, since these are more robust to outliers (e.g. Kaplan (1989), Barber/Lyon (1996), Loughran/Ritter (1997), McLaughlin/Safieddine/Vasudevan (1998)).

As can be seen from Table 9, the median ECO parent in the sample is relatively large with sales of EUR 2,966 million in the pre-ECO fiscal year. A comparison of averages and medians indicates that the size-distribution is significantly right-skewed. The median ECO subsidiary is considerably smaller at EUR 152 million sales in the pre-ECO fiscal year. Concerning the relative size of parent and subsidiary, four ratios are presented: relative sales, total assets, market capitalization, and book value. While the median subsidiary represent less than 10% of the median parent in terms of sales and total assets, it represents more than 30% in terms of market capitalization, reflecting higher valuation multiples of the subsidiary. This is also indicated by the median market-to-book ratio of the ECO subsidiaries, which at 3.2 is nearly 50% above the median market-to-book ratio of the ECO parents.

---

[141] Example of the application of industry-adjusted operating ratios from diverse areas in empirical corporate finance and accounting research are Healy/Palepu (1988), Asquith/Healy/Palepu (1989), Kaplan (1989); Healy/Palepu (1990); Smith (1990); Dann/Masulis/Mayers (1991); Healy/Palepu/Ruback (1992); Denis/Denis (1993); DeGeorge/Zeckhauser (1993); Mikkelson/Partch (1994); Healy/Palepu/Ruback (1994); McLaughlin/Safiedinne/Vasudevan (1996); Loughran/Ritter (1997); Desai/Jain (1999)

Table 9: ECO operating ratios

Sample averages, pre-ECO fiscal year end	ECO Parent		ECO Subsidiary	
	Average	Median	Average	Median
Sales, EUR million	12,421	2,966	756	152
Total Assets, EUR million	11,730	1,592	660	170
Book Value, EUR million	4,126	402	462	94
Market Capitalization, EUR million	12,873	666	2,174	253
Subsidiary Sales/Parent Sales			16.5%	7.0%
Subsidiary Total Assets/Parent Total Assets			18.5%	9.4%
Subsidiary Market Cap/Parent Market Cap			38.2%	30.8%
Subsidiary Book Value/Parent Book Value			29.3%	18.3%
Leverage	71.1%	74.4%	68.6%	72.5%
Market-to-book Ratio	3.5	2.1	4.1	3.2
EBITDA margin	12.0%	10.6%	-1.0%	11.5%
Return on assets	11.4%	9.6%	3.1%	13.8%
Industry-adjusted EBITDA margin	-2.5%	-1.6%	-23.0%	-0.6%
Industry-adjusted Return on assets	-0.9%	-1.0%	-15.6%	-0.2%
Capex/Sales	4.5%	4.5%	83.1%	7.8%
Industry-adjusted Capex/Sales	-2.1%	-2.8%	28.4%	-0.5%
Tobin's Q	2.2	1.3	5.2	3.4
Industry-adjusted Tobin's Q	0.1	0.0	1.4	0.7

Definitions
Market-to-book ratio = market capitalization / book value
Leverage = (total assets - book value) / total assets
Tobin's Q = (market capitalization + total assets - book value) / total assets
EBITDA margin = (Betriebsergebnis + Abschreibungen) / sales
Asset utilization = sales / (total assets$_t$ + total assets$_{t-1}$) / 2
Return on assets = EBITDA margin * asset utilization
Capex/sales = (Anlagevermögen$_t$ + Anlagevermögen$_{t-1}$ + Abschreibungen$_t$) / sales$_t$

In terms of leverage, ECO parents and subsidiaries are relatively similar. Concerning operating performance, the median ECO subsidiary has a slightly higher EBITDA margin and a significantly higher return on assets than the median ECO parent. However, both ECO parents and subsidiaries underperform their respective industries, if only marginally.

Median ECO parents and subsidiaries also invest less than their respective industry counterparts, as indicated by the negative industry-adjusted capex/sales ratios. This is particularly pronounced concerning ECO parents. However, Tobin's Q, as a measure of investment opportunities, shows that ECO parents have about industry-average investment opportunities, while ECO subsidiaries have superior investment opportunities than their industry.[142]

Summarizing the descriptive evidence presented, a distinctive pattern of corporations involved in ECO transactions emerges: ECOs on German exchanges are particularly likely to be undertaken by groups of companies in the engineering and machinery or diversified industry sectors, with slightly below-average operating performance, and underinvestment pre-ECO. ECO subsidiaries are particularly likely to be from the software and services sector, have below-average operating performance, but enjoy superior valuation ratios and investment opportunities.

4.3 Methodology

4.3.1 Overarching empirical design

4.3.1.1 Operationalization of efficiency criterion

Reiterating the efficiency criterion developed in section 2.5.1, *ECOs constitute an efficient form of restructuring if they are associated with a reduction in agency costs, proxied for by the change in equity value related to the transaction.*

The change in equity value is the difference between equity value measured after the transaction, and the (unobservable) equity value if the ECO had not taken place. Under the null hypothesis, the equity value is assumed to be unaffected by the ECO. In informal terms:

(9) $$H_0\text{: } \textit{Equity value}_{\textit{Post-ECO}} - \textit{Equity value}_{\textit{No ECO}} = 0$$

(10) $$H_1\text{: } \textit{Equity value}_{\textit{Post-ECO}} - \textit{Equity value}_{\textit{No ECO}} \neq 0$$

In order to evaluate the null hypothesis empirically, an operative definition of equity value is needed, covering four aspects: return measurement, measurement interval, measurement scope, and identification of expected return, which are discussed in turn below. Finally, an operative definition has to encompass a method for testing above hypothesis.

142 Properties of Tobin's Q and its calculation are reviewed in Lindenberg/Ross (1981), Perfect/Wiles (1994), and Lewellen/Baldrinath (1997)

Return Measurement: Equity value is commonly measured as the market capitalization, which is defined as the share price multiplied by the number of shares outstanding. However, this definition has the disadvantage of being sensitive to e.g. capital increases or share buybacks. Therefore, changes in equity value are therefore not measured as changes in market capitalization, but as returns to shareholders over a time period. The returns to shareholders incorporate both changes in share price and dividends (e.g. Strong (1992) for a concise definition). Formally, where Pit is the stock price and Divit is the dividend of firm i at period t:

(11) $$R_{it} = (P_{it} + Div_{it} - P_{it-1}) / P_{it-1})$$

The change in equity value due to ECOs is thus defined as the difference between the return to shareholders measured in case of an ECO and the (unobservable) return to shareholders if the ECO had not taken place. As is common in the literature, discrete returns instead of continually compounded returns are used (e.g. Thompson (1988), Kothari/Warner (1997)).

Measurement interval: In defining a time period for measuring stock returns, a trade-off must be made. On the one hand, a short time period can potentially capture the effect of ECOs with more precision, since extraneous or confounding information is excluded. On the other hand, the effect of ECOs potentially materializes over an extended period, which is not captured when stock returns are measured over a short time period (e.g. Brown/Warner (1980), McWilliams/Siegel (1997)). Two methodical alternatives have been developed: the (short term) event study (e.g. Fama et al. (1969)), and the analysis of long term returns after event (e.g. Ritter (1991)). The theoretical basis for the two different approaches has been discussed in Section 2.5.1. The event study analyzes the immediate short-term stock price response surrounding the announcement of an event. The underlying assumption is that an efficient capital market immediately and fully adjusts its expectations on the announcement (e.g. Fama (1970), MacKinlay (1997)). Under this assumption, the full economic effect of ECOs can be captured by analyzing the short-term capital market response. While long-term abnormal returns over extended time periods are hardly reconcilable with capital market efficiency (e.g. Fama (1998)), empirical studies on various types of events (e.g. IPOs (Ritter (1991)), SEOs (Loughran/Ritter (1995)) have found significant long-term abnormal returns. Therefore, an investigation of both short-term and long-term capital market response is instructive. In the short-term event study, event periods of up to 30 days surrounding the announcement of the ECO are analyzed. In the long-term returns study, returns up to 3 years post-ECO are analyzed.[143]

Measurement scope: While prior to the ECO, only the parent shares are traded, after the ECO, parent and subsidiary shares are traded separately. Consequently, two series of returns to shareholders can be calculated. Potential effects of an ECO on equity value can therefore materialize in either or both of the two return series. In order to capture the full economic effects of the ECO, both return series thus have to be incorporated into an aggregated returns measure, namely the return on a weighted portfolio formed by parent and subsidiary (e.g. Cusatis/Miles/Woolridge (1993) or Desai/Jain (1999) for similar approaches in the spin-off literature). In analyzing the specific sources of potential effects, however, it can be instructive to look at parent and subsidiary returns separately. Formally, the weight wPar on the parent in the weighted parent-subsidiary portfolio is given as follows, where MVPar is the market capitalization of the parent at the ECO date, MVSub is the market capitalization of subsidiary at the ECO date, and OWN_PAR is the ownership of the parent in the subsidiary immediately post-ECO:

$$w_{Par} = \frac{MV_{Par} - MV_{Sub} * OWN\_PAR}{MV_{Par} + MV_{Sub} - MV_{Sub} * OWN\_PAR} \qquad (12)$$

In cases where the parent market capitalization is lower than the imputed value of the parent's stake in the subsidiary, the parent weight is set to zero. While such cases are fundamentally irreconcilable with market efficiency, examples exist for ECOs in technology-related sectors during the 1999/2000 period (e.g. Lamont/Thaler (2003), Schill/Zhou (2001), Cornell/Liu (2001)).

Identification of expected return: Assuming that the ECO is not anticipated by market participants, the Equity valueNo ECO is the expected equity value at the end of the chosen time period. The return to shareholders over that time period is the expected return. Since the expected return obviously cannot be directly measured, it needs to be approximated (e.g. Brown/Warner (1980)). For example, the expected return can be estimated via an asset pricing model (e.g. the Sharpe (1964)-Lintner (1965)-Mossin (1966) CAPM, or the Fama/French (1991) three-factor model). More simply, the return on a portfolio of com-

[143] Where long term returns for a sample firm are not available for the entire period under consideration due to a merger or a delisting, the return is substituted by the expected return (e.g. Barber/Lyon (1997) for a discussion of filling in vs. truncating)

parable companies that have not undergone an ECO can be interpreted as a proxy for the expected return (e.g. Barber/Lyon (1997)).[144]

Summarizing above discussion in more formal terms, the null hypothesis becomes the following, where P stands for share price and [0;1] are time subscripts:

(13) $$H_0 : \frac{P_1^{Portfolio} - P_0^{Portfolio}}{P_0^{Portfolio}} - \frac{E\left[P_1^{Portfolio}\right] - P_0^{Portfolio}}{P_{t0}^{Portfolio}} = 0$$

(14) $$H_1 : \frac{P_1^{Portfolio} - P_0^{Portfolio}}{P_0^{Portfolio}} - \frac{E\left[P_1^{Portfolio}\right] - P_0^{Portfolio}}{P_0^{Portfolio}} \neq 0$$

Defining R as the return and AR as the abnormal return, the null hypothesis simplifies to (e.g. Strong (1992) for a similar exposition):

(15) $$H_0 : R_t^{Portfolio} - E\left[R_t^{Portfolio}\right] \equiv AR_t^{Portfolio} = 0$$

(16) $$H_1 : R_t^{Portfolio} - E\left[R_t^{Portfolio}\right] \equiv AR_t^{Portfolio} \neq 0$$

Hypothesis tests: Above equations provide a concise operationalization of the efficiency criterion in terms of abnormal return. In order to identify what drives abnormal returns, the hypotheses concerning the change in agency costs related to ECOs developed in Section 3 need to be empirically tested. In such tests, the following most general functional form can be assumed:

(17) $$AR_t = f(\textit{investment efficiency, information asymmetries and disclosure, incentive compensation, ownership concentration, error})$$

The abnormal returns are thus the dependent variable, whereas the proxies for agency cost changes are the independent variables. Applying the simplifying assumption of a linear functional form, this can be expressed as:

(18) $$AR_t = a + \beta_1 \textit{ (investment efficiency)} + \beta_2 \textit{ (information asymmetries and disclosure)} + \beta_3 \textit{ (incentive compensation)} + \beta_4 \textit{ (ownership concentration)} + e_t$$

Under the null hypothesis, the hypothesized agency cost changes are unrelated to abnormal returns. The null hypothesis can thus be expressed as

(19) $$H_0 : \beta_1 = \beta_2 = \beta_3 = \beta_4 = 0$$

(20) $$H_1 : |\beta_1| + |\beta_2| + |\beta_3| + |\beta_4| \neq 0$$

---

[144] See Section 4.3.3.3 for more details

4.3.1.2 *Methods used in the ECO literature and their imitations*

The overarching empirical design discussed in the previous section is composed of elements also used in the previous ECO literature. Table 10 summarizes methodological choices made in the ECO literature concerning the five aspects discussed above.

As can be seen in from Table 10, previous authors unanimously use equity value as the *efficiency criterion* for ECOs. This choice is valid under the general assumptions underlying corporate finance applications developed in Section 2.4, in particular that the value of liabilities remains unchanged as a consequence of ECOs. The possibility of a change in value of liabilities is discussed in the literature (e.g. Schipper/Smith (1986)), based on wealth-transfer arguments from the spin-off literature (e.g. Hite/Owers (1983), Schipper/Smith (1983)) but rejected. Some authors (Hulburt/Miles/Woolridge (2002), Powers (2003)) analyze operating performance of ECOs in addition to equity value. While it is instructive to analyze operating performance as a potential source of changes in equity value, its use as an efficiency criterion is inconsistent with the underlying theoretical framework of the present study: Markets are assumed to be efficient, and expected changes in operating ratios due to ECOs are thus assumed to be impounded in stock prices.

As far as *returns measurement* is concerned, previous authors unanimously make use of discrete abnormal stock returns. The use of continuously compounded returns is rejected for various reasons, such non-zero expected sample mean (e.g. Barber/Lyon (1997) for a discussion in the context of long-term abnormal returns). The only exception is Kaserer/Ahlers (2000), who introduce a methodological refinement consisting of weighting abnormal returns by the relative of size of ECO parent and subsidiary. This methodological variation builds on the plausible assumption that short-term abnormal returns on the ECO announcement should be the greater in magnitude the larger the size of the subsidiary relative to the parent. However, this refinement is not established in the literature and has not been taken up in more recent studies.

The *measurement interval* for abnormal returns used in the ECO literature varies between short-term event studies and long-term returns studies.

The measurement scope for long-term returns in most previous ECO work is generally limited to either parent or subsidiary abnormal returns. Portfolio approaches borrowed from the spin-off literature (e.g. Desai/Jain (1999)) have only recently been applied in Brettel/Junker/Pinker (2004).

Diverse models for the *identification of expected return* are used in the previous ECO literature. For short-term abnormal returns, the market model clearly dominates, while some authors have recently used even simpler market-index adjusted returns (Hulburt/Miles/Woolridge (2002), Vijh (2002)), given the robustness of short-term abnormal returns to the chosen return generating process. For long-term abnormal returns, however, a dominant model does not exist. Approaches used in the literature included market index returns, market model returns, matching firm returns, reference portfolio returns, and calendar-time portfolio returns coupled with an asset pricing model (refer to Section 4.3.3.3 for a more detailed discussion). The heterogeneity of methods reflects the more general controversial methodological discussion on the measurement of long-term abnormal returns (e.g. Fama (1998), Mitchell/Stafford (2000), Loughran/Ritter (2000), Lyon/Barber/Tsai (1999)).

Hypothesis tests in the ECO literature are generally based on two-sample difference-in-means t-tests, or on cross-sectional regression analysis. The two-sample t-tests partition the sample into two (or more) subsamples, based on some transaction characteristic such as the planned use of ECO proceeds, and compare the abnormal returns of the two subsamples (e.g. Allen/McConnell (1998) for a good example of this approach). However, since these tests are essentially univariate in nature, variable interactions cannot be detected, and firm characteristics, such as size or profitability, cannot be controlled for. In a cross-sectional regression, the sample cross-section of abnormal returns is regressed on a set of variables representing transaction or firm characteristics, as explained in the previous section. A good example of this approach is Vijh (2002).

Summarizing above discussion, the overarching empirical design of the present study follows the dominant approach in the previous literature where there is relative unanimity on the correct approach, namely as far as efficiency criterion, returns measurement, and hypothesis tests are concerned. Where the previous ECO literature uses different approaches, namely as far as measurement interval, measurement scope, and identification of expected return are concerned, the present study employs multiple approaches in order to ensure robustness of results against methodological differences.

Table 10: Methodological approaches in the ECO literature

	U.S. studies					
Author (Year)	Schip-per/ Smith (1986)	Klein/ Rosen-feld/Be-ranek (1991)	Slovin/ Sushka/ Ferraro (1995)	Allen/ McCon-nell (1998)	Vijh (1999)	Prezas/ Tarim-cilar/ Vasudevan (2000)
Sample period	1963-1983	1966-1983	1980-1991	1978-1993	1981-1995	1986-1995
Sample size	76	52	36	188	628	251
Efficiency criterion						
Equity value	X	X	X	X	X	X
Operating performance						
Return measurement						
Abnormal returns	X	X	X	X	X	X
Other						
Measurement interval						
Short-term	X	X	X	X		
Long-term		X			X	X
Measurement scope (LT)						
Parent					X	
Sub		X			X	X
Portfolio						
Expected Return: Short-term						
Market index						
Market model	X	X	X	X		
Expected Return: Long-term						
Market index					X	
Market model						
Reference portfolio						
Matched firm					X	X
Calendar-time portfolio					X	
Hypothesis tests						
Two-sample t		X		X	X	
Cross-sectional regression				X	X	X
None	X		X			

Table 10 (continued)

German studies								
Hulburt/ Miles/ Wool-ridge (2002)	Vijh (2002)	Powers (2003)	Kaserer/ Ahlers (2000)	Langen-bach (2001)	Löffler (2001)	Elsas/ Löffler (2003)	Brettel/ Junker/ Pinker (2004)	Present study
1981-1994	1980-1997	1981-1996	1984-1997	1984-1999	1984-1996	1984-2000	1984-2000	1984-2001
185	337	181	23	32	19	37	50	55
X	X	X	X	X	X	X	X	X
X		X						
X	X	X	X	X	X	X	X	X
			X					
X	X		X	X	X	X	X	X
		X	X	X			X	X
X			X				X	X
X		X		X			X	X
							X	X
X	X							
	X		X	X	X	X	X	X
							X	X
			X					
		X						X
							X	X
X				X	X			
	X	X			X	X		X
			X				X	

4.3.2 Measurement of short-term abnormal returns: event study

4.3.2.1 Concept and relevance of event studies

The effect of ECOs on firm value is first analyzed based on short-term abnormal stock returns via an event study of ECO announcements.

As discussed above, an informationally efficient capital market immediately and fully incorporates the new information contained in the event announcement into the stock price (e.g. Fama (1991)). Thus, the short-term abnormal stock price reaction on announcement of an event constitutes a valid measure of the total economic effect of an event.[145]

The development of event study methodology is generally associated with the seminal studies by Ball/Brown (1968) and Fama et al. (1969), who studied the effect of earnings announcements, and stock splits, respectively. Today, the event study is one of the most popular empirical methods in finance (e.g. Peterson (1989), Shleifer/Vishny (1997)).[146] To a certain part, its popularity is due to the robustness of its results against violations of its underlying statistical assumptions (e.g. Henderson (1990), Thompson (1988)), which has been repeatedly proven in simulation studies (e.g. the often-cited studies by Brown/Warner (1980, 1985) and Dyckman/Philbrick/Stephan (1984)). Another factor is computational convenience: A measure of the event's economic impact can be constructed using stock returns over a short time period, as opposed to the observation of direct productivity related measures (such as e.g. operating earnings) over several years following the event (MacKinlay (1997)).

Irrespective of methodical variations, an event study involves the following steps (e.g. McWilliams/Siegel (1997), MacKinlay (1997)):

- Definition of event and event period
- Estimation of expected returns
- Calculation of abnormal returns and test for significance

---

[145] It must be further assumed that the event is unanticipated (e.g. McWilliams/Siegel (1997)); and that there are no contemporaneous confounding events (Thompson (1988)), or that the mean effect of contemporaneous confounding events is zero (Armitage (1995))

[146] Seiler/Chakornpipat (1997) count 97 event studies published in the Journal of Financial Economics between 1980 and 1992 alone, which is equal to 23% of total articles

In the following, these three steps are reviewed in more detail. Given the ample availability of excellent reviews of event study methodology (e.g. Peterson (1989), Henderson (1990), Kritzman (1994), Armitage (1995), Thompson (1996), McWilliams/Siegel (1997), MacKinlay (1997), Binder (1998), McWilliams/McWilliams (2000)) and of simulation studies analyzing the relative performance of different methodologies (e.g. Brown/Warner (1980, 1985), Cowan (1992), Cowan/Sergeant (1996), Savickas (2003)), the methodological review is held relatively brief.

4.3.2.2 Definition of event and event period

The event of interest in this study is the first public announcement of an ECO. The first public announcement is defined as a press article or news ticker report based on information originating from the parent company.[147] This event definition is consistent with the U.S. literature (e.g. Schipper/Smith (1986), Vijh (1999)) and also dominates the more recent German literature (e.g. Elsas/Löffler (2003), Brettel/Junker/Pinker (2004), or Bühner/Digmayer (2003) on sell-offs).[148]

A natural definition of the event period would be the event date, i.e. the day of announcement. However, this definition leads to two potential problems:

- *Announcement uncertainty.* The capital market reaction on announcement of an ECO is given by the product of the expected economic effect of the ECO and the estimated probability of the ECO occurring. If the capital market estimates that the probability of the ECO occurring is smaller than one, the short-term stock price reaction thus underestimates the true expected economic effect of the ECO. Regularly, companies engage in multiple announcement of ECO plans over time, each with increasing concreteness. Copeland/Lemgruber/Mayers (1987) find that spin-offs are announced an average 2.5 times, and abnormal returns can be identified for up to six announcements. An exclusive focus on the first announcement therefore underestimates the capital market assessment of the economic effect of ECOs.

[147] Yau/Ferri/Sugrue (1994) provide evidence that event study results are generally robust to gaps in press coverage by comparing conclusions reached based on using different news sources

[148] Pellens (1993), Hasselmann (1997), and Kaserer/Ahlers (2000) define the ECO itself as the event. This definition is inconsistent with capital market theory, as discussed in e.g. in Löffler (2001), p. 160 and Brettel/Junker/Pinker (2004)

- *Event date uncertainty.* It cannot be ruled out that capital market participants gain information on an impending ECO before such reports are published in the press. If information gradually leaks into the capital market in the period before the actual announcement, there will also be a gradual stock price adjustment. Thus, the stock price reaction on the announcement date underestimates the capital market assessment of the economic effect of ECOs.

While the first problem, announcement uncertainty, is generally ignored in the literature, two different solutions have been proposed to the second problem, event date uncertainty.

The first solution is a simple extension of the event period. When a longer event period is used, the effects of the event are more likely to be captured. On the other hand, an extension of the event period leads to a decline in power of statistical tests (e.g. the simulation evidence presented by Brown/Warner (1980)). Also, a misspecification of the model of the expected return has more severe consequences over longer periods (Fama (1998)). As a sensible trade-off, multiday event periods extending up to 50 days surrounding the announcement have become common in the literature (e.g. Armitage (1995)).

The second solution involves the use of statistical techniques to identify the day where the announcement is most likely to have occurred. Such techniques include maximum likelihood estimation (Ball/Torous (1988)) or tests indicating structural breaks in time series of residuals (Brockett/Chen/Garven (1999)). For example, Brockett/Chen/Garven (1999) determine uncertain event dates based on a cumulative sum of squares (CUSUM) test involving one-step ahead forecast errors: When the one-step ahead forecast error based on model parameters from the estimation period is significantly different from zero, they conclude that the observation in question must be generated from a different model, and thus belong to the event period. Since simulation studies could not demonstrate an advantage over traditional techniques in terms of test specification or power (Boehmer/Musumeci/Poulsen (1991); MacKinlay (1997) for a similar reading of the evidence), the simple extension of the event period continues to dominate the literature.

In the present study, different event periods, ranging up to 30 days before and after the identified publication date of the press announcement are used. This event period definition is consistent with the U.S. literature and most of the German literature.[149]

4.3.2.3 *Estimation of expected return*

In section 4.3.1.1, the following null hypothesis for the economic impact of ECOs was developed:[150]

(21) $$H_0 : R_t - E[R_t] \equiv AR_t = 0$$

(22) $$H_1 : R_t - E[R_t] \equiv AR_t \neq 0$$

In order to test the hypothesis, a model for estimating the expected return E[Rt] thus has to be developed. In a correctly specified model, the expected value of the abnormal return must be zero since on an efficient capital market, the actual returns cannot be systematically different from the expected returns calculated by the model. Formally (Brown/Warner (1980), p. 209) :

(23) $$E[AR_{it}] = \\ (E[AR_{it} \mid Inf = 0]) * p(Inf = 0) + (E[AR_{it} \mid Inf = 1]) * p(Inf = 1) = 0$$

The expected value of the abnormal return AR_{it} of company i at time t is thus given by the weighted average of the abnormal return conditional on an announcement *Inf* and conditional on no announcement, where the probability of an announcement is given by *p*.

Apart from this prerequisite, model selection is largely an empirical question (Brown/Warner (1985)). The selected model of the expected return should minimize the variance of the abnormal return in order to facilitate significance tests. Simulation evidence shows that the theoretically more appealing model does not necessarily perform better as a basis for empirical research, as simulation evidence by Brown/Warner (1985) shows.

---

[149] Counter to the literature, Kaserer/Ahlers (2000) in their study of ECOs define the event not as the announcement but as the transaction itself, based on the presumption that problems with announcement and event date uncertainty preclude any valid inference based on announcement dates.

[150] The portfolio subscripts have been dropped since the short-term stock price reaction refers to the parent company only

In the literature, the simple market model overwhelmingly dominates (e.g. Armitage (1995), Binder (1998), for examples of application in the ECO literature, see e.g. Schipper/Smith (1986), Vijh (2002)). The market model estimates assumes that expected returns linearly depend on the market return. Formally the expected return of firm i at time t (where R_{mt} is the market return and ε_{it} is an error term):[151]

(24) $$E[R_{it}] = a_i + \beta_i R_{mt} + \varepsilon_{it}$$

The parameters of the market model are estimated via OLS regression over an estimation period generally preceding the event (MacKinlay (1997)).

Other models that can be used to estimate the expected return include the CAPM, the APT (Ross (1976)), and the Fama-French three-factor model (Fama/French (1992)[152]). Empirical comparisons of models in simulation studies show however, that the gains to more elaborate models are minimal (e.g. Cable/Holland (1999), Brown/Weinstein (1985), or Brenner (1979) for a comparison of different models in the context of stock splits). Strong (1992) provides a review of different expected return models.[153]

The present study thus uses the market model to estimate abnormal returns. Following the dominant approach in the literature, parameters are estimated via OLS regression based on a 100-day estimation period ending 50 days before the ECO announcement. A discussion of different alternative definitions of the estimation period is contained in Henderson (1990). Corrado/Zivney (1992) show via simulation that event study results are generally not sensitive to the length of estimation period.[154]

The market return is defined as the daily return on the CDAX performance index. A brief discussion of the advantages of using capital-weighted versus equal-weighted indexes, and broad market indexes versus sector indexes is contained in Brettel/Junker/Pinker (2004). Simulation evidence shows that results are generally unaffected by the choice of capital-

---

151 As is common in the literature and as discussed in Section 4.3.1.1, discrete returns are used, for simulation evidence the use of discrete versus continuously compounded returns see Thompson (1988)

152 Ziegler et al. (2003) is one of the first German applications of the Fama-French three factor model

153 Contrary to the literature, Pettengill/Clark (1999) recommend the use of the CAPM instead of the market model because the market model intercept may be biased for momentum stocks

154 Aktas/de Bodt/Cousin (2003) argue that parameter estimates can be biased when other firm specific events unrelated to the event of interest lead to variance increases in the estimation period. In order to correct for such variance increases, the authors propose to use a Markov-switching-regime procedure to estimate the market model

weighted versus equal-weighted (Brown/Warner (1980)) or broad market versus sector index (Thompson (1988)).

A further issue concerning estimation of expected returns is thin trading. Thinly traded securities are defined as securities which are not traded at least at daily intervals. For thinly traded securities it is common to observe a higher than usual proportion of zero returns and of extreme returns (Scholes/Williams (1977)). This is due to the fact that recorded stock prices are not result of a transaction at days where no trading in the respective stock takes place. As a consequence, daily returns of thinly traded stocks are autocorrelated, and their covariance with the market return is substantially underestimated (Dimson (1979)). Consequently, the market model β-factor is downwardly biased. Furthermore, estimates of return variance are distorted (Campbell/Wasley (1993)).

Different modifications to the market model have been suggested to correct for this bias. The Scholes-Williams (SW) method proceeds by estimating three separate regressions, using different lags and leads of market returns (e.g. Moore/Peterson/Peterson (1986) for an application). Formally:

(25) $$E[R_{it}] = a_i + \beta_{ik} R_{mt+k} + \varepsilon_{it}, \quad k = -1,\ 0,\ 1$$

The aggregate SW-parameters for firm i are then calculated as follows, where ϱ is the first-order autocorrelation coefficient of the market return during the estimation period, and T is the number of days in the estimation period:

(26) $$\beta_i^{SW} = \left(\sum_{k=-1}^{1} \beta_{ik} \right) / (1 + 2\varrho)$$

(27) $$a_i^{SW} = \frac{1}{T-2} \left(\sum_{t=2}^{T} R_{it} - \beta_i^{SW} * \sum_{t=2}^{T} R_{mt} \right)$$

An alternative procedure is proposed by Dimson (Dim). Dimson's aggregated coefficients method proceeds by introducing different lags and leads of market returns into the market model regression (e.g. Bhagat (1983) for an application). Formally:

(28) $$E[R_{it}] = a_i + \sum_{k=-n}^{n} \beta_{in} R_{mt+n} + \varepsilon_{it}$$

The number of lags and leads n can be freely chosen, depending on the severity of non-trading. A common choice is to use one lead and one lag (Peterson (1989)). The aggregate parameters are then calculated as follows:

(29) $$\beta_i^{Dim} = \sum_{k=-n}^{n} \beta_{ik}$$

(30) $$a_i^{Dim} = \frac{1}{T-2}\left(\sum_{t=2}^{T} R_{it} - \beta_i^{Dim} * \sum_{t=2}^{T} R_{mt}\right)$$

Assessments of the relative merits of the Scholes-Williams and Dimson methods in Fowler/Rorke (1983) and McInish/Wood (1986) come to the conclusion that the two methods are largely equivalent. Other methods for dealing with thin trading include filling in missing returns (e.g. Heinkel/Kraus (1994) for a procedure for estimating the variance of unobserved returns), or eliminating thinly traded securities from the sample altogether (e.g. Elsas/Löffler (2003)).

Simulation evidence shows that event study results based on monthly stock returns are generally unaffected by applying the Scholes-Williams or Dimson procedure (Brown/Warner (1980)). In a more general context, Jain (1986) finds that the difference between abnormal returns calculated using Scholes-Williams versus standard OLS beta estimates is minimal. Cowan/Sergeant (1996) in contrast, find that thin trading influences event study test specification, based on additional simulation evidence using daily stock returns.

Therefore, both the Scholes-Williams and Dimson methods are applied in addition to the market model in the present study to demonstrate robustness of results.

4.3.2.4 Abnormal return calculation and tests for significance

4.3.2.4.1 The standard model and extensions

Based on the market model, the abnormal return AR_{it} of company i at time t is given by the difference between the actual return and the market model expected return:

(31) $$AR_{it} = R_{it} - \hat{a}_i - \hat{\beta}_i R_{mt}$$

The average abnormal return AR_t of the entire sample of N companies is the simple arithmetic average of abnormal returns calculated by separately regressing each sample company's return on the market return:[155]

(32) $$AR_t = \frac{1}{N}\sum_{i=1}^{N} AR_{it}$$

A simple t-statistic is calculated by dividing the sample average abnormal return at event date t by the time-series standard deviation of sample abnormal returns during the estimation period. Because sample abnormal returns are used in order to calculate the standard deviation, this method is sometimes called the portfolio-time series method (Armitage (1995)). Formally (where τ is a time subscript designating the estimation period and T the number of days in the estimation period):

(33) $$t = \frac{AR_t}{\sqrt{\frac{1}{T-1}\sum_{t=1}^{T}\left(AR_t - \frac{1}{T}\sum_{\tau=1}^{T} AR_\tau\right)^2}}$$

For multiday event periods, the daily average abnormal returns are summed over the k days of the event period to form cumulative average abnormal returns CAR:

(34) $$CAR = \sum_{t=1}^{k} AR_t$$

(35) $$t = \frac{CAR}{\sqrt{\sum_{t=1}^{k}\left[\frac{1}{T-1}\sum_{t=1}^{T}\left(AR_t - \frac{1}{T}\sum_{\tau=1}^{T} AR_\tau\right)^2\right]}}$$

In order for the above procedure to be statistically valid, several assumptions need to be met. The estimation of the expected return via the market model requires that the standard assumption of OLS regression are fulfilled. Within the market model, it is assumed that stock returns are independent and identically distributed for each firm and independent across firms (MacKinlay (1997)). The potential violation of this assumption leads to three econometric problems concerning the variance of abnormal returns specific to event studies. These problems may require a modification of the standard model:

---

155 The following exposition follows Brown/Warner (1985)

- Unequal residual variance
- Event-induced variance
- Cross-sectional dependence

Unequal residual variance. Since not all stocks are equally volatile, the distribution of abnormal returns is generally not identical across all sample firms. As a consequence, the t-test introduced above is not correctly specified: In order for the null hypothesis of zero abnormal return to be rejected, more volatile stocks need the same absolute abnormal return as less volatile stocks. In the literature, it is therefore common to use standardized residuals. This standardization procedure was introduced into the event study literature by Patell (1976) and popularized in the finance literature by Dodd/Warner (1983).

Using the standardization procedure, abnormal returns are divided by the standard deviation of the forecast (e.g. Strong (1992), MacKinlay (1997) for detailed expositions). The standard deviation of the forecast is the adjusted standard deviation of abnormal returns during the estimation period. The adjustment is necessary because the abnormal returns are not true residuals, but rather prediction errors (parameters from the estimation period are used to calculate event period abnormal returns). The longer the estimation period, the smaller is the error in the out of sample forecast, and thus the closer to one the adjustment term (Henderson (1990)). This standardization creates standardized prediction errors (SPEs), with an expected mean of zero and a standard deviation of one. Thus, standardized prediction errors are identically distributed across firms, eliminating the problem of unequal residual variance. Formally (where s_i is the standard deviation of abnormal returns for firm i during the estimation period, and S_{it} is the adjusted standard deviation):

(36) $$SPE_{it} = AR_{it} / S_{it}$$

(37) $$s_i = \sqrt{(1/T-2)\sum_{t=1}^{T} AR_{it}^2}$$

(38) $$S_{it} = s_i \sqrt{1 + \frac{1}{T} + \frac{(R_{mt} - \overline{R}_m)^2}{\sum_{t=1}^{T}(R_{mt} - \overline{R}_m)^2}}$$

(39) $$\overline{R}_m = \frac{1}{T}\sum_{t=1}^{T} R_{mt}$$

The average standardized prediction error SPE_t on event day t is then calculated as a simple arithmetic average:

(40)
$$SPE_t = \frac{1}{N}\sum_{i=1}^{N} SPE_{it}$$

The standard t-statistic is given by the following formula:

(41)
$$t = \sqrt{N} * SPE_t$$

For multiday event periods, daily abnormal returns are summed over the k days of the event period per sample company i to form cumulative abnormal returns CAR_i, and then standardized by the multiday standard deviation of the forecast SD_i, leading to cumulative standardized prediction errors $CSPE_i$. Formally:

(42)
$$CSPE_i = CAR_i / SD_i$$

(43)
$$CAR_i = \sum_{t=1}^{k} AR_{it}$$

(44)
$$SD_i = s_i \sqrt{k + \frac{k^2}{T} + \frac{\sum_{t=1}^{k} R_{mt} - k(\bar{R}_m)^2}{\sum_{t=1}^{T} (R_{mt} - \bar{R}_m)^2}}$$

(45)
$$t = \frac{1}{\sqrt{N}}\sum_{i=1}^{N} CSPE_i$$

This method for cumulating standardized prediction errors was first proposed by Mikkelson/Partch (1988) and applied in e.g. Mais/Moore/Rogers (1991) or Meznar/Nigh/Kwok (1994). The calculation of a multiday standard error of the forecast accounts for the serial correlation of daily abnormal returns. Therefore, this method, recommended in e.g. Binder (1998) or McWilliams/McWilliams (2000), is generally preferable to other methods which progress by directly cumulating SPEs (as presented in e.g. McWilliams/Siegel (1997)).

Event-induced variance. Within the market model framework, it is generally assumed that parameters are stationary (e.g. Binder (1998)),[156] i.e. they do not change over time and are identical between estimation period and event period. However, there has long been evidence that variance increases around various types of events (e.g. Beaver (1968) on earnings announcements, Dann (1981) on common stock repurchases, or Mikkelson (1981) on convertible securities calls). Brown/Warner (1985) study the impact of event-induced variance on event study tests and find that variance increases lead to a significant overrejection of the null hypothesis of zero abnormal return.

In the earlier literature, the use of the cross-sectional standard deviation of abnormal returns during the event period instead of the time-series standard deviation across the estimation period was suggested as a remedy for the event-induced variance problem (e.g. Penman (1982)). This method is commonly called the ordinary cross-sectional method (Armitage (1995)). Formally, the t-statistic is given by:

(46)
$$t = \frac{AR_t}{\sqrt{\frac{1}{N(N-1)}\sum_{i=1}^{N}\left(AR_{it} - \frac{1}{N}\sum_{i=1}^{N} AR_{it}\right)^2}}$$

While the ordinary cross-sectional method can thus handle event-induced variance shifts, it is misspecified in case of unequal residual variance, similarly to the portfolio time-series method. In response, Boehmer/Musumeci/Poulsen (1991) have developed the standardized cross-sectional method, which is a hybrid between Patell's standardized prediction error method and Penman's ordinary cross-sectional method. The advantage of this method is that estimation period information is incorporated via the standardization of abnormal returns. Formally, the t-statistic is given by:

(47)
$$t = \frac{SPE_t}{\sqrt{\frac{1}{N(N-1)}\sum_{i=1}^{N}\left(SPE_{it} - \frac{1}{N}\sum_{i=1}^{N} SPE_{it}\right)^2}}$$

Simulation evidence in Boehmer/Musumeci/Poulsen (1991) shows that their test is well specified in the presence of event-induced variance, and has higher power than the ordinary cross-sectional test. In the context of thin trading, Campbell/Wasley (1993) and Cowan/Sergeant (1996) show that event-induced variance increases are particularly likely

[156] Coutts/Mills/Roberts (1997) show that parameter estimates are not generally stable over the estimation

since events lead to strong increases in trading volume for thinly-traded stocks. Thus, the traditional portfolio-time series and the standardized prediction error method are particularly likely to suffer from misspecification in thinly traded samples. Simulation evidence (Seiler (2000)) confirms the superior power and specification of the standardized cross-sectional method under conditions of event-induced variance.

Cross-sectional dependence. A standard assumption in event study research is that abnormal returns are independent across firms. In formal terms, the cross-sectional correlation of market model residuals must be zero. Non-zero correlations are likely when sample companies experience a common event (e.g. a regulatory change), or when event periods of different companies overlap. Therefore, cross-sectional dependence is commonly referred to as event clustering in the literature (Brown/Warner (1980)).

While Brown/Warner (1985) do not detect severe misspecification of test statistics when events are clustered, but methods are used that do not account for cross-sectional covariance, Collins/Dent (1984) find significant overrejections of the null hypothesis of zero abnormal return when sample firms are from the same industry. A thorough discussion of the impact of event clustering on inference is provided in Bernard (1987).

Among the methods discussed so far, the standardized prediction error, ordinary cross-sectional and standardized cross-sectional method are misspecified when abnormal returns are dependent. Only the portfolio-time series method can incorporate cross-sectional covariance, since it uses the standard deviation of portfolio abnormal returns.

4.3.2.4.2 Seemingly unrelated regression

The previous section has discussed three econometric problems related to the variance of abnormal returns in event studies, and has described modifications to test statistics to accommodate the problems described. However, none of the proposed modifications can handle all three problems at once. In response, methods based on Zellner's (1962) seemingly unrelated regression (SUR) framework have been proposed. Table 11 summarizes the properties of different methods.[157]

The seemingly unrelated regression framework allows for cross-sectional dependence between the residuals of different equations. It is called seemingly unrelated because the

---

period, but document that results are generally robust.

equations do not share common explanatory variables, as in standard simultaneous equation models, but are only related via their errors. Its introduction into empirical finance research is associated with Schipper/Thompson (1983) and Binder (1985). The generalization of the approach to non-contemporaneous events is due to Malatesta (1986). Variants and extensions have been proposed by Collins/Dent (1984), Schipper/Thompson (1985), and Thompson (1985).

Table 11: Abilities of different event-study methods to handle econometric issues

Method	Unequal residual variance	Event-induced variance	Cross-sectional dependence
Portfolio-time series			X
Standardized prediction error	X		
Ordinary cross-sectional		X	
Standardized cross-sectional	X	X	
Seemingly unrelated regression	X	X	X
X: issue can be accomodated by method			

In general, event study adaptations of SUR are implemented as follows. First, a modification to the expected return estimation for each sample company is made. The traditional method has two steps: In the first step, the parameters of the market model equation are estimated using estimation period data. In a second step, the event period abnormal return is calculated. Event studies based on the SUR method, in contrast, proceed in a single step. An event period dummy variable is introduced into the market model equation (e.g. Schipper/Thompson (1983)). This dummy variable takes the value of one during the event period, and of zero at all other times. The market model equation is then estimated based on both the estimation and event period data. The coefficient on the dummy variable is a measure of the abnormal return. Formally, where D_{it} is the dummy variable for firm i and event day t:

(48) $$R_{it} = a_i + \beta_i R_{mt} + \delta_{it} D_{it} + \varepsilon_{it}$$

Under the common assumption of weak stationarity of the return generating process, the traditional method and the dummy variable approach are equivalent, although parameter

[157] Table 11 has been adapted from Armitage (1995), p. 41

estimates based on the dummy-variable approach are slightly more efficient because all return data is used for parameter estimation (Thompson (1985)).

The SUR method then proceeds by jointly estimating a system of N stacked market model equations for the entire sample. Formally:

$$
\text{(49)} \qquad
\begin{aligned}
R_{1t} &= a_1 + \beta_1 R_{mt} + \delta_{1t} D_{1t} + \varepsilon_{1t} \\
R_{2t} &= a_2 + \beta_2 R_{mt} + \delta_{2t} D_{2t} + \varepsilon_{2t} \\
R_{3t} &= a_3 + \beta_3 R_{mt} + \delta_{3t} D_{3t} + \varepsilon_{3t} \\
&\vdots \\
R_{nt} &= a_n + \beta_n R_{mt} + \delta_{nt} D_{nt} + \varepsilon_{nt}
\end{aligned}
$$

More generally, the system of equations can be written as follows in matrix notation;

$$
\text{(50)} \qquad
\begin{bmatrix} Y_1 \\ Y_2 \\ \vdots \\ Y_N \end{bmatrix} =
\begin{bmatrix} X_1 & 0 & \cdots & 0 \\ 0 & X_2 & \cdots & 0 \\ \vdots & \vdots & \ddots & \vdots \\ 0 & 0 & \cdots & X_N \end{bmatrix}
\begin{bmatrix} \Gamma_1 \\ \Gamma_2 \\ \vdots \\ \Gamma_N \end{bmatrix} +
\begin{bmatrix} \varepsilon_1 \\ \varepsilon_2 \\ \vdots \\ \varepsilon_N \end{bmatrix}
$$

where in our case N is the number of firms in the sample, Y_i is a $T \times 1$ vector of returns for firm i, X_i is a $T \times 3$ matrix of explanatory variables for firm i (the constant, the market return, and the dummy variable), Γ_i is a 3×1 vector of coefficients for firm i, and ε_i is a $T \times 1$ vector of errors. Omitting the firm subscripts, this set of equations can be written as:

$$
\text{(51)} \qquad Y = X\Gamma + \varepsilon
$$

The residuals ε are assumed to have the following variance-covariance matrix Σ, where $\sigma_{ij} = E\,[\varepsilon_{it}\,\varepsilon_{jt}]$:

$$
\text{(52)} \qquad
\Sigma = \begin{bmatrix} \sigma_{11} & \sigma_{12} & \cdots & \sigma_{1N} \\ \sigma_{21} & \sigma_{22} & \cdots & \sigma_{2N} \\ \vdots & \vdots & \ddots & \vdots \\ \sigma_{N1} & \sigma_{N2} & \cdots & \sigma_{NN} \end{bmatrix}
$$

The efficient estimator of the vector of firm-specific coefficients Γ is then given by the following equation, where I is a T × T unit matrix: (see Zellner (1962) for the derivation):[158]

(53) $$\hat{\Gamma} = \left(X'\left(\hat{\Sigma}^{-1} \otimes I\right)X\right)^{-1}\left(X'\left(\hat{\Sigma}^{-1} \otimes I\right)Y\right)$$

Since the true variance-covariance matrix of the residuals Σ is not known, it is estimated using the residuals estimated from a separate equation-by-equation application of OLS. The estimated variance-covariance matrix of residuals $\hat{\Sigma}$ is then used to generate joint generalized least squares (JGLS) estimates of the equation parameters (e.g. Thompson (1985)). If the variance-covariance matrix is diagonal, i.e. the covariances are zero, the parameter estimates will be identical to the OLS parameter estimates (e.g. McDonald (1987)).

After the system of equations has been estimated, hypothesis testing proceeds by imposing across-equation linear constraints on the system of equations. Linear restrictions in SUR can be tested using three different test statistics, namely the Wald test, the Lagrange Multiplier (LM) test, and the Likelihood Ratio (LR) test (e.g. Engle (1984) for a review and derivation).[159] The properties of the different alternative test statistics in a SUR framework are analyzed via simulation in Binder (1985). While the three tests are asymptotically equivalent (e.g. Engle (1984)), Binder (1985) finds that test statistics can have poor finite sample properties under certain conditions. In the present study, the Wald test is applied because it has the least computational cost.[160]

In the simple case, where the null hypothesis states that all parameters in question are zero, the Wald statistic is defined as follows: Let $h(\theta)$ be a vector valued function of the k parameters, $\hat{\theta}$ the unconstrained parameter estimate, and $\tilde{\theta}$ the constrained estimate, such that $(h(\tilde{\theta}) = 0)$. Then let $\hat{V}$ be the estimate of the covariance matrix of $\hat{\theta}$, and $A(\theta)$

---

[158] For a general derivation of the GLS estimator and a discussion of its properties, see e.g. Hayashi (2000), Section 1.6

[159] In Zellner's (1962) original paper, Appendix A, a likelihood ratio test is developed

[160] In contrast to the LM and LR statistics, the calculation of the constrained parameter estimates is not required.

$= \partial h(\theta)/\partial\theta$. The Wald-statistic, Chi-square distributed with k degrees of freedom, is then given by (e.g. Engle (1984), p. 780):

$$\xi_{W} = h'(\theta)\left(A(\hat{\theta})\hat{V}A'(\hat{\theta})\right)^{-1}h(\hat{\theta}) \qquad (54)$$

In the present case, however, the relevant null hypothesis is that the *sum* of coefficients on the dummy variable is zero. Formally:

$$H_0 : \sum_{i=1}^{N} \delta_i = 0 \qquad (55)$$

$$H_1 : \sum_{i=1}^{N} \delta_i \neq 0 \qquad (56)$$

Thus, the relevant null hypothesis represents a case of adding-up restrictions. In that case, a modification to the Wald statistic is required, because the covariance matrix of disturbances is singular. Testing in such an environment commonly proceeds by deleting an equation from the SUR system. Ray/Ravikumar/Savin (2000) derive the modified Wald statistic and provide an algebraical proof of its invariance to the equation deleted.

The gain of using SUR over standard OLS regression via separate regressions depends on the degree of cross-sectional correlation: The estimation of the variance-covariance matrix of residuals introduces estimation error, which can outweigh any gains achieved over OLS when cross-sectional correlation is small (Thompson (1985); Grubb/Magee (1988) provide some rules of thumb for deciding between OLS and estimated GLS).[161] Bhushan (1993) emphasizes that the impact of estimation error can be particularly severe when there are few time-series observations available to estimate the residual variance-covariance matrix. Ultimately, the choice of model is thus an empirical question, which can be analyzed using simulation. Based on simulation evidence, Malatesta (1986) finds that parameter estimates using standard OLS and JGLS are virtually identical, and test statistics used in conjunction with JGLS are not more powerful. He thus concludes that there is no practical payoff to using JGLS in the typical event study context. However,

[161] In order to establish that the amount of cross-sectional correlation is nontrivial, for example a Breusch/Pagan (1980) test can be used.

Thompson (1985, p. 167) rightly cautions against drawing conclusions from simulation experiments:

> "The design chosen in these experiments naturally leads to the sort of independence that renders econometric modeling unnecessary, however. Firms are typically picked at random. Event dates are selected independent of the market return. Only a single event is examined within each simulation."

Still, McDonald (1987), who extends Malatesta's (1986) study using companies that have experienced an actual event in order to counter skepticism that the covariance structure is not adequately modeled in simulation studies based on randomly selected stocks, equally does not find advantages of JGLS over OLS. Teets/Parks (1992) equally come to overall mixed results. In contrast, Ingram/Ingram (1993), introducing a higher degree of cross-sectional correlation into their simulation data, confirm that OLS is misspecified for realistic levels of cross-sectional correlation, while JGLS remains well-specified.

While SUR is theoretically superior to OLS, its advantages in a practical context have thus not been convincingly proven. Its use has therefore been largely limited to regulatory event studies, where all sample firms share a common event data or belong to the same industry, and cross-sectional correlation of residuals is therefore particularly likely (e.g. Schipper/Smith (1983) on the introduction of new merger regulation). MacKinlay (1997, p. 27) termed this case "total clustering".

In the present study, firms do not share announcement dates, but there is some overlap in event periods when these are extended up to 30 days prior to the announcement date. Further, there is industry concentration in software/high technology for 1999/2000. Therefore, the SUR framework is applied as a robustness test in addition to hypothesis tests based on the standard market model.

4.3.2.4.3 GARCH

Within the market model, the standard OLS assumption of homoskedastic errors applies. Assuming a random walk, the best estimate of the conditional variance h_t at time t is its own historical value, where v_t is an error term (Poon/Granger (2003), Appendix A, contains a thorough review of volatility models):

(57) $$\hat{h}_t = h_{t-1} + v_t$$

While the previous section has discussed a modification of the t-statistic to handle event-induced variance shifts, it is a well-known empirical fact that the volatility of stock returns in general is not constant: Large returns have a tendency to be followed by large returns, and small returns have a tendency to be followed by small returns (Mandelbrot (1963), Fama (1965)). Thus, the level of volatility tends to exhibit positive autocorrelation. This effect is commonly called volatility clustering (e.g. Bollerslev/Engle/Nelson (1994)).[162]

Numerous time-series models have been developed in order to incorporate the stochastic behavior of the volatility of economic time series. Two particularly prominent classes of models are the autoregressive conditional heteroskedasticity (ARCH) model (Engle (1982)) and the generalized autoregressive conditional heteroskedasticity (GARCH) model (Bollerslev (1986)).[163] Reviews of the use of ARCH models in finance are Bollerslev/Chou/Kroner (1992), Engle (2001), Palm (1996), and Bera/Higgins (1993).

Under an ARCH(q) model, the conditional variance h_t depends on the previous q realizations of the squared error (Engle (1982)). In the original article (Engle (1982)), an ARCH model is applied to explain the time series behavior of inflation. Formally, where y_t is the dependent variable, x_t is a vector of explanatory variables, b is a vector of unknown parameters, ε_t is a discrete-time stochastic process, and Ψ_{t-1} is the information set at time t-1:[164]

(58) $$y_t = x'_t b + \varepsilon_t; \quad \varepsilon_t \mid \Psi_{t-1} \sim N(0, h_t)$$

(59) $$h_t = a_0 + \sum_{i=1}^{q} a_i \varepsilon_{t-i}^2$$

Early applications of ARCH processes to model economic time series have shown that it is regularly necessary to incorporate multiple lags in order to take account of the long memory typically found (e.g. Bera/Higgins (1993), Bollerslev/Engle/Nelson (1994)). For example, Engle/Kraft (1983) use an ARCH(8)-model in their work on U.S. inflation. However, the presence of multiple lags has led typical applications to assume a (plausible,

---

162 Bollerslev/Engle/Nelson (1994) provide a concise review of empirical regularities in stock returns, such as leptokurtosis, skewness, volatility clustering and leverage

163 Models of stochastic volatility in continuous time can also be found in the derivatives pricing literature (e.g. Hull/White (1987))

164 In general the non-negativity constraints $\alpha_0 > 0$ and $\alpha_i \geq 0$ for i=1,...,q must hold

but arbitrary) linear declining lag structure, since estimating a free lag distribution could have led to the violation of the non-negativity constraints for the parameters.

This criticism has led to the development of the GARCH-model (Bollerslev (1986)), which is able to model the behavior of economic time series using a more parsimonious parameterization with fewer lags. Under a GARCH(p,q) model, the conditional variance h_t depends on the previous q realizations of the squared error and on its previous p own squared lags (Bollerslev (1986)):[165]

(60) $$y_t = x'_t b + \varepsilon_t; \quad \varepsilon_t \mid \Psi_{t-1} \sim N(0, h_t)$$

(61) $$h_t = a_0 + \sum_{i=1}^{q} a_i \varepsilon_{t-i}^2 + \sum_{i=1}^{p} \beta_i h_{t-i}^2$$

ARCH and GARCH models are usually estimated via the method of maximum likelihood (e.g. Palm (1996) for a brief exposition).[166] Maximum likelihood estimates of ARCH and GARCH models are obtained using iterative numerical procedures, such as the Berndt/Hall/Hausman (1974) algorithm.[167]

Empirical applications of GARCH models to stock returns document strong evidence for ARCH effects (e.g. French/Schwert/Stambaugh (1987), who analyze daily S&P500 excess returns over the T-bill rate).[168] Akgiray (1989) fits a variety of time series models to CRSP index returns and finds that GARCH(1,1) exhibits the best forecast accuracy. A number of papers study the importance of adjusting for ARCH effects in the residuals of the market model. Morgan/Morgan (1987), for example, find that the estimate of the small firm effect is significantly altered when the conditional variance of returns is corrected for.

The application of GARCH modeling in an event study context is proposed by Savickas (2003). Assuming a GARCH(1,1,) model, the market model equation can be extended as follows (Savickas (2003)), where *D* is a dummy variable denoting the event period:

---

[165] Non-negativity constraints analogous to the ARCH-model are required to hold, i.e. $\alpha_0 > 0$, $\alpha_i \geq 0$ for $i=1,\ldots,q$, and $\beta_i \geq 0$ for $i=1,\ldots,p$ (see Nelson/Cao (1992) how these sufficient conditions for nonnegative conditional variance can be weakened)

[166] Estimation via the General Method of Moments (GMM) is also feasible, e.g. Rich/Raymond/Butler (1991) and is not dependent on the conditional normality assumption

[167] Derivations of the log-likelihood functions and the estimation algorithm are provided in the original papers (Engle (1982), Bollerslev (1986))

[168] Brief reviews of the empirical GARCH literature can be found in Bollerslev/Chou/Kroner (1992) and in Wang (2003), Section 3.5

(62) $$R_{it} = a_i + \beta_i R_{mt} + \delta_{it} D_{it} + \varepsilon_{it} \qquad \varepsilon_{it} \sim N(0, h_{it})$$

(63) $$h_{it} = a_i + b_i h_{it-1}^2 + c_i \varepsilon_{it-1}^2 + d_{it} D_t$$

After estimating the equation via maximum likelihood, the coefficient estimates of δ_{it}, the abnormal return during the event period, are standardized by the conditional variance to obtain GARCH Prediction Errors (GPE):

(64) $$GPE_{it} = \frac{\delta_{it}}{\sqrt{h_{it}}}$$

The test statistic is obtained by averaging the GARCH Prediction Errors and dividing them by the cross-sectional standard deviation:

(65) $$GPE_t = \frac{1}{N} \sum_{i=1}^{N} GPE_{it}$$

(66) $$t = \frac{GPE_t}{\sqrt{\frac{1}{N(N-1)} \sum_{i=1}^{N} \left(GPE_{it} - \frac{1}{N} \sum_{i=1}^{N} GPE_{it} \right)^2}}$$

The advantage of the GPE method over other event study methods is that it can accommodate unequal residual variance between sample firms, event induced variance shifts and stochastic variance at the same time. Simulation evidence presented in Savickas (2003) shows that the GARCH-based approach is generally well-specified and has the highest power among the different methods surveyed.

While there are very few examples of application of GARCH modeling in event studies due to the novelty of the approach,[169] the present study applies the GARCH-based method as a final robustness check, given the convincing empirical evidence on GARCH effects in stock returns.

4.3.2.4.4 Nonparametric tests and bootstrap

Hypothesis testing using standard t-tests requires that the parameter to be tested is normally distributed in order for the test statistic to follow a t-distribution. In the present

---

[169] For example Cyree/DeGennaro (2001) apply a variant of the ARCH model to study the returns to banks announcing an acquisition; Hilliard/Savickas (2002) develop a GARCH-model to detect event effects on unsystematic volatility

context, this implies that market model residuals (abnormal returns) be normally distributed.

While it is an accepted empirical fact that stock returns are leptokurtic and slightly skewed (e.g. Fama (1965)), this does not immediately imply that residuals are also non-normal. Based on simulation evidence, Brown/Warner (1980) cannot reject that the t-statistic follows a t-distribution. In further simulation evidence provided by Brown/Warner (1985) and Berry/Gallinger/Henderson (1990) it is also shown that market model residuals converge to a normal distribution for sufficiently large sample sizes. Consequently, the traditional t-statistic overwhelmingly dominates the earlier event study literature, and alternative approaches are regarded as unnecessary complications (e.g. Henderson (1990)).

In the newer literature, however, a consensus has formed that t-statistics can be sensitive to violations of the normality assumption particularly in small samples (e.g. McWilliams/Siegel (1997), MacKinlay (1997)). Two different testing approaches have thus been proposed which do not rely on the normality assumption: nonparametric tests, and bootstrapping.

Nonparametric tests such as the sign test or the rank test make less restrictive distributional assumptions. Thus, they potentially exhibit superior specification in the absence of normality. Their use is therefore generally recommended as a robustness check (e.g. McWilliams/Siegel (1997), MacKinlay (1997), McWilliams/McWilliams (2000)). Simulation evidence in Berry/Gallinger/Henderson (1990), however, shows that the traditional sign test and the rank test, which both assume a symmetric abnormal return distribution, are generally misspecified in an event study context. Therefore, different nonparametric tests have been proposed that do not rely on the assumption of a symmetric distribution (e.g. Serra (2002) for a review of the different test statistics).

Corrado (1989) develops a generalized rank test that transforms the distribution of abnormal returns into a uniform distribution across possible rank values, regardless of the properties of the original distribution. In simulation evidence, Corrado (1989) shows that his generalized rank test is well-specified and has superior power compared to the traditional t-statistic.[170] In Corrado/Zivney (1992), the generalized rank test is compared to the traditional t-test and a generalized sign test, which equally does not require a symmetric

---

[170] Similar evidence can be found in Seiler (2000) for the case of Equity Real Estate Investment Trust (EREIT) return data

abnormal return distribution. Via simulation, it is shown that both the generalized rank and the generalized sign test are well-specified, while the t-test suffers from misspecification, especially when the sample size is smaller than 50, or the estimation period is shorter than 90 days. In terms of power, the generalized rank test is found to be marginally superior to the generalized sign test.

Cowan (1992), however, finds that the generalized sign test has higher power than the generalized rank test when there is an event-induced variance increase, and for multiday-event windows. Also, the generalized sign test appears more robust to outliers than the generalized rank test. Cowan/Sergeant (1996) confirm these findings with respect to samples of thinly traded stocks, which are especially likely to be subject to an event period variance increase.

The present study therefore applies the generalized sign test as a robustness check for the results obtained from the application of the t-tests discussed in the previous sections. The z-distributed generalized sign statistic is given as follows (e.g. Cowan (1992)), where *pos* is the number of stocks with positive abnormal return in the event window, N is the number of stocks in the sample, T is the number of days in the estimation period, $\hat{p}$ is the expected fraction of positive abnormal returns calculated from the estimation period, and $AR_{it}^{+} = 1$ if the abnormal return of firm i at day t is positive and zero otherwise:

(67) $$z = \frac{(pos - N\hat{p})}{\sqrt{N\hat{p}(1-\hat{p})}}; \quad \hat{p} = \frac{1}{N}\sum_{i=1}^{N}\frac{1}{T}\sum_{t=1}^{T} AR_{it}^{+};$$

The generalized sign statistic thus does not assume that the fraction of positive abnormal returns under the null hypothesis is equal to 50% and can therefore accommodate skewed distributions.

Bootstrapping has been introduced into event study methodology as an alternative testing procedure when the distribution of residuals is non-normal and the sampling distribution of the t-statistic is therefore unknown. McWilliams/Siegel (1997) recommend the application of bootstrap methods for small samples where normality assumptions cannot be relied on. The bootstrap is due to Efron (1979), textbook expositions are provided in e.g.

Efron/Tibshirani (1993) and Davison/Hinkley (1997), review articles are Hinkley (1988), Maddala/Li (1996) and Hall (1994).[171]

The bootstrap is a special form of Monte Carlo simulation which assumes that the unknown distribution of a parameter can be approximated by a discrete distribution giving equal weight to each residual from the original estimation. Thus, no a priori assumption is made about the distribution of the parameter. In order to calculate a bootstrap distribution, repeated random samples of the parameter are drawn with replacement from the set of original estimated parameter values. Formally, an unknown distribution function is replaced by its empirical estimator (Hall (1994)). For the purpose of hypothesis testing, the test statistic in question is then calculated for each of the resamples. Critical values from the bootstrap distribution are then used for hypothesis testing (e.g. Maddala/Li (1996)).

Formally, let the null hypothesis and the alternative hypotheses be the following:[172]

(68) $$H_0 : \theta = \theta_0$$

(69) $$H_1 : \theta \neq \theta_0$$

Then, let $\hat{\theta}$ be a parameter value estimated as a function of a sample $X_1,\dots,X_N$, and let $\hat{\theta}*$ be a parameter value computed from the resample $X*_1,\dots,X*_N$.[173] Let $\hat{\sigma}*$ denote the parameter variance calculated from the resample. From the bootstrap distribution, calculate a number $\hat{t}$ such that (where *a* is the desired Type I error):

(70) $$Pr* = \left(\frac{\left|\hat{\theta}* - \hat{\theta}\right|}{\hat{\sigma}*} > \hat{t} \right) = a$$

In effect, the bootstrap distribution is thus used to calculate a new critical t-value $\hat{t}$. The null hypothesis is rejected, if the conventional t-value $\left|\hat{\theta} - \theta_0\right| / \hat{\sigma}$ exceeds the critical value $\hat{t}$.

---

[171] A historical account of the bootstrap's development and its influence on statistics is Efron (2000)

[172] This exposition closely follows Hall/Wilson (1991)

[173] For example, θ could be an average abnormal return AR_t and $X_1,\dots,X_N$ could be a sample of event day t abnormal returns for firm 1 to N

In the calculation of the critical value, two aspects merit attention: First, the bootstrap distribution is based on the difference between the resampled parameter value and the original estimated parameter value, not the parameter value of the null hypothesis. This has the effect of considerably increasing the power of the test. Second, resampling is based on the variance of the resampled parameters, not on the original estimated variance. This is known as bootstrap pivoting and has the effect of reducing the error in the level of significance. These two guidelines have been proposed by Hall/Wilson (1991). The importance of pivoting is more formally derived in Hall (1994).

Since the present study is based on a relatively small sample size, bootstrapped t-statistics are calculated as a further robustness test in addition to the conventional t-statistics.[174] As is common in the literature (e.g. Hinkley (1988)), 10,000 resamples are of size N are drawn.[175] Examples for similar applications of the bootstrap in related finance literature are relatively rare, but include e.g. Johnston/Hamill (2000) on dividend initiations, Gorton/Schmid (in press) on codetermination, and Aktas/de Bodt/Roll (in press) on M&A regulation.

4.3.2.5 Summary of empirical design

The empirical design used for the short-term abnormal returns measurement is summarized in Table 12.

Results are first presented for the full sample of observations. In a second step, the sample is split into two subsamples, ECO announcements 1984-1997, and ECO announcements 1998-2001, in order to identify potential differences in the capital market reaction to transactions surrounding the 1999-2000 period of sustained positive stock market performance.

---

174 An exception are the SUR results. The SUR results are not bootstrapped because, although Hein/Westfall (2004) propose an algorithm that could be adapted in order to bootstrap the SUR, such methods have not yet been firmly established in practice

175 The ideal number of bootstrap replications would be infinity. A method for determining the minimum number of bootstrap replications to reach a predetermined level of precision is proposed by Andrews/Buchinsky (2000); in their simulations, the minimum number of replications sufficient to justify conventional significance levels nowhere exceeds 4,000

Table 12: Summary of empirical design of short-term event study

Presentation of results	Full sample, two subsamples (1984-1997; 1998-2001)
Event definition	ECO announcement
Event period	Days -5, -4, -3, -2, -1, 0, 1, 2, 3, 4, 5 Multiday periods of different lengths surrounding ECO announcement -30 0, -25 0, -20 0, -15 0, -10 0, -5 0, 1 5, 1 10, 1 15, 1 20, 1 25, 1 30
Expected return calculation	Standard market model Scholes-Williams market model Dimson market model Market model estimated via SUR Market model with GARCH effects
Estimation details	Estimation period length of 100 days, ending 50 days prior to the event; Underlying market index: CDAX composite

Test statistics	Port-folio time-series t	Standar-dized predic-tion error t	Ordi-nary cross-sectio-nal t	Standar-dized cross-sectio-nal t	Genera-lized sign test	Wald test	Garch predic-tion error t
Standard market model	X*	X*	X*	X*	X		
Scholes-Williams market model	X*	X*	X*	X*	X		
Dimson market model	X*	X*	X*	X*	X		
Market model estimated via SUR						X	
Market model with GARCH effects							X*

* denotes bootstrapped version of test statistic is also calculated

4.3.3 Measurement of long-term abnormal returns

4.3.3.1 Concept and relevance of long-term returns analysis

In addition to the short-term abnormal returns surrounding the ECO announcement, the present study analyzes long term returns after ECOs. The assumption underlying event studies is that on an efficient capital market, the stock price response to an event is immediate, and can thus be fully captured via the analysis of short-term abnormal returns (refer back to Section 4.3.1.1).

However, over the past two decades, a separate literature has developed, which argues that stock prices adjust only slowly to the information conveyed by an event. Thus, the study of long-term returns after an event is of interest. A review of this literature and its implications for market efficiency is provided in Fama (1998).

The earliest long-term returns studies commonly identified in the literature are Jaffe (1974) and Mandelker (1974), who studied the returns to merging firms. However, it was not until the early 1990s that the long-term returns literature established itself as a field of study, which continues a lively development until today. Abundant of the study of long-term returns after corporate events are Ritter (1991) and more recently Gompers/Lerner (2003) on IPOs, Loughran/Ritter (1995) and Spiess/Affleck-Graves (1995) on SEOs,[176] Cusatis/Miles/Woolridge (1993) on spin-offs, Desai/Jain (1997) and Byun/Rozeff (2003) on stock splits, Agrawal/Jaffe/Mandelker (1992) on merging firms, Lakonishok/Vermaelen (1990) on tender offers, Ikenberry/Lakonishok/Vermaelen (1995) on open market share repurchases, Spiess/Affleck-Graves (1999) and Billett/Flannery/Garfinkel (2001) on debt offerings and loan announcement, Vijh (1999) on ECOs, Hertzel et al. (2002) on private placements of equity, Boehme/Sorescu (2002) on dividend initiations, and Eberhart/Maxwell/Siddique (2004) on R&D increases. More recent studies go beyond the simple measurement of long-term returns to identify their underlying drivers, such as e.g. market timing (Clarke/Dunbar/Kahle (2002), Schultz (2003)), insider trading (Clarke/Dunbar/Kahle (2001)), pre-event earnings and earnings management (Rangan (1998), Teoh/Welch/Wong (1998a/1998b), Yi (2001),), investment strategy (Jeanneret (2000)), institutional investment (Gibson/Safieddine/Sonti (2003)), prior information (Kadiyala/Rau (2004)). The study of long-term returns has also garnered interest in the German literature (e.g. Sapusek (2000), Stehle/Ehrhardt (1999), Stehle/Ehrhardt/Przyborowski (2000), Gerke/Fleischer (2001), Kiss/Stehle (2002)).

Based on the above studies, three different patterns of reaction can be identified in long-term returns: Efficient reaction, i.e. zero long-term abnormal returns, overreaction to in-

---

[176] The U.S. evidence of long-term underperformance of IPOs and SEOs has also proven relatively robust in an international context, e.g. Spain: Alvarez/Gonzalez (2002); Canada: Kooli/L'Her/Suret (2004); U.K.: Abhyankar/Ho (2001), Espenlaub/Gregory/Tonks (2000); Denmark: Jakobsen/Sorensen (2001); Switzerland: Drobetz/Kammermann/Waelchli (2003); also see Loughran/Ritter/Rydqvist (1994) and Ritter (2003) for international comparisons

formation (first discussed in DeBondt/Thaler (1985) on returns to "past winners"), and underreaction. For example, the evidence on stock splits documents long-term positive abnormal returns both before and after the event (Desai/Jain (1997)). Thus, the positive abnormal returns after the split represent underreaction to the positive information conveyed by the split. In contrast, the evidence on SEOs documents strong stock returns before the event due to strong earnings realizations, and negative long-term abnormal returns after the event (e.g. Loughran/Ritter (1995)). Thus, the positive returns pre-SEO can be interpreted as an overreaction of the market to positive information (strong earnings), which is only gradually corrected after the event (when earnings mean-revert).

In order to rationalize the patterns of overreaction and underreaction, several behavioral models have been developed (e.g. Barberis/Shleifer/Vishny (1998), Daniel/Hirshleifer/ Subrahmanyam (1998), Hong/Stein (1999)). These models relax some of the assumptions common to the efficient capital markets literature, such as e.g. costless short selling, and explain observed return patterns by certain cognitive features of investors, such as e.g. overconfidence or loss aversion (e.g. Hirshleifer (2001) and Barberis/Thaler (2003) for general surveys of behavioral finance and asset pricing).

In defense of market efficiency, Fama (1998) argues that a random split between overreaction and underreaction can be consistent with market efficiency: If the split is indeed random, an investor can earn no abnormal returns on average by conditioning on the occurrence on certain events. Furthermore, Fama (1998) argues that the inferences drawn from long-term returns studies are extremely sensitive to the methodology employed. In fact, a test for long-term abnormal returns is a test of the joint hypothesis that the long-term abnormal returns are indeed zero, and that the return generating model is correct (e.g. Fama (1970)). The joint hypothesis problem is particularly acute in long-term returns studies (e.g. Lyon/Barber/Tsai (1999)), since in the traditional short-term event study, the expected return over the event window is usually close to zero, and the return generating model therefore does not have a strong effect on results. Similar in spirit to Fama (1998), Eckbo/Masulis/Norli (2000) argue that the nonzero long-term abnormal returns found in most studies are spurious results, caused by a failure of the common long-term returns measurement methods to properly account for risk. Brav/Geczy/Gompers (1999) come to a similar conclusion.

The sensitivity of results to methodology and the heterogeneity of methods employed in empirical work has spurred the publication of several studies dedicated to the methodology of long-term returns studies (Kothari/Warner (1997), Barber/Lyon (1997),

Lyon/Barber/Tsai (1999), Brav (2000), Cowan/Sergeant (2001), Ehrhardt/Koerstein (2001), Mitchell/Stafford (2000), Ang/Zhang (2004)). In these studies, three core issues have been identified:

- Calculation of long-term returns
- Estimation of expected return
- Tests for significance

These three areas are discussed in more detail in the following. Recommendations from the methodological literature are summarized in Table 13.

4.3.3.2 Calculation of long-term returns

Three fundamentally different methods for the calculation of long-term abnormal returns are commonly discussed in the literature:

- Cumulative abnormal returns (CARs)
- Buy-and-hold abnormal returns (BHARs)
- Calendar-time portfolio abnormal returns (CTARs)

Table 13, Panel A, shows that most methodological studies recommend the use of BHARs. Mitchell/Stafford (2000, p. 296) write that

> "Buy-and-hold abnormal returns have become the standard method of measuring long-term abnormal returns."

However, some authors suggest the use of CTARs. In particular, Fama (1998) strongly advocates the calendar-time approach. Given this controversy, the three methods are discussed in more detail below.

Table 13: Methodological recommendations in the long-term returns literature

	Kothari/ Warner (1997)	Barber/Lyon (1997)	Lyon/Barber/ Tsai (1999)
Panel A: Calculation of long-term return			
BHAR			**X**
BHAR rebalanced	X	**X**	X
Winsorized BHAR			
CAR	X	X	
CTAR			**X**
Panel B: Estimation of expected return			
Market index	**X**		
Reference Portfolio		X	**X**
Matching firm		**X**	X
Asset pricing model			
Market model	X		
CAPM	X		
FF three-factor model	X	X	X
Panel C: Tests for significance			
Cross-sectional t	X	**X**	X
Time-series t	X		
Bootstrapped skewness-adjusted t			**X**
Bootstrapped p-values			**X**
Dependence adjusted t			
Two-sample t			
Sign test			

X: method tested. Recommended method printed in bold

Table 13 (continued)

Loughran/ Ritter (2000)	Mitchell/ Stafford (2000)	Cowan/ Sergeant (2001)	Ehrhardt/ Koerstein (2001)	Ang/Zhang (2004)
X	X	X	**X**	**X**
			X	
		X		
X	**X**			X
X			X	
X	X	**X**	**X**	X
		X	X	**X**
X	**X**			
X		X	X	X
			X	X
	X			
	X			
		X		
				X

In order to calculate *cumulative abnormal returns*, security-specific abnormal returns are averaged per subperiod t over the sample, and then summed over the event period T (e.g. Kothari/Warner (1997)). Formally:

(71) $$AR_{it} = R_{it} - E[R_{it}]$$

(72) $$AR_t = \frac{1}{N}\sum_{i=1}^{N} AR_{it}$$

(73) $$CAR_T = \sum_{t=1}^{T} AR_t$$

While regularly employed in the earlier literature (e.g. in DeBondt/Thaler (1985)), CARs are used more sparsely today because of biases introduced through the additive cumulation procedure. The additive cumulation leads to an upward bias in CARs, which is an increasing function of the bid-ask spread of sample firms (Conrad/Kaul (1993)). Furthermore, CARs imply a periodic rebalancing of the sample each period t to equal weights (Barber/Lyon (1997)). Thus, a test of the null hypothesis of zero CARs over the event period is not a test that the return of holding a portfolio of the sample stocks over the entire event period is zero, but a test that the average per-subperiod t abnormal return is zero (Ritter (1991)).

In response to these perceived deficiencies, *buy-and-hold abnormal returns* came to dominate as a return measure that more closely mimics the actual investor experience (e.g. Dimson/Marsh (1986)) in the more recent literature. Examples of the application of BHARs in the applied long-term returns literature include e.g. Ikenberry/Lakonishok/Vermaelen (1995), Teoh/Welch/Wong (1998a/1998b), Spiess/Affleck-Graves (1995, 1999), Schultz (2003) or Sapusek (2000) and Stehle/Ehrhardt/Przyborowski (2001) in the German literature. Instead of adding abnormal returns, BHARs are formed by multiplying per-subperiod returns over the event period (e.g. Barber/Lyon (1997) for each firm. Then, BHARs are averaged over the sample. Formally (e.g. Ehrhardt/Koerstein (2001)), the buy-and-hold abnormal return over the event period T is given by:

(74) $$BHAR_T = \frac{1}{N}\sum_{i=1}^{N} BHAR_{iT}$$

(75) $$BHAR_{iT} = \left(\prod_{t=1}^{T}(1 + R_{it}) - \prod_{t=1}^{T}(1 + E[R_{it}])\right)$$

Thus, BHARs compare the returns to buying and holding the sample of event firms to buying and holding a benchmark. Since they ignore the effect of compounding, CARs are biased predictors of BHARs (Barber/Lyon (1997)). Consequently, there are few examples of the use of CARs in the recent applied literature.

A third method for computing long-term abnormal returns is *calendar-time portfolio abnormal returns*. The origins of this method stretch back to Jaffe (1974) and Mandelker (1974). While the CAR method and the BHAR method both align the sample firms in event time, the CTAR method operates in calendar time. Thus, a rolling portfolio is formed each period including all sample firms that have completed an event within the prior k periods (e.g. Mitchell/Stafford (2000)). The returns of this calendar-time portfolio are then either compared to the returns on a reference portfolio, or they are analyzed via an asset pricing model such as the Fama-French three-factor model, and the regression intercept measures the average per-period abnormal return on the portfolio of the event firms (Lyon/Barber/Tsai (1999)). Examples of the application of CTARs in the applied long-term returns literature include Brav/Geczy/Gompers (2000), Schultz (2003) or Kadiyala/Rau (2004). Figure 20 provides a graphical comparison of BHAR and CTAR method.

The relative merits of BHAR and CTAR are discussed controversially in the methodological literature. The calculation of BHARs assumes that abnormal returns of sample firms are independent (e.g. Lyon/Barber/Tsai (1999)). In case of cross-sectional dependence, test statistics based on BHARs can therefore be severely overstated (Mitchell/Stafford (2000)). A solution to the cross-sectional dependence problem similar to the SUR framework for the analysis of long-term returns. At the same time, the cross-sectional dependence problem is likely to be more severe because an overlap in event periods is the more likely the longer the event period under study.[177] CTARs, on the other hand, do not suffer from the cross-sectional dependence problem, since cross-sectional dependence is accommodated via the aggregation of sample securities into portfolios (Fama (1998)). When there is reason to believe that the cross-sectional dependence problem is severe due to the characteristics of the sample under study, part of the literature therefore tends to

[177] Modifications to the conventional t-statistic in order to accommodate cross-sectional dependence are discussed in Section 4.3.3.4

Figure 20: Comparison of BHAR and CTAR methods

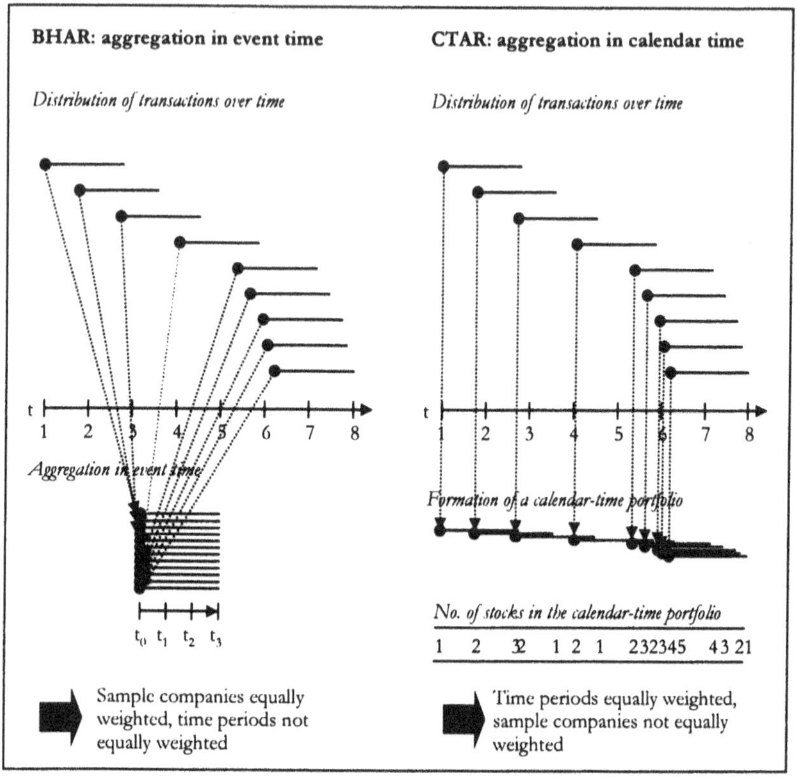

recommend CTARs over BHARs (Lyon/Barber/Tsai (1999), Mitchell/Stafford (2000), Ang/Zhang (2004)).

In contrast, Loughran/Ritter (2000) forcefully argue against the use of CTARs. The researcher must take into account that BHARs and CTARs in fact test two different null hypotheses: BHARs test the null hypothesis that the mean long-term abnormal return across the sample of firms is zero. Thus, each sample firm receives equal weight (value-weighting is of course possible, e.g. Mitchell/Stafford (2000)). CTARs test the null hypothesis that the mean long-term abnormal return over the event period is zero. Thus, each time period receives equal weight. Consequently, firms that experience events during periods where many other firms also experience events receive a lower weight than firms that experience events during time periods where few other firms experience events. This is a consequence of the rolling calendar portfolio having a different number of members per subperiod (Lyon/Barber/Tsai (1999)). In the context of the present study, the Metallgesellschaft/Kolbenschmidt ECO, which was the sole ECO that happened in 1984, would thus receive 20 times the weight of the ECOs in 1999, where 20 ECOs took place. Loughran/Ritter (2000) argue, and confirm via simulation, that the equal weighting of time periods leads to CTAR-based tests having low power. In addition, it is argued that a further reduction in power is caused when CTARs are used in conjunction with asset pricing models such as the Fama-French three-factor model, and contaminated portfolios are used to estimate the factors in the regression.[178] Furthermore, the CTAR approach in conjunction with an asset pricing model potentially suffers from a heteroskedasticity problem due to the changing number of stocks in the calendar-time portfolio (e.g. Ang/Zhang (2004)).

In light of the above discussion, the present study employs BHARs as a core measure of long-term abnormal returns, with CARs as an additional measure to ensure robustness. CTARs are not employed. In the ECO literature, Vijh (1999) uses a similar approach.

4.3.3.3 Estimation of expected return

In the preceding section, the dominance of the market model for the estimation of expected return in the short-term event study has been discussed. A similar consensus does not exist in the long-term returns literature, as can be seen from the diverging recommendations in Table 13, Panel B. In the methodological literature, the choice of return generating model is viewed as a largely empirical question, to be solved via simulation experiments comparing the properties of different models. Four main approaches for the estimation of expected return have been proposed (e.g. Barber/Lyon (1997)):

- Market index

[178] The most simple case of contamination is that the return on the market index used in the market model equation also contains firms that have experienced an event, and which should theoretically be excluded. The same applies to the additional factors in the Fama-French three-factor model, e.g. the SML factor, the return on a portfolio of small stocks less the return on a portfolio of large stocks, which is calculated based on portfolios that include firms that have experienced an event

- Asset pricing model
- Matching firm
- Reference portfolio

Based on simulation evidence, the methodological literature has come to mixed recommendations. While the choice of method is guided by the principle that sample firms must be matched to benchmarks composed of firms whose riskiness or return-generating characteristics are similar, a theory of long-term returns does not exist (Brav/Geczy/Gompers (2000)). The choice of model is therefore largely based on the properties of different methods in terms of Type I and Type II error found in simulation studies. A typical simulation study (e.g. Ehrhardt/Koerstein (2001)) proceeds in two steps: Specification is analyzed by testing if rejection frequencies of the null hypothesis of zero abnormal returns conform to their theoretical level in portfolios of randomly drawn securities (Type I error). Power is analyzed by testing rejection frequencies of the null hypothesis in portfolios where abnormal returns have been artificially induced (Type II error).

In the following, the relative merits of the four models are discussed in more detail. From Table 13, it can be seen that most methodological papers recommend the use of reference portfolios.

Using a *market index*, the expected return of a sample firm is simply the return on a stock market index (e.g. Kothari/Warner (1997), Ehrhardt/Koerstein (2001)). Formally:

$$E[R_{it}] = R_{mt} \quad i = 1,\ldots n \qquad (76)$$

The estimation of expected returns via market indexes is generally not recommended in the literature. Since the same expected return is assumed for all sample firms, firm-specific characteristics that affect expected returns are not taken into account. Not surprisingly, test based on abnormal returns relative to market indexes are generally not well specified (e.g. Barber/Lyon (1997)). Canina et al. (1998) further cautions against potential biases from the use of equal-weighted index returns. Still, applications of market indexes for the estimation of expected returns can be found in e.g. Brav/Geczy/Gompers (2000) or Sapusek (2000), or in Langenbach (2001) as far as the ECO literature is concerned.

Given the recommendations in the methodological literature, however, abnormal returns based on a market index are used for comparison purposes only in the present study. As in the short-term event study, the CDAX Composite is chosen as the relevant market index.

Using an *asset pricing model*, the expected return of a sample firm is the return calculated from an asset pricing model, such as the market model, or the Fama-French three-factor model (Fama/French (1992, 1995, 1996a)). For example, within the Fama-French three-factor model, the expected return on the calendar time portfolio Rct is (where Rft is the risk-free rate, Rmt is the market return, SMB is the return on a portfolio of small stocks less the return on a portfolio of large stocks, and HML is the return on a portfolio of high book-to-market value stocks less the return on a portfolio of low book-to-market value stocks):

(77) $$E[R_{ct}] = R_{ft} + \beta(R_{mt} - R_{ft}) + sSMB_t + hHML_t$$

Model parameters are estimated via regression based on a pre-event estimation period, similar to short-term event studies (e.g. Kothari/Warner (1997)), or estimated post-event (e.g. Mitchell/Stafford (2000)). Simulation evidence in Kothari/Warner (1997) shows that tests based on CARs and three different asset pricing models, namely the market model, the CAPM, and the Fama-French three-factor model, all suffer from severe misspecification. This evidence is confirmed in Barber/Lyon (1997) for the Fama-French three-factor model. Simulation evidence in Lyon/Barber/Tsai (1999) on the use of the Fama-French three-factor model in conjunction with CTARs also indicates a potential for misspecification, particularly for non-random samples, e.g. samples with low market-to-book ratio. Ang/Zhang (2004), in contrast, find that tests based on the Fama-French three-factor model in conjunction with CTARs are generally well specified, but they find lower power compared to tests based on reference portfolios or matching firms. Similar findings are reported in Loughran/Ritter (2000), who explain the low power of the Fama-French three-factor model with the contamination of factor portfolios with event firms, and the equal-weighting of time periods.

Consequently, asset pricing models are not employed in the present study in order to estimate long-term abnormal returns.

Using a *matching firm*, the expected return of a sample firm is the return on a similar firm, the matching firm. Formally, where j is the matching firm:

(78) $$E[R_{it}] = R_{jt} \quad i = 1,...n; \; j = 1,...,n$$

Similarity is commonly determined using such criteria as size, market-to-book ratio, or industry code (e.g. Barber/Lyon (1997), Lyon/Barber/Tsai (1999)). The use of these criteria is motivated empirical evidence that has identified these firm characteristics as determinants of stock returns (e.g. Daniel/Titman (1995), and of course Fama/French (1992,1995, 1996a)). Therefore, this approach is also sometimes termed characteristic-based pricing model. In order to accommodate momentum, a matching on past stock performance is also sometimes recommended (Ang/Zhang (2004)). Simulation studies find that tests based on the matching firm approach lead to well-specified test statistics (Barber/Lyon (1997), Lyon/Barber/Tsai (1999), Cowan/Sergeant (2001), Ehrhardt/Koerstein (2001)). However, the power of tests is generally somewhat lower than with tests based on reference portfolios, since the use of matching firms leads to a high cross-sectional variance of abnormal returns. The literature also discusses the impact of different matching procedures. Barber/Lyon (1997) find that the impact of altering the matching procedure is generally relatively small, and recommend choosing a matching firm based on size (market capitalization) and market-to-book ratio.

The present study follows the recommendation from the literature and uses on abnormal returns calculated using matching firms. The matching procedure used is similar to Barber/Lyon (1997): The universe of stocks traded on German exchanges is ranked according to market capitalization for each year of the sample period (record date: June 30 of each respective year), and 5 size portfolios are formed. In order to counter contamination problems, stocks experiencing ECOs are purged from the size portfolios. Then, a stock is chosen as a matching firm which has the closest market-to-book value to the respective sample firm and is in the same size portfolio. When the chosen matching firm delists during the event period, its return is replaced by the market return for the subsequent periods.[179]

Using a *reference portfolio*, the expected return of a sample firm is the return on a portfolio of similar firms, the reference portfolio (e.g. Barber/Lyon (1997),

---

[179] Survivorship bias in long-term event studies and the implications of filling in the market return vs. truncating the return series are discussed in Kothari/Warner (1997) and Barber/Lyon (1997). The potential impact of missing delisting returns in financial databases are discussed in Shumway (1997)

Mitchell/Stafford (2000)). Formally, where RPt is the return on the reference portfolio:

$$E[R_{it}] = R^{i}_{Pt} \quad ; i = 1;...; n \tag{79}$$

Similarity is commonly determined by such criteria as size, market-to-book ratio, industry code, or beta. For example, Barber/Lyon (1997) form reference portfolios based on size (market capitalization) and market-to-book ratio: The population of stocks is categorized into 10 size deciles and 5 market-to-book quintiles. On this basis, 5 × 10 = 50 reference portfolios are formed. The expected return of a sample firms is the return on the reference portfolio in the same size and market-to-book ratio category.

In the literature, different approaches have been proposed for calculating the return on the reference portfolio. The return on the reference portfolio can be calculated assuming monthly rebalancing of the portfolio, or assuming a buy-and-hold strategy. Reference portfolio returns were mostly calculated under a periodic-rebalancing assumption in the earlier methodological literature (e.g. Barber/Lyon (1997), Kothari/Warner (1997)). Formally, assuming equal weighting, the return on a periodically rebalanced reference portfolio is given by the following equation, where M is the number of stocks in the reference portfolio:

$$R^{RB}_{P} = \prod_{t=1}^{T} \left(\frac{\sum_{j=1}^{M} R_{jt}}{M} + 1 \right) - 1 \tag{80}$$

The *rebalancing bias* resulting from the assumption of periodic rebalancing of a portfolio was identified by Blume/Stambaugh (1983) and Roll (1983). Depending on the extent of autocorrelation of security-specific returns, rebalancing creates an upward bias in portfolio returns. Applying these results, periodic rebalancing is commonly dropped in the more recent literature, and a buy-and-hold strategy is instead assumed (Lyon/Barber/Tsai (1999), Mitchell/Stafford (2000), Cowan/Sergeant (2001), Ehrhardt/Koerstein (2001)). Assuming equal weighting, the return on the reference portfolio is then given as the arithmetic average of the M stocks in the reference portfolio. Formally:

$$(81) \qquad R_P^{EW} = \sum_{j=1}^{M} \frac{\prod_{t=1}^{T}\left(1+R_{jt}\right)-1}{M}$$

A further methodological refinement that is commonly recommended in the more recent literature concerns the computation of a value-weighted return on the reference portfolio (e.g. Ehrhardt/Koerstein (2001), Cowan/Sergeant (2001)), where MV_{j0} is the market value of security j at time 0:

$$(82) \qquad R_P^{EW} = \frac{1}{\sum_{j=1}^{M} MV_{j0}} \sum_{j=1}^{M} MV_{j0} \prod_{t=1}^{T}\left(1+R_{jt}\right)-1$$

In simulation studies, tests based on reference portfolios as the expected return model generally perform well. The use of reference portfolios is recommended in Lyon/Barber/Tsai (1999), Cowan/Sergeant (2001), and Ehrhardt/Koerstein (2001). Particularly for small sample sizes, tests based on reference portfolios have higher power compared to the matching-firm approach (Ehrhardt/Koerstein (2001)). However, potential biases must be avoided via careful construction of the reference portfolio and the choice of an appropriate testing procedure. Apart from the rebalancing bias, Barber/Lyon (1996) identify the new listing bias and the skewness bias. The new listing bias refers to a downward bias in the reference portfolio returns from including new listings, which have been shown to underperform in the years following the IPO (Ritter (1991)). The skewness bias refers to skewness in reference portfolio returns, which can lead to misspecified test statistics. Both the rebalancing bias and the new listing bias are eliminated by using buy-and-hold reference portfolios that exclude new listings. The skewness bias is accommodated via appropriate modifications to the test statistics, discussed in the next section.

Following the recommendations in the literature, the present study uses both equal-weighted and value-weighted reference portfolios. Due to their conceptual superiority and higher degree of conservatism, value-weighted reference portfolios are considered as the main benchmark. Reference portfolios are formed by categorizing the population of German stocks into 5 size quintiles and 5 market-to-book quintiles each year of the sample period (record date: June 30 of each respective year). On this basis, $5 \times 5 = 25$ reference portfolios are formed for each year of the sample period. The return on the reference portfolio in the same size and market-to-book ratio category as the simple firm in the year of the ECO is the assigned expected return.

4.3.3.4 *Tests for significance*

Recommendations for tests of significance of long-term abnormal returns from the methodological literature are summarized in Table 13, Panel C. Conventionally, the significance of abnormal returns can be tested using standard t-statistics. CARs are standardized using either the time-series standard deviation over the event period (e.g. Kothari/Warner (1997)) or the cross-sectional standard deviation over the sample (e.g. Barber/Lyon (1997)). In this study, the cross-sectional standard deviation is applied. Formally, the test statistic is given as follows:

$$s(CAR_{iT}) = \sqrt{\frac{1}{(N-1)}\left(\sum_{i=1}^{N}(CAR_{iT} - CAR_T)^2\right)} \tag{83}$$

$$t = \frac{CAR_T}{\sqrt{N} * s(CAR_{iT})} \tag{84}$$

BHARs are commonly standardized using the cross-sectional standard deviation over the sample, since the calculation of a time-series standard deviation is infeasible (e.g. Lyon/Barber/Tsai (1999)). Formally, the test statistic is given as follows:

$$s(BHAR_{iT}) = \sqrt{\frac{1}{(N-1)}\left(\sum_{i=1}^{N}(BHAR_{iT} - BHAR_T)^2\right)} \tag{85}$$

$$t = \frac{BHAR_T}{\sqrt{N} * s(BHAR_{iT})} \tag{86}$$

While the central limit theorem should guarantee that the distribution of abnormal returns across the sample converges to the normal, although individual abnormal returns are not normally distributed (e.g. Sawyer/Gygax (2001)), simulation evidence points to misspecification of test statistics even for large samples (e.g. Cowan/Sergeant (2001)). In the literature, two issues have been identified which require modifications to the conventional test statistics given above:

- Skewness
- Cross-sectional dependence

Simulation evidence indicates that considerable *skewness* is present in BHARs (e.g. Barber/Lyon (1997), Cowan/Sergeant (2001), Ehrhardt/Koerstein (2001)). This problem originates from the comparison of single-security returns (the sample firm) to portfolio returns (the reference portfolio), which have different distributional properties. Consequently, conventional t-statistics that assume a normal distribution are misspecified. In order accommodate skewness, the literature (Lyon/Barber/Tsai (1999), Ehrhardt/Koerstein (2001) thus recommends the use of a skewness-adjusted t-statistic developed by Johnson (1978). In order to improve specification further, it is recommended to bootstrap the skewness-adjusted t-statistic (Sutton (1993)). A different recommendation to accommodate skewness is made in Cowan/Sergeant (2001). These authors recommend to winsorize abnormal returns at three standard deviations above and below the mean, respectively. This procedure successfully reduces skewness, since there are considerably more extreme positive than extreme negative abnormal returns.

The present study uses Johnson's bootstrapped skewness-adjusted t-statistic. Winsorization is not applied since the procedure effectively truncates the abnormal return distribution, which could, in the extreme, be interpreted as manipulation of the data. Johnson's skewness-adjusted t-statistic is given as follows, where t_c denotes the conventional t-statistic (Equation 86) and γ is an estimate of the coefficient of skewness:

(87) $$t_J = \sqrt{N}\left(t_c + \frac{1}{3}t_c^2\gamma + \frac{1}{6N}\gamma\right)$$

(88) $$\gamma = \frac{\sum_{i=1}^{N}(BHAR_{iT} - BHAR_T)^3}{n * s(BHAR_{iT})^3}$$

The bootstrapping procedure applied to the statistic is similar to the procedure described in Section 4.3.2.4.4 for the short-term event study. However, following a recommendation in Lyon/Barber/Tsai (1999), bootstrap resamples of size N/4 instead of N are drawn. This adjustment is due to the skewness adjustment affecting test specification (Shao (1996) and Bickel/Götze/van Zwet (1997) for further theoretical discussion; Ang/Zhang (2004) find that the resample size does not materially affect inferences). An alternative bootstrapping procedure has been developed by Brock/Lakonishok/LeBaron (1992) and Ikenberry/Lakonishok/Vermaelen (1995). This method does not bootstrap a test statistic, but calculates empirical p-values from a simulated distribution of long-term abnormal returns calculated from random samples of (non-event) firms. Lyon/Barber/Tsai (1999) find that both alternative bootstrap methods are well-specified and have comparable power. Therefore, the present study, for the sake of easier comparability with the short-term event study results, employs the bootstrapped skewness-adjusted t-statistic.

The presence of *cross-sectional dependence* of abnormal returns is particularly likely in long-term event studies due to the overlap of event periods. One solution to cross-sectional dependence is the calendar-time portfolio approach, which is not applied in the present study due to reasons discussed above (Section 4.3.3.2). However, within the BHAR approach, modifications to the test statistics can be made in order to accommodate cross-sectional dependence.[180]

Mitchell/Stafford propose a dependence-adjusted test statistic. Assuming cross-sectional dependence, the standard deviation of BHARs includes a covariance term, where ϱ_{ij} is the average pairwise correlation of the BHARs of two sample firms:

(89)
$$s_D(BHAR_{iT}) = \left[\frac{1}{(N-1)} \left(\sum_{i=1}^{N} (BHAR_{iT} - BHAR_T)^2 \right) + \frac{N-1}{N} \varrho_{ij} * s(BHAR_{iT}) * s(BHAR_{jT}) \right]^{0.5}$$

Under the simplifying assumption of equal variances of individual BHARs, a dependence-adjusted t-statistic can be calculated, which is corrected by the ratio of the two standard deviation s and sD:

(90)
$$t_{MS} = \frac{BHAR_T}{\sqrt{N} * s(BHAR_{iT})} * \frac{1}{\sqrt{1 + (N-1)\varrho_{ij}}}$$

In order to calculate the correlation coefficient ϱ, a simplified linear correlation structure is assumed: First, the correlation coefficient of BHARs is estimated for sample firms with completely overlapping event periods. Second, for sample firms with non-overlapping event periods, a correlation coefficient of zero is assumed. Third, it is assumed that the correlation coefficient declines linearly with the length of the overlap of the event period. Fourth and finally, the estimated correlation coefficients are averaged over all possible pairs of sample firms in order to calculate the overall average correlation coefficient (see Mitchell/Stafford (2000), Appendix A, for an example).

---

[180] As a further alternative, Brav (2000) proposes a Bayesian estimation approach that accommodates cross-sectional dependence, with prior beliefs generated from OLS-estimates of an asset pricing model

Cowan/Sergeant (2001) propose a two-groups t-statistic, where R_{iT} is the return on sample firm i, and R_{BT} is the return on the benchmark B, e.g. the reference portfolio or the matching firm for firm i:

(91) $$t = \frac{BHAR_i}{\sqrt{\frac{1}{N(N-1)}\left(\sum_{i=1}^{N}(R_{iT} - R_T)^2\right) + \frac{1}{N(N-1)}\left(\sum_{B=1}^{N}(R_{BT} - R_B)^2\right)}}$$

Cowan/Sergeant (2001) themselves admit that such a test is a relatively crude approach because it ignores both pairwise dependence (in contrast to the conventional t-statistic) and cross-sectional dependence. However, the two types of dependences have opposite effects on variance: Ignoring cross-sectional dependence (as the conventional t-statistic does) upwardly biases test statistics, while ignoring pairwise dependence leads to a downward bias in test statistics. In the two-groups test, these two biases (potentially) approximately cancel out.

In simulation experiments where cross-sectional dependence has been artificially induced into the data, both the Cowan/Sergeant (2001) and the Mitchell/Stafford (2000) test statistics are well-specified, while conventional t-statistics tend to be overstated.[181] Given the significant event period overlap in the sample of the present study, both the Cowan/Sergeant (2001) and the Mitchell/Stafford (2000) test statistics are applied as robustness tests in addition to the conventional t-statistics.

4.3.3.5 *Summary of empirical design*

The design of the long-term returns analysis of this study is summarized in Table 14.

Results are first presented for the full sample of observations. In a second step, the sample is split into two subsamples, ECOs announced in 1984-1997, and ECOs announced in 1998-2001, and selected results are presented in order to identify potential differences in the capital market reaction to transactions surrounding the 1999-2000 period of sustained positive stock market performance.

---

[181] The effect of ignoring cross-sectional dependence on the conventional t-statistic can be immediately seen from Equation (89): the overstatement is due to an underestimate of the standard deviation of BHARs, due to the assumption of zero covariance between sample firms

Table 14: Summary of empirical design of long-term returns analysis

Presentation of results	Full sample, two subsamples (1984-1997; 1998-2001)
Measurement interval	Periods of different lengths up to three years after ECO: +6M, +12M, +18M, +24M, +30M, +36M
Measurement scope	Abnormal returns calculated for parent, subsidiary, and weighted parent-subsidiary portfolio
Return calculation	Buy-and-hold abnormal returns, not rebalanced; Cumulative abnormal returns as robustness test
Expected return estimation	Market index (CDAX Composite) Reference portfolio, value-weighted, based on size and market-to-book ratio Reference portfolio, equal-weighted, based on size and market-to-book ratio Matching firm, based on size and market-to-book ratio
Test statistics	Conventional t-statistic, based on cross-sectional standard deviation Johnson's skewness-adjusted t-statistic Bootstrapped Johnson's skewness-adjusted t-statistic Mitchell/Stafford dependence-adjusted t-statistic Cowan/Sergeant two-sample t-statistic

4.3.4 Hypothesis tests: cross-sectional regression

4.3.4.1 Concept and relevance of cross-sectional regression analysis

Hypotheses on the determinants of abnormal returns are tested via cross-sectional regression.

Cross-sectional regression models are the standard method used in the corporate finance literature in order to investigate the association between the magnitude of abnormal returns and the characteristics of a transaction or the firms involved in the transaction (e.g. MacKinlay (1997), Binder (1998)). An early example of the use of this approach is Asquith/Mullins (1986), who analyze announcement returns to seasoned equity offerings, using such explanatory variables as offering size and prior stock returns (further examples are e.g. Vermaelen (1984) on stock repurchases, or Eckbo (1985) on corporate control). In the ECO literature, relevant examples of cross-sectional regression analysis include Allen/McConnell (1998), Vijh (2002), Powers (2003), and Elsas/Löffler (2003).

4.3.4.2 *Regression assumptions and diagnostic tests*

Typically, cross-sectional regression models are estimated via OLS (e.g. Vijh (2002), Allen/McConnell (1998) for examples from the ECO literature). The set of standard assumptions to be met for the OLS estimator to be the best linear unbiased estimator (BLUE) has been extensively discussed in the statistics literature (e.g. Hayashi (2000), Chapter 1), and is therefore not repeated here. In the following, only those assumptions likely to be violated in cross-sectional regressions with abnormal returns as the dependent variable are discussed:

- The regressors are orthogonal to the error term for all observations
- The error terms are spherical
- The error terms follow a normal distribution

The discussion that follows assumes a linear regression model of the following form, where y is a n×1 vector of dependent variables, X is an n×K data matrix, β is a K×1 vector of explanatory variables, and ε is a n×1 vector of errors:

(92) $$y = X\beta + \varepsilon$$

The first assumption is that *the regressors are orthogonal to the error term for all observations.*

The orthogonality assumption can be stated as follows in formal terms, where xjk is an independent variable k referring to observation j:

(93) $$E[x_{jk}\ \varepsilon_i] = 0;\ i, j = 1, 2, \ldots, n;\ k = 1, \ldots, K$$

Because of the assumption of the zero-mean error term, the orthogonality assumption implies that the regressors are contemporaneously uncorrelated with the error term.

In the context of the present study, this represents a potential problem: If some firms are more likely than others to undertake an event due to certain firm characteristics such as e.g. profitability, investors can use firm characteristics to rationally forecast the likelihood of the event. However, when the event is anticipated, abnormal announcement returns will be smaller in magnitude because the impact of the event has already been (partially) impounded into stock prices prior the announcement. Consequently, residuals are no longer independent from regressors, and the orthogonality assumption is violated. Thus, OLS estimators are no longer consistent. An example of anticipated events is provided by Malatesta/Thompson (1985) in the context of acquisitions. Acharya (1988) develops an econometric model that uses firm characteristics in order to forecast the probability of event announcements and incorporate it into abnormal return estimates. Eckbo/Maksimovic/Williams (1990) develop a maximum-likelihood approach that allows consistent cross-sectional estimation of abnormal returns for partially anticipated events, again in a mergers and acquisitions context. Prabhala (1997), however, shows that standard OLS remains applicable, and that conventional t-statistics represent a conservative measure of significance in the case of anticipated events, since the announcement effect underestimates the true effect of the event.

In line with the previous ECO literature, the present study therefore employs standard OLS procedures.

The next assumption is that *error terms are spherical*. The assumption of spherical error terms has two elements. The first is that the conditional variance of the error terms is constant. This is the familiar homoskedasticity assumption, which can be formally stated as follows:

$$(94) \qquad E[\varepsilon_i^2 | X] = \sigma^2 < \infty; i = 1, 2, \ldots, n$$

The second is that the conditional covariance between error terms is zero. In a time-series context, this assumption is also regularly stated as zero serial correlation or autocorrelation. In formal terms:

$$(95) \qquad E[\varepsilon_i \varepsilon_j | X] = 0; i, j = 1, 2, \ldots, n; i \neq j$$

The presence of heteroskedasticity or autocorrelation implies that the OLS estimator remains consistent, but is no longer efficient.

The presence of heteroskedasticity can be detected using a White-test (White (1980)). The strength of the White-test is that it specifically tests whether the variance-covariance matrix of the OLS estimator is affected by heteroskedasticity.[182] The White-test proceeds by conducting an auxiliary regression, where the squared residuals obtained from the original regression equation to be tested are the dependent variable, and the original explanatory variables, their squares and their cross-products are the explanatory variables. The auxiliary regression serves to determine if the variance of the residuals from the original regression equation varies systematically with any of the variables included in the original regression equation. Then, a Lagrange Multiplier test can be conducted of the joint hypothesis that all coefficients in the auxiliary regression equation are zero.[183] The test statistic is obtained by multiplying the coefficient of determination R^2 of the auxiliary regression by the number of observations N. The test statistic is Chi-square distributed, with degrees of freedom equal to the number of regressors in the auxiliary regression equation. Formally:

$$N * R^2 \sim \chi^2(m) \tag{96}$$

The presence of autocorrelation can be detected using a Durbin-Watson test (Durbin/Watson (1951)) or a Breusch-Godfrey test (Godfrey (1978), Breusch (1978), Breusch/Godfrey (1981)). The Durbin-Watson statistic tests for first-order autocorrelation. Under the null hypothesis, the error term is independent from its immediately previous value. Formally, the test statistic is given as follows, where the error terms ε are obtained from the original regression equation:

$$DW = \frac{\sum_{i=2}^{N} (\varepsilon_i - \varepsilon_{i-1})^2}{\sum_{i=2}^{N} \varepsilon_i^2} \tag{97}$$

The distribution of the Durbin-Watson statistic depends on the values of the independent variables, and an exact distribution is therefore not available; however, the distribution can be shown to lie between a lower and an upper distribution.

The Durbin-Watson test has been criticized on two aspects: It can only detect first-order autocorrelation, and it contains a substantive inconclusive region, namely the region between the lower and the upper distribution, where the null hypothesis can be neither accepted nor rejected. The more general Breusch-Godfrey test is not affected by these deficiencies. The Breusch-Godfrey test proceeds by conducting an auxiliary regression, where the residuals obtained from the original regression equation are the dependent variable, and the explanatory variables are the explanatory

---

182 Alternative tests for heteroskedasticity include the Goldfeld-Quandt test (Goldfeld/Quandt (1965)) and the Breusch-Pagan test (Breusch/Pagan (1979))

183 Engle (1984) contains a general discussion of Lagrange Multiplier (LM) tests

variables from the original regression equation, plus the lagged values of the residuals from the original regression equation. The number of lagged residual terms to be included in the second regression equation can be determined by the researcher. Then, a Lagrange Multiplier test can be conducted of the joint hypothesis that all coefficients in the auxiliary regression equation are zero. The test statistic then given as follows, where q is the number of lagged terms included in the regression:

$$(N-r)*R^2 \sim \chi^2(q) \tag{98}$$

In the present study, the White, Durbin-Watson and Breusch-Godfrey test statistics are reported in order to detect potential violations of the assumption of spherical error terms.

Implications and remedies for heteroskedasticity and cross-sectional correlation of residuals in the estimation of abnormal returns have been discussed in Section 4.3.2.4.1 of the present study. In Section 4.3.2.4.2, the SUR model has been introduced as a solution that can handle unequal residual variance, event-induced variance shifts, and cross-sectional covariance at once. As already pointed out in Gonedes/Dopuch (1974), heteroskedasticity of the error terms in a cross-sectional regression is probable when the abnormal return estimators are heteroskedastic. The violation of the homoskedasticity assumption is thus likely in typical cross-sectional event study contexts (e.g. Sefcik/Thompson (1990)). In contrast, there is no reason to expect autocorrelation in a purely cross-sectional model (although models of e.g. spatial autocorrelation in regional cross-section data have been developed, see Anselin (1988) for a general introduction). However, in the present study, there is significant calendar clustering, and event periods overlap especially in the long-term returns analysis. Thus, a certain degree of autocorrelation cannot be ruled out a priori.

Therefore, statistical techniques that correct for heteroskedasticity and potentially for autocorrelation are required in the present study. A natural solution would consist in extending the SUR approach in order to include explanatory variables for the abnormal returns. For example, in a similar setting, Sefcik/Thompson (1990), develop an estimated generalized least squares (EGLS) estimator to account for both heteroskedasticity and cross-sectional correlation. Their method involves the aggregation of event firms into a portfolio, and is thus applicable only to the case of contemporaneous events.

However, Karafiath (1994), based on Monte Carlo simulation evidence comparing different types of estimators, finds that OLS is generally well-specified in cross-sectional regressions with abnormal returns as the dependent variable for degrees of heteroskedasticity and autocorrelation typically found in an event study context. Karafiath (1994) also finds that the gain in power from using more sophisticated techniques is negligible. In a later paper, Karafiath (2004) broadly confirms her earlier results based on actual stock return data: OLS is uniformly well-specified, while weighted least squares (WLS) offers a gain in power over OLS, but shows a tendency to overreject the null hypothesis.

In light of the above evidence, the present study does not rely on EGLS procedures, but employs standard OLS. However, in order to guarantee correct inference, standard errors are adjusted for heteroskedasticity. White (1980) and MacKinnon/White (1985) have developed a heteroskedasticity-consistent covariance matrix estimator, and Newey/West (1987) have developed an estimator that can both accommodate heteroskedasticity and autocorrelation. Long/Ervin (2000) recommend the use of White's (1980) heteroskedasticity-consistent standard errors for smaller samples regardless of the result of diagnostic tests for heteroskedasticity, since these tests are found to have low power in simulations.

Under homoskedasticity, using Equation (92), the variance of the OLS estimator is given by:

(99) $$Var(\hat{\beta} \mid X) = (X'X)^{-1} X'(\sigma^2 I_N) X(X'X)^{-1}$$

which simplifies as follows:

(100) $$Var(\hat{\beta} \mid X) = \sigma^2 (X'X)^{-1} X'X(X'X)^{-1} = \sigma^2 (X'X)^{-1}$$

White's consistent estimator of the variance-covariance matrix is then given as follows, where k is the number of regressors:[184]

(101) $$\hat{\Sigma} = \frac{N}{N-k}(X'X)^{-1}\hat{\Omega}(X'X)^{-1}$$
$$\hat{\Omega} = \sum_{i=1}^{N} \varepsilon_i^2 x_i x_i'$$

---

[184] This estimator differs from the estimator suggested in White's (1980) original paper in that it contains a degree-of-freedom adjustment, namely the term N/(N-k), see MacKinnon/White (1985)

The Newey-West estimator is similar to the White estimator, but contains an adjustment for autocorrelation, where q is the number of lagged terms employed:

(102)
$$\hat{\Sigma} = \frac{N}{N-k}(X'X)^{-1}\hat{\Omega}(X'X)^{-1};$$
$$\hat{\Omega} = \frac{N}{N-k}\left[\sum_{i=1}^{N}\varepsilon_i^2 x_i x_i' + \sum_{j=1}^{q}\left(\left(1-\frac{j}{q+1}\right)\sum_{i=j+1}^{N}\left(x_i\varepsilon_i\varepsilon_{i-j}x_{i-j}' + x_{i-j}\varepsilon_{i-j}\varepsilon_i x_i'\right)\right)\right]$$

The present study thus generally employs White's (1980) heteroskedasticity consistent covariance matrix in all regression models. The Newey/West matrix (1987) is also used for comparison purposes or where diagnostic tests indicated the presence of autocorrelation. As discussed in Thompson (1996), the use of White's (1980) method has become a common approach in testing for cross-sectional relationships in the event-study literature. An applied example can be found in e.g. Dann/Masulis/Mayers (1991). In the ECO literature, White's estimator is applied in e.g. Elsas/Löffler (2003) and Powers (2003)

The third and final assumption is that *the error terms follow a normal distribution.* This assumption is not required in order for the OLS estimator to have BLUE properties. However, it is required in order for inferences from parametric hypothesis tests such as the t-test to be valid. Formally:

(103)
$$\varepsilon_i \,|X \sim N(0, \sigma^2);\ i = 1, 2, \ldots, n$$

The normality of the error term is commonly tested via the Jarque-Bera statistic (Bera/Jarque (1981)). The Jarque-Bera statistic tests whether the coefficients of skewness and of excess of a distribution kurtosis are jointly zero. It is Chi-square distributed, with 2 degrees of freedom. Formally it is given as follows, where the first term represents the coefficient of skewness, and the second term represents the coefficient of kurtosis:

(104)
$$JB = N\left[\frac{1}{6}\left(\frac{\frac{1}{N}\sum_{i=1}^{N}\varepsilon_i^3}{\left(\sqrt{\sum_{i=1}^{N}\varepsilon_i^2}\right)^3}\right)^2 + \frac{1}{24}\left(\left(\frac{\frac{1}{N}\sum_{i=1}^{N}\varepsilon_i^4}{\sum_{i=1}^{N}\varepsilon_i^2}\right)-3\right)^2\right]$$

Remedies for non-normal distributions include bootstrapping, as already discussed in Section 4.3.2.4.4. The application of bootstrap techniques to regression models is due to Freedman (1981). In the present study, bootstrapping techniques are applied in order to calculate confidence intervals for regression coefficients. In the ECO literature, a similar technique has been applied by Elsas/Löffler (2003).[185] The bootstrap procedure is similar to that described in Section 4.3.2.4.4 and proceeds as follows: N vectors are formed of the dependent variable observations yi and the associated data vector xi of explanatory variables for each i = 1, 2, …, N. Then, 10,000 random resamples of size N are drawn with replacement from the N vectors. This resampling procedure preserves the association between explanatory and dependent variable observations. For each of the random resamples, the regression equation is estimated, and a t-value is calculated from the regression coefficient and its associated standard error. The t-statistic for each resample is recorded, and critical values from the bootstrap t-distribution are calculated, similarly to Equation (70). Formally, the critical t-value $\hat{t}$ is given as follows, where β represents the original regression coefficient, β^* the bootstrap estimate, se^* its associated bootstrap standard error, and a the type I error:

(105) $$Pr^* = \left(\frac{\left|\hat{\beta}^* - \hat{\beta}\right|}{\hat{se}^*} > \hat{t} \right) = a$$

The confidence interval for the regression coefficient is then given as follows, where se is the original coefficient standard error:

(106) $$\left[\hat{\beta} - \hat{t}^{(1-a/2)}\hat{se},\ \hat{\beta} - \hat{t}^{(a/2)}\hat{se} \right]$$

The regression coefficient is significantly different from zero if the confidence interval does not include zero at the chosen significance level. The bootstrap procedure is applied in the present study as a robustness test or where the Bera-Jarque test indicates non-normality.

4.3.4.3 Model specification

Once the appropriateness of OLS estimation has been established based on the diagnostic tests discussed in the previous section, the specific regression model has to be estimated. Model specification refers to the process of selecting the functional form

---

[185] Elsas/Löffler (2003) also apply a methodological refinement to the bootstrap that adjusts for calendar clustering of events, but report no material difference in results compared to the unadjusted procedure

and the explanatory variables to be included in the regression equation to be estimated. A review of different approaches to model specification is provided by Leamer (1983), Nakamura/Nakamura/Duleep (1990), MacKinnon (1992), and in Kennedy (2000), Chapter 5. Conventionally, model specification is understood as an iterative process, where improvements of specification criteria such as goodness-of-fit are sought, while constantly ensuring fulfillment of OLS assumptions (e.g. Nakamura/Nakamura/Duleep (1990)). In the present study, a general-to-specific approach is used, where specification starts with a full model including all explanatory variables, from which redundant variables are successively eliminated (a thorough review is provided in Hendry (1993)).

A variety of tests is commonly used in order to guide model specification (e.g. Long/Trivedi (1992), Krämer/Sonnberger (1986)): Tests for the significance of individual regression coefficients and the overall significance of the model, goodness-of-fit and information criteria, tests of functional form, omitted and redundant variable tests, stability tests, and tests for multicollinearity. In the context of the present study, the following test statistics are employed in order to guide model specification:

- The statistical significance of individual regression coefficients is assessed based on conventional t-tests, and on robust t-tests using heteroskedasticity- or heteroskedasticity- and autocorrelation-consistent standard errors. T-tests are supplemented by bootstrapped confidence intervals (refer back to Section 0). The overall statistical significance of the regression is assessed based on an F-test.

- The goodness-of-fit of the regression model is assessed based on adjusted R^2, which measures the variation of the dependent variable around its mean linearly explained by the variation of the explanatory variables, adjusted for loss in degrees of freedom from the inclusion of additional explanatory variables. In addition, information criteria are used as measures striking a balance between overfitting and goodness-of-fit. These statistics are the Akaike information criterion AIC (Akaike (1973)) and the Schwarz information criterion BIC (Schwarz (1978)). Formally, the information criteria are given as follows, where k is the number of explanatory variables, N is the number of observations, and L is the sample log-likelihood:

(107) $$AIC = -2\,ln(L) + 2k$$

(108) $$BIC = -2\,ln(L) + ln(N)k$$

The rule for model selection is to choose the model specification which minimizes the respective information criterion. While the information criteria were originally developed in connection with time-series regressions, a review of the use of information criteria for model selection in cross-sectional regression is provided in (Gagné/Dayton (2002)) and in (Dayton (2003)). As can be immediately seen from the formulae, the Schwarz information criterion imposes a heavier penalty for the inclusion of additional explanatory variables.

- The stability of model specification across the sample is assessed based on a CUSUM test (Brown/Durbin/Evans (1975)). CUSUM (cumulative sum) tests are based on recursive residuals, the standardized discrepancy between the actual value of the dependent variable for observation j and the optimal forecast using only the information contained in the previous j-1 observations (applications of recursive residuals are reviewed in Kianifard/Swallow (1996)). The advantage of CUSUM tests over the Chow (1960) test is that neither the number nor the timing of possible parameter shifts have to be previously known (e.g. Krämer/Sonnberger (1986), Chapter 4, for a detailed discussion of the two tests).

  Formally, recursive residuals w_j are defined as follows:

(109) $$w_j = \frac{y_j - x_j{}'\beta_{j-1}}{\sqrt{\left(1 + x_j{}'\left(X'_{j-1}\,X_{j-1}\right)^{-1} x_j\right)}};$$
$$j = k+1,\ \ldots,\ N;\ \ X'_{j-1} = \left[x_1,\ \ldots,\ x_{j-1}\right]$$

The CUSUM statistic W_J for the first J observations is defined as follows, where the scale factor S_N is an estimate of the standard deviation of the residuals:

(110) $$W_J = \frac{1}{\sqrt{S_N}} \sum_{k+1}^{J} w_j;\quad E\left[W_J\right] = 0$$

(111) $$S_N = \frac{\sum_{k+1}^{N}\left(w_j - \sum_{k+1}^{N}\frac{w_j}{N-k}\right)^2}{N-k-1}$$

The obtained CUSUM statistic for each successive observation is then graphed. The critical values of the CUSUM statistic have been derived in Brown/Durbin/Evans (1975) based on the probability of Brownian motion sample paths exceeding certain critical values (an alternative treatment has recently been provided by Zeileis (2000)).

- Potential multicollinearity issues are detected by inspection of the correlation matrix of explanatory variables and based on the variance inflation factor (VIF). The correlation matrix of explanatory variables is based on the Pearson correlation coefficient. Formally, it is given as follows, where *x* and *y* are the variables under consideration (e.g. Wooldridge (2000), p. 714) :

(112)
$$r = \frac{\sum_{i=1}^{N} x_i y_i - \frac{1}{N}\sum_{i=1}^{N} x_i \sum_{i=1}^{N} y_i}{\sqrt{\left(\sum_{i=1}^{N} x_i^2 - \frac{1}{N}\left(\sum_{i=1}^{N} x_i\right)^2\right) * \left(\sum_{i=1}^{N} y_i^2 - \frac{1}{N}\left(\sum_{i=1}^{N} y_i\right)^2\right)}}$$

The null hypothesis of r=0 is tested with a simple t-test:

(113)
$$t = \frac{r}{\sqrt{\left(1 - r^2\right)/(N-2)}}$$

The variance inflation factor (VIF) is calculated based on the unadjusted R^2 of auxiliary regressions: Each explanatory variable is chosen as the dependent variable in turn, and regressed on all other explanatory variables. Formally:

(114)
$$VIF = \frac{1}{1 - R^2}$$

A VIF exceeding 10 is commonly interpreted as a sign of severe multicollinearity (e.g. Kleinbaum et al. (1998), p. 237).

As a final caveat, the common approach to model specification has been criticized for having the data itself instead of theoretical hypotheses guide model specification. Leamer/Leonard (1983, p. 306) write:

> "Empirical results reported in economics journals are selected from a large set of estimated models. Journals, through their editorial policies, engage in some selection, which in turn stimulates extensive model searching and prescreening by prospective authors. Since this process is well known to professional readers, the reported results are widely regarded to overstate the precision of estimates, and

> probably to distort them as well. As a consequence, statistical analyses are either greatly discounted or completely ignored."

In the same spirit, automated specification search processes such as stepwise regression are not commonly considered conceptually valid in econometrics (e.g. Leamer (1983)): A distinct danger in conducting extensive searches for the optimal model specification is data mining (Lovell (1983)): When a large number of different explanatory variables is selected at random to form regression models, a certain number of these regression models will show significant coefficients by pure chance, even if the variables are totally unrelated on theoretical grounds. Lovell (1983) shows this empirically.

In the present study, dangers of data mining are countered by the general-to-specific modeling approach, where no additional variables are added at later stages. Also, robustness is tested by using alternative specifications of the dependent variable.

4.3.4.4 *Explanatory variable definitions*

4.3.4.4.1 *Summary of explanatory variables*

In the following, the explanatory variables employed for the empirical test of the hypotheses developed in Section 3 are defined. Table 15 presents the list of explanatory variables employed, sorted by the hypothesis they relate to. In the following, the definition of the explanatory variables to test hypotheses relating to each value lever is discussed in turn. Subsequently, control variables are discussed.

4.3.4.4.2 *Variables relating to focus and investment efficiency*

In the following, the hypotheses relating to focus and investment efficiency developed in Section 3.3 are reiterated and operationalized by providing the relevant variable definitions.

In the U.S. literature on diversification, as discussed in Section 3.3.2.2, divestiture transactions such as spin-offs or sell-offs are related to reductions in the heterogeneity of divisional investment opportunities, leading to improvements in investment efficiency, in turn leading to an increase in firm value (Burch/Nanda (2003), Gertner/Powers/Scharfstein (2003), Dittmar/Shivdasani (2003), Ahn/Denis (2004)).

Investment efficiency in diversified groups of companies is measured by analyzing transfers between divisions, where transfers to segments with weak investment opportunities are interpreted as evidence of inefficient capital reallocations (e.g. the relative investment efficiency measure developed by Rajan/Servaes/Zingales (2000)).

Unfortunately, similar empirical specifications cannot be implemented for German datasets, since data on segment investment and cash flows is required. Such data is generally not available before the introduction of mandatory segment reporting in 1998 (refer back to Section 3.4.4) Therefore, the present study adopts an adapted specification, where investment efficiency is not directly measured, but assessed based on different approximate measures.

H1A: The effect of ECOs on firm value is positively related to a reduction in the heterogeneity of divisional investment opportunities post-ECO

An improvement in investment efficiency is assumed if the heterogeneity of the group of companies' investment opportunities is reduced as a consequence of the ECO. A reduction in the heterogeneity of investment opportunities is expected to improve investment efficiency by curbing inefficient transfers between segments (refer back to Section 3.3.3 for the theoretical arguments and empirical evidence supporting this relationship).

In the literature, heterogeneity (or conversely, relatedness) is assessed based on different measures, such as Herfindahl indexes, the entropy measure, qualitative classifications, or commodity flow data (for a discussion of the properties of different measures, e.g. Gorecki (1974), Fan/Lang (2000), Sambharya (2000)).

Heterogeneity measures used in the literature on investment efficiency commonly rely on segment financial data. For example, Lamont/Polk (2002) use measures of the dispersion of industry Q across the group of companies' segments, weighted by some measure of segment size, such as sales. As discussed, such measures cannot be constructed for German datasets due to the absence of segment financial data. Therefore, in a further simplification, a specification based on industry classification schemes is adopted in the present study.

Table 15: Summary of explanatory variable definitions

Hypothesis	Variable name	Description
H1A	FOCUS	Reduction in heterogeneity of investment opportunities, measured as reduction in the number of different (secondary) industry codes
H1B	OVINV	Overinvestment, measured as the industry-adjusted capex/sales ratio
H1C	DEBT_RED	Use of ECO proceeds for leverage reduction, measured as the percentage reduction in absolute debt of the group of companies
H1C	DIV_PAYOUT	Use of ECO proceeds for dividend payout, measured as the change in the dividend payout ratio of the group of companies
H2A	ASYM	Pre-ECO information asymmetrics, measured as the standard deviation of market model residuals for the parent stock in the pre-ECO year
H2B	TRANSP	Reduction in information asymmetries via the ECO, measured as the matching-firm adjusted change in the standard deviation of market model residuals
H2B	ANALYSTS	Reduction in information asymmetries via the ECO, measured as the industry-adjusted increase in the number of covering analysts
H3A	ALIGN	Interest alignment via management ownership in the subsidiary post-ECO, measured as a dummy variable taking the value of one if management owns stock in the subsidiary, zero otherwise
H3B	INFL	Influence of management on the pay setting process, measured as the combined representation of parent management on the subsidiary supervisory and management boards relative to parent ownership in the subsidiary
H3B	INFL_AR	Influence of management on the pay setting process, measured as the representation of parent management on the subsidiary supervisory board relative to parent ownership in the subsidiary
H3B	INFL_VS	Influence of management on the pay setting process, measured as the c representation of parent management on the subsidiary management board relative to parent ownership in the subsidiary
H4A	OWN_PAR	Parent control of the subsidiary, measured as parent percentage ownership in the subsidiary post-ECO
H4B	FLOAT	Relinquishment of parent control of the subsidiary, measured as the percentage free float of subsidiary stock post-ECO
H1C	DEBT_RED* OVINV	Interaction variable of overinvestment and debt reduction
H1C	DIV_PAYOUT* OVINV	Interaction variable of overinvestment and dividend payout
H1D	OWN_PAR* OVINV	Interaction variable of overinvestment and parent ownership
H1D	FLOAT* OVINV	Interaction variable of overinvestment and subsidiary free-float

The variable FOCUS thus measures the percentage reduction in the number of different industry codes of the group of companies related to the separation from the subsidiary due to the ECO. Industry codes are defined at the NACE 5-digit level and obtained from Hoppenstedt Firmendatenbank. The NACE classification contains both a primary code, which denotes the primary industry sector of the company in question, and secondary codes, which denote further industry sectors where the company in question has activities.[186] Formally, where *NOC* is the number of different NACE 5-digit industry codes:

$$FOCUS = 1 - \frac{NOC_{-1}^{Par}}{NOC_{-1}^{Par} + NOC_{-1}^{Sub}} \tag{115}$$

H1B: The effect of ECOs on firm value is negatively related to the presence of overinvestment

The presence of pre-ECO overinvestment is assumed to be negatively related to the effect on firm value since the inflow of capital due to the ECO potentially further exacerbates overinvestment. Different specifications of the variable OVINV are supposed to measure the extent of overinvestment pre-ECO, and of persistent overinvestment post-ECO.

Different alternative specifications of overinvestment are used in the empirical finance literature, mostly developed in the context of diversification research. Overinvestment in diversified firms is commonly measured by relating each division's capital expenditures to the average of stand-alone firms in the division's industry sector, and aggregating over divisions (e.g. Burch/Nanda (2003)). Overinvestment is assumed to be present if the aggregated capital expenditures/assets ratio of the diversified firm exceeds the capital expenditures/assets ratio of a portfolio of stand-alone firms from the relevant industries. Again, a simplified measure must be used in the present study due to the unavailability of segment data.

The variable OVINV is the industry-adjusted capital expenditures/sales ratio, pre-ECO, where the relevant industry is the 3-digit FTSE industry classification sector of the ECO parent (a similar measure is used in e.g. Lamont (1997)). Formally, where M is the number of firms in the ECO parent industry sector, and the time subscript -1 denotes the pre-ECO fiscal year:

---

186 For example, Siemens has 9 secondary NACE codes

(116) $$OVINV = \frac{Capex_{-1}^{Par}}{Sales_{-1}^{Par}} - \frac{1}{M}\sum_{j=1}^{M}\frac{Capex_{-1}^{j}}{Sales_{-1}^{j}}$$

For the cross-sectional regression of long-term returns, investment is measured over the three years following the ECO. Arithmetic averages of the three post-ECO years are used.

A shortcoming of this definition is that it cannot differentiate between above industry-average investment due to overinvestment, or due to superior investment opportunities. However, since segment data is not available, a more precise measure cannot be constructed.

H1C: The effect of ECOs on firm value is positively related to a payout to shareholders/ debtholders of the proceeds from the ECO

A payout of ECO proceeds is assumed to enhance value since it reduces potential overinvestment. As discussed in Section 3.3.3, the existence of internal capital markets in groups of companies increases the potential of value-destroying empire-building activities by self-interested managers.

Two variables are used in order to test H1C: DEBT_RED and DIV_PAYOUT are supposed to measure the payout of ECO proceeds to debtholders and shareholders, respectively.

The payout of ECO proceeds to debtholders is measured via the variable DEBT_RED. DEBT_RED measures the reduction in absolute debt of the group of companies, based on the pre- and post-ECO fiscal year ends. Thus, the variable captures a debt paydown contemporaneous to an ECO. It is possible that such a contemporaneous debt paydown is unrelated to the ECO itself. An ideal measure would thus directly capture the use of ECO proceeds. However, such data is generally unavailable. IPO prospectuses generally do not describe the intended use of proceeds with sufficient quantitative clarity. In an effort to directly capture the use of proceeds, press reports mentioning the planned use of ECO proceeds are sometimes used in the literature as indicator for a payout to debtholders (e.g. Allen/McConnell (1998), Vijh (2002)). However, this type of definition has the disadvantage that the precise extent of debt paydown remains unspecified. The present study therefore approximates the payout of ECO proceeds to debtholders by measuring the contemporaneous reduction in absolute debt, where debt is defined as total assets less the book value of equity. If the ECO subsidiary is consolidated, the change in absolute debt is simply the change in the group of companies' debt, based on the consolidated financial statements. If the ECO subsidiary is not consolidated post-ECO because parent ownership is reduced below the relevant threshold levels, the change in subsidiary debt is added to the change in ECO parent debt. Formally, where the time subscripts -1 and +1 denote the pre- and post-ECO fiscal years:

$$(117)\quad DEBT\_RED = \begin{cases} \dfrac{Debt_{-1}^{Par}}{Debt_{+1}^{Par}} - 1 & ;\ \textit{if sub consolidated} \\[2ex] \dfrac{Debt_{-1}^{Par}}{Debt_{+1}^{Par} + Debt_{+1}^{Sub}} - 1; & \textit{if sub unconsolidated post} - ECO \end{cases}$$

The payout of ECO proceeds to shareholders is measured via the variable DIV_PAYOUT. DIV_PAYOUT measures the change in the dividend payout ratio from the pre-ECO to the post-ECO fiscal year. Again, it is possible that a contemporaneous change in the dividend payout ratio is unrelated to the ECO itself. However, the change in the dividend payout ratio appears to be the closest possible approximation based on the data available. In calculating the change in the dividend payout ratio, special care must be taken to avoid double-counting: the ECO parent receives dividends from the ECO subsidiary, which in turn can be paid out to parent shareholders. The aggregate payout ratio of the group is thus defined as the pro-forma consolidated dividend payment, i.e. all dividends accruing to outside shareholders, divided by consolidated profits. Consolidated profits are the sum of the parent's net income after minority interest and the subsidiary's net income multiplied by the ownership stake of outside shareholders. Similarly, consolidated dividends are the parent's dividends plus the subsidiary's dividends accruing to outside shareholders. Formally, where Div denotes dividends, NI denotes net income, and the time subscripts -1 and +1 denote the pre- and post-ECO fiscal years:

$$(118)\quad DIV\_PAYOUT = \frac{Div_{+1}^{Par} + Div_{+1}^{Sub} * (1 - OWN_{+1}^{Par})}{NI_{+1}^{Par} + NI_{+1}^{Sub} * (1 - OWN_{+1}^{Par})} - \frac{Div_{-1}^{Par} + Div_{-1}^{Sub} * (1 - OWN_{-1}^{Par})}{NI_{-1}^{Par} + NI_{-1}^{Sub} * (1 - OWN_{-1}^{Par})}$$

In order to capture the role of overinvestment, the interaction terms between the payout variables and overinvestment measures are also examined. Following standard recommendations from the econometrics literature (e.g. Kleinbaum et al. (1998), Chapter 11), variables are centered around their sample means before calculating the interaction term. Formally, the interaction term is thus defined as follows, where the subscripts i and j denote firms i and j, and N is the number of firms in the sample:

$$DEBT\_RED*OVINV \equiv$$

(119) $$\left(DEBT\_RED_i - \frac{1}{N}\sum_{j=1}^{N} DEBT\_RED_j\right)*\left(OVINV_i - \frac{1}{N}\sum_{j=1}^{N} OVINV_j\right)$$

$$DIV\_PAYOUT*OVINV \equiv$$

(120) $$\left(DIV-PAYOUT_i - \frac{1}{N}\sum_{j=1}^{N} DIV\_PAYOUT_j\right)*\left(OVINV_i - \frac{1}{N}\sum_{j=1}^{N} OVINV_j\right)$$

H1D: The effect of ECOs on firm value is positively related to the creation of effective impediments against continued inefficient reallocations post-ECO via a separation of parent and subsidiary

The impact of ECOs on investment policy is not only assumed to depend on the payout of ECO proceeds and the reduction of the heterogeneity of investment opportunities. It is further hypothesized that efficiency gains from decreased heterogeneity and a smaller internal capital market can only materialize when parent and subsidiary are effectively separated post transaction. In order to test H1D empirically, the interaction effect between overinvestment (variable OVINV) and parent ownership in the subsidiary post-transaction (variable OWN_PAR, see below), and free-float of the subsidiary (variable FLOAT, see below) is analyzed. As above, variables are centered around their sample means before calculating the interaction term. Formally, the interaction term is thus defined as follows, where the subscripts i and j denote firms i and j and N is the number of firms in the sample:

$$OVINV*OWN\_PAR_i \equiv$$

(121) $$\left(OVINV_i - \frac{1}{N}\sum_{j=1}^{N} OVINV_j\right)*\left(OWN\_PAR_i - \frac{1}{N}\sum_{j=1}^{N} OWN\_PAR_j\right)$$

$$OVINV*FLOAT_i \equiv$$

(122) $$\left(OVINV_i - \frac{1}{N}\sum_{j=1}^{N} OVINV_j\right)*\left(FLOAT_i - \frac{1}{N}\sum_{j=1}^{N} FLOAT_j\right)$$

4.3.4.4.3 Variables relating to information asymmetries and disclosure

In the following, the hypotheses relating to information asymmetries and disclosure developed in Section 3.4 are reiterated, and operationalized by providing the relevant variable definitions.

H2A: The effect of ECOs on firm value is positively related to the extent of information asymmetries among investors and between investors and management prior to the transaction.

The presence of information asymmetries pre-ECO is assumed to be positively related to value creation, since the increase in mandatory disclosure due to the ECO is especially valuable when there are severe information asymmetries present prior to the transaction (refer back to Section 3.4.4).

Since information asymmetries cannot be directly measured, different empirical proxies are used in the literature (e.g. Krishnaswami/Subramaniam (1999) for a review). A particularly widely used measure is the quality of analyst coverage (e.g. Gebhardt/Lee/Swaminathan (2000), Gode/Mohanram (2003) for recent applied examples). The use of this measure builds on empirical studies on analyst recommendations.[187] Studies on the quality of analyst forecasts come to the conclusion that, despite the biases found, analyst recommendation have investment value under certain conditions. In the theoretical information asymmetries literature, Barry/Brown (1985) thus suggest the dispersion of analyst earnings forecast as an empirical measure for information asymmetries, while Merton (1987) suggests the number of analysts covering a firm. Holthausen/Verrecchia (1990) differentiate between two measures of the quality of analyst coverage, namely informedness (the prediction error of the average earnings forecast), and consensus (the dispersion of earnings forecasts). In the spin-off literature, Gilson et al. (2001) and Krishnaswami/Subramaniam (1999) show that the quality of analyst coverage improves post-transaction, and that the announcement effect is positively related to such improvement.

Unfortunately, the quality of analyst coverage is not a precise measure of information asymmetries in the context of a study on the German capital market, with a sample period beginning in the mid-1980s. The analyst culture being a relatively recent phenomenon in Germany, few companies were covered by analysts in the 1980s (see

---

[187] The earlier literature compares the prediction error of analyst forecasts to those generated by time series models (e.g. Brown/Rozeff (1978), Crichfield/Dyckman/Lakonishok (1978), Collins/Hopwood (1980), Givoly/Lakonishok (1984)). Later studies analyze systematic biases in analyst estimates (e.g. Butler/Lang (1991), Abarbanell/Bernard (1992), Easterwood/Nutt (1999), Lim (2001)), and examine if abnormal returns can be generated by trading strategies based on analyst recommendations (e.g. Womack (1996), Barber (2001)). The determinants of analyst coverage are the subject of e.g. Bhushan (1989), O'Brien/Bhushan (1990), O'Brien (1990), Stickel (1992), Sinha/Brown/Das (1997). The effect of diversification on the quality of analyst coverage is analyzed in Zuckerman (2000) and Erwin/Perry (2000)

Gerke/Oerke (1998) for a review of the importance of analysts on the German capital market). Thus, a valid measure of the quality of analyst coverage can hardly be constructed for the present dataset (e.g. Elsas/Löffler (2003) for a similar argument).

Therefore, an alternative measure of information asymmetry is used: the standard deviation of market model residuals. This measure was proposed in Bhagat/Marr/Thompson (1985) in the context of equity issuing costs and applied in e.g. Blackwell/Marr/Spivey (1990), Krishnaswami/Spindt/Subramaniam (1999), Krishnaswami/Subramaniam (1999), and Elsas/Löffler (2003). Assuming that different investor groups and firm management are equally well-informed about economy-wide factors influencing the firm's value, the unexplained (residual) volatility in stock returns is a measure of the amount of value-relevant information that is not shared by the market (Krishnaswami/Subramaniam (1999)).

The present study thus measures information asymmetries based on the standard deviation of market model residuals. The standard deviation of market model residuals for the ECO parent is calculated via OLS regression over the year (250 trading days) preceding the ECO announcement (refer back to Section 4.3.2.3 for a discussion of the market model equation). In order to test H2A empirically, the variable ASYM is defined. Formally, where ε_{t_1} is the market model residual at trading day t of the pre-ECO year:

(123)
$$ASYM = \sqrt{\frac{1}{250-1}\sum_{t_1=1}^{250}\varepsilon_{t_1}^2}$$

H2B: The effect of ECOs on firm value is positively related to the reduction of information asymmetries among investors and between investors and management after to the transaction.

Apart from the level of information asymmetries prior to the ECO, a reduction in information asymmetries thanks to the ECO is also assumed to be positively related to firm value. Concerning the measurement of a reduction in information asymmetries, the same arguments apply as for the measurement of the level of information asymmetries. Thus, in order to test H2B, the reduction in information asymmetries is measured by the reduction in the standard deviation of market model residuals from the pre-ECO to the post-ECO period. In order to capture potential industry-wide developments in the extent of information asymmetry, the reduction in market model residuals is adjusted by a matching firm. This matching firm is the firm from the same 3-digit FTSE industry classification code that is closest in market capitalization to the sample firm (ECO parent). The variable TRANSP is thus defined as follows, where $\varepsilon_{t_1}^{match}$ is the market model residual of the matching firm in the pre-ECO year, $\varepsilon_{t_2}^{match}$ is the market model residual of the matching firm in the post-ECO year, and the superscript *Par* denotes the ECO-parent:[188]

(124)
$$TRANSP = \left(\sqrt{\frac{1}{250-1}\sum_{t_2=1}^{250}\left(\varepsilon_{t_2}^{Par}\right)^2} - \sqrt{\frac{1}{250-1}\sum_{t_1=1}^{250}\left(\varepsilon_{t_1}^{Par}\right)^2} \right) - \left(\sqrt{\frac{1}{250-1}\sum_{t_2=1}^{250}\left(\varepsilon_{t_2}^{match}\right)^2} - \sqrt{\frac{1}{250-1}\sum_{t_1=1}^{250}\left(\varepsilon_{t_1}^{match}\right)^2} \right)$$

In addition, an alternative specification based on analyst coverage is used. While such a specification is expected to contain substantial measurement error due to the gaps in analyst coverage in Germany discussed above, it is nevertheless expedient to have an alternative specification as a robustness check. Due to limited data availability, the measure relies on the number of analysts covering the sample firm, and not on more complex measures of analyst informedness or consensus. The variable ANALYSTS is defined as the matching-firm adjusted change in the number of analysts covering the group of companies (ECO-parent as well as ECO-subsidiary) from the pre-ECO period to the post-ECO period. The number of analysts is identified from IBES, via Datastream (Philbrick/Ricks (1991) comment on the use of IBES data). The matching firm is identified using the same procedure employed for the variable TRANSP. The matching firm adjustment is important since the presence of analysts on the German capital market has substantially increased over the sample period, and an analysis of the unadjusted change would thus create an upward bias. Formally, where NOA_{-1} is the number of analysts covering one year prior to the ECO, and NOA_{+1} is the number of analysts covering one year post ECO, and Par, Sub, and match denote ECO-parent, ECO-subsidiary, and matching firm, respectively:

(125)
$$ANALYSTS = \frac{NOA_{+1}^{Par} + NOA_{+1}^{Sub} - NOA_{-1}^{Par}}{NOA_{-1}^{Par}} - \frac{NOA_{+1}^{match} - NOA_{-1}^{match}}{NOA_{-1}^{match}}$$

188 Alternative specifications where the standard deviation is not measured using the ECO-parent, but a portfolio of ECO-parent and ECO-subsidiary are also possible, but do not materially affect results

4.3.4.4.4 *Variables relating to incentive compensation*

In the following, the hypotheses relating to incentive compensation developed in Section 3.5 are reiterated and operationalized by providing the relevant variable definitions.

H3A: The effect of ECOs on firm value is positively related to the introduction of a stock options program or managerial equity ownership

The presence of a stock options program for ECO subsidiary management, or direct ownership of ECO subsidiary equity by the management are expected to reduce the interest divergence between management and shareholders, and thus increase firm value (refer back to Section 3.5.4).

Since stock options programs for management are a relatively recent phenomenon in Germany, a combined measure of stock options and managerial equity ownership is adopted. Also, the exact number of stock options allotted to subsidiary management cannot be determined in general:[189] Since German disclosure rules only require the disclosure of total management board compensation, precise data on individual compensation from stock options is not available Regularly, stock options programs are implemented via a conditional capital increase ("genehmigtes Kapital"). From the original Handelsregister report indicating the conditional capital increase, however, it cannot be inferred if the conditional capital increase is exploited in full, and to whom the stock options are finally granted.

In light of the above discussion, H3A is tested using a simplified measure of interest alignment: The variable ALIGN is defined as a dummy variable, equal to one when there is a stock options program for subsidiary management post-ECO, or subsidiary management directly owns a nontrivial share of subsidiary equity (>0.1%), and zero otherwise. Formally:

$$(126) \qquad ALIGN = \begin{cases} 1 & \textit{if stock options exist or managerial stock ownership} > 0.1\% \\ 0 & \textit{otherwise} \end{cases}$$

[189] For example, Epcos indicated in its IPO prospectus that it planned to grant stock options for *up to* 2,480,000 shares

H3B: The effect of ECOs on firm value is negatively related to managerial influence over the pay setting process in the subsidiary

According to the managerial power approach, self-interest managers are assumed to use their influence over the pay-setting process in order to gain excess compensation. Thus, managerial influence over the pay-setting process in the ECO subsidiary is assumed to be negatively related to firm value creation from the ECO (refer back to Section 3.5.4).

In the literature, different measures for managerial influence over the pay setting process have been developed. For example, Tosi/Gomez-Mejia (1989) used survey-based evidence, where Chief Compensation Officers were asked to rate the influence different parties on the pay-setting process. In a later paper, Tosi/Gomez-Mejia (1994) present a measure of for the monitoring of CEO compensation, based on 17 items. In another example, Finkelstein (1992) develops a measure of managerial power based on 13 items, including such elements as ownership power (derived from managerial stock ownership), or prestige power (derived from elite education or board mandates). Further examples for measures of managerial influence in the management literature can be found in Barkema/Pennings (1998) and Finkelstein/Boyd (1998).

In order to measure the concept of managerial influence over the pay setting process without using questionnaire-based qualitative data, a simpler operationalization is necessary. The present study assumes that effective control of the pay-setting process is particularly likely when ECO parent management is strongly represented on the ECO subsidiary supervisory board. It is assumed that such strong representation reduces subsidiary management influence, and thus reins in excessive pay-levels. Thus, a strong representation of parent management on the subsidiary supervisory boards is expected to be negatively related to the effect of ECOs on firm value. While this is a novel variable definition, it builds on arguments and empirical evidence from the managerial power approach: Werner/Tosi (1995) find that pay levels are lower at owner-controlled firms, and a similar conclusion is reached in Tosi/Gomez-Mejia (1994).

On the other hand, a similar effect is not expected for ECO parent management presence on the subsidiary management board: When a self-interested parent manager is present on both management boards, he cannot be assumed to have an interest in constraining subsidiary management compensation. This mirrors similar findings from the management literature, showing that manager-controlled firms are subject to higher pay levels (e.g. Barkema/Pennings (1998)).

Data on board composition is obtained from Hoppenstedt Aktienführer. The representation of parent management on the subsidiary supervisory and management boards is analyzed by manual counting of cross-mandates. H3B is then tested using three variables, namely INFL_AR, measuring the representation on the supervisory board, INFL_VS, measuring the representation on the management board, and INFL, an aggregate variable measuring the total representation on both supervisory and management board. All variables refer to the fiscal year following the ECO. Also, all variables are adjusted for the level of parent ownership in the subsidiary. Concerning the supervisory board, only the mandates pertaining to shareholder representatives are counted, the mandates of employee representatives are disregarded. Formally, where OWN_PAR_1 is the ECO parent ownership in the ECO subsidiary one year post ECO, and *NAR* is the number of shareholder representatives on the subsidiary supervisory board, *NVS* is the number of members of the subsidiary management board, *PAR* is the number of shareholder representatives on the subsidiary supervisory board that are parent management board members, and *PVS* is the number of subsidiary management board members that are also parent management board members:

(127) $$INFL\_AR = \frac{PAR / NAR}{OWN\_PAR_1}$$

(128) $$INFL\_VS = \frac{PVS / NVS}{OWN\_PAR_1}$$

(129) $$INFL = \frac{INFL\_AR + INFL\_VS}{2}$$

4.3.4.4.5 *Variables relating to ownership concentration*

In the following, the hypotheses relating to ownership concentration developed in Section 3.6 are reiterated, and operationalized by providing the relevant variable definitions.

H4A: The effect of ECOs on firm value is positively related to the fraction of ownership retained by the parent company in the subsidiary immediately post-ECO

It is assumed that alternative control structures develop only over time, and that the beneficial effects of blockholder monitoring thus outweigh potential expropriation of subsidiary shareholders based on collusion of parent and subsidiary management in the short-term (refer back to Section 3.6.4)

In order to test H4A, the variable OWN_PAR is employed. OWN_PAR measures the fraction of ownership retained by the ECO parent in the subsidiary, immediately post ECO. In the ECO literature, similar variable definitions are used in e.g. Allen/McConnell (1998).

H4B: The effect of ECOs on firm value is positively related to a subsequent relinquishment of parent control

In the longer term, it is assumed that the detrimental effects of blockholder control dominate the beneficial effects of monitoring. Thus, firm value is expected to increase when the parent relinquishes control subsequent to the ECO.

The variable FLOAT is employed in order to test H4B. FLOAT measures the proportion of shares that are free-float (i.e. not owned by a blockholder), three years after the ECO. The three-year period corresponds to the event period chosen in the long-term returns analysis. Free-float is defined as any shares that are not owned by the ECO parent, management, or an outside blockholder with at least a 5% stake. The 5% threshold is common in the literature on ownership concentration (e.g. Morck/Shleifer/Vishny (1988)).

4.3.4.4.6 Control variables: Operating ratios and market timing

In addition to the explanatory variables related to agency theory discussed in the previous section, control variables are included in the regression model. Control variables do not relate to the agency-cost related hypotheses on the effect of ECOs on firm value, but control for firm characteristics or capital market conditions unrelated to agency considerations which might influence abnormal returns. The inclusion of control variables in cross-sectional regression models is common in the ECO literature (e.g. Elsas/Löffler (2003), Vijh (2002)). Table 16 presents the list of control variables.

The control variables are chosen in order to capture potential effects on abnormal returns originating from certain operating ratios, and from market timing.

As far as operating ratios are concerned, the variable LEVERAGE refers to the ECO parent leverage at the fiscal year end prior to the ECO. The variable RELSIZE refers to the relative size of the subsidiary, and is defined as subsidiary total assets divided by parent total assets, both at the fiscal year end prior to the ECO. The variable PSIZE refers to the ECO parent size, measured as total assets at the fiscal year end preceding the ECO. The variable ROA refers to the industry-adjusted ECO parent return on assets over the fiscal year preceding the ECO.[190]

As far as market timing is concerned, five potential indicator variables are included. Baker/Wurgler (2002) describe market timing as the practice of "issuing shares at high prices and repurchasing at low prices" (p. 1). Market timing has been repeatedly identified as a reason for the clustering of IPOs in certain periods, the so-called "hot issue periods", during which capital market conditions are particularly favorable for equity issuance (e.g. Ibbotson/Jaffe (1975), Ritter (1984); Wasserfallen/Wittleder (1994) present German evidence). In the recent literature, a lively debate has developed on the potentially far-reaching and persistent impact of market timing on capital structure (Baker/Wurgler (2002), Huang/Ritter (2004), Alti (2004), Flannery/Rangan (2004), Hovakimian (2004), Kayhan/Titman (2004)).

Three potential explanations for the clustering of equity issuance have been developed: the time-variation of capital demand along macroeconomic cycles (Choe/Masulis/Nanda (1993)); the time-variation in the adverse selection costs of issuing equity in the spirit of Myers/Majluf (1984), analyzed in Lucas/McDonald (1990) and Bayless/Chaplinsky (1996); and the time-variation in investor sentiment (e.g. Lowry (2003)), where equity issuance is concentrated in periods of overoptimism.

The three theoretical explanations for market timing lead to different predictions concerning the pattern of abnormal returns surrounding ECOs. The macroeconomic explanation does not predict abnormal returns. The adverse selection explanation, refined by Nanda (1991) for the application to ECOs, predicts a positive abnormal announcement return since the undervaluation signal concerning the (larger) parent outweighs the overvaluation signal concerning the (smaller) subsidiary; but zero long-term abnormal returns, since the announcement effect ensures correct pricing of the

---

[190] In order to calculate industry-adjustment, the equal-weighted arithmetic average ROA of firms in the same 3-digit FTSE industry sector is deducted from parent ROA

issue. The investor sentiment explanation predicts a positive abnormal announcement return since investors overreact to the positive news conveyed by the announcement, and negative long-term abnormal returns, when arbitrageurs gradually correct the initial overreaction.

Within the ECO literature, market timing has been analyzed in Hand/Skantz (1998), Vijh (2002), Wagner (2004) and Fucks (2004). While Hand/Skantz (1998) find that ECOs, similarly to IPOs, are clustered in periods of favorable market conditions, they do not examine the potential relationship between ECO market timing and abnormal returns. Vijh (2002), as already reviewed, finds contradictory evidence to Nanda's (1991) model. Wagner (2004) does not find an influence of market timing on short-term abnormal returns for German ECO announcements. Fucks (2004) does not find an influence of market timing on the fraction of ownership offered for German ECOs. In a more general context, Lowry (2003) does not find a significant relationship between market timing and post-IPO long-term abnormal returns.

While the existence of market timing of equity issues is accepted by most researchers, and its potential influence on issuing patterns and capital structure is extensively discussed, an influence of market timing on post-issue *abnormal* returns (as opposed to *absolute* returns) therefore cannot be a priori expected.

Following the literature, different variables are used as market timing indicators. The variable CDAXPRIOR measures the CDAX performance during the calendar year preceding the ECO, based on e.g. Lucas/McDonald (1990), predicting an increase in equity issuance after a period of sustained superior market performance. The variable CDAXPOST measures the CDAX performance during the calendar year succeeding the ECO, based on e.g. Baker/Wurgler (2000), who identified equity issuance as a predictor of a drop in stock market performance. The variable CDAXPRIOR-CDAXPOST is the difference between pre- and post-issue market performance (following e.g. Hand/Skantz (1998)). The variable IPOSPRIOR measures the number of IPOs in the calendar year preceding the ECO, based on e.g. Bayless/Chaplinsky (1996), who analyzed the clustering of equity issuance in "hot" and "cold" markets, or Fucks (2004) in an ECO context. Finally, the variable CDAX_PE measures the price-earnings ratio of the CDAX composite index on the ECO announcement day, assuming that equity issuance is clustered in periods where the market is highly valued compared to historical averages.

Table 16: Control variables

Hypothesis	Variable name	Description
Control	LEVERAGE	Parent leverage pre-ECO
Control	RELSIZE	Relative size of subsidiary, measured as subsidiary total assets relative to parent total asset pre-ECO
Control	PSIZE	Parent size, measured as parent assets pre-ECO
Control	ROA	Parent Return on Assets pre-ECO, industry-adjusted
Control	CDAXPRIOR	Market timing indicators, measured as CDAX performance in the year prior to the ECO, in the year post ECO, the difference between prior and posterior performance, the number of IPOs in the year prior to the ECO, and the CDAX price-earnings ratio on the announcement day
Control	CDAXPOST	
Control	CDAXPRIOR-CDAXPOST	
Control	IPOSPRIOR	
Control	CDAX_PE	

4.3.4.5 *Dependent variable definitions*

The cross-sectional regression models estimated in the present study employ both short-term and long-term measures of abnormal returns as dependent variables. While under the concept of capital market efficiency, long-term abnormal returns cannot be systematically different from zero, and the agency variables defined above are therefore by definition unrelated to long-term abnormal returns, a long-term analysis is instructive for the reasons discussed in Section 2.5.1: Relaxing the assumption of capital market efficiency, the short-term capital market reaction cannot be equated with the full economic effect of an event, and the long-term reaction is therefore the ultimate yardstick for value creation.

In order to test the significance of ***short-term abnormal returns***, cumulative standardized prediction errors (CSPEs) of the ECO parent are used as the dependent variable. The rationale for choosing CSPEs instead of cumulative abnormal returns is to make abnormal performance directly comparable across sample firms with different return volatility. Cumulative abnormal returns are also used as a robustness test. Reiterating Equation (42) from Section 4.3.2.4.1, the cumulative standardized prediction error of firm i is defined as:

(130)
$$CSPE_i = CAR_i / SD_i = \sum_{t=1}^{k} AR_{it} \Bigg/ \sqrt{\left[\left(\frac{1}{T-2}\right)\sum_{t=1}^{T} AR_{it}^2\right]\left[k + \frac{k^2}{T} + \frac{\sum_{t=1}^{k} R_{mt} - k(\bar{R}_m)^2}{\sum_{t=1}^{T}(R_{mt} - \bar{R}_m)^2}\right]}$$

Event windows of different lengths are used to form CSPEs in order to ensure robustness of results. However, longer event windows are generally preferred because of the likelihood of gradual information transmission discussed in Section 4.3.2.2. Thus, CSPE -30 0, the cumulative standardized prediction error calculated over the 30 days preceding the ECO announcement, constitutes the main dependent variable of interest.

In order to test the significance of ***long-term abnormal returns***, CSPEs are used as the dependent variable as well. Long-term CSPEs are calculated similarly to short-term CSPEs, however, the adjustment term for out-of sample forecast can be eliminated since a separate estimation period does not exist. Formally, the cumulative standardized prediction error for firm i is then given as follows, where T represents the number of days in the event period:

$$CSPE_i^{LT} = CAR_i / s_i = \sum_{t=1}^{T} AR_{it} \Bigg/ \sqrt{\left(\frac{1}{T-2}\right)\sum_{t=1}^{T} AR_{it}^2} \tag{131}$$

As a robustness check, different estimation procedures for the expected return, as discussed in Section 4.3.3.3, are used. Also, BHARs are employed in place of CSPEs.

4.3.4.6 Expected signs of explanatory variables

The expected signs of the dependent variables are summarized in Table 17. While the expected signs of the variables in models relating to the short-term capital market reaction immediately follow from the hypotheses developed in Section 3 and the variable definitions discussed above, care must be taken concerning models relating to the long-term capital market reaction.

As discussed above, a cross-sectional analysis of the determinants of long-term returns is instructive despite the apparent contradiction to the assumption of capital market efficiency. In the present study, the assumption of capital market efficiency is maintained insofar as variables relating to information that is fully revealed to the capital market on the ECO announcement are expected to be unrelated to long-term abnormal returns. For example, the variable FOCUS is assumed to be unrelated to long-term abnormal returns, since industry codes of parent and subsidiary are known on the ECO announcement.

Table 17: Expected signs of explanatory variables

Hypothesis	Variable name	Expected sign	
		Short-term	Long-term
H1A	FOCUS	+	
H1B	OVINV	-	-
H1C	DEBT_RED	+	
H1C	DIV_PAYOUT	+	
H2A	ASYM	+	
H2B	TRANSP	-	-
H2B	ANALYSTS	-	-
H3A	ALIGN	+	
H3B	INFL	+	+
H3B	INFL_AR	+	+
H3B	INFL_VS	+/-	
H4A	OWN_PAR	+	
H4B	FLOAT		+
H1C	DEBT_RED*OVINV	+	
H1C	DIV_PAYOUT*OVINV	+	
H1D	OWN_PAR*OVINV	-	
H1D	FLOAT*OVINV		+

The same applies to DEBT_RED and DIV_PAYOUT (planned use of the proceeds is disclosed on announcement), ASYM (extent of pre-ECO information asymmetry is known), ALIGN (planned use of stock-based compensation is disclosed), and OWN_PAR (parent stake sold in ECO is disclosed). In contrast, variables where additional information is revealed post-ECO, and where full anticipation of this information cannot be assumed, are expected to be related to long-term abnormal returns. For example, it is not known whether overinvestment is maintained post-ECO (variable OVINV). Similar arguments apply to TRANSP and ANALYSTS (the actual reduction in information asymmetry is revealed over time), INFL (it cannot be fully anticipated to what extent the parent maintains board mandates in the subsidiary), and FLOAT (it cannot be anticipated if and when the parent relinquishes control of the subsidiary).[191] These considerations lead to the expected dependent variable signs in the long-term analysis shown in Table 17.

[191] Under strict capital market efficiency, the capital market would form rational expectations on the development of these variables, and these expectations could not be systematically in error.

4.3.4.7 *Summary of empirical design*

The empirical design of the cross-sectional regression analysis is summarized in Table 18. Due to the limited sample size, results are presented exclusively for the full sample; subsample regressions, similar to the analysis of subsample short-term and long-term abnormal returns, are not performed. Instead, the stability of regression results across sample periods is evaluated based on CUSUM tests (refer back to Section 4.3.4.3).

Table 18: Summary of empirical design of cross-sectional regression

Estimation Technique	Multivariate OLS Regression
Modeling approach	General-to-specific
Dependent Variables	Cumulative standardized prediction errors; Short term: -30 0 Long term: +36M
Regression diagnostics	Heteroskedasticity: White test Autocorrelation: Durbin-Watson test, Breusch-Godfrey test (3 lags) Normality: Jarque-Bera Test
Model specification criteria	Overall significance: F-test Coefficient significance: t-test Goodness-of-fit: Adjusted R^2 Information criteria: Akaike, Schwarz Stability: CUSUM test Multicollinearity: Variance inflation factor
Robustness checks	Alternative definitions of dependent variable: Cumulative abnormal returns, event periods of different lenghts, thin-trading adjustments Bootstrapped confidence intervals Alternative standard errors: conventional, White heteroskedasticity-consistent, Newey-West autocorrelation and heteroskedasticity-consistent

4.4 Results

4.4.1 Abnormal returns

4.4.1.1 Short-term abnormal returns

4.4.1.1.1 Results for the full sample

In the following, the results of the short-term abnormal returns analysis for the full sample are presented. First, results based on OLS market model regressions are reported. Table 19 presents short-term abnormal returns surrounding the ECO announcement as calculated from the standard market model. Table 20 presents the results for the Scholes-Williams market model, and Table 21 presents the results for the Dimson market model. The three tables are identically structured: Panel A reports average abnormal returns (AR), and Panel B reports standardized prediction errors (SPE) for five days surrounding the ECO announcement day (day 0). Panel C reports cumulative average abnormal returns (CAR) over multiday event periods preceding and following the ECO announcement, and Panel D report cumulative standardized prediction errors. Below the return data, t-statistics are reported. In Panels A and C, a t-statistic based on the portfolio time-series standard deviation (Equation (33)), and an ordinary cross-sectional t (Equation (46)) are reported. In Panels B and D, a standardized t-statistic (Equation (43)) and a standardized cross-sectional t (Equation (47)) are reported. Below the conventional t-statistics, bootstrapped t-statistics are reported.[192] In addition, a non-parametric sign-test is presented (Equation (67)). Following standard notation, * denotes statistical significance at the 10%-level, ** at the 5% level, and *** at the 1% level.

The following discussion begins with Table 19, the standard market model. As shown in Panel A, there is an average abnormal return of 1.26% on the day of the ECO announcement. This positive abnormal return is statistically significant based on all the

[192] In the literature, bootstrap results are often presented by reporting the percentile of the bootstrap distribution in which the conventional t-statistic falls. In the present study, however, a bootstrapped t-statistic is reported for easier comparison with the conventional t-statistic. This statistic is arrived at by first calculating the percentile of the boostrap distribution, and then calcuating the t-statistic corresponding to the percentile under the assumption that the test statistic is t-distributed

alternative measures employed, although only at the 10% level based on the ordinary cross-sectional t. Neither of the five days preceding or succeeding the announcement day exhibits robust abnormal returns in either direction. The analysis of standardized prediction errors in Panel B confirms these results. Looking at the bootstrapped standardized cross-sectional t, which should be considered the main significance measure for methodological reasons (refer back to the discussion in Section 4.3.2.4.4), the announcement day SPE of 0.49 is significant at the 5%-level with a t-value of 2.61. Again, neither of the preceding or succeeding days shows significant standardized prediction errors.

Turning to the analysis of cumulative abnormal returns, Panel C shows a strongly significant cumulative abnormal return of 11.09% during the 30 days up to and including the ECO announcement day. Shorter multiday event periods preceding the announcement day also exhibit highly significant abnormal returns, considering all alternative measures of significance. For example, over the 15 days up to and including the ECO announcement day, the abnormal return is 9.08%. No significant abnormal returns can be detected in post-announcement periods.

A graphical analysis of cumulative abnormal returns, presented in Figure 21, confirms this pattern. Apparently, an upward trend in abnormal returns begins on around day -20: the capital market thus seems to anticipate the public ECO announcement. The reaction on the actual (public) announcement day is only related to the least informed investors who have received no prior information via other channels, or related to a further increase in the probability of the planned transaction actually taking place associated with a public announcement. The implications of this pattern for the informational efficiency of the capital market are discussed in more detail in Section 4.5.3.1.

Panel D, the cumulative standardized prediction errors, further confirms these results: CSPEs are significantly positive in pre-announcement periods, but not significantly different from zero in post-announcement periods.

Table 19: Short-term abnormal returns, standard market model

Panel A: Abnormal Returns	-5	-4	-3	-2	-1
AR	0.54%	0.58%	-0.22%	0.36%	0.49%
Portfolio time-series t	1.58	1.72 *	-0.64	1.07	1.46
Bootstrapped value	1.03	1.06	-0.71	0.79	1.20
Ordinary cross-sectional t	1.00	1.05	-0.71	0.78	1.18
Bootstrapped value	1.03	1.07	-0.73	0.78	1.20
Sign test	2.97 ***	0.78	0.23	-0.04	0.23

Panel B: Standardized Prediction Errors	-5	-4	-3	-2	-1
SPE	0.23	0.43	-0.08	0.10	0.11
Standardized t	1.68 *	3.14 ***	-0.61	0.74	0.83
Bootstrapped value	1.54	1.19	-0.93	0.85	0.94
Standardized cross-	1.59	1.17	-0.95	0.89	0.95
Bootstrapped value	1.56	1.20	-0.94	0.85	0.92

Panel C: Cumulative Abnormal Returns	-30 0	-25 0	-20 0	-15 0	-10 0	-5 0
CAR	11.09%	10.20%	9.44%	9.18%	6.33%	3.01%
Portfolio time-series t	5.89 ***	5.91 ***	6.09 ***	6.79 ***	5.64 ***	3.64 ***
Bootstrapped value	2.70 ***	3.00 ***	3.15 ***	3.00 ***	2.68 **	2.19 **
Ordinary cross-sectional t	3.10 ***	3.24 ***	3.40 ***	3.76 ***	3.02 ***	2.09 **
Bootstrapped value	3.33 ***	3.52 ***	3.71 ***	4.21 ***	3.17 ***	2.18 **
Sign test	2.70 ***	2.97 ***	2.70 ***	3.79 ***	2.15 **	2.97 ***

Panel D: Cumulative Standardized Prediction Errors	-30 0	-25 0	-20 0	-15 0	-10 0	-5 0
CSPE	0.57	0.62	0.60	0.67	0.60	0.52
Standardized t	4.24 ***	4.62 ***	4.45 ***	4.99 ***	4.44 ***	3.86 ***
Bootstrapped value	3.06 ***	3.17 ***	3.06 ***	3.11 ***	2.80 ***	2.45 **
Standardized cross-	5.48 ***	5.53 ***	4.83 ***	5.16 ***	4.57 ***	4.10 ***
Bootstrapped value	5.04 ***	5.08 ***	4.44 ***	4.74 ***	4.21 ***	4.00 **

Table 19 (continued)

0	1	2	3	4	5
1.26%	-0.40%	-0.23%	0.17%	0.41%	0.19%
3.72 ***	-1.19	-0.68	0.50	1.20	0.55
1.88 *	-0.86	-1.03	0.45	0.99	0.54
1.81 *	-0.83	-1.00	0.44	0.97	0.54
1.84 *	-0.87	-1.02	0.45	0.98	0.56
3.79 ***	-0.59	-0.86	1.05	1.05	-0.04

0	1	2	3	4	5
0.49	-0.16	-0.02	-0.02	0.20	0.01
3.63 ***	-1.15	-0.12	-0.13	1.50	0.06
2.65 ***	-1.17	-0.20	-0.13	1.58	0.09
2.65 **	-1.20	-0.20	-0.12	1.59	0.10
2.61 **	-1.18	-0.19	-0.11	1.60	0.10

1 5	1 10	1 15	1 20	1 25	1 30
0.13%	-0.11%	1.95%	0.94%	-0.20%	-0.57%
0.17	-0.10	1.49	0.62	-0.12	-0.31
0.17	-0.80	0.17	0.01	-0.01	-0.03
0.05	-0.74	0.46	-0.29	-0.93	-1.07
0.05	-0.75	0.47	-0.29	-0.95	-1.08
0.23	1.60	2.15**	1.05	0.51	0.78

1 5	1 10	1 15	1 20	1 25	1 30
0.01	0.02	0.15	0.08	0.00	0.01
0.05	0.16	1.12	0.56	0.02	0.05
0.05	0.23	1.43	0.58	0.02	0.06
0.14	0.47	1.50	0.73	0.12	0.33
0.14	0.46	1.47	0.73	0.12	0.33

Table 20: Short-term abnormal returns, Scholes-Williams market model

Panel A: Abnormal Returns

	-5	-4	-3	-2	-1
AR	0.47%	0.47%	-0.36%	0.37%	0.23%
Portfolio time-series t	1.33	1.33	-1.04	1.07	0.65
Bootstrapped value	0.91	0.84	-1.13	0.83	0.50
Ordinary cross-sectional t	0.87	0.82	-1.11	0.81	0.48
Bootstrapped value	0.90	0.84	-1.13	0.80	0.49
Sign test	1.91 *	0.82	-0.01	0.27	-0.28

Panel B: Standardized Prediction Errors

	-5	-4	-3	-2	-1
SPE	0.19	0.40	-0.11	0.09	0.08
Standardized t	1.42	2.94 ***	-0.82	0.68	0.56
Bootstrapped value	1.31	1.10	-1.22	0.80	0.61
Standardized cross-	1.34	1.09	-1.25	0.83	0.63
Bootstrapped value	1.37	1.11	-1.28	0.83	0.64

Panel C: Cumulative Abnormal Returns

	-30 0	-25 0	-20 0	-15 0	-10 0	-5 0
CAR	9.60%	8.72%	8.26%	8.43%	5.52%	2.43%
Portfolio time-series t	4.92 ***	4.88 ***	5.14 ***	6.01 ***	4.74 ***	2.83 ***
Bootstrapped value	2.47 **	2.75 ***	2.76 ***	2.82 ***	2.37 **	1.75 *
Ordinary cross-sectional t	2.38 **	2.48 **	2.70 ***	3.18 ***	2.34 **	1.50
Bootstrapped value	2.51 **	2.62 **	2.84 ***	3.22 ***	2.41 **	1.53
Sign test	2.73 **	1.64	2.19 **	3.83 ***	2.19 **	2.19 **

Panel D: Cumulative Standardized Prediction Errors

	-30 0	-25 0	-20 0	-15 0	-10 0	-5 0
CSPE	0.50	0.54	0.53	0.62	0.53	0.45
Standardized t	3.70 ***	4.02 ***	3.90 ***	4.58 ***	3.95 ***	3.37 ***
Bootstrapped value	2.97 ***	3.12 ***	2.95 ***	3.14 ***	2.51 **	2.12 **
Standardized cross-	3.57 ***	3.71 ***	3.52 ***	3.99 ***	3.11 ***	2.18 **
Bootstrapped value	4.68 ***	4.21 ***	4.00 ***	4.21 ***	3.33 ***	2.26 **

Table 20 (continued)

0	1	2	3	4	5
1.26%	-0.49%	-0.32%	0.26%	0.30%	0.04%
3.60 ***	-1.40	-0.91	0.75	0.86	0.10
1.86 *	-1.02	-1.33	0.66	0.70	0.10
1.81 *	-1.00	-1.00	-1.29	0.65	0.69
1.86 *	-1.03	-1.33	0.66	1.30	0.72
3.28 ***	-0.01	-1.10	1.09	0.54	0.27

0	1	2	3	4	5
0.50	-0.17	-0.04	0.01	0.19	-0.03
3.67 ***	-1.28	-0.31	0.09	1.38	-0.22
2.64 **	-1.33	-0.51	0.09	1.45	-0.34
2.70 ***	-1.35	-0.52	0.08	1.46	-0.35
2.78 ***	-1.39	-0.53	0.08	1.49	-0.36

1 5	1 10	1 15	1 20	1 25	1 30
-0.21%	-1.10%	0.59%	-0.39%	-1.69%	-1.88%
-0.27	-0.99	0.44	-0.25	-0.96	-0.98
-0.26	-0.72	0.74	0.16	-0.52	-0.50
-0.38	-1.61	-0.49	-1.05	-1.69 *	-1.65 *
-0.40	-1.67	-0.50	-1.05	-1.73 *	-1.61 *
-0.01	1.64	1.36	0.82	-0.28	0.54

1 5	1 10	1 15	1 20	1 25	1 30
-0.02	-0.06	0.06	0.01	-0.06	-0.04
-0.17	-0.47	0.44	0.04	-0.45	-0.26
-0.20	-0.52	0.51	0.04	-0.59	-0.39
-0.30	-0.90	0.15	-0.25	-1.00	-0.78
-0.32	-0.92	0.16	-0.25	-1.02	-0.79

Table 21: Short-term abnormal returns, Dimson market model

Panel A: Abnormal Returns					
	-5	-4	-3	-2	-1
AR	0.25%	0.13%	-0.43%	0.17%	0.23%
Portfolio time-series t	0.64	0.33	-1.08	0.43	0.58
Bootstrapped value	0.46	0.21	-1.26	0.36	0.50
Ordinary cross-sectional t	0.45	0.21	-1.24	0.36	0.50
Bootstrapped value	0.48	0.23	-1.27	0.35	0.52
Sign test	0.77	1.05	-1.93 *	-0.31	-0.85

Panel B: Standardized Prediction Errors					
	-5	-4	-3	-2	-1
SPE	0.09	0.10	-0.15	0.04	0.04
Standardized t	0.67	0.75	-1.13	0.29	0.30
Bootstrapped value	0.46	1.13	-1.48	0.34	0.23
Standardized cross-	0.66	0.53	-1.80 *	0.40	0.36
Bootstrapped value	0.64	0.53	-1.75 *	0.38	0.34

Panel C: Cumulative Abnormal Returns						
	-30 0	-25 0	-20 0	-15 0	-10 0	-5 0
CAR	11.47%	9.75%	9.49%	8.73%	5.97%	1.72%
Portfolio time-series t	5.17 ***	4.80 ***	5.20 ***	5.48 ***	4.52 ***	1.76 *
Bootstrapped value	3.08 ***	2.74 ***	2.75 ***	2.88 ***	3.60 ***	1.78 *
Ordinary cross-sectional t	3.23 ***	3.03 **	3.35 **	3.36 ***	2.61 **	0.90
Bootstrapped value	4.00 ***	3.52 ***	3.78 ***	3.87 ***	2.93 ***	0.96
Sign test	3.21 ***	2.94	2.94	2.67 **	2.67 **	1.59

Panel D: Cumulative Standardized Prediction Errors						
	-30 0	-25 0	-20 0	-15 0	-10 0	-5 0
CSPE	0.50	0.48	0.47	0.49	0.42	0.23
Standardized t	3.75 ***	3.59 ***	3.51 ***	3.65 ***	3.18 ***	1.75 *
Bootstrapped value	3.87 ***	3.78 ***	3.31 ***	3.42 ***	3.60 ***	2.49 **
Standardized cross-	4.42 ***	4.09 ***	3.97 ***	3.82 ***	3.01 ***	1.21
Bootstrapped value	4.28 ***	3.96 ***	3.84 ***	3.70 ***	2.91 ***	1.18

Table 21 (continued)

0	1	2	3	4	5
1.37%	-0.26%	0.14%	-0.03%	0.31%	0.56%
3.43 ***	-0.64	0.35	-0.07	0.78	1.27
1.93 *	-0.48	0.53	-0.07	0.76	1.18
1.92 *	-0.47	0.54	-0.06	0.76	1.16
2.14 **	-0.59	0.59	-0.06	0.99	1.52
3.48 ***	-0.31	-0.04	1.05	0.23	0.77

0	1	2	3	4	5
0.46	-0.07	0.08	-0.01	0.13	0.09
3.40 ***	-0.49	0.61	-0.07	0.93	0.69
3.52 ***	-0.79	0.69	-0.09	1.45	0.70
2.82 ***	-0.53	1.01	-0.08	1.20	1.09
2.74 ***	-0.50	0.99	-0.08	1.16	1.07

1 5	1 10	1 15	1 20	1 25	1 30
0.67%	0.09%	2.26%	1.67%	0.64%	0.35%
0.76	0.07	1.47	0.94	0.32	0.16
0.71	0.06	1.34	0.82	0.27	0.15
0.86	-0.22	0.81	0.25	-0.31	-0.42
1.01	-0.25	0.94	0.29	-0.36	-0.48
0.23	1.86 *	1.32	1.05	0.23	1.32

1 5	1 10	1 15	1 20	1 25	1 30
0.22	0.07	0.20	0.16	0.08	0.07
0.75	0.56	1.50	1.20	0.58	0.56
0.98	0.70	1.99 *	1.65	0.80	0.60
1.20	0.74	1.81 *	1.15	0.38	0.41
1.18	0.71	1.76 *	1.12	0.38	0.40

Figure 21: Cumulative average abnormal returns surrounding ECO announcement, full sample

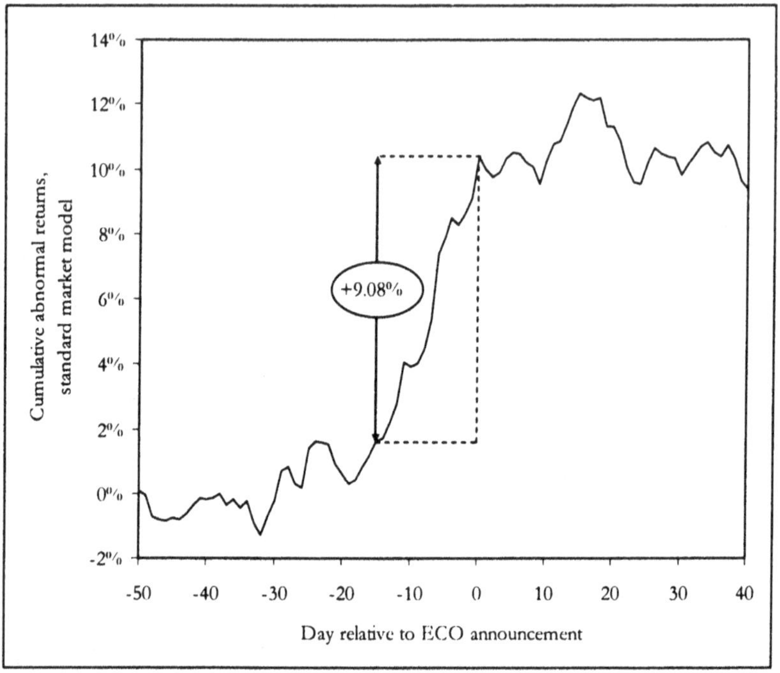

From a methodological viewpoint, the following points deserve highlighting:

- Results are generally robust to variations in testing methodology. The non-parametric sign-test confirms the results of parametric t-tests.
- The use of standardized prediction errors instead of abnormal returns generally results in a gain of statistical significance.
- The accommodation of event-induced variance shifts via the application of the Boehmer/Musumeci/Poulsen (1991) cross-sectional procedures reduces statistical significance: Part of the abnormal return is accounted for by an event-related variance increase.

- The application of bootstrapping procedures mostly results in a loss of statistical significance, which is especially pronounced for portfolio-time series t. This pattern is due to the high degree of non-normality of abnormal returns.

Table 20 repeats the analysis based on the Scholes-Williams market model, while Table 21 shows the results based on the Dimson market model. In general, the impact of the adjustments for thin-trading based on either method is relatively minor: Under the standard market model, the announcement day average abnormal return is 1.26%, while it is an identical 1.26% under Scholes-Williams, and 1.37% under Dimson. Standardized prediction errors are also very similar, with an announcement day SPE of 0.49 under the standard market model, 0.50 under Scholes-Williams, and 0.46 under Dimson. Consequently, levels of statistical significance are largely comparable under the Scholes-Williams and the Dimson method.

Table 22 compares parameter estimates under the three OLS market model approaches: standard, Scholes-Williams, and Dimson. Consistent with theoretical predictions, the standard market model beta estimates are significantly lower than both the Scholes-Williams and Dimson estimates: The average standard market model beta is 0.69, but 0.98 applying Scholes-Williams, and 1.45 applying Dimson. This pattern reflects the underestimate of systematic risk due to thin trading. Also, the goodness-of-fit of the regression is marginally increased using both the Scholes-Williams and Dimson methods.

Thus, while parameter estimates are substantially changed by the application of both the Scholes-Williams and the Dimson methods, abnormal returns are relatively unaffected. This result is a confirmation of findings from simulation studies (Brown/Warner (1980, 1985)), which have confirmed that event study results are insensitive to the expected return model. Also, this results mirrors similar findings from the methodological literature, which has repeatedly confirmed the minor impact of thin-trading adjustments on short-term event studies (e.g. Peterson (1989)). The conclusions from the abnormal returns analysis based on the standard market model discussed above are therefore entirely unchanged by the application of thin-trading adjustments.

Results of the abnormal returns analysis based on seemingly unrelated regression (SUR) are reported in Table 23. Panel A reports abnormal returns, and Panel B shows cumulative abnormal returns. Statistical significance is evaluated by a Wald test

Table 22: Market model regression parameters

	Average	Min	Max	Not significant at 5% level
Standard				
Beta	0.69	-0.47	1.76	21
Alpha	0.00	0.00	0.01	54
R^2	15.3%	0.0%	62.2%	
F	23.11	0.00	161.38	14
Scholes-Williams				
Beta	0.98	-0.48	3.32	16
Alpha	0.00	0.00	0.01	49
R^2	20.9%	0.0%	67.2%	
F	23.11	0.00	161.38	14
Dimson				
Beta	1.45	-0.68	3.61	23
Alpha	0.00	0.00	0.01	47
R^2	19.7%	0.7%	67.3%	
F	10.59	0.21	64.58	13

reported below. In terms of abnormal returns, results are very similar to the standard OLS market model: The SUR-based announcement day abnormal return is 1.24% (compared to 1.26% under the OLS standard market model), and the cumulative average abnormal return over the 30 days up to the announcement is 11.74% (compared to 11.09% under the OLS standard market model).

The SUR-based announcement day abnormal return is highly statistically significant as indicated by the Wald-test. SUR-based cumulative abnormal returns for all periods preceding the announcement day are also highly significant based on the Wald-test.

These results lead to the following conclusions from a methodological point of view:

- The simultaneous correction for unequal residual variance, event-induced variance shifts, and cross-sectional covariance in SUR does not result in materially different parameter estimates compared to standard OLS procedures in the present study.

- Statistical significance levels under SUR are also largely unaffected when compared to the standardized cross-sectional t-statistic.

- As discussed in Section 4.3.2.4.2, the methodological literature mostly argues that gains from using SUR over OLS are marginal in event studies with non-contemporaneous event periods, as cross-sectional covariance is generally minor. These findings are thus confirmed.

Results from the abnormal returns analyzed incorporating GARCH effects are presented in Table 24. Panel A presents GARCH prediction errors (GPE), while Panel B reports cumulative GARCH prediction errors (CGPE). Statistical significance is evaluated by a t-test. The GARCH prediction error at the announcement day is a highly statistically significant 2.07. The average daily GARCH prediction error over the 30 days up to the ECO announcement is an equally highly significant 0.53. However, significance levels decline for shorter event periods. None of the post-announcement period GARCH prediction errors are statistically significant. Bootstrapping does not materially affect significance levels. Thus, results are again fundamentally unaffected by the application: While the incorporation of the stochastic development of volatility marginally reduces significance levels, especially for the shorter multiday event periods, the positive short-term abnormal performance persists.

As the application of various different statistical methods has documented, ECOs lead to a robust positive short-term abnormal return which materializes over the thirty days preceding the announcement. A thorough discussion of this result, including a comparison with previous literature, follows in Section 4.5.1.1.

4.4.1.1.2 Results for the two subsamples

In order to evaluate the stability of results across the sample period, the sample has been split into two subsamples, ECOs announced between 1984 and 1997 (25 observations), and ECOs announced between 1998 and 2001 (28 observations). An analysis of the two subsamples is especially interesting in light of the unequal distribution of ECO announcements over the sample period (refer back to Figure 2).

The strong representation of ECOs from the 1999-2000 period in the sample quite naturally leads to the question if results for the full sample are entirely driven by this subset of observations.

Table 25 presents short-term abnormal returns for the two subsamples: Panel A presents the 1984-1997 ECO announcements, while Panel B reports the 1998-2001

Table 23: Short-term abnormal returns, SUR

Panel A: Abnormal Returns						
		-5	-4	-3	-2	-1
AR		0.47%	0.57%	-0.21%	0.28%	0.49%
Wald statistic		1.20	1.79	0.23	0.41	1.29

Panel B: Cumulative Abnormal Returns						
	-30 0	-25 0	-20 0	-15 0	-10 0	-5 0
CAR	11.74%	9.50%	6.05%	-0.02%	0.92%	-2.24%
Wald statistic	19.40 ***	18.73 ***	20.78 ***	26.76 ***	17.52 ***	7.79 ***

Table 24: Short-term abnormal returns, GARCH

Panel A: Prediction Errors						
		-5	-4	-3	-2	-1
GPE		0.67	0.47	0.32	0.55	1.12
t		1.43	0.37	0.60	1.47	1.12
Bootstrapped value		1.41	0.33	0.58	1.39	0.86

Panel B: Cumulative Prediction Errors						
	-30 0	-25 0	-20 0	-15 0	-10 0	-5 0
CGPE	0.53	0.52	0.43	0.35	0.39	0.35
t	3.26 ***	3.83 ***	3.03 ***	1.98 *	2.12 **	2.00 *
Bootstrapped value	3.20 ***	4.00 ***	3.07 ***	1.97 *	2.15 **	1.99 *

Table 23 (continued)

0	1	2	3	4	5
1.24%	-0.42%	-0.28%	0.13%	0.40%	0.15%
8.76 ***	0.95	0.44	0.08	0.89	0.12

1 5	1 10	1 15	1 20	1 25	1 30
-0.02%	-0.72%	0.92%	-0.61%	-2.24%	-3.29%
0.00	0.27	0.28	0.09	0.96	1.68

Table 24 (continued)

0	1	2	3	4	5
2.07	0.10	0.29	0.60	-0.16	0.41
2.78 ***	0.23	0.53	1.09	-0.21	0.66
2.69 ***	0.23	0.51	1.07	0.00	0.62

1 5	1 10	1 15	1 20	1 25	1 30
-0.07	0.03	0.06	0.10	-0.21	-0.17
-0.39	0.20	0.45	0.66	-1.45	-1.14
-0.38	0.20	0.45	0.66	-1.44	-1.15

Table 25: Short-term abnormal returns, standard market model, subsample analysis

Panel A: Subsample 1984-1997

		-5	-4	-3	-2	-1
AR		0.34%	0.31%	-0.25%	0.27%	-0.27%
Portfolio time-series t		1.01	0.93	-0.74	0.80	-0.81
Ordinary cross-sectional t		1.05	0.93	-0.90	1.40	-0.98

	-30 0	-25 0	-20 0	-15 0	-10 0	-5 0
CAR	4.77%	5.17%	3.29%	3.32%	2.13%	1.37%
Portfolio time-series t	2.57 **	3.04 ***	2.15 **	2.49 **	1.93 *	1.68
Ordinary cross-sectional t	2.35 **	2.59 **	1.96 *	2.26 **	1.82 *	1.40

Panel B: Subsample 1998-2001

		-5	-4	-3	-2	-1
AR		0.68%	0.80%	-0.23%	0.42%	1.17%
Portfolio time-series t		1.05	1.23	-0.35	0.65	1.80 *
Ordinary cross-sectional t		0.67	0.78	-0.44	0.47	1.58

	-30 0	-25 0	-20 0	-15 0	-10 0	-5 0
CAR	15.85%	13.95%	14.40%	14.06%	9.83%	4.33%
Portfolio time-series t	4.39 ***	4.22 ***	4.85 ***	5.42 ***	4.57 ***	2.73 **
Ordinary cross-sectional t	2.15 **	2.16 **	2.76 **	3.01 ***	2.66 **	1.73 *

Panel C: Two-sample t-tests for differences of means

AR		-5	-4	-3	-2	-1
t		0.26	0.36	0.01	0.12	1.07

CAR	-30 0	-25 0	-20 0	-15 0	-10 0	-5 0
t	3.48 ***	2.88 ***	3.85 ***	3.98 ***	3.14 **	1.41

Table 25 (continued)

0	1	2	3	4	5
0.97%	-0.80%	0.21%	0.13%	-0.03%	-0.02%
2.91 ***	-2.41 **	0.64	0.39	-0.09	-0.07
1.92 *	-1.76 *	0.75	0.36	-0.10	-0.09

1 5	1 10	1 15	1 20	1 25	1 30
-0.51%	-0.09%	-0.37%	-0.65%	-1.82%	-1.84%
-0.68	-0.08	-0.28	-0.43	-1.09	-1.01
-0.37	0.21	-0.12	-0.40	-1.42	-1.32

0	1	2	3	4	5
1.49%	-0.07%	-0.68%	0.18%	0.77%	0.34%
2.30 **	-0.10	-1.04	0.27	1.19	0.53
1.18	-0.08	-2.05 *	0.26	1.01	0.58

1 5	1 10	1 15	1 20	1 25	1 30
0.55%	-0.49%	3.56%	1.70%	0.41%	-0.46%
0.38	-0.24	1.42	0.59	0.13	-0.13
-0.12	-1.26	0.08	-0.71	-1.12	-1.28

0	1	2	3	4	5
0.39	0.54	-0.66	0.03	0.60	0.27

1 5	1 10	1 15	1 20	1 25	1 30
0.52	-0.17	1.48	0.82	0.74	0.44

ECO announcements. In light of the robustness of short-term abnormal returns against methodological variations, and in the interest of brevity, only the abnormal returns and cumulative abnormal returns, calculated via the standard market model are reported.

As is immediately evident from Table 25, the short-term capital market reaction differs between the two subsamples: For the 1984-1997 period, there is only a marginally positive announcement effect. Over the fifteen days up to the ECO announcement, there is a positive and significant abnormal return of 3.32%, compared to 9.08% for the full sample (refer back to Table 19).

In contrast, ECOs announced in 1998-2001 report a strongly significant positive announcement effect of 14.06% over the fifteen days up to the ECO announcement. As the two-sample t-test in Panel C shows, the difference in short-term capital market reaction between the two subperiods is also statistically significant when analyzing extended event periods of at least ten days in length, although it is insignificant when analyzing individual event days.A graphical analysis (Figure 22) of cumulative average abnormal returns provides further intuition. While statistically significant cumulative average abnormal returns are detected for both subsamples, this effect is considerably stronger for the 1998-2001 subsample.

In conclusion, the analysis of the two subsamples confirms results for the full sample insofar as significant positive short-term abnormal returns are detected for both periods under study. However, it also shows that short-term abnormal returns are significantly larger for the 1998-2001 subsample.

4.4.1.2 *Long-term abnormal returns*

4.4.1.2.1 *Results for the full sample*

Results of the analysis of long-term abnormal returns for the full sample are presented in four tables. The four tables differ in the estimation of expected return: Table 26 is based on value-weighted reference portfolios, Table 27 is based on equal-weighted reference portfolios, Table 28 is based on matching firms, and Table 29 is based on a market index (CDAX Composite).

The tables are identically structured: Panel A reports abnormal returns for the ECO parent, Panel B reports abnormal returns for the ECO subsidiary, Panel C reports

Figure 22: Cumulative average abnormal returns surrounding ECO announcement, subsamples

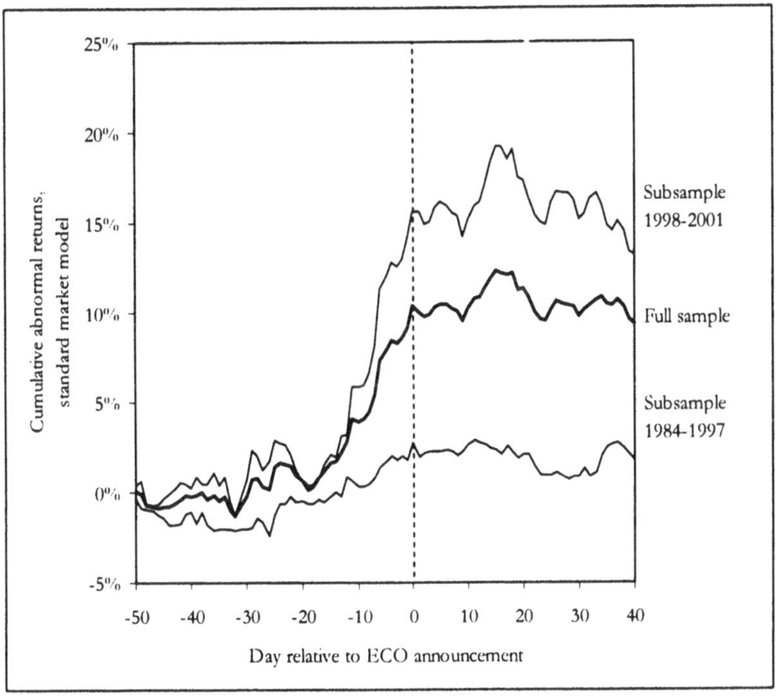

abnormal returns for the weighted parent/subsidiary portfolio. Both BHARs and CARs are presented. Concerning BHARs, five different test statistics are presented: a simple t-statistic (Equation (86)), Johnson's skewness-adjusted t-statistic (Equation (87)), a bootstrapped version of Johnson's skewness-adjusted t-statistic, the cross-sectional dependence-adjusted t-statistic proposed in Mitchell/Stafford (2000) (Equation(90)), and the two-groups t-statistic proposed in Cowan/Sergeant (2001) (Equation (91)). Concerning CARs, a simple t-statistic is presented (Equation (84)).

In light of the recommendations from the methodological literature discussed in Section 4.3.3.3, the following discussion is mostly based on Table 26, the value-weighted reference portfolio-adjusted long term abnormal returns.

Table 26 : Long-term abnormal returns, value-weighted reference portfolio adjusted

Panel A: Parent, Value-Weighted Reference Portfolios		
	+6M	+12M
BHAR	-3.98%	-2.20%
Simple t-statistic	-0.89	-0.38
Johnson's Skewness-adjusted t-statistic	-0.81	-0.35
Bootstrapped Johnson's t-statistic	-0.78	-0.33
Mitchell-Stafford adjusted t-statistic	-0.43	-0.18
Cowan-Sergeant cross-sectional t-statistic	-0.65	-0.29
CAR	-6.95%	-7.70%
Simple t-statistic	-1.43	-1.07

Panel B: Subsidiary, Value-Weighted Reference Portfolios		
	+6M	+12M
BHAR	41.50%	31.60%
Simple t-statistic	2.68 ***	2.31 **
Johnson's Skewness-adjusted t-statistic	3.55 ***	2.95 ***
Bootstrapped Johnson's t-statistic	1.64	1.64
Mitchell-Stafford adjusted t-statistic	1.74 *	1.50
Cowan-Sergeant cross-sectional t-statistic	2.42 **	2.08 **
CAR	26.64%	24.42%
Simple t-statistic	2.63 **	2.31 **

Panel C: Parent-Subsidiary-Portfolio, Value-Weighted Reference Portfolios		
	+6M	+12M
BHAR	12.99%	9.18%
Simple t-statistic	1.31	1.12
Johnson's Skewness-adjusted t-statistic	1.64	1.26
Bootstrapped Johnson's t-statistic	1.08	1.12
Mitchell-Stafford adjusted t-statistic	0.73	0.62
Cowan-Sergeant cross-sectional t-statistic	1.15	0.94
CAR	2.83%	-0.47%
Simple t-statistic	0.42	-0.06

Table 26 (continued)

+18M	+24M	+30M	+36M
-6.62%	-15.60%	-20.72%	-27.27%
-1.38	-2.46 **	-3.05 ***	-3.94 ***
-1.10	-2.50 **	-3.13 ***	-4.18 ***
-1.06	-2.06 **	-2.76 ***	-3.12 ***
-0.56	-1.20	-1.48	-1.92 *
-0.81	-1.66	-1.96 *	-2.43 **
-13.70%	-20.16%	-16.95%	-15.99%
-1.50	-2.07 **	-1.91 *	-1.49

+18M	+24M	+30M	+36M
13.83%	2.97%	1.52%	-12.15%
0.90	0.30	0.15	-1.37
1.62	0.36	0.20	-1.23
1.39	0.33	0.19	-1.08
0.94	0.20	0.10	-0.89
1.24	0.24	0.11	-1.01
24.20%	18.23%	16.97%	11.06%
2.35 **	1.66	1.49	0.93

+18M	+24M	+30M	+36M
0.41%	-8.48%	-10.84%	-22.05%
-0.35	-1.19	-1.46	-3.85 ***
0.09	-1.00	-1.20	-3.97 ***
0.09	-0.92	-1.09	-4.90 ***
0.03	-0.66	-0.81	-2.14 **
0.05	-0.83	-0.97	-2.16 **
-3.81%	-13.81%	-15.76%	-20.74%
-0.49	-1.51	-1.61	-2.02 **

Table 27: Long-term abnormal returns, equal-weighted reference portfolio adjusted

Panel A: Parent, Equal-Weighted Reference Portfolios

	+6M	+12M
BHAR	-3.38%	-2.46%
Simple t-statistic	-0.76	-0.42
Johnson's Skewness-adjusted t-statistic	-0.70	-0.39
Bootstrapped Johnson's t-statistic	-0.60	-0.34
Mitchell-Stafford adjusted t-statistic	-0.38	-0.21
Cowan-Sergeant cross-sectional t-statistic	-0.55	-0.32
CAR	-6.24%	-7.66%
Simple t-statistic	-1.28	-1.06

Panel B: Subsidiary, Equal-Weighted Reference Portfolios

	+6M	+12M
BHAR	40.23%	28.59%
Simple t-statistic	2.62 **	2.07 **
Johnson's Skewness-adjusted t-statistic	3.48 ***	2.60 **
Bootstrapped Johnson's t-statistic	1.72 *	1.65
Mitchell-Stafford adjusted t-statistic	1.84 *	1.46
Cowan-Sergeant cross-sectional t-statistic	2.34 **	1.87 *
CAR	25.52%	21.39%
Simple t-statistic	2.56 **	2.00 *

Panel C: Parent-Subsidiary-Portfolio, Equal-Weighted Reference Portfolios

	+6M	+12M
BHAR	13.24%	8.40%
Simple t-statistic	1.34	1.02
Johnson's Skewness-adjusted t-statistic	1.69 *	1.14
Bootstrapped Johnson's t-statistic	1.11	1.04
Mitchell-Stafford adjusted t-statistic	0.76	0.58
Cowan-Sergeant cross-sectional t-statistic	1.18	0.86
CAR	3.16%	-1.25%
Simple t-statistic	0.47	-0.16

Table 27 (continued)

+18M	+24M	+30M	+36M
-5.64%	-14.18%	-19.94%	-26.33%
-1.15	-2.26 **	-2.78 ***	-3.53 ***
-0.92	-2.23 **	-2.89 ***	-3.60 ***
-0.81	-1.95 *	-2.54 **	-3.12 ***
-0.48	-1.14	-1.40	-1.78 *
-0.70	-1.58	-1.96 *	-2.49 **
-12.45%	-18.99%	-15.54%	-14.79%
-1.34	-1.90 *	-1.70 *	-1.29

+18M	+24M	+30M	+36M
12.49%	3.28%	2.39%	-8.05%
0.83	0.33	0.23	-0.96
1.42	0.39	0.28	-0.85
1.21	0.25	0.14	-0.89
0.90	0.23	0.16	-0.68
1.12	0.27	0.18	-0.69
22.15%	17.35%	16.74%	14.31%
2.10 **	1.53	1.45	1.29

+18M	+24M	+30M	+36M
0.99%	-7.39%	-10.34%	-20.09%
-0.18	-1.00	-1.30	-3.31 ***
0.18	-0.85	-1.11	-3.13 ***
0.16	-0.67	-1.04	-2.93 ***
0.08	-0.57	-0.74	-1.88 *
0.11	-0.75	-0.95	-2.08 **
-3.45%	-13.31%	-15.29%	-19.11%
-0.44	-1.41	-1.53	-1.88 *

Table 28: Long-term abnormal returns, matching-firm adjusted

Panel A: Parent, Matching-firm adjusted		
	+6M	+12M
BHAR	-4.42%	-4.13%
Simple t-statistic	-0.81	-0.52
Johnson's Skewness-adjusted t-statistic	-0.77	-0.50
Bootstrapped Johnson's t-statistic	-0.68	-0.37
Mitchell-Stafford adjusted t-statistic	-0.53	-0.35
Cowan-Sergeant cross-sectional t-statistic	-0.66	-0.51
CAR	-9.02%	-14.42%
Simple t-statistic	-1.50	-1.50

Panel B: Subsidiary, Matching-firm adjusted		
	+6M	+12M
BHAR	36.97%	29.02%
Simple t-statistic	2.14 **	1.74 *
Johnson's Skewness-adjusted t-statistic	2.65 **	2.07 **
Bootstrapped Johnson's t-statistic	1.68 *	1.60
Mitchell-Stafford adjusted t-statistic	2.04 **	1.66
Cowan-Sergeant cross-sectional t-statistic	2.09 **	1.79 *
CAR	20.76%	22.32%
Simple t-statistic	1.77 *	1.61

Panel C: Parent-Subsidiary-Portfolio, Matching-firm adjusted		
	+6M	+12M
BHAR	11.17%	9.01%
Simple t-statistic	1.03	0.90
Johnson's Skewness-adjusted t-statistic	1.23	0.98
Bootstrapped Johnson's t-statistic	0.99	0.95
Mitchell-Stafford adjusted t-statistic	0.69	0.60
Cowan-Sergeant cross-sectional t-statistic	0.97	0.90
CAR	-0.70%	-5.62%
Simple t-statistic	-0.09	-0.53

Table 28 (continued)

+18M	+24M	+30M	+36M
-12.04%	-21.17%	-19.76%	-26.04%
-0.94	-1.46	-1.83 *	-2.52 **
-1.14	-2.00	-2.22 **	-3.20 ***
-0.94	-1.59	-1.72 *	-2.22 **
-0.61	-0.96	-1.21	-1.66
-0.92	-1.37	-1.43	-1.87
-18.72%	-22.30%	-15.39%	-17.40%
-1.50	-1.61	-1.27	-1.29

+18M	+24M	+30M	+36M
17.06%	8.46%	10.77%	1.81%
1.15	0.79	1.11	0.23
1.55	0.83	1.20	0.24
1.28	0.64	0.99	0.10
1.43	0.75	1.06	0.22
1.31	0.62	0.74	0.14
30.80%	29.52%	30.07%	26.46%
2.26 **	2.04 **	1.68 *	1.38

+18M	+24M	+30M	+36M
4.28%	-3.90%	-3.57%	-13.32%
0.44	-0.43	-0.39	-1.96 *
0.49	-0.40	-0.36	-2.18 **
0.49	-0.35	-0.25	-2.07 **
0.31	-0.29	-0.26	-1.31
0.45	-0.35	-0.29	-1.18
-5.76%	-13.61%	-14.35%	-19.90%
-0.53	-1.22	-1.44	-2.35 **

Table 29: Long-term abnormal returns, index-adjusted

Panel A: Parent, Index-adjusted	+6M	+12M
BHAR	0.18%	-4.26%
Simple t-statistic	0.03	-0.59
Johnson's Skewness-adjusted t-statistic	0.05	-0.55
Bootstrapped Johnson's t-statistic	0.12	-0.52
Mitchell-Stafford adjusted t-statistic	0.01	-0.26
Cowan-Sergeant cross-sectional t-statistic	0.03	-0.58
CAR	-2.98%	-11.28%
Simple t-statistic	-0.48	-1.26

Panel B: Subsidiary, Index-adjusted	+6M	+12M
BHAR	44.23%	26.32%
Simple t-statistic	2.62 **	1.77 *
Johnson's Skewness-adjusted t-statistic	3.45 ***	2.13 **
Bootstrapped Johnson's t-statistic	1.66	1.62
Mitchell-Stafford adjusted t-statistic	1.28	0.87
Cowan-Sergeant cross-sectional t-statistic	2.60 **	1.76 *
CAR	28.89%	16.53%
Simple t-statistic	2.57 **	1.37

Panel C: Parent-Subsidiary-Portfolio, Index-adjusted	+6M	+12M
BHAR	16.61%	5.78%
Simple t-statistic	1.53	0.62
Johnson's Skewness-adjusted t-statistic	1.91 *	0.67
Bootstrapped Johnson's t-statistic	1.30	0.68
Mitchell-Stafford adjusted t-statistic	0.75	0.31
Cowan-Sergeant cross-sectional t-statistic	1.49	0.60
CAR	6.20%	-5.85%
Simple t-statistic	0.77	-0.61

Table 29 (continued)

+18M	+24M	+30M	+36M
-18.66%	-33.94%	-40.86%	-44.39%
-2.60 **	-3.90 ***	-4.66 ***	-5.58 ***
-2.17 **	-3.87 ***	-4.60 ***	-4.99 ***
-1.89 *	-2.93 ***	-3.49 ***	-4.22 ***
-0.99	-1.71 *	-2.04 **	-2.45 **
-2.19 **	-3.44 ***	-4.15 ***	-5.00 ***
-26.61%	-38.86%	-40.14%	-40.08%
-2.28 **	-3.28 ***	-4.04 ***	-3.99 ***

+18M	+24M	+30M	+36M
-4.83%	-24.93%	-29.96%	-38.83%
-1.34	-2.32 **	-2.64 **	-3.85 ***
-0.45	-2.13 **	-2.38 **	-3.09 ***
-0.37	-1.88 *	-1.99 *	-2.42 **
-0.23	-1.14	-1.29	-1.89 *
-0.42	-1.93 *	-2.23 **	-3.42 ***
2.94%	-12.18%	-21.10%	-25.76%
0.25	-1.06	-1.80 *	-2.63 **

+18M	+24M	+30M	+36M
-13.15%	-29.12%	-34.18%	-42.20%
-2.11 **	-3.38 ***	-3.73 ***	-5.33 ***
-1.53	-3.33 ***	-3.55 ***	-4.90 ***
-1.46	-2.87 ***	-2.68 ***	-4.22 ***
-0.78	-1.67	-1.84 *	-2.63 **
-1.41	-2.68 ***	-3.07 ***	-4.75 ***
-19.20%	-35.62%	-43.69%	-49.37%
-1.95 *	-3.29 ***	-3.77 ***	-4.65 ***

Panel A of Table 26 shows that ECO parents experience a negative buy-and-hold abnormal return of -27.27% in the 36 months following the ECO. The negative 36-month BHAR is highly statistically significant based on the simple t-statistic, Johnson's skewness-adjusted t-statistic, and the bootstrapped version of Johnson's skewness-adjusted t-statistic. While the two t-statistics that adjust for cross-sectional dependence, the Mitchell-Stafford statistic, and the Cowan-Sergeant statistic, indicate lower significance levels, the negative 36-month BHAR remains statistically significant under all variants of test statistics.

As can be seen from the inspection of shorter periods post-ECO, the negative abnormal return is largely concentrated in the second and third year following the ECO. The first significant negative long-term abnormal return is detected in the 24-month period following the ECO, and statistical significance increases when analyzing longer post-ECO periods up to 36 months.

A markedly different picture emerges when looking at the ECO subsidiary abnormal returns (Panel B). The 6-month BHAR is an economically highly significant 41.50%. The 12-month BHAR is still positive at 31.50%, but not significant based on Johnson's bootstrapped skewness-adjusted t-statistic. The BHAR turns negative at around 30 months post-ECO, and comes in at a statistically insignificant -12.15% after 36 months. Thus, a significant abnormal return cannot be detected for the average ECO subsidiary over the three post-ECO years.

The BHARs on the weighted ECO parent-subsidiary portfolio (Panel C) relatively closely resemble the ECO parent BHARs, reflecting the overweight of parent stocks in the portfolio. The 36-month BHAR is a negative and statistically highly significant -22.05%.

The analysis of cumulative abnormal returns as a robustness check tentatively confirms the BHAR analysis, but leads to somewhat different results: The parent 36-month CAR is a negative but statistically insignificant -15.99%, while the parent/subsidiary portfolio 36-month CAR at a statistically significant -20.74% comes in very close to the BHAR. In contrast to the BHAR, the subsidiary 36-month CAR is positive at 11.06%, but equally statistically insignificant. Thus, the results from the analysis are not substantially changed.

From a methodological point of view, several comments are in order:

- The skewness-adjustment in Johnson's t-statistic improves power relative to the simple t-statistic, reflecting skewness of the return distribution. Johnson's bootstrapped skewness-adjusted t-statistics generally indicate lower significance levels than the non-bootstrapped version, which is a reflection of properties of the return distribution not captured by the skewness-adjustment, such as leptokurtosis (e.g. Sutton (1993)).
- As expected, the t-statistics correcting for cross-sectional dependence indicate substantially lower significance levels, reflecting positive cross-sectional correlation of abnormal returns in the sample due to overlap of event periods
- Cumulative abnormal returns can deviate upwards or downwards from BHARs, as discussed in the methodological literature (e.g. Barber/Lyon (1997)). Tests based on CARs generally have lower power than tests based on BHARs, consistent with results from the methodological literature (again Barber/Lyon (1997)).

As a robustness check, different models for estimating expected long-term returns have been applied. Table 27 reports long-term abnormal returns based on the return on equal-weighted reference portfolios as expected return. The equal-weighting of reference portfolios as opposed to value-weighting does not significantly alter results. The parent 36-month BHAR is a negative and highly significant -26.33% (compared to -27.27% based on value-weighted reference portfolios). The subsidiary 36-month BHAR is insignificant at -8.05%, and the portfolio 36-month BHAR is a negative and significant -20.09%. In general, equal-weighting of reference of reference portfolios as opposed to value-weighting reduces abnormal performance in either direction. Also the positive subsidiary 6-month and 12-month BHARs are slightly less pronounced compared to the value-weighted reference portfolio analysis.

Table 28 reports long-term abnormal returns based on the return on a matching firm as expected return. The use of matching firms leaves results virtually unchanged for parent returns: The 36-month BHAR is a negative -26.04%. Significance levels are slightly lower than for the reference portfolio analysis, owing to the greater variance of matching firm returns, leading to a greater variance of BHARs. In contrast, subsidiary abnormal returns are substantially affected. While the approaches based on reference portfolios find negative (if insignificant) subsidiary 36-month BHARs, the matching-firm approach results in a positive 1.81% 36-month subsidiary BHAR. A potential explanation for this finding is that numerous ECO subsidiaries in the sample are small firms, from high-growth industries, especially software (refer back to the sample descriptive statistics in Section 4.2.2). Apparently, the expected return on these firms is better captured by selecting appropriate matching firms than by reference portfolios. Thus, the subsidiary underperformance disappears. Consequently, the parent/subsidiary portfolio 36-month BHAR based on matching firms, at -13.32%, is less negative than the BHAR based on reference portfolios. However, the parent/subsidiary portfolio BHAR is still statistically significant, at least using the t-statistics not accounting for cross-sectional dependence.

Finally, Table 29 reports long-term abnormal returns based on the CDAX return as expected return. While the approaches discussed previously are preferable on theoretical grounds (as discussed in Section 4.3.3.3), market-adjusted returns are included for comparison purposes, and since they are regularly reported in the previous ECO literature (e.g. Langenbach (2001)). Using the CDAX return as the expected return, both parent and subsidiary 36-month BHARs are significantly negative, with parent underperformance being particularly pronounced at -44.39%. However, these results should not be taken at face value: as explained in Section 4.3.3.3, the use of the market return as the expected return does not make any adjustment for firm-specific risk factors. Thus, the apparent pattern of subsidiary overperformance, followed by underperformance relative to the market, merely reflects sample characteristics: The sample being heavily weighted in 1999 and 2000, and concentrated in small firms from growth sectors, BHARs reflect the outperformance of this industry sector relative to the total stock market in 1999 and early 2000, and the subsequent downturn. The analyses based on reference portfolios, and especially on matching firms, are not affected since the appropriate risk adjustments are made via the matching procedure.

In order to illustrate results, long-term BHARs are finally presented graphically, comparing all four methods for the estimation of abnormal returns employed Figure 23 presents parent BHARs, Figure 24 presents subsidiary BHARs, Figure 25 and presents parent/subsidiary portfolio BHARs. As already discussed, it can be seen that the reference portfolio and matching firm methods lead to very similar results for the parent and portfolio BHARs, and to moderately similar results for the subsidiary BHARs.

Figure 23: Parent long-term BHARs, full sample

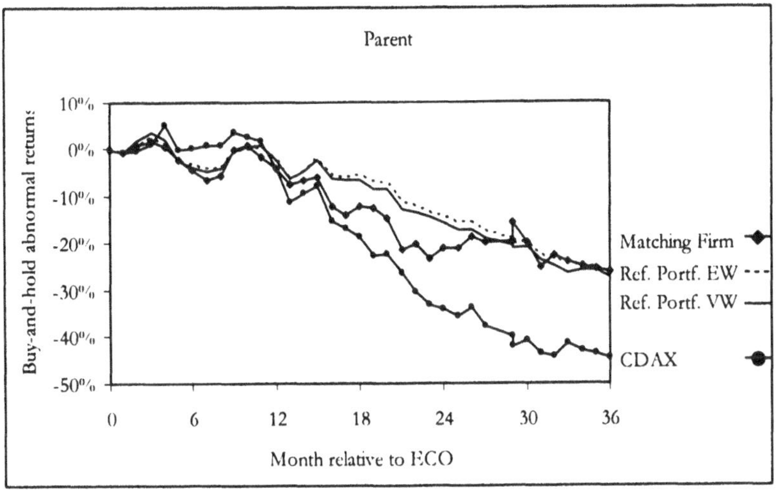

Figure 24: Subsidiary long-term BHARs, full sample

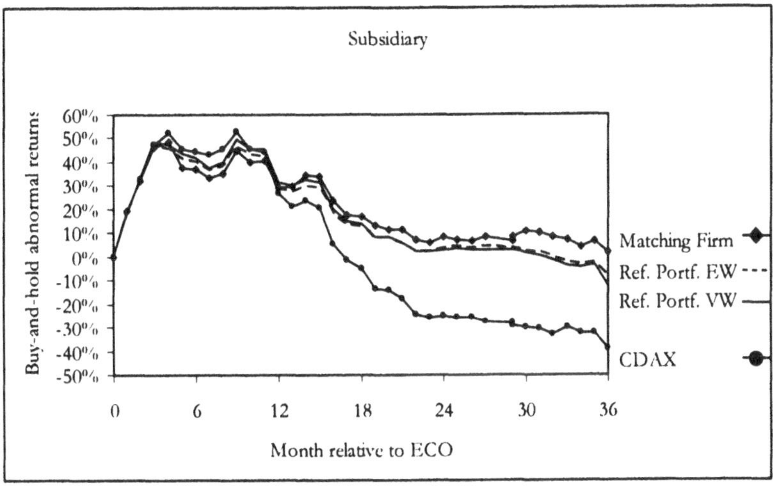

Figure 25: Parent/subsidiary portfolio long-term BHARs, full sample

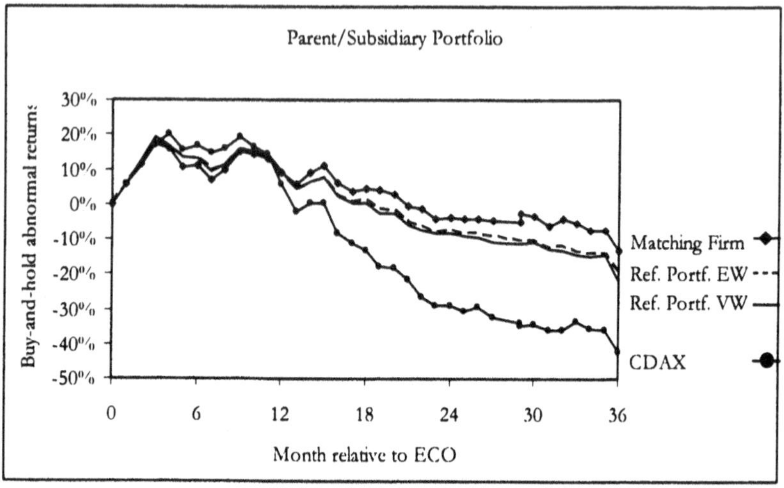

In conclusion, weighted parent/subsidiary portfolios exhibit a robust negative long-term abnormal return during the three post-ECO years, as documented under the application of several methodological variations to return measurement, expected return estimation and significance testing. This result is further discussed and contrasted with previous literature in Section 4.5.1.2.

4.4.1.2.2 Results for the two subsamples

Analogously to the analysis of short-term abnormal returns, the sample has been split into two subsamples, ECOs announced between 1984 and 1997 (25 observations), and ECOs announced between 1998 and 2001 (28 observations), in order to evaluate the stability of long-term abnormal returns across sample periods.

For the sake of brevity, two alternative methods for estimating expected returns are selected out of the four applied above for the full sample analysis: Value-weighted reference portfolios, and matching firms. Equal-weighted reference portfolios are dropped because of their close similarity to value-weighted reference portfolios, and the CDAX as benchmark is dropped on theoretical grounds (as discussed in Section 4.3.3.3).

Results are presented in Table 30 and Table 31 (value-weighted reference portfolio-adjusted returns), and in Table 32 and Table 33 (matching firm-adjusted returns).

As expected, significance levels generally decline compared to the analysis of the full sample due to smaller sample size. However, conclusions reached based on the full sample are essentially valid for both subsamples:

- The parent underperforms significantly over the three years following the ECO, although underperformance is stronger for the 1984-1997 subsample (at 27.99% and 33.82%, depending on the benchmark used), than for the 1998-2001 subsample (at 24.03% and 21.42%, depending on the benchmark used).
- The subsidiary does not exhibit significant underperformance over the three years following the ECO in either of the two subperiods, and based on either of the two benchmarks. However, the pattern of subsidiary abnormal returns differs between the two subsamples: the positive abnormal returns detected in the first six months after the ECO in the full sample analysis are entirely due to the 1998-2001 subsample, while the 1984-1997 subsample exhibits a very stable development in line with the benchmark during the three year period.
- The parent/subsidiary portfolio abnormal return over the three years following the ECO for the 1984-1997 sample period is a negative and significant -26.37% (value-weighted reference portfolio-adjusted), or -21.47% (matching firm-adjusted), respectively. The results for the 1998-2001 subsample are less clear: While the abnormal return is negative and significant at -18.71% using value-weighted reference portfolios as benchmark, it is insignificantly different from zero at -7.22% under the matching firm adjustment..

Thus, parent and parent/subsidiary portfolio exhibit long-term negative abnormal returns in the three years following the ECO in both subsamples. However, results are not fully robust to benchmark variation as far as the parent/subsidiary portfolio performance of the 1998-2001 subsample is concerned.

In order to illustrate results, subsample long-term BHARs are finally presented graphically, comparing the two subsamples. Figure 26 presents parent BHARs, Figure 27 presents subsidiary BHARs, Figure 28 and presents parent/subsidiary portfolio BHARs.

Table 30: Long-term abnormal returns, value-weighted reference portfolio-adjusted, subsample 1984-1997

Panel A: Parent, Value-weighted reference portfolio-adjusted

	+6M	+12M
BHAR	-3.66%	-1.34%
Simple t-statistic	-1.06	-0.23
Johnson's Skewness-adjusted t-statistic	-1.00	-0.23
Bootstrapped Johnson's t statistic	-0.64	-0.24
Mitchell-Stafford adjusted t-statistic	-0.51	-0.11
Cowan-Sergeant cross-sectional t-statistic	-0.68	-0.18
CAR	-4.06%	-2.21%
Simple t-statistic	-1.10	-0.39

Panel B: Subsidiary, Value-weighted reference portfolio-adjusted

	+6M	+12M
BHAR	17.56%	17.92%
Simple t-statistic	1.57	1.66
Johnson's Skewness-adjusted t-statistic	2.05 *	1.91 *
Bootstrapped Johnson's t statistic	1.07	1.21
Mitchell-Stafford adjusted t-statistic	1.02	1.08
Cowan-Sergeant cross-sectional t-statistic	1.49	1.67
CAR	12.80%	14.76%
Simple t-statistic	1.59	1.68

Panel C: Value-weighted reference portfolio-adjusted

	+6M	+12M
BHAR	8.65%	8.24%
Simple t-statistic	0.85	0.90
Johnson's Skewness-adjusted t-statistic	1.15	1.09
Bootstrapped Johnson's t statistic	0.42	0.60
Mitchell-Stafford adjusted t-statistic	0.47	0.50
Cowan-Sergeant cross-sectional t-statistic	0.80	0.82
CAR	4.04%	4.48%
Simple t-statistic	0.61	0.64

Table 30 (continued)

+18M	+24M	+30M	+36M
-3.25%	-11.74%	-26.71%	-33.82%
-0.79	-1.11	-2.29 **	-2.70 **
-0.44	-1.14	-2.38 **	-2.83 ***
-0.50	-1.72 *	-2.24 **	-2.58 **
-0.21	-0.54	-1.12	-1.31
-0.40	-0.92	-1.64	-1.90 *
-3.44%	-11.18%	-27.66%	-32.23%
-0.45	-1.23	-2.65 **	-2.86 ***

+18M	+24M	+30M	+36M
20.32%	21.03%	20.10%	-2.02%
1.32	1.13	1.07	-0.14
1.60	1.33	1.25	-0.08
1.11	0.83	0.80	-0.05
0.91	0.73	0.70	-0.09
1.37	1.09	0.95	-0.11
14.53%	12.20%	8.65%	-1.93%
1.45	1.10	0.78	-0.20

+18M	+24M	+30M	+36M
6.24%	1.57%	-6.00%	-26.37%
0.47	0.12	-0.44	-3.44 ***
0.74	0.19	-0.34	-3.60 ***
0.42	0.05	-0.24	-3.01 ***
0.35	0.07	-0.24	-1.91 *
0.57	0.11	-0.34	-1.78 *
2.33%	-3.34%	-11.70%	-22.75%
0.30	-0.37	-1.23	-2.95 ***

Table 31: Long-term abnormal returns, value-weighted reference portfolio-adjusted, subsample 1998-2001

Panel A: Parent, Value-weighted reference portfolio-adjusted	+6M	+12M
BHAR	-4.26%	2.39%
Simple t-statistic	-0.54	0.24
Johnson's Skewness-adjusted t-statistic	-0.48	0.27
Bootstrapped Johnson's t statistic	0.27	0.15
Mitchell-Stafford adjusted t-statistic	-0.26	0.12
Cowan-Sergeant cross-sectional t-statistic	-0.40	0.18
CAR	-9.54%	-7.27%
Simple t-statistic	-1.10	-0.58

Panel B: Subsidiary, Value-weighted reference portfolio-adjusted	+6M	+12M
BHAR	61.14%	67.62%
Simple t-statistic	2.28 **	2.32 **
Johnson's Skewness-adjusted t-statistic	2.97 ***	3.09 ***
Bootstrapped Johnson's t statistic	1.79 *	1.46
Mitchell-Stafford adjusted t-statistic	1.48	1.51
Cowan-Sergeant cross-sectional t-statistic	2.03 *	2.05 **
CAR	38.08%	46.47%
Simple t-statistic	2.19 **	2.60 **

Panel C: Parent-Subsidiary-Portfolio,Value-weighted reference portfolio-adjusted	+6M	+12M
BHAR	16.03%	19.30%
Simple t-statistic	0.98	1.25
Johnson's Skewness-adjusted t-statistic	1.25	1.48
Bootstrapped Johnson's t statistic	0.69	0.51
Mitchell-Stafford adjusted t-statistic	0.54	0.69
Cowan-Sergeant cross-sectional t-statistic	0.85	1.05
CAR	1.44%	2.72%
Simple t-statistic	0.13	0.20

Table 31 (continued)

+18M	+24M	+30M	+36M
-9.68%	-16.89%	-15.37%	-21.42%
-1.13	-2.17 **	-2.00 *	-3.11 ***
-0.96	-2.00 *	-1.91 *	-2.89 ***
0.68	1.46	1.61	2.11 **
-0.51	-1.06	-0.97	-1.51
-0.74	-1.41	-1.34	-2.08 **
-23.51%	-25.07%	-7.39%	-1.49%
-1.60	-1.62	-0.53	-0.09

+18M	+24M	+30M	+36M
11.20%	-11.45%	-12.26%	-18.31%
0.02	-1.24	-1.47	-1.73 *
0.92	-1.10	-1.36	-1.69
0.49	0.60	0.94	1.32
0.52	-0.81	-0.96	-1.12
0.70	-0.98	-1.06	-1.52
31.59%	23.54%	24.81%	23.44%
1.80 *	1.37	1.31	1.15

+18M	+24M	+30M	+36M
-5.30%	-18.20%	-15.84%	-18.71%
-1.11	-2.38 **	-2.26 **	-2.25 **
-0.51	-2.11 **	-2.15 **	-2.31 **
0.40	1.37	1.82 *	1.68
-0.31	-1.32	-1.25	-1.25
-0.40	-1.51	-1.37	-1.74 *
-12.89%	-22.35%	-19.29%	-19.01%
-0.95	-1.61	-1.18	-1.06

Table 32: Long-term abnormal returns, matching firm-adjusted, subsample 1984-1997

Panel A: Parent, Matching firm-adjusted	+6M	+12M
BHAR	-2.04%	-0.25%
Simple t-statistic	-0.51	-0.05
Johnson's Skewness-adjusted t-statistic	-0.49	-0.05
Bootstrapped Johnson's t statistic	-0.31	-0.04
Mitchell-Stafford adjusted t-statistic	-0.25	-0.02
Cowan-Sergeant cross-sectional t-statistic	-0.32	-0.03
CAR	-2.31%	-2.14%
Simple t-statistic	-0.56	-0.47

Panel B: Subsidiary, Matching firm-adjusted	+6M	+12M
BHAR	15.26%	15.79%
Simple t-statistic	1.22	1.32
Johnson's Skewness-adjusted t-statistic	1.45	1.44
Bootstrapped Johnson's t statistic	1.04	1.16
Mitchell-Stafford adjusted t-statistic	0.80	0.86
Cowan-Sergeant cross-sectional t-statistic	1.19	1.35
CAR	10.99%	11.83%
Simple t-statistic	1.22	1.19

Panel C: Parent-Subsidiary-Portfolio, Matching firm-adjusted	+6M	+12M
BHAR	7.58%	6.61%
Simple t-statistic	0.69	0.68
Johnson's Skewness-adjusted t-statistic	0.88	0.81
Bootstrapped Johnson's t statistic	0.56	0.63
Mitchell-Stafford adjusted t-statistic	0.38	0.38
Cowan-Sergeant cross-sectional t-statistic	0.65	0.61
CAR	3.58%	2.76%
Simple t-statistic	0.48	0.36

Table 32 (continued)

+18M	+24M	+30M	+36M
1.71%	-1.53%	-20.90%	-27.99%
0.05	-0.17	-1.31	-1.60
0.27	-0.17	-1.65	-2.03 *
0.53	-0.99	-1.35	-2.10 **
0.14	-0.08	-0.64	-0.78
0.17	-0.10	-0.93	-1.18
2.31%	-0.07%	-14.43%	-17.86%
0.39	-0.01	-1.37	-1.49

+18M	+24M	+30M	+36M
21.37%	23.39%	22.77%	3.26%
1.55	1.37	1.31	0.25
1.59	1.57	1.47	0.25
1.28	1.09	1.11	0.24
0.93	0.89	0.85	0.16
1.35	1.14	0.97	0.16
14.97%	15.19%	13.31%	4.81%
1.26	1.16	0.95	0.35

+18M	+24M	+30M	+36M
10.29%	8.27%	-0.89%	-20.90%
1.03	0.61	-0.05	-1.71 *
1.05	0.73	-0.02	-1.96 *
0.73	0.30	-0.02	-1.75 *
0.49	0.34	-0.03	-0.95
0.86	0.52	-0.04	-1.17
6.35%	2.50%	-5.31%	-17.12%
0.69	0.26	-0.48	-1.72 *

Table 33: Long-term abnormal returns, matching firm -adjusted, subsample 1998-2001

Panel A: Parent, Matching firm adjusted		
	+6M	+12M
BHAR	-6.55%	-2.74%
Simple t-statistic	-0.67	-0.19
Johnson's Skewness-adjusted t-statistic	-0.63	-0.16
Bootstrapped Johnson's t statistic	-0.51	-0.44
Mitchell-Stafford adjusted t-statistic	-0.32	-0.09
Cowan-Sergeant cross-sectional t-statistic	-0.57	-0.20
CAR	-15.01%	-19.27%
Simple t-statistic	-1.40	-1.17

Panel B: Subsidiary, Matching firm adjusted		
	+6M	+12M
BHAR	54.84%	61.14%
Simple t-statistic	1.82 *	1.73 *
Johnson's Skewness-adjusted t-statistic	2.23 **	2.14 **
Bootstrapped Johnson's t statistic	1.65	1.21
Mitchell-Stafford adjusted t-statistic	1.19	1.13
Cowan-Sergeant cross-sectional t-statistic	1.77 *	1.78 *
CAR	28.88%	40.04%
Simple t-statistic	1.42	1.60

Panel C: Parent-Subsidiary-Portfolio, Matching firm adjusted		
	+6M	+12M
BHAR	13.28%	17.80%
Simple t-statistic	0.74	0.91
Johnson's Skewness-adjusted t-statistic	0.91	1.04
Bootstrapped Johnson's t statistic	0.55	0.45
Mitchell-Stafford adjusted t-statistic	0.41	0.51
Cowan-Sergeant cross-sectional t-statistic	0.69	0.96
CAR	-5.00%	-7.02%
Simple t-statistic	-0.36	-0.38

Table 33 (continued)

+18M	+24M	+30M	+36M
-27.94%	-42.63%	-18.75%	-24.30%
-0.99	-1.22	-1.25	-2.00 *
-1.36	-1.72 *	-1.51	-2.53 **
-1.15	-1.17	-1.54	-2.61 **
-0.52	-0.59	-0.61	-0.98
-1.12	-1.27	-1.21	-1.83 *
-40.41%	-37.93%	-16.26%	-17.00%
-1.93 *	-1.56	-0.77	-0.73

+18M	+24M	+30M	+36M
14.80%	-7.27%	2.36%	2.65%
0.32	-0.52	0.24	0.28
0.91	-0.56	0.23	0.30
0.70	-0.33	0.34	0.32
0.56	-0.33	0.16	0.18
0.77	-0.45	0.18	0.22
40.67%	37.95%	44.73%	45.78%
1.69	1.67	1.44	1.37

+18M	+24M	+30M	+36M
-2.88%	-14.70%	-6.18%	-7.22%
-0.34	-1.08	-0.74	-1.07
-0.19	-1.23	-0.73	-1.05
-0.21	-1.30	-0.73	-1.10
-0.11	-0.60	-0.41	-0.59
-0.21	-1.04	-0.54	-0.71
-21.19%	-25.49%	-21.83%	-22.17%
-1.13	-1.40	-1.38	-1.67

Figure 26: Parent long-term BHARs, subsamples

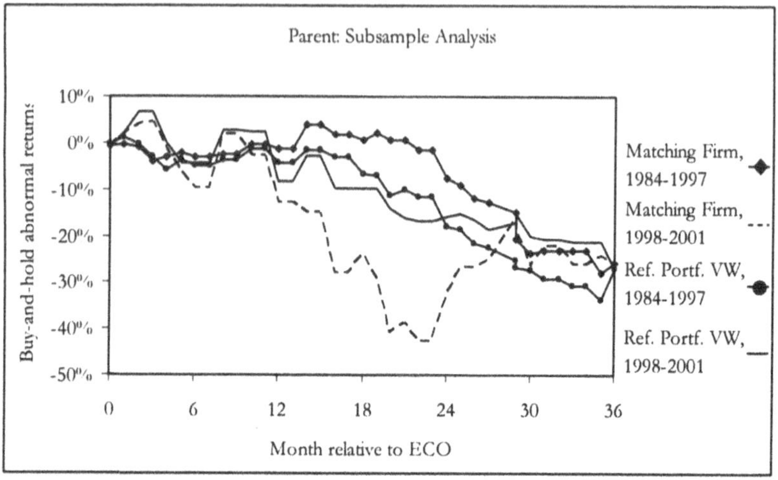

Figure 27: Subsidiary long-term BHARs, subsamples

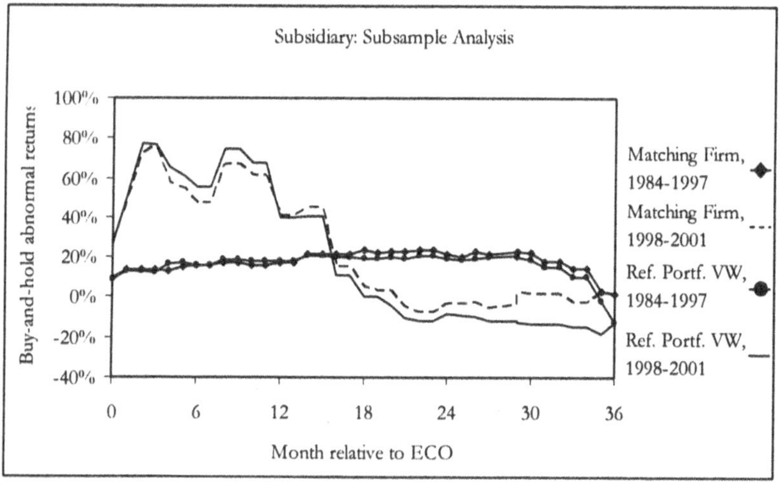

Figure 28: Parent/subsidiary portfolio long-term BHARs, subsamples

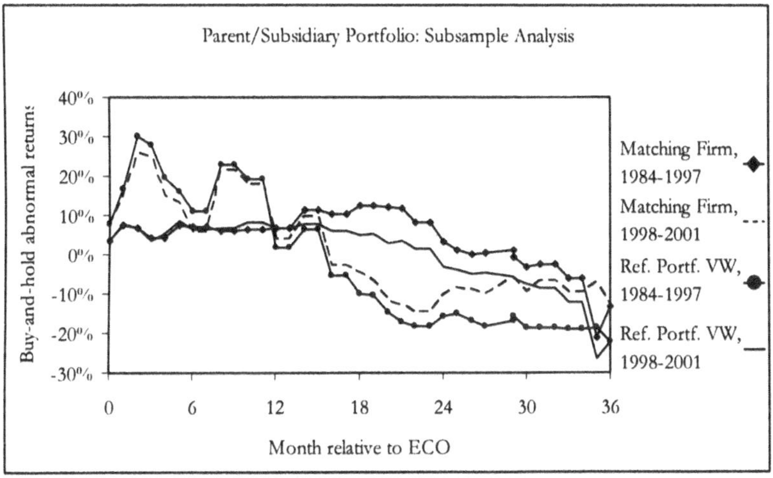

From the graphs, it can be seen that returns during the three year period differ substantially in the intermediate term, but seem to converge towards the end of the three year period.

In conclusion, the negative long-term abnormal performance of parent and parent/subsidiary portfolios is overall relatively robust to variations in sample period. ECOs from the 1998-2001 period do not exhibit return patterns materially different in nature.

4.4.2 *Cross-sectional regression*

4.4.2.1 *Explanatory variable descriptive statistics*

Descriptive statistics of the explanatory variables and of the control variables defined in Section 4.3.4.4 are provided in Table 34. Several facts merit comment:[193]

---

[193] Minimal differences to the sample descriptive statistics (Section 4.2.2 , Table 9) are possible since the cross-sectional regression analysis is based on a subsample of 49 observations (excluding financial institutions), while the descriptive statistics are based on the entire sample of 53 observations for which data are availle

- ECOs lead to a substantial decline in the heterogeneity of the group of companies: the number of different industry codes, as measured by the variable FOCUS, is reduced by an average of 37.1%. This indicates that parent and subsidiary in the ECO sample are mostly not in the same industry.

  Before the ECO, ECO parents on average invest marginally less than their industry counterparts, as measured by the variable OVINV. Post-ECO, parent investment is increased towards the industry average, while subsidiary investment is considerably above industry average. At face value, this pattern does not support the pattern discussed in Section 3.3.4, namely the increase in investment efficiency thanks to ECOs, due a reduction of empire-building overinvestment present in diversified groups of companies.

Table 34: Explanatory variable descriptive statistics

Variable	Specification	Mean	Median	Maximum	Minimum
FOCUS		37.1%	40.0%	75.0%	0.0%
OVINV	Parent, pre-ECO	-2.1%	-2.8%	44.9%	-45.6%
	Parent, post-ECO	0.0%	-1.0%	27.5%	-24.8%
	Sub, Post-ECO	8.5%	0.5%	341.1%	-121.4%
	Portfolio, Post-ECO	-1.1%	-0.9%	24.4%	-36.0%
DEBT_RED		-18.1%	-22.0%	130.3%	-95.7%
DIV_PAYOUT		-31.1%	0.0%	122.2%	-759.4%
ASYM		2.8%	2.3%	13.2%	1.1%
TRANSP		-0.5%	-0.4%	3.1%	-8.2%
ANALYSTS		68%	33%	700%	-125%
ALIGN		0.4	0.0	1.0	0.0
INFL		27.5%	19.3%	313.4%	0.0%
INFL_AR		48.5%	37.0%	626.7%	0.0%
INFL_VS		6.5%	0.0%	77.9%	0.0%
OWN_PAR		54.2%	60.3%	95.8%	0.0%
FLOAT		44.7%	32.7%	100.0%	0.0%
LEVERAGE		71.7%	76.4%	97.0%	14.0%
RELSIZE		11.8%	10.0%	111.9%	0.0%
PSIZE		11.7	1.6	136.1	0.0
ROA		-0.9%	-1.0%	51.0%	-27.0%
CDAXPRIOR		21.7%	26.2%	51.4%	-21.8%
CDAXPOST		12.4%	12.1%	59.8%	-39.4%
CDAXPRIOR-CDAXPOST		9.3%	7.7%	62.3%	-54.8%
IPOSPRIOR		87.9	68.0	188.0	8.0
CDAX_PE		20.1	19.8	28.1	14.8

- On average, debt increases and dividend payout ratios are reduced post-ECO, as measured by the variables DEBT_RED and DIV_PAYOUT. Thus, ECO proceeds are commonly not paid out to debtholders or shareholders. To the contrary, ECOs are on average accompanied by an increase in debt and an increase in earnings retainment. This is consistent with the increased industry-adjusted post-ECO investment levels just described.
- Information asymmetries, as measured by the industry-adjusted change in the standard deviation of market model residuals, the variable TRANSP, decreases substantially post-ECO. Also, the industry-adjusted number of analysts covering the group of companies increases significantly, at an average of 68%
- Incentive compensation in the form of direct management ownership in the subsidiary or stock options programs is introduced in 23 out of 49 ECOs in the sample: While it is very common for ECOs from 1999 onwards, it is rarely observed in the first half of the sample period.
- The ECO parent retains substantially less seats on the ECO subsidiary supervisory board than explained by its ownership in the subsidiary. An even stronger effect can be detected concerning the subsidiary management board: double management board mandates are extremely rare in the sample.
- Parent ownership in the subsidiary immediately post-ECO is an average 54.2%. Three years post ECO, free float is an average 44.7%. Thus, most ECO subsidiaries are subject to blockholder control during the period under observation.

Table 35 is the correlation matrix of explanatory variables. As discussed in Section 4.3.4.3, a high degree of correlation between two explanatory variables can be indicative of multicollinearity. Table 35 reveals that the correlation between explanatory variables is mostly minor. Pearson correlation coefficients significantly different from zero at the 5% level are printed in bold. In the following, correlation coefficients exceeding 0.5 in absolute value are discussed in more detail:

- The correlation between OVINV, Parent, post-ECO and OVINV, Portfolio, post-ECO is 0.85. Since investment of the pro-forma consolidated portfolio of parent and subsidiary post-ECO is largely determined by the parent due to

Table 35: Correlation matrix of explanatory variables

	FOCUS	OVINV, Parent, pre-ECO	OVINV, Parent, post-ECO	OVINV, Sub, post-ECO	OVINV, Portfolio, post-ECO	DEBT_RED	DIV_PAYOUT	ASYM	TRANSP	ANALYSTS
FOCUS	1.00	0.02	0.06	0.19	-0.07	0.00	-0.07	0.03	-0.18	-0.23
OVINV Parent, pre-ECO		1.00	**0.34**	-0.12	0.19	-0.16	0.18	-0.16	0.25	-0.21
OVINV Parent, post-ECO			1.00	**0.32**	**0.85**	-0.13	-0.04	-0.20	0.23	-0.08
OVINV Sub, post-ECO				1.00	**0.45**	-0.09	0.09	0.26	-0.25	-0.11
OVINV Portfolio, post-ECO					1.00	-0.19	-0.14	-0.16	0.25	-0.05
DEBT_RED						1.00	-0.07	-0.22	0.10	0.12
DIV_PAYOUT							1.00	0.10	0.04	-0.02
ASYM								1.00	**-0.50**	-0.10
TRANSP									1.00	0.02
ANALYSTS										1.00
ALIGN										
INFL										
INFL_AR										
INFL_VS										
OWN_PAR										
FLOAT										
LEVERAGE										
RELSIZE										
PSIZE										
ROA										
CDAXPRIOR										
CDAXPOST										
CDAXPRIOR-CDAXPOST										
IPOSPRIOR										
CDAX_PE										

Table 35 (continued)

ALIGN	INFL	INFL_AR	INFL_VS	OWN_PAR	FLOAT	LEVERAGE	RELSIZE	PSIZE	ROA	CDAXPRIOR	CDAXPOST	CDAXPRIOR-CDAXPOST	IPOSPRIOR	CDAX_PE
-0.26	-0.14	-0.16	0.06	0.20	-0.23	-0.17	0.06	-0.09	-0.03	**-0.48**	-0.28	-0.20	**-0.39**	0.18
-0.07	-0.08	-0.06	-0.15	0.11	0.10	-0.14	-0.17	0.04	0.13	-0.12	0.00	-0.18	-0.11	-0.02
-0.10	0.03	0.01	0.14	0.15	-0.09	0.14	0.16	-0.23	**0.35**	-0.01	-0.03	0.04	-0.18	-0.01
0.10	-0.08	-0.08	-0.06	0.08	-0.17	0.10	-0.05	0.28	-0.02	-0.06	0.06	0.23	0.03	0.09
-0.01	0.03	0.00	0.19	0.20	-0.01	0.09	0.01	-0.21	**0.36**	0.07	-0.06	0.14	-0.08	-0.02
-0.22	0.09	0.07	0.07	-0.08	-0.12	**0.43**	**0.34**	0.03	-0.18	0.00	0.00	0.02	-0.21	-0.03
-0.05	0.02	0.10	**-0.44**	-0.05	-0.03	0.04	0.09	0.11	0.08	-0.15	-0.33	-0.10	-0.11	-0.05
0.50	-0.09	-0.06	-0.15	-0.20	-0.11	-0.40	-0.03	-0.04	-0.21	**0.42**	0.15	0.16	**0.48**	0.10
-0.07	0.06	0.07	-0.04	-0.08	0.26	-0.02	0.04	0.05	**0.48**	-0.01	0.13	-0.25	0.03	0.06
0.25	0.35	0.37	-0.08	-0.31	0.16	0.04	-0.12	-0.05	0.09	0.17	0.09	0.07	0.09	-0.04
1.00	0.06	0.11	-0.28	**-0.44**	0.17	-0.42	-0.08	0.06	-0.01	**0.55**	**0.39**	**0.11**	**0.84**	0.23
	1.00	**0.98**	0.16	-0.13	-0.07	0.01	0.08	-0.07	0.07	0.02	0.07	-0.03	0.01	-0.07
		1.00	-0.02	-0.19	-0.04	-0.04	0.04	-0.05	0.07	0.03	0.08	-0.03	0.06	-0.06
			1.00	**0.34**	-0.18	**0.29**	0.21	-0.11	0.02	-0.02	-0.02	0.00	-0.24	-0.05
				1.00	**-0.39**	0.27	0.05	-0.14	**0.34**	**-0.40**	-0.03	-0.27	**-0.40**	-0.22
					1.00	-0.13	**-0.35**	-0.05	-0.07	0.03	-0.03	0.05	0.23	**0.39**
						1.00	0.19	0.31	0.11	-0.13	-0.17	0.08	**-0.41**	-0.11
							1.00	-0.04	0.00	0.05	0.19	-0.12	-0.04	-0.14
								1.00	0.04	0.07	-0.16	0.20	0.25	0.05
									1.00	-0.11	0.09	-0.13	0.02	0.10
										1.00	0.22	**0.61**	**0.63**	0.06
											1.00	**-0.64**	**0.43**	-0.14
												1.00	0.15	0.15
													1.00	0.18
														1.00

its larger size, the substantial correlation is expected. Multicollinearity is not an issue since the two variables do not enter the same regression equation.

- The correlation between ASYM and TRANSP is -0.50. Thus, strong information asymmetry pre-ECO is associated with a strong reduction in information asymmetry due to the ECO. This is consistent with the theoretical arguments from Section 3.4.4: the increase in mandatory disclosure engendered by an ECO is particularly important where strong managerial incentives for effective voluntary disclosure do not exist.
- The correlation between ASYM and ALIGN is 0.50. Thus, managerial equity ownership or stock options programs are likely to be used by firms being subject to substantial information asymmetries. This pattern is consistent with the core paradigm of agency theory: Monitoring and incentive compensation are alternative mechanisms to decrease agency costs, and incentive compensation is particularly important under circumstances where information asymmetry prevents effective monitoring (refer back to Section 2.5.2).
- The correlation between ALIGN and CDAXPRIOR is 0.55, and the correlation between ALIGN and IPOSPRIOR is even 0.84. This follows from the fact that incentive compensation mechanisms were primarily used in the 1999-2000 years, where prior stock market performance was positive and numerous IPOs took place.
- The correlation between CDAXPRIOR and IPOSPRIOR is 0.63, reflecting the fact that IPOs were clustered around periods of superior market performance. Also, not surprisingly, the correlations between CDAXPRIOR and CDAXPOST, respectively, and their difference CDAXPRIOR-CDAXPOST, are high.
- Finally, the correlation between INFL and INFL_AR is 0.98. The nearly perfect correlation is due to the fact that the variable INFL is constructed from INFL_AR and INFL_VS, and INFL_VS has very low variance since there are extremely few double management board mandates, as discussed above.

In conclusion, an inspection of the correlation matrix of explanatory variables indicates that major multicollinearity issues need not be expected, given the relatively small number of significant correlation coefficients. However, more precise evidence on potential multicollinearity is provided below in the calculation of Variance Inflation Factors.

4.4.2.2 *Short-term abnormal returns regressions*

4.4.2.2.1 *Results for the full model*

Results of the cross-sectional regression on short-term abnormal returns are presented in Table 36 and Table 37. In the leftmost column of the tables, the expected signs of the variables are indicated. Below the coefficients, t-statistics based on White heteroskedasticity-consistent standard errors are reported in parentheses. In addition, diagnostic tests and specification indicators are shown in the bottom panel of the tables.

As explained in Section 4.3.4.3, a general-to-specific model specification approach has been followed, where, starting with a full model, irrelevant variables have been excluded from the equation in order to arrive at a more parsimonious specification. Also, different alternative specifications are reported as a robustness check.

Table 36 shows Model (1), the full model, which includes all explanatory variables discussed in Section 3. The adjusted R^2 of 75.16% indicates a high goodness-of-fit, and the F-statistic is strongly significant at 10.08. Diagnostic tests do not indicate heteroskedasticity, autocorrelation, or non-normality of the residuals. The maximum VIF is relatively high at 7.85, but below the threshold value of 10, and thus does not indicate the presence of multicollinearity. The CUSUM test shows no evidence of structural breaks (Figure 29). As far as the size, sign, and significance of coefficients are concerned, Model (1) indicates the following:

- *Focus and investment efficiency:* The coefficient on FOCUS is positive and strongly significant. A reduction in the diversity of investment opportunities is positively related to short-term abnormal returns. For example, a 10% reduction increases the cumulative standardized prediction error by 0.18, which compares to a cumulative standardized prediction of 0.57 (over the 30 days up to the ECO announcement). Thus, H1A is supported. The coefficient on OVINV is negative and strongly significant. Sample parents with above

Table 36: Short-term cross-sectional regression, full model

	Expected sign	Full model	
Model		1	
Dependent Variable		CSPE -30 0	
Constant		2.60	
		(2.47)	**
FOCUS	+	1.80	
		(3.00)	***
OVINV	-	-7.52	
		(-4.50)	***
DEBT_RED	+	0.92	
		(2.54)	**
DIV_PAYOUT	+	-0.51	
		(-4.42)	***
DEBT_RED*OVINV	+		
DIV_PAYOUT*OVINV	+		
ASYM	+	-15.46	
		(-1.82)	*
TRANSP	-	5.68	
		(0.64)	
ALIGN	+	0.93	
		(2.82)	***
OWN_PAR	+	1.53	
		(2.31)	**
OWN_PAR*OVINV	-	-35.50	
		(-5.52)	***

INFL_AR	+	0.23	
		(2.76)	***
INFL_VS	+/-	1.10	
		(1.00)	
LEVERAGE	+/-	-5.18	
		(-4.56)	***
RELSIZE	+/-	0.09	
		(0.63)	
PSIZE	+/-	6.30	
		(5.28)	***
ROA	+/-	-3.45	
		(-3.19)	***
CDAXPRIOR	+/-	1.02	
		(1.30)	
Adjusted R^2		75.16%	
F		10.08	***
White statistic		1.10	
Breusch-Godfrey statistic		0.00	
Durbin-Watson statistic		2.30	
Jarque-Bera statistic		1.34	
Akaike information criterion		2.5817	
Schwarz information criterion		3.238	
CUSUM significant at 5% level		No	
Maximum VIF		7.85	
Average VIF		2.79	

Figure 29: CUSUM graph, Model (1)

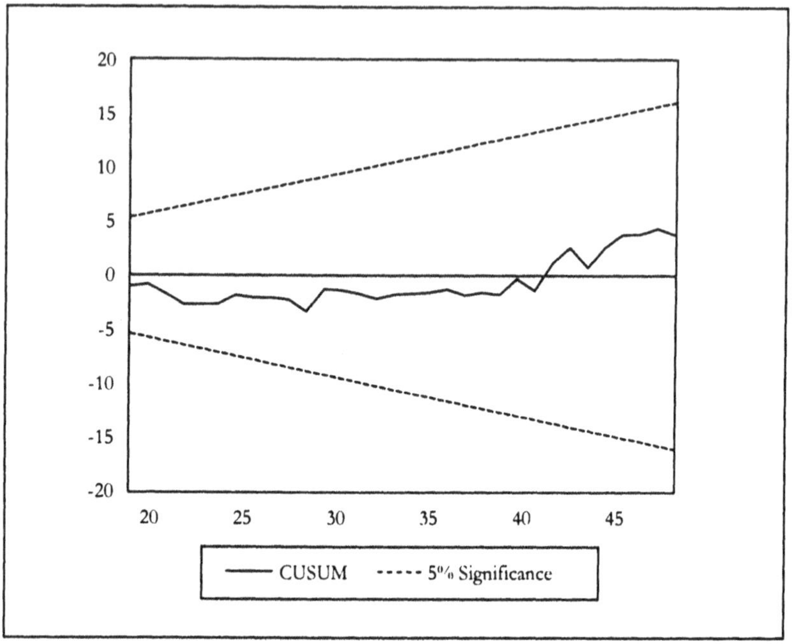

industry-average investment pre-ECO thus have significantly lower short-term abnormal returns. This supports H1B. In terms of coefficient magnitude, a 1% increase in the industry-adjusted capex/sales ratio leads to a decrease of 0.08 of the cumulative standardized prediction error. The coefficient on DEBT_RED is positive and significant, while the coefficient on DIV_PAYOUT is negative and strongly significant. Thus, a payout of ECO proceeds to debtholders appears to be positively related to short-term abnormal returns, while a payout to shareholders appears to be negatively related. Therefore, H1C is only partially supported. Finally, the coefficient on OVINV*OWN_PAR is negative and strongly significant. Consistent with H1D, the negative effect of pre-ECO overinvestment is particularly severe when the parent retains a high fraction of ownership in the subsidiary, and effective impediments against inefficient capital reallocations are thus not created.

- *Information asymmetry:* The coefficient on ASYM is negative and weakly significant. This result is in contradiction to H2A. While it is hypothesized that strong pre-ECO information asymmetries should be positively related to short-term abnormal returns, the opposite is the case. While H2A is based on the assumption that the increase in mandatory disclosure caused by an ECO is particularly valuable in environments with high information asymmetry, this pattern is apparently not borne out by the data. The coefficient on TRANSP is positive and insignificant. Thus, a decrease in information asymmetry post-ECO is not significantly related to short-term abnormal returns. Therefore, H2B can neither be supported nor rejected. A potential explanation is the strong negative correlation between ASYM and TRANSP, as already discussed above. In alternative model specifications, the two variables are thus analyzed separately.

- *Incentive compensation:* The coefficient on ALIGN is positive and strongly significant. Sample ECOs where subsidiary management is incentivized via direct stock ownership or a stock options program enjoy significantly higher announcement returns. The influence of incentive compensation on short-term abnormal returns is very strong: Sample parents with incentive compensation have a CSPE which is 0.93 higher than that of those without incentive compensation for subsidiary managers. Consequently, H3A is supported. The coefficient on INFL_AR is also positive and strongly significant, pointing to an effective control of managerial influence over the pay-setting process via parent representation on the subsidiary supervisory board. Thus, H3B is equally supported. However, despite the strong statistical significance, the influence of INFL_AR on short-term abnormal returns is not very strong economically. Assuming an average supervisory board size of 8 shareholder representatives, and 50% parent ownership in the subsidiary, each additional board seat for the ECO parent increases the CSPE by only 0.05. An influence of INFL_VS cannot be detected. The coefficient on INFL_VS is positive but insignificant.

- *Ownership concentration:* The coefficient on OWN_PAR is positive and significant. Thus, a higher parent ownership in the subsidiary post-ECO is positively related to the announcement return, supporting H4A. The magnitude of the coefficient is quite high at 1.53: For example, 20% higher

Table 37: Short-term cross-sectional regression, reduced models

	Expected sign	Reduced models including CDAXPRIOR			
Model		2	3	4	5
Dependent Variable		CSPE -30 0	CSPE -30 0	CSPE -30 0	CSPE -30 0
Constant		2.46	1.55	2.09	0.73
		(2.27) **	(1.45)	(1.95) *	(0.59)
FOCUS	+	1.81	1.76	2.95	2.70
		(3.28) ***	(2.69) ***	(3.98) ***	(3.18) ***
OVINV	-	-7.87	-7.29	-4.59	-5.08
		(-5.78) ***	(-4.81) ***	(-2.76) ***	(-2.69) ***
DEBT_RED	+	1.02	0.77		
		(3.63) ***	(1.72) *		
DIV_PAYOUT	+	-0.56	-0.54		
		(-7.10) ***	(-5.57) ***		
DEBT_RED*OVINV	+			4.13	2.65
				(1.86) *	(1.04)
DIV_PAYOUT*OVINV	+			1.77	1.84
				(4.50) ***	(4.09) ***
ASYM	+	-17.49		-37.93	
		(-2.69) ***		(-4.42) ***	
TRANSP	-		20.28		27.92
			(2.27) **		(2.58) **
ALIGN	+	0.87	0.65	0.91	0.74
		(2.80) ***	(2.11) **	(2.45) **	(1.76) *
OWN_PAR	+	1.66	1.41	2.36	2.55
		(2.69) ***	(2.16) **	(2.99) ***	(2.71) ***
OWN_PAR*OVINV	-	-36.63	-34.74	-17.09	-21.11
		(-6.42) ***	(-5.10) ***	(-2.46) **	(-2.69) ***

OWN_PAR*OVINV	-	-36.63	-34.74	-17.09	-21.11
		(-6.42) ***	(-5.10) ***	(-2.46) **	(-2.69) ***
INFL_AR	+	0.26	0.27	0.13	0.19
		(3.59) ***	(2.04) **	(0.87)	(1.09)
INFL_VS	+/-				
LEVERAGE	+/-	-4.98	-4.00	-5.38	-4.35
		(-4.07) ***	(-3.57) ***	(-4.71) ***	(-3.42) ***
RELSIZE	+/-				
PSIZE	+/-	6.29	5.77	3.78	3.92
		(4.93) ***	(3.88) ***	(2.48) **	(2.25) **
ROA	+/-	-2.97	-3.42	-3.34	-4.86
		(-3.78) ***	(-3.36) ***	(-3.05) ***	(-3.09) ***
CDAXPRIOR	+/-	1.19	1.02	2.36	1.28
		(1.73) *	(1.29)	(2.56) **	(1.28)
Adjusted R^2		75.60%	76.00%	67.38%	57.32%
F		12.44 ***	12.69 ***	8.63 ***	5.96 ***
White statistic		0.63	0.79	0.78	0.50
Breusch-Godfrey statistic		0.41	0.00	0.09	0.20
Durbin-Watson statistic		2.28	2.11	1.83	1.71
Jarque-Bera statistic		1.01	1.76	2.05	10.11 ***
Akaike information criterion		2.5312	2.5146	2.8214	3.0903
Schwarz information criterion		3.0717	3.0551	3.3619	3.6309
CUSUM significant at 5% level		No	No	No	No
Maximum VIF		6.62	6.12	5.52	5.35
Average VIF		2.49	2.44	2.24	2.27

Table 37 (continued)

	Expected sign	Reduced models excluding CDAXPRIOR			
Model		6	7	8	9
Dependent Variable		CSPE -30 0	CSPE -30 0	CSPE -30 0	CSPE -30 0
Constant		2.80	2.04	2.69	1.20
		(2.67) **	(2.02) **	(2.34) **	(1.01)
FOCUS	+	1.30	1.33	2.06	2.22
		(2.77) ***	(2.34) **	(2.92) ***	(2.88) ***
OVINV	-	-8.16	-7.62	-4.79	-5.13
		(-5.91) ***	(-5.05) ***	(-2.69) ***	(-2.69) ***
DEBT_RED	+	1.14	0.91		
		(4.29) ***	(2.07) **		
DIV_PAYOUT	+	-0.61	-0.58		
		(-7.98) ***	(-6.21) ***		
DEBT_RED*OVINV	+			5.15	3.37
				(2.20) **	(1.34)
DIV_PAYOUT*OVINV	+			1.93	1.92
				(4.62) ***	(4.29) ***
ASYM	+	-12.32		-30.78	
		(-2.40) **		(-3.53) ***	
TRANSP	-		16.31		26.60
			(1.93) *		(2.45) **
ALIGN	+	0.99	0.82	1.16	0.93
		(3.43) ***	(2.88) ***	(3.01) ***	(2.32) **
OWN_PAR	+	1.41	1.25	1.83	2.26
		(2.42) **	(1.93) *	(2.24) **	(2.45) **
OWN_PAR*OVINV	-	-38.28	-36.22	-17.57	-20.76
		(-6.66) ***	(-5.35) ***	(-2.35) **	(-2.63) **

INFL_AR	+	0.24	0.25	0.08	0.15
		(3.25) ***	(1.90) *	(0.51)	(0.88)
INFL_VS	+/-				
LEVERAGE	+/-	-4.86	-4.09	-5.00	-4.25
		(-4.08) ***	(-3.64) ***	(-4.10) ***	(-3.31) ***
RELSIZE	+/-				
PSIZE	+/-	6.45	5.97	3.61	3.80
		(5.03) ***	(4.00) ***	(2.20) **	(2.16) **
ROA	+/-	-2.81	-3.23	-3.11	-4.72
		(-3.62) ***	(-3.19) ***	(-2.65) **	(-2.97) ***
CDAXPRIOR	+/-				
Adjusted R^2		74.91%	75.56%	62.33%	56.55%
F		12.94 ***	13.37 ***	7.62 ***	6.21 ***
White statistic		0.62	0.77	0.59	0.36
Breusch-Godfrey statistic		0.00	0.00	0.22	0.11
Durbin-Watson statistic		2.17	2.04	1.59	1.57
Jarque-Bera statistic		0.86	1.40	9.55 ***	17.13 ***
Akaike information criterion		2.5462	2.5199	2.9525	3.0954
Schwarz information criterion		3.0481	3.0218	3.4543	3.5973
CUSUM significant at 5% level		No	No	No	No
Maximum VIF		6.41	6.11	5.51	5.35
Average VIF		2.33	2.39	2.15	2.21

parent ownership increases the CSPE -30 0 by 0.30. Thus, blockholder control of the subsidiary by the parent immediately post-ECO has a strong positive effect on firm value.

- *Control variables*: An inspection of the coefficients on the control variables reveals that short-term abnormal returns are negatively and significantly related to leverage and profitability, positively and significantly related to parent size, and unrelated to the relative size of the subsidiary and the prior year CDAX performance.

Summarizing the above evidence, all variables with the exception of DIV_PAYOUT and ASYM have the expected signs. Hypotheses concerning focus and investment efficiency, incentive compensation, and ownership concentration are supported. There is not support for the hypothesized effects of information asymmetries and disclosure on ECO value creation. To the contrary, the evidence (if weakly) points towards a negative effect of pre-ECO information asymmetry on short-term abnormal returns.

A thorough discussion of the evidence and a comparison to previous results from the ECO literature follows in Section 4.5.2.

4.4.2.2.2 *Results for the reduced models*

In what follows, the general model is reduced towards a more parsimonious specification, and alternative model specifications are proposed. On the basis of redundant variables tests, a set of reduced models has been developed Table 37:

- Models (2)-(5) exclude the insignificant variables INFL_VS and RELSIZE.
- The variables relating to information asymmetry enter into the models separately: Models (2) and (4) include ASYM, while models (3) and (5) include TRANSP.
- In order to examine the marginal effect of pre-ECO overinvestment on the payout of ECO proceeds, models (4) and (5) include the respective interaction terms.

Models (6) to (9) are identical to models (2) and (5), except that the variable CDAXPRIOR is eliminated in addition.

Short of a discussion of every coefficient, the following points deserve highlighting. As expected, the exclusion of redundant variables does not affect R^2. Adjusted R^2 remains at around 75% for Models (2), (3), (6), and (7). The inclusion of the interaction term between overinvestment and the payout variables leads to a decline in adjusted R^2, in the order of 10% to 15%. In terms of the Schwarz information criterion, Model (7) is the best model, while the Akaike information criterion is minimized by Model (3). Both information criteria decline thanks to the exclusion of redundant variables The F-test indicates strong overall significance for all model specifications. Also, the diagnostic tests do not indicate heteroskedasticity, autocorrelation or non-normality, with the exception of models (4), (8) and (9), where the Jarque-Bera statistic indicates strong non-normality. The CUSUM tests do not find evidence for structural breaks. Variance inflation factors are benign, with none of the maximum values exceeding 7.

Concerning the regression coefficients, the models appear robust to the changes in specification. None of the variables changes sign, and the magnitude of the coefficients is relatively stable. Significance levels are also relatively unaffected. With the exception of INFL_AR, which becomes insignificant in the models including the interaction term between overinvestment and the payout variables, all variables remain significant. Thus, the conclusions discussed above remain fully intact. The reduced models differ in the following respects:

- Included separately, the coefficient on the variable TRANSP is positive and significant. Thus, the effect of ECOs on firm value is positively related to an increase in information asymmetry, measured by the industry-adjusted standard deviation of market model residuals. This is in direct contradiction to H2B. The coefficient on the variable ASYM remains negative and significant when included separately. Thus, as in the full model, H2A is rejected. Strong pre-ECO information asymmetry is negatively related to short-term abnormal returns. Apparently, the relationship between short-term abnormal returns and information asymmetry is different than hypothesized.

- The coefficients on the interaction terms OVINV*DEBT_RED and OVINV*DIV_PAYOUT are both positive. While the coefficient on OVINV*DIV_PAYOUT is significant in all four models where it is included, the coefficient on OVINV*DEBT_RED is only significant in the two Models (4) and (8) that include the variable ASYM. Overall, this pattern provides further support for H1C. The marginal effect of a payout of ECO proceeds is the more positively related to ECO value creation the more severe pre-ECO overinvestment. Thus, while the overall effect of an increase in the dividend payout ratio post-ECO is negative, it is less so for sample companies that overinvested pre-ECO.

- The coefficient on CDAXPRIOR is positive and significant in models (2) and (4). While this does not provide very strong evidence on an influence of the prior-year CDAX performance on ECO value creation, given its insignificance in the alternative model specifications, it weakly points towards a potential role of market timing. As already suggested by the stronger announcement effect for the 1998-2001 ECO subsample compared to the 1984-1997 subsample discussed in Section 4.4.1.1.2, there appears to be a clustering of ECOs in periods where they lead to a positive short-term capital market reaction. However, the evidence appears to be rather weak, given the insignificance of CDAXPRIOR in various model specifications.

Summarizing the above discussion, hypotheses concerning focus and investment efficiency, incentive compensation, and ownership concentration are solidly supported. As far as information asymmetries and disclosure is concerned, both H2A and H2B are rejected.

4.4.2.2.3 Robustness checks

In order to test the robustness of the preliminary conclusions reached in the previous section, the regression models are subjected to six different robustness checks:

- Conventional and Newey-West standard errors are used instead of White standard errors;
- bootstrapped confidence intervals for the regression coefficients are calculated;
- CSPEs based on the Scholes/Williams and Dimson adjustments are used as the dependent variable instead of CSPEs calculated based on the standard market model;
- CARs are used as the dependent variable instead of CSPEs;

- CSPEs over different event periods are used as the dependent variable; and finally,
- alternative definitions of explanatory variables are applied.

Robustness tests are generally based on Model (2). Further (unreported) robustness tests based on different base models do not materially alter conclusions.

Table 38 compares the t-statistics calculated based on three alternative standard errors (refer back to Section 4.3.4): White heteroskedasticity-consistent standard errors, conventional OLS standard errors, and Newey-West autocorrelation and heteroskedasticity consistent standard errors. Following a recommendation by Long/Ervin (2000), heteroskedasticity- consistent standard errors are generally used despite the White test not indicating the presence of heteroskedasticity due to the low power of the test in small samples. As Table 38 shows, t-statistics differ between the three alternative methods. However, only two variables are materially affected: the coefficient on INFL_AR is strongly significant using White and Newey-West, but only weakly so using standard OLS; the coefficient on CDAXPRIOR is significant using White and Newey-West, but not significant using standard OLS. Thus, overall conclusions are unaffected by the method for calculating standard errors.

Table 39 presents bootstrapped confidence intervals for the regression coefficients for the models discussed so far. Bootstrapped confidence intervals at the 1%, 5%, and 10% level of significance are reported in square brackets below the regression coefficients. A regression coefficient is significantly different from zero if the zero is not included in the respective confidence interval (refer back to Section 4.3.4).

The application of bootstrapped confidence intervals does not fundamentally affect conclusions based on parametric tests. However, significance levels are in general somewhat lower based on bootstrapped confidence intervals, and three coefficients become insignificant as a consequence:

- The coefficient on INFL_AR is insignificant, except in Model (1).
- The coefficient on ALIGN is only weakly significant in some of the models.
- The coefficient on the interaction DEBT_RED*OVINV is insignificant in all models.

Table 38: Short-term cross-sectional regression, alternative standard errors

	Expected sign	White standard errors		Conven-tional standard errors		Newey-West standard errors	
Model		2		2b		2c	
Dependent Variable		CSPE -30 0		CSPE -30 0		CSPE -30 0	
Constant		2.46		2.46		2.46	
		(2.27)	**	(2.48)	**	(2.07)	**
FOCUS	+	1.81		1.81		1.81	
		(3.28)	***	(-2.70)	***	(3.32)	***
OVINV	-	-7.87		-7.87		-7.87	
		(-5.78)	***	(-5.38)	***	(-5.49)	***
DEBT_RED	+	1.02		1.02		1.02	
		(3.63)	***	(2.49)	**	(4.42)	***
DIV_PAYOUT	+	-0.56		-0.56		-0.56	
		(-7.10)	***	(-5.83)	***	(-7.69)	***
ASYM	+	-17.49		-17.49		-17.49	
		(-2.69)	***	(-2.12)	**	(-2.99)	***
ALIGN	+	0.87		0.87		0.87	
		(2.80)	***	(2.72)	***	(3.19)	***
OWN_PAR	+	1.66		1.66		1.66	
		(2.69)	***	(2.44)	**	(2.94)	***
OWN_PAR*OVINV	-	-36.63		-36.63		-36.63	
		(-6.42)	***	(-5.57)	***	(-6.86)	***
INFL_AR	+	0.26		0.26		0.26	
		(3.59)	***	(1.91)	*	(3.55)	***
LEVERAGE	+/-	-4.98		-4.98		-4.98	
		(-4.07)	***	(-4.59)	***	(-3.39)	***
PSIZE	+/-	6.29		6.29		6.29	
		(4.93)	***	(4.35)	***	(5.73)	***
ROA	+/-	-2.97		-2.97		-2.97	
		(-3.78)	***	(-3.12)	***	(3.20)	***
CDAXPRIOR	+/-	1.19		1.19		1.19	
		(1.73)	*	(1.42)		(2.08)	**

Table 39: Short-term cross-sectional regression, bootstrapped confidence intervals

Model	1			
Dependent Variable	CSPE -30 0			
Significance level	1% level	5% level	10% level	
Constant	2.60			
	[-1.50;6.49]	[0.00;5.19]	[0.53;4.73]	*
FOCUS	1.80			
	[0.22;4.27]	[0.68;3.46]	[0.84;3.11]	***
OVINV	-7.52			
	[-15.70;-0.70]	[-13.08;-3.06]	[-12.00;-3.97]	***
DEBT_RED	0.92			
	[-0.27;2.56]	[0.18;2.01]	[0.32;1.74]	**
DIV_PAYOUT	-0.51			
	[-1.17;-0.02]	[-0.96;-0.17]	[-0.86;-0.24]	***
DEBT_RED*OVINV				
DIV_PAYOUT*OVINV				
ASYM	-15.46			
	[-46.16;15.37]	[-35.97;5.92]	[-32.44;2.28]	
TRANSP	5.68			
	[-22.56;38.39]	[-14.05;28.44]	[-9.25;24.51]	
ALIGN	0.93			
	[-0.06;2.54]	[0.18;1.85]	[0.35;1.62]	**
OWN_PAR	1.53			
	[-0.53;4.86]	[0.03;3.49]	[0.38;3.14]	**
OWN_PAR*OVINV	-35.50			
	[-61.72;-12.53]	[-54.11;-19.70]	[-50.15;-23.09]	***
INFL_AR	0.23			
	[-0.06;0.50]	[0.02;0.41]	[0.06;0.37]	**
INFL_VS	1.10			
	[-3.83;5.33]	[-2.24;4.43]	[-1.51;3.70]	
LEVERAGE	-5.18			
	[-10.69;-0.87]	[-8.28;-2.42]	[-7.62;-3.01]	***
RELSIZE	0.09			
	[-0.61;0.74]	[-0.36;0.51]	[-0.21;0.43]	
PSIZE	6.30			
	[2.56;11.75]	[4.21;10.38]	[4.54;9.84]	***
ROA	-3.45			
	[-8.66;-0.22]	[-6.96;-1.08]	[-6.05;-1.62]	***
CDAXPRIOR	1.02			
	[-1.32;3.36]	[-0.71;2.83]	[-0.27;2.47]	

Bootstrapped confidence intervals are reported in square brackets below the regression coefficients

Table 39 (continued)

Model	2			
Dependent Variable	CSPE -30 0			
Significance level	1% level	5% level	10% level	
Constant	2.46			
	[-1.28;6.75]	[-0.12;5.25]	[0.40;4.81]	*
FOCUS	1.81			
	[0.19;3.63]	[0.51;3.30]	[0.79;3.09]	***
OVINV	-7.87			
	[-13.55;-3.14]	[-12.22;-4.20]	[-11.27;-4.86]	***
DEBT_RED	1.02			
	[-0.12;2.36]	[0.20;1.96]	[0.37;1.80]	**
DIV_PAYOUT	-0.56			
	[-1.17;-0.18]	[-1.01;-0.32]	[-0.88;-0.37]	***
DEBT_RED*OVINV				
DIV_PAYOUT*OVINV				
ASYM	-17.49			
	[-48.62;12.11]	[-37.15;3.77]	[-33.13;-0.46]	*
TRANSP				
ALIGN	0.87			
	[-0.25;2.21]	[-0.02;1.69]	[0.13;1.54]	*
OWN_PAR	1.66			
	[-0.48;4.48]	[0.24;3.62]	[0.54;3.25]	**
OWN_PAR*OVINV	-36.63			
	[-59.53;-16.85]	[-55.41;-20.71]	[-50.87;-24.29]	***
INFL_AR	0.26			
	[-0.18;0.64]	[-0.07;0.55]	[-0.01;0.49]	
INFL_VS				
LEVERAGE	-4.98			
	[-9.57;-0.54]	[-8.19;-2.24]	[-7.53;-2.83]	***
RELSIZE				
PSIZE	6.29			
	[2.05;12.93]	[3.19;11.42]	[3.88;10.65]	***
ROA	-2.97			
	[-6.82;-0.33]	[-5.67;-1.19]	[-5.15;-1.42]	***
CDAXPRIOR	1.19			
	[-0.94;3.64]	[-0.47;3.06]	[-0.23;2.62]	

Bootstrapped confidence intervals are reported in square brackets below the regression coefficients

Table 39 (continued)

Model	3			
Dependent Variable	CSPE -30 0			
Significance level	1% level	5% level	10% level	
Constant	1.55			
	[-2.27;5.14]	[-0.87;4.05]	[-0.50;3.49]	
FOCUS	1.76			
	[-0.21;3.80]	[0.29;3.21]	[0.57;2.94]	**
OVINV	-7.29			
	[-12.94;-2.29]	[-11.40;-3.67]	[-10.61;-4.25]	***
DEBT_RED	0.77			
	[-0.54;2.25]	[-0.23;1.63]	[0.00;1.50]	
DIV_PAYOUT	-0.54			
	[-1.09;-0.22]	[-0.93;-0.29]	[-0.85;-0.33]	***
DEBT_RED*OVINV				
DIV_PAYOUT*OVINV				
ASYM				
TRANSP	20.28			
	[-2.77;53.28]	[2.52;44.25]	[6.29;39.55]	**
ALIGN	0.65			
	[-0.43;1.84]	[-0.12;1.40]	[0.05;1.24]	*
OWN_PAR	1.41			
	[-0.41;3.84]	[0.04;3.21]	[0.40;2.89]	**
OWN_PAR*OVINV	-34.74			
	[-56.63;-13.30]	[-52.33;-20.18]	[-49.32;-22.45]	***
INFL_AR	0.27			
	[-0.25;0.62]	[-0.05;0.53]	[0.02;0.48]	
INFL_VS				
LEVERAGE	-4.00			
	[-8.67;-0.19]	[-7.14;-1.40]	[-6.31;-1.77]	***
RELSIZE				
PSIZE	5.77			
	[1.08;11.88]	[2.53;9.96]	[3.27;9.39]	***
ROA	-3.42			
	[-7.92;-0.86]	[-6.13;-1.58]	[-5.64;-1.92]	***
CDAXPRIOR	1.02			
	[-1.27;3.61]	[-0.50;2.69]	[-0.22;2.43]	

Bootstrapped confidence intervals are reported in square brackets below the regression coefficients

Table 39 (continued)

Model	4		
Dependent Variable	CSPE -30 0		
Significance level	1% level	5% level	10% level
Constant	2.09		
	[-1.24;6.15]	[-0.45;5.19]	[-0.14;4.36] *
FOCUS	2.95		
	[0.84;7.54]	[1.60;6.17]	[1.82;5.59] ***
OVINV	-4.59		
	[-9.99;3.01]	[-8.39;1.14]	[-7.61;-0.02] *
DEBT_RED			
DIV_PAYOUT			
DEBT_RED*OVINV	4.13		
	[-8.67;16.04]	[-5.34;12.94]	[-3.30;10.88]
DIV_PAYOUT*OVINV	1.77		
	[-0.71;3.90]	[0.26;3.17]	[0.67;2.90] **
ASYM	-37.93		
	[-79.22;-9.39]	[-69.48;-20.83]	[-62.74;-24.88] ***
TRANSP			
ALIGN	0.91		
	[-0.34;2.07]	[-0.06;1.73]	[0.10;1.59] *
OWN_PAR	2.36		
	[0.14;5.45]	[0.83;4.46]	[1.08;4.10] ***
OWN_PAR*OVINV	-17.09		
	[-35.98;18.27]	[-28.83;8.32]	[-26.11;4.12]
INFL_AR	0.13		
	[-0.53;0.80]	[-0.37;0.59]	[-0.28;0.51]
INFL_VS			
LEVERAGE	-5.38		
	[-10.10;-2.39]	[-9.06;-2.87]	[-8.26;-3.19] ***
RELSIZE			
PSIZE	3.78		
	[-3.67;10.26]	[-1.09;8.17]	[-0.30;7.53]
ROA	-3.34		
	[-8.00;-0.17]	[-6.72;-1.11]	[-5.77;-1.59] ***
CDAXPRIOR	2.36		
	[-0.21;6.90]	[0.72;5.83]	[1.03;5.20] **

Bootstrapped confidence intervals are reported in square brackets below the regression coefficients

Table 39 (continued)

Model	5			
Dependent Variable	CSPE -30 0			
Significance level	1% level	5% level	10% level	
Constant	0.73			
	[-3.64;5.50]	[-2.63;3.57]	[-1.98;2.99]	
FOCUS	2.70			
	[0.86;7.15]	[1.25;6.00]	[1.54;5.37]	***
OVINV	-5.08			
	[-12.10;4.18]	[-9.92;1.65]	[-8.88;0.69]	
DEBT_RED				
DIV_PAYOUT				
DEBT_RED*OVINV	2.65			
	[-10.20;15.86]	[-6.57;13.20]	[-4.32;10.55]	
DIV_PAYOUT*OVINV	1.84			
	[-0.98;4.80]	[0.15;3.95]	[0.58;3.55]	**
ASYM				
TRANSP	27.92			
	[-0.75;80.56]	[6.44;71.64]	[12.45;64.52]	***
ALIGN	0.74			
	[-0.71;2.10]	[-0.32;1.71]	[-0.15;1.52]	
OWN_PAR	2.55			
	[-0.35;5.70]	[0.80;5.17]	[1.16;4.77]	**
OWN_PAR*OVINV	-21.11			
	[-50.34;17.20]	[-38.49;10.47]	[-34.48;4.85]	
INFL_AR	0.19			
	[-0.57;0.66]	[-0.37;0.57]	[-0.27;0.51]	
INFL_VS				
LEVERAGE	-4.35			
	[-9.53;-0.08]	[-7.97;-1.13]	[-7.07;-1.78]	***
RELSIZE				
PSIZE	3.92			
	[-3.83;10.90]	[-1.42;8.45]	[-0.51;7.62]	
ROA	-4.86			
	[-11.72;-0.99]	[-9.63;-2.12]	[-9.02;-2.79]	***
CDAXPRIOR	1.28			
	[-1.00;5.25]	[-0.42;4.34]	[-0.15;3.60]	

Bootstrapped confidence intervals are reported in square brackets below the regression coefficients

Table 39 (continued)

Model	6			
Dependent Variable	CSPE -30 0			
Significance level	1% level	5% level	10% level	
Constant	2.80			
	[-0.14;7.84]	[0.51;5.85]	[0.91;5.10]	**
FOCUS	1.30			
	[-0.21;2.85]	[0.20;2.55]	[0.36;2.31]	**
OVINV	-8.16			
	[-13.45;-3.19]	[-11.87;-4.85]	[-11.24;-5.53]	***
DEBT_RED	1.14			
	[-0.23;2.23]	[0.34;1.97]	[0.47;1.83]	**
DIV_PAYOUT	-0.61			
	[-1.15;-0.22]	[-1.00;-0.36]	[-0.90;-0.42]	***
DEBT_RED*OVINV				
DIV_PAYOUT*OVINV				
ASYM	-12.32			
	[-36.61;15.58]	[-29.90;5.52]	[-26.81;1.53]	
TRANSP				
ALIGN	0.99			
	[0.01;2.18]	[0.27;1.68]	[0.37;1.54]	***
OWN_PAR	1.41			
	[-0.49;4.08]	[0.06;3.34]	[0.29;3.01]	**
OWN_PAR*OVINV	-38.28			
	[-64.04;-18.70]	[-55.03;-23.38]	[-51.81;-25.80]	***
INFL_AR	0.24			
	[-0.25;0.67]	[-0.10;0.54]	[-0.01;0.48]	
INFL_VS				
LEVERAGE	-4.86			
	[-10.67;-1.01]	[-8.30;-2.38]	[-7.55;-2.83]	***
RELSIZE				
PSIZE	6.45			
	[1.84;13.25]	[3.40;11.65]	[4.25;10.72]	***
ROA	-2.81			
	[-6.90;-0.46]	[-5.81;-1.00]	[-4.93;-1.34]	***
CDAXPRIOR				

Bootstrapped confidence intervals are reported in square brackets below the regression coefficients

Table 39 (continued)

Model	7			
Dependent Variable	CSPE -30 0			
Significance level	1% level	5% level	10% level	
Constant	2.04			
	[-1.15;5.14]	[-0.24;4.38]	[0.19;3.97]	*
FOCUS	1.33			
	[-0.16;2.91]	[0.17;2.46]	[0.38;2.23]	**
OVINV	-7.62			
	[-13.05;-2.80]	[-11.61;-4.17]	[-11.14;-4.75]	***
DEBT_RED	0.91			
	[-0.40;2.11]	[0.00;1.75]	[0.21;1.60]	**
DIV_PAYOUT	-0.58			
	[-1.19;-0.25]	[-0.98;-0.33]	[-0.89;-0.38]	***
DEBT_RED*OVINV				
DIV_PAYOUT*OVINV				
ASYM				
TRANSP	16.31			
	[-14.44;47.74]	[-0.95;39.82]	[2.84;34.38]	*
ALIGN	0.82			
	[-0.16;1.84]	[0.13;1.49]	[0.25;1.36]	**
OWN_PAR	1.25			
	[-0.45;3.56]	[-0.09;3.00]	[0.15;2.68]	*
OWN_PAR*OVINV	-36.22			
	[-61.95;-14.58]	[-53.47;-19.83]	[-50.18;-23.66]	***
INFL_AR	0.25			
	[-0.19;0.61]	[-0.07;0.50]	[-0.01;0.46]	
INFL_VS				
LEVERAGE	-4.09			
	[-8.56;-0.45]	[-6.88;-1.32]	[-6.29;-1.83]	***
RELSIZE				
PSIZE	5.97			
	[1.07;12.83]	[2.90;10.49]	[3.54;9.87]	***
ROA	-3.23			
	[-7.27;-0.41]	[-5.96;-1.39]	[-5.48;-1.72]	***
CDAXPRIOR				

Bootstrapped confidence intervals are reported in square brackets below the regression coefficients

Table 39 (continued)

Model	8			
Dependent Variable	CSPE -30 0			
Significance level	1% level	5% level	10% level	
Constant	2.69			
	[-0.74;6.83]	[0.31;5.96]	[0.80;5.30]	**
FOCUS	2.06			
	[0.60;5.93]	[1.02;4.46]	[1.13;4.14]	***
OVINV	-4.79			
	[-11.37;3.48]	[-9.52;0.60]	[-8.50;-0.33]	*
DEBT_RED				
DIV_PAYOUT				
DEBT_RED*OVINV	5.15			
	[-10.64;19.68]	[-6.23;16.46]	[-4.02;13.29]	
DIV_PAYOUT*OVINV	1.93			
	[-0.37;4.48]	[0.20;3.58]	[0.63;3.30]	**
ASYM	-30.78			
	[-82.48;-11.45]	[-59.60;-16.22]	[-54.35;-19.25]	***
TRANSP				
ALIGN	1.16			
	[0.04;2.59]	[0.28;2.10]	[0.39;1.90]	***
OWN_PAR	1.83			
	[-0.55;4.35]	[0.13;3.60]	[0.41;3.30]	**
OWN_PAR*OVINV	17.57			
	[-41.40;24.88]	[-30.33;11.48]	[-26.88;7.08]	
INFL_AR	0.08			
	[-0.90;0.59]	[-0.62;0.49]	[-0.48;0.41]	
INFL_VS				
LEVERAGE	-5.00			
	[-9.59;-0.87]	[-8.35;-2.10]	[-7.76;-2.69]	***
RELSIZE				
PSIZE	3.61			
	[-3.60;10.00]	[-1.42;8.25]	[-0.81;7.17]	
ROA	-3.11			
	[-8.47;-0.31]	[-6.62;-1.13]	[-5.83;-1.46]	***
CDAXPRIOR				

Bootstrapped confidence intervals are reported in square brackets below the regression coefficients

Table 39 (continued)

Model	9			
Dependent Variable	CSPE -30 0			
Significance level	1% level	5% level	10% level	
Constant	1.20			
	[-2.25;5.04]	[-1.57;4.02]	[-1.01;3.50]	
FOCUS	2.22			
	[0.49;5.84]	[0.96;4.91]	[1.16;4.61]	***
OVINV	-5.13			
	[-11.55;3.02]	[-9.49;1.17]	[-8.54;0.19]	
DEBT_RED				
DIV_PAYOUT				
DEBT_RED*OVINV	3.37			
	[-12.43;18.39]	[-7.65;14.34]	[-4.38;11.81]	
DIV_PAYOUT*OVINV	1.92			
	[-0.64;4.85]	[0.12;4.21]	[0.66;3.78]	**
ASYM				
TRANSP	26.60			
	[2.69;85.11]	[8.89;69.55]	[12.94;64.22]	***
ALIGN	0.93			
	[-0.35;2.19]	[-0.04;1.83]	[0.10;1.62]	*
OWN_PAR	2.26			
	[-0.30;5.45]	[0.47;4.56]	[0.82;4.28]	**
OWN_PAR*OVINV	-20.76			
	[-42.81;22.24]	[-34.42;11.91]	[-31.58;6.57]	
INFL_AR	0.15			
	[-0.65;0.67]	[-0.50;0.53]	[-0.37;0.46]	
INFL_VS				
LEVERAGE	-4.25			
	[-9.51;-0.42]	[-7.75;-1.43]	[-7.17;-1.80]	***
RELSIZE				
PSIZE	3.80			
	[-3.73;10.53]	[-1.90;8.29]	[-0.92;7.60]	
ROA	-4.72			
	[-11.50;-0.99]	[-9.46;-2.02]	[-8.94;-2.63]	***
CDAXPRIOR				

Bootstrapped confidence intervals are reported in square brackets below the regression coefficients

Overall though, bootstrapped confidence intervals confirm the results obtained from parametric t-tests. The lower power of the bootstrap procedure is expected, since the Jarque-Bera statistic indicates normality of the residuals in most models. In the literature, the superior power of parametric tests under circumstances where the normality assumption is fulfilled has been repeatedly documented.

Further robustness checks consist in variations of the dependent variable. Table 40 presents regression results where instead of CSPEs based on the standard market model, and CSPEs based on the Scholes-Williams and Dimson adjustments for thin trading are used. The base model is again Model (2). As can be seen from the table, the magnitude and significance of coefficient estimates is essentially unaffected by the use of CSPEs adjusted for thin trading. The only exception is the insignificant coefficient on CDAXPRIOR in the Dimson-adjusted model (Model (11)). Thus, conclusions reached based on standard market model CSPEs are confirmed.

Table 41 presents regression results where cumulative abnormal returns (CARs) are used as dependent variable instead of cumulative standardized prediction errors (CSPEs). The base models are Model (2), (3), (6), and (7), respectively. The goodness-of-fit of the models declines markedly, with adjusted R^2 of around 62% for Models (2f) and (6b), and around 67% for Models (3b) and (7b), compared to around 75% for the base models. Diagnostic tests do not indicate autocorrelation or structural breaks, but strong non-normality for all models, and mild heteroskedasticity for some models. However, the regression coefficients mostly remain significant. The exceptions are the following:

- The coefficient on DIV_PAYOUT is insignificant in three of the four models
- The coefficient on ASYM is insignificant in both model (2f) and (6b)
- The coefficient on INFL_AR is insignificant in both model (3b) and (7b)

Thus, no influence of dividend payout ratios on cumulative abnormal returns can be detected, weakening the contradiction to H1C. Also, no impact of pre-ECO information asymmetry can be detected on cumulative abnormal returns, and H2A is again not supported. Finally, support for H3B is weakened, since parent supervisory board mandates do not have an effect on cumulative abnormal returns. This last result is similar to the evidence from bootstrapping discussed above.

Table 40: Short-term cross-sectional regression, with thin-trading adjustments

	Expected sign	Thin-trading adjustments			
Model		2d		2e	
Dependent Variable		CSPE -30 0, SW		CSPE -30 0, Dimson	
Constant		1.24		2.31	
		(1.03)		(2.28)	**
FOCUS	+	2.17		1.92	
		(4.35)	***	(3.85)	***
OVINV	-	-7.58		-7.25	
		(-5.44)	***	(-6.19)	***
DEBT_RED	+	0.87		0.84	
		(3.06)	***	(3.74)	***
DIV_PAYOUT	+	-0.52		-0.55	
		(-7.04)	***	(-7.68)	***
ASYM	+	-18.12		-16.42	
		(-2.80)	***	(-2.83)	***
ALIGN	+	0.95		0.83	
		(2.71)	***	(2.88)	***
OWN_PAR	+	1.90		1.37	
		(2.98)	***	(2.39)	**
OWN_PAR*OVINV	-	-33.57		-34.02	
		(-5.83)	***	(-6.57)	***
INFL_AR	+	0.29		0.21	
		(3.89)	***	(3.21)	***
LEVERAGE	+/-	-3.99		-4.50	
		(-2.97)	***	(-4.00)	***
PSIZE	+/-	5.88		5.87	
		(4.3)	***	(5.07)	***
ROA	+/-	-2.95		-2.99	
		(-3.48)	***	(-4.05)	***
CDAXPRIOR	+/-	1.63		1.03	
		(2.56)	**	(1.50)	
Adjusted R^2		73.88%		75.28%	
F		11.44	***	12.25	***
White statistic		0.54		0.44	
Breusch-Godfrey statistic		1.01		0.91	
Durbin-Watson statistic		2.24		2.13	
Jarque-Bera statistic		0.79		1.64	
Akaike information criterion		2.5319		2.4682	
Schwarz information criterion		3.0724		3.0087	
CUSUM significant at 5% level		No		No	
Maximum VIF		6.62		6.62	
Average VIF		2.49		2.49	

Table 41: Short-term cross-sectional regression, CARs as dependent variable

	Expected sign	Cumulative abnormal returns			
Model		2f	3b	6b	7b
Dependent Variable		CAR -30 0	CAR -30 0	CAR -30 0	CAR -30 0
Constant		0.85	0.57	0.91	0.71
		(3.00) ***	(2.27) **	(3.35) ***	(2.97) ***
FOCUS	+	0.39	0.44	0.29	0.31
		(2.71) ***	(2.87) ***	(2.60) **	(2.35) **
OVINV	-	-1.39	-1.11	-1.44	-1.21
		(-5.83) ***	(-3.14) ***	(-6.08) ***	(-3.31) ***
DEBT_RED	+	0.31	0.20	0.33	0.24
		(3.52) ***	(1.91) *	(4.10) ***	(2.31) **
DIV_PAYOUT	+	-0.04	-0.02	-0.05	-0.04
		(-1.54)	(-1.07)	(-1.69) *	(1.61)
DEBT_RED*OVINV	+				
DIV_PAYOUT*OVINV	+				
ASYM	+	-2.90		-1.89	
		(-1.29)		(-0.99)	
TRANSP	-		6.24		5.11
			(3.00) ***		(2.56) **
ALIGN	+	0.21	0.16	0.23	0.21
		(2.97) ***	(2.28) **	(3.33) ***	(3.15) ***
OWN_PAR	+	0.34	0.32	0.29	0.27
		(3.05) ***	(2.09) **	(2.62) **	(1.79) *
OWN_PAR*OVINV	-	-7.17	-5.85	-7.50	-6.28
		(-5.76) ***	(-3.68)	(-6.27) ***	(-3.92) ***

INFL_AR	+	0.04	0.04	0.04	0.03
		(2.27) **	(1.23)	(2.13) **	(1.05)
INFL_VS	+/-				
LEVERAGE	+/-	-1.53	-1.26	-1.51	-1.29
		(-4.50) ***	(-4.82) ***	(-4.51) ***	(-4.84) ***
RELSIZE	+/-				
PSIZE	+/-	1.43	1.19	0.00	1.25
		(5.25) ***	(3.43) ***	(5.48) ***	(3.54) ***
ROA	+/-	-0.52	-0.75	-0.49	-0.70
		(-3.18) ***	(-3.16) ***	(-2.92) ***	(-2.90) ***
CDAXPRIOR	+/-	0.23	0.29		
		(1.25)	(1.58)		
Adjusted R^2		62.06%	68.13%	61.84%	66.81%
F		7.04 ***	8.89 ***	7.48 ***	9.05 ***
White statistic		1.58	1.50	1.82 *	1.71 *
Breusch-Godfrey statistic		0.45	1.11	0.52	1.08
Durbin-Watson statistic		2.17	1.88	2.13	1.91
Jarque-Bera statistic		23.07 ***	15.16 ***	22.45 ***	17.93 ***
Akaike information criterion		-0.2181	-0.3926	-0.2251	-0.3645
Schwarz information criterion		0.3223	0.1479	0.2768	0.1374
CUSUM significant at 5% level		No	No	No	No
Maximum VIF		6.62	6.12	6.41	6.11
Average VIF		2.49	2.44	2.33	2.39

Table 42: Short-term cross-sectional regressions, alternative event periods

	Expected sign	Different event periods		
Model		2g	2h	2i
Dependent Variable		CSPE -25 0	CSPE -20 0	CSPE -15 0
Constant		1.47	1.02	0.89
		(1.30)	(0.80)	(0.78)
FOCUS	+	1.56	1.53	1.77
		(2.85) ***	(2.65) **	(2.47) **
OVINV	-	-7.05	-7.45	-7.53
		(-4.97) ***	(-5.49) ***	(-4.97) ***
DEBT_RED	+	0.64	0.83	0.93
		(1.80) *	(2.51) **	(2.43) **
DIV_PAYOUT	+	-0.68	-0.70	-0.63
		(-8.01) ***	(-8.72) ***	(-6.9) ***
ASYM	+	-13.80	-10.92	-17.12
		(-2.00) *	(-1.65)	(-2.14) **
ALIGN	+	0.59	0.74	0.75
		(1.77) *	(2.12) **	(2.41) **
OWN_PAR	+	1.09	1.35	2.23
		(1.77) *	(2.30) **	(3.30) ***
OWN_PAR*OVINV	-	-32.15	-31.51	-30.81
		(-5.15) ***	(-5.20) ***	(-4.50) ***
INFL_AR	+	0.22	0.22	0.14
		(2.64) **	(2.86) ***	(1.64)
LEVERAGE	+/-	-3.06	-3.03	-3.50
		(-2.38) **	(-2.10) **	(-2.48) **
PSIZE	+/-	4.76	4.85	4.76
		(3.54) ***	(3.31) ***	-3.10 ***
ROA	+/-	-2.79	-2.36	-3.84
		(-3.28) ***	(-2.81) ***	(-3.51) ***
CDAXPRIOR	+/-	1.23	1.27	2.27
		(1.64)	(1.86) *	(2.48) **
Adjusted R^2		67.65%	72.88%	69.48%
F		8.72 ***	10.92 ***	9.41 ***
White statistic		0.27	1.01	0.54
Breusch-Godfrey statistic		1.03	0.65	0.00
Durbin-Watson statistic		2.29	2.32	2.29
Jarque-Bera statistic		10.28 ***	1.48	2.31
Akaike information criterion		2.8206	2.6349	2.9161
Schwarz information criterion		3.3612	3.1754	3.4567
CUSUM significant at 5% level		No	No	No
Maximum VIF		6.62	6.62	6.62
Average VIF		2.49	2.49	2.49

Table 42(continued)

2j	2k
CSPE -10 0	CSPE -5 0
0.24	0.15
(0.17)	(0.12)
1.73	1.40
(2.13) **	(2.11) **
-8.62	-8.11
(-3.77) ***	(-2.89) ***
1.10	0.50
(2.36) **	(1.06)
-0.56	-0.74
(-2.28) **	(-4.15) ***
-10.83	-17.59
(-0.95)	(-1.33)
0.72	0.25
(1.85) *	(0.55)
2.11	2.02
(1.95) *	(1.42)
-32.96	-28.90
(-3.56) ***	(-2.67) **
0.20	0.30
(1.68) *	(2.23) **
-2.60	-2.20
(-1.25)	(-0.94)
4.92	4.54
(2.44) **	(1.86) *
-3.51	-2.87
(-2.31) **	(-1.45)
1.51	1.67
(1.23)	(1.51)
51.55%	57.90%
4.93 ***	6.08 ***
1.33	1.78
0.36	0.38
1.56	1.83
1.60	2.70
3.4378	3.443
3.9783	3.8848
No	No
6.62	6.62
2.49	2.49

Table 43: Short-term cross-sectional regression, alternative specifications

	Expected sign	Alternative model specifications					
Model		2l	2m	2n	2o	2p	2q
Dependent Variable		CSPE -30 0	CSPE -30 0	CSPE -30 0	CSPE -30 0	CSPE -30 0	CSPE -30 0
Constant		2.89	2.27	2.75	1.36	2.52	2.52
		(2.91) ***	(1.79) *	(2.84) ***	(0.99)	(2.37) **	(2.29) **
FOCUS	+	1.19	1.52	1.41	1.04	1.81	1.81
		(2.00) *	(2.28) **	(2.46) **	(1.75) *	(3.27) ***	(3.10) ***
OVINV	-	-8.31	-7.91	-8.22	-8.17	-7.90	-7.58
		(-5.57) ***	(-5.19) ***	(-5.66) ***	(-5.66) ***	(-5.90) ***	(-5.17) ***
DEBT_RED	+	1.21	1.05	1.18	1.12	1.03	1.00
		(2.86) ***	(2.43) ***	(2.91) ***	(2.80) ***	(3.76) ***	(3.52) ***
DIV_PAYOUT	+	-0.61	-0.59	-0.59	-0.60	-0.54	-0.56
		(-6.53) ***	(-5.96) ***	(-6.36) ***	(-6.58) ***	(-7.20) ***	(-6.83) ***
ASYM	+	-11.39	-14.12	-13.67	-12.48	-17.41	-19.11
		(-1.49)	(-1.76) *	(-1.83) *	(-1.69) *	(-2.69) ***	(-2.74) ***
ALIGN	+	1.06	0.76	1.02	0.90	0.88	0.92
		(3.18) ***	(1.66)	(3.27) ***	(2.83) ***	(2.83) ***	(2.82) ***
OWN_PAR	+	1.44	1.45	1.58	1.68	1.63	1.55
		(2.14) **	(2.15) **	(2.35) **	(2.47) **	(2.68) **	(2.37) **
OWN_PAR*OVINV	-	-39.42	37.03	-39.00	-38.11	-36.95	-34.77
		(-5.79) ***	(-5.38) ***	(-5.98) ***	(-5.90) ***	(-6.61) ***	(-5.26) ***
INFL_AR	+	0.25	0.25	0.26	0.27		0.27
		(1.83) *	(1.81) *	(1.92) *	(1.98) *		(3.73) ***
LEVERAGE	+/-	-4.91	-4.41	-4.99	-4.95	-5.06	-4.89
		(-4.44) ***	(-3.42) ***	(-4.58) ***	(-4.59) ***	(-4.25) ***	(-3.81) ***

PSIZE	+/-	6.44	5.74	6.36	6.48	6.39	5.92
		(4.37) ***	(3.17) ***	(4.39) ***	(4.50) ***	(5.18) ***	(4.00) ***
ROA	+/-	-2.72	-2.93	-2.77	-3.07	-2.97	-2.94
		(-2.80) ***	(-2.98) ***	(-2.92) ***	(-3.20) ***	(-3.88) ***	(-3.61) ***
CDAXPRIOR	+/-					1.17	1.19
						(1.17)	(1.71) *
CDAXPOST	+/-	-0.44					
		(-0.71)					
IPOSPRIOR	+/-		0.28				
			(0.67)				
CDAXPRIOR-CDAXPC	+/-			0.60			
				(1.31)			
CDAX_PE	+/-				0.07		
					(1.48)		
INFL	+					0.54	
						(3.79) ***	
ANALYSTS	+						-0.07
							(-0.77)
Adjusted R^2		74.56%	74.53%	75.40%	75.73%	76.09%	75.19%
F		11.82 ***	11.80 ***	12.32 ***	12.52 ***	12.75 ***	11.39 ***
White statistic		0.80	0.46	0.97	1.11	0.66	0.61
Breusch-Godfrey statistic		0.21	0.00	0.51	0.40	0.31	0.49
Durbin-Watson statistic		2.18	2.19	2.24	2.26	2.29	2.35
Jarque-Bera statistic		0.84	0.93	0.87	2.52	1.09	1.07
Akaike information criterion		2.5728	2.5741	2.5391	2.5259	2.511	2.5598
Schwarz information criterion		3.1134	3.1147	3.0796	3.0665	3.0515	3.1389
CUSUM significant at 5% level		No	No	No	No	No	No
Maximum VIF		6.41	6.52	6.37	6.51	6.31	7.45
Average VIF		2.47	2.62	2.44	2.52	2.57	2.60

In a further variation of the dependent variable, Table 42 presents regression results for successively shorter event periods. Again, the base model is Model (2). As can be expected, goodness-of-fit and significance levels show a tendency of declining as the event period is shortened, since shorter event periods do not capture the full economic effects of the ECO. However, none of the adjusted R^2 falls under 50%, and the model based on the shortest event period surveyed, the five days up to the announcement, has an adjusted R^2 of 57.90%. The magnitude of coefficient estimates is altered as the dependent variable changes, but all coefficients retain their original signs. Significance levels of individual coefficients generally decline somewhat. The most robust coefficients, remaining significant regardless of event period length, are those on FOCUS, OVINV, DIV_PAYOUT, OWN_PAR*OVINV, and PSIZE. Also robust, significant in four of the five models, are the coefficients on DEBT_RED, ALIGN, OWN_PAR, INFL_AR, and ROA. Thus, the conclusions drawn above based on the event period of thirty days up to the ECO announcement are confirmed. Coefficients not robust to variations in the length of the event period are those on ASYM, LEVERAGE, and CDAXPRIOR. This pattern again confirms the weak contradictory evidence on H2A, the role of pre-ECO information asymmetry.

As a final robustness check, several alternative explanatory variable specifications are tested, and alternative market timing indicators are introduced. The variable INFL_AR is replaced by the aggregate measure INFL as a measure of managerial influence on the pay-setting process. The variable TRANSP is replaced by the variable ANALYSTS as measure of the reduction in information asymmetry due to the ECO. The variable CDAXPRIOR as an indicator for potential market timing is replaced by the variables CDAXPOST, IPOSPRIOR, CDAXPRIOR-CDAXPOST, and CDAX_PE as alternative market timing indicators.

The base model is model (2), and results are presented in Table 43. The analysis of alternative specifications leads to mixed conclusions: On the one hand, the magnitude and significance of the coefficients on the unchanged variables remains stable. Goodness-of-fit and diagnostic statistics also remain well-behaved. These are clear signs of model robustness. On the other hand, the coefficients on ANALYSTS is insignificant. This may indicate that ANALYSTS is an inferior of information asymmetry, or that the variable is measuring something different. The behavior of the variable INFL is not materially different from the measure INFL_AR.

As far as the market timing indicators are concerned, all four alternative indicators are insignificant. Taken together with the weak significance of CDAXPRIOR found in prior robustness checks, this evidence speaks against a material role of market timing as a determinant of short-term abnormal returns.

Summarizing the results from the robustness checks, conclusions are robust to changes in standard error calculation, the application of bootstrapping procedures, and various changes in the dependent variable definition, including thin-trading adjustments, the use of cumulative abnormal returns, and shorter event periods. Also, conclusions remain essentially unaltered when various explanatory variables are replaced by alternative measures, although alternative measures are generally insignificant. Evidence for a material role of market timing is not found.

A more general discussion of the results and of their implications follows in Section 4.5.2.1.

4.4.2.3 *Long-term abnormal returns regressions*

4.4.2.3.1 *Results for the full and reduced models*

Results of the cross-sectional regressions on long-term abnormal returns are presented in Table 44. The table is identically structured as the tables for the short-term abnormal returns regressions. However, for each regression three variants are reported, representing a measure of parent/subsidiary portfolio, parent, and subsidiary abnormal return, respectively. T-statistics are based on White heteroskedasticity-consistent standard errors.

As discussed in Section 4.3.4.6, the long-term regressions employ a reduced set of variables, since a significant relation to abnormal returns is only expected for those variables where additional information is revealed post-ECO.

Table 44 first presents models that are directly based on Model (3) from the short-term analysis. Model (10a) presents results for the parent/subsidiary portfolio. The adjusted R^2 of 33.42% indicates reasonable fit, and results of diagnostic tests show that none of the OLS assumptions is violated. Overall, results from the short-term analysis are confirmed:

- *Focus and investment efficiency*: As expected, the coefficients on the variables FOCUS, DEBT_RED, and DIV_PAYOUT are insignificant since no new information is disclosed post-ECO. Contrary to expectations, the coefficient on OVINV is positive and highly significant, indicating that above-industry average investment is positively related to long-term abnormal returns. This contradicts H1C. However, the coefficient on the interaction between OVINV and FLOAT is positive as expected, indicating that overinvestment coupled with ineffective barriers against cross-subsidization also impacts abnormal returns negatively in the long-term, further supporting H1D.

- *Information asymmetries and disclosure*: Neither the coefficient on ASYM nor the coefficient on TRANSP is significant. As previously discussed, this result is caused by the significant negative correlation between the two coefficients. In further models, TRANSP is included separately.
- *Incentive compensation*: As expected, the coefficient on ALIGN is insignificant, since no new information is revealed post-ECO. The coefficient on INFL_AR is positive and highly significant, indicating that effective impediments against excessive managerial compensation positively impact long-term abnormal returns (H2B).
- *Ownership concentration*: The coefficient on FLOAT is positive and highly significant. Thus, a relinquishment of control by the parent positively influences abnormal returns, in support of H4B.
- *Control variables*: Leverage is clearly negatively related to long-term abnormal returns, while parent size is positively related. Prior year market performance is not significantly related to long-term abnormal returns.

Model (10b) repeats the analysis for parent long-term abnormal returns. All coefficients have the same signs and similar significance levels as in the analysis of portfolio returns, which is not surprising due to the heavy weight of the parent in the portfolio.

While hypotheses are thus largely confirmed in the long-term analysis (with exception of H1C) as far as parent and parent/subsidiary portfolio abnormal returns are concerned, no such relationship can be detected for subsidiary abnormal returns: Model (10c) has a negative adjusted R^2, and the F-statistic is insignificant. Apparently though, subsidiary long-term abnormal returns are unrelated to changes in agency costs.

Table 44: Long-term cross-sectional regression

	Expected sign	Full model (=Model (2) in short-term regression)		
Model		10a: Portfolio	10b: Parent	10c: Sub
Dependent Variable		CSPE 0 36M	CSPE 0 36M	CSPE 0 36M
Constant		1.36	2.04	0.18
		(1.34)	(1.76) *	(0.15)
FOCUS		-0.13	0.30	-0.30
		(-0.21)	(0.42)	(-0.40)
OVINV	-	7.55	4.00	-0.37
		(5.98) ***	(2.73) ***	(-0.78)
DEBT_RED		0.17	0.32	-0.41
		(0.47)	(0.79)	(-0.93)
DIV_PAYOUT		0.03	-0.06	0.07
		(0.36)	(-0.79)	(0.63)
ASYM		-0.08	-9.62	6.99
		(0.00)	(-0.82)	(0.74)
TRANSP	-	-11.04	-18.92	-0.16
		(-0.82)	(-1.40)	(-0.02)
ALIGN		0.00	0.19	-0.01
		(0.00)	(0.49)	(-0.02)
FLOAT	+	1.01	0.52	-0.08
		(3.05) ***	(1.46)	-(0.56)
FLOAT*OVINV	-	18.61	10.27	-0.01
		(4.62) ***	(2.77) ***	(-0.02)
INFL_AR	+	0.20	0.19	0.77
		(2.58) **	(2.85) ***	(1.85) *
LEVERAGE	+/-	-2.65	-3.64	-0.30
		(-2.73) ***	(-3.30) ***	(-0.22)
PSIZE	+/-	3.11	3.16	-0.12
		(3.69) ***	(2.99) ***	(-0.08)
ROA	+/-	-0.56	-0.51	0.30
		(-0.52)	(-0.43)	(0.27)
CDAXPRIOR	+/-	-0.91	-0.22	-0.88
		(-1.29)	(-0.27)	(-0.95)
Adjusted R^2		33.42%	17.94%	-4.66%
F		2.72 ***	1.75 *	0.85
White statistic		0.58	0.35	0.61
Breusch-Godfrey statistic		2.43	0.25	0.00
Durbin-Watson statistic		2.54	2.29	2.00
Jarque-Bera statistic		0.47	3.83	0.84
Akaike information criterion		2.4630	2.5456	2.7665
Schwarz information criterion		3.0421	3.1247	3.3456
CUSUM test significant at 5% level		No	No	No
Maximum VIF		3.18	4.22	5.85
Average VIF		2.08	2.09	2.54

Table 44 (continued)

	Expected sign	Reduced model w/ CSPE30		
Model		11a: Portfolio	11b: Parent	11c: Sub
Dependent Variable		CSPE 0 36M	CSPE 0 36M	CSPE 0 36M
Constant		0.68	1.01	1.10
		(1.25)	(1.96) *	(1.58)
FOCUS				
OVINV	-	6.69	3.32	-0.01
		(6.21) ***	(2.68) **	(-0.03)
DEBT_RED				
DIV_PAYOUT				
ASYM				
TRANSP	-	-11.75	-13.56	0.23
		(-2.64) **	(2.20) **	(0.07)
ALIGN				
FLOAT	+	0.85	0.52	0.59
		(2.65) **	(1.92) *	(1.22)
FLOAT*OVINV	-	18.35	8.34	0.35
		(7.02) ***	(3.65) ***	(0.42)
INFL_AR	+	0.24	0.22	-0.07
		(3.84) ***	(4.24) ***	(-1.22)
LEVERAGE	+/-	-2.03	-2.54	-1.52
		(-3.26) ***	(-4.01) ***	(-1.80) *
PSIZE	+/-	2.65	2.71	-0.04
		(2.93) ***	(2.96) ***	(-0.05)
ROA	+/-			
CSPE30	+/-	0.03	0.12	-0.13
		(0.47)	(1.71) *	(-2.01) *
Adjusted R^2		37.12%	29.43%	0.71%
F		4.84 ***	3.55 ***	1.04
White statistic		0.76	0.47	1.03
Breusch-Godfrey statistic		0.94	0.22	0.37
Durbin-Watson statistic		2.40	2.25	2.22
Jarque-Bera statistic		0.80	3.48	0.48
Akaike information criterion		2.3234	2.2895	2.6828
Schwarz information criterion		2.6580	2.6337	3.0269
CUSUM test significant at 5% level		No	No	No
Maximum VIF		2.02	1.72	4.22
Average VIF		1.38	1.31	1.95

Table 44 (continued)

Reduced model		
12a: Portfolio	12b: Parent	12c: Sub
CSPE 0 36M	CSPE 0 36M	CSPE 0 36M
0.71	1.38	0.69
(1.31)	(5.10) ***	(0.92)
6.53	3.06	0.00
(6.06) ***	(2.67) **	(0.01)
-10.71	-9.51	-2.80
(-2.66) **	(1.71) *	(-0.33)
0.83	0.47	0.62
(2.68) **	(1.73) *	1.57
18.11	8.22	0.37
(7.29) ***	(3.39) ***	(0.32)
0.23	0.20	-0.05
(4.00) ***	(4.54) ***	(-0.36)
-2.03	-2.90	-1.11
(-3.16) ***	(-4.18) ***	(-1.14)
2.58	2.60	-0.02
(2.88) ***	(2.84) ***	(-0.01)
38.24%	26.67%	-2.44%
5.60 ***	3.55 ***	0.83
0.91	0.34	1.15
0.91	0.35	0.16
2.41	2.32	2.11
0.94	1.47	0.84
2.2901	2.3120	2.6982
2.5875	2.6179	3.0041
No	No	No
1.91	1.70	4.22
1.35	1.27	2.05

Models (11) and (12) are reduced models where insignificant variables have been eliminated. While the reduced models have a significantly improved goodness-of-fit (adjusted R^2 of up to 38.24%), coefficient signs remain unchanged, and magnitudes and significance levels do not change materially. The sole exception is the coefficient on the variable TRANSP, which is negative and significant in Models (11a), (11b), (12a), and (12b): Thus, a reduction in information asymmetry is positively related to abnormal returns in the long-term, in support of H2B.

In order to assess the relationship between short-term and long-term abnormal returns, Models (11) contain short-term abnormal returns (CSPE30) as additional control variable. Interestingly, the short-term abnormal return is positively related to parent long-term abnormal returns, while it is negatively related to subsidiary long-term abnormal returns. However, the coefficients are only marginally significant in both models.

4.4.2.3.2 *Robustness checks*

The results of the cross-sectional regressions on long-term abnormal returns are subjected to three robustness checks: First, bootstrapped confidence intervals are calculated in place of the White heteroskedasticity-consistent standard errors. Second, BHARs are used in place of CSPEs as the dependent variable.[194] Third, alternative market timing indicators are employed.

Bootstrapped confidence intervals are reported in Table 45 (Models (11), (12)). While significance levels decline somewhat compared to the parametric t-tests, coefficients generally remain significant under the application of the bootstrap procedure. There are two exceptions: The coefficients on TRANSP and FLOAT*OVINV in Model (12b) become insignificantly different from zero. In conclusion, results of the long-term regression analysis are robust, and are not driven by distortions of the test statistics due to non-normality of the residuals.

Regression results with BHARs as the dependent variable are reported in Table 46 (Models (11), (12)). As can be seen from the table, goodness-of-fit of the regressions declines markedly, in the order of 10% as measured by the adjusted R^2. Also, there

---

[194] In unreported regressions, alternative variable specifications were also tested, i.e. CDAXPOST and IPOSPRIOR instead of CDAXPRIOR, INFL instead of INFL_AR, and ANALYSTS instead of TRANSP. Results were not materially affected.

are signs of severe non-normality of the residuals, as indicated by the significant values of the Jarque-Bera statistic.

Consequently, statistical significance of individual regression coefficients deteriorates. While all coefficients retain the same signs and remain significant in the analysis of portfolio returns (Models (11d), (12d)), the coefficients on OVINV, TRANSP, and FLOAT become insignificant in the analysis of parent returns (Models (11e), (12e)). In conclusion, results of the cross-sectional regression on parent long-term abnormal returns have to be interpreted with some caution.

Alternative specifications of the market timing indicator variable, namely CDAXPOST, CDAXPRIOR-CDAXPOST, IPOSPRIOR, and CDAX_PE, based on Model (12), are reported in Table 47. Also, the variable CDAXPRIOR is included separately in the reduced model.

The variables CDAXPOST, IPOSPRIOR, and CDAX_PE are insignificant throughout. Thus, subsequent market returns, the preceding-year frequency of IPOs, and the announcement day market price-earnings-ratio are not significantly related to long-term abnormal returns of either parent/subsidiary portfolio, parent, or subsidiary.

As far as prior-year market returns are concerned, a negative and significant relationship appears to exist to parent/subsidiary portfolio abnormal returns, but not to either parent or subsidiary returns alone. This relationship appears to be consistent with the investor sentiment explanation of market timing: The correction of initial investor overoptimism. However, further (unreported) analyses show that the relationship is spurious and disappears when alternative specifications of the abnormal return are used.[195]

---

[195] In more detail: The dependent variable (CSPE 0 36) is based on the use of value-weighted reference portfolio returns as expected returns. This benchmark indicates underperformance of the subsidiary for the 1998-2001 sample period (but not for the 1984-1997 sample period). This effect is due to the special industry distribution of ECO subsidiaries for the 1998-2001 sample, which is not properly captured by the reference portfolios. The underperformance disappears when matching firms are used instead. Consequently, the significant coefficient on CDAXPRIOR also becomes insignificant.

Table 45: Long-term cross-sectional regression, bootstrapped confidence intervals

Model	11a			11b			11c		
Entity	Portfolio			Parent			Sub		
Dependent Variable	CSPE 0 36M			CSPE 0 36M			CSPE 0 36M		
Constant	0.68			1.01			1.10		
	[-1.03;2.99]	[-0.39;2.16]	[-0.17;1.82]	[-0.41;2.86]	[0.01;2.23]	[0.19;1.95] **	[-0.98;3.49]	[-0.29;3.03]	[0.04;2.62] *
OVINV	6.69			3.32			-0.01		
	[3.56;10.04]	[4.57;9.23]	[4.91;8.79] ***	[-0.30;8.47]	[0.37;6.71]	[0.88;6.13] ***	[-1.34;1.11]	[-1.02;0.80]	[-0.78;0.62]
TRANSP	-11.75			-13.56			0.23		
	[-25.27;0.88]	[-22.25;-3.26]	[-20.34;-4.71] **	[-38.53;6.85]	[-28.89;0.67]	[-25.07;-1.30] *	[-8.39;8.98]	[-6.29;6.55]	[-4.97;5.52]
FLOAT	0.85			0.52			0.59		
	[-0.07;1.65]	[0.15;1.44]	[0.26;1.33] **	[0.08;0.35]	[0.12;0.31]	[0.14;0.29] ***	[-0.25;0.10]	[-0.20;0.05]	[-0.18;0.03]
FLOAT*	18.35			8.34			0.35		
OVINV	[10.60;27.79]	[13.10;24.71]	[14.24;23.68] ***	[-0.17;1.25]	[-0.03;1.03]	[0.05;0.96] *	[-0.97;2.09]	[-0.52;1.70]	[-0.33;1.44]
INFL_AR	0.24			0.22			-0.07		
	[0.05;0.47]	[0.10;0.40]	[0.13;0.37] ***	[1.24;15.29]	[3.22;13.04]	[4.28;12.18] ***	[-2.79;3.65]	[-1.95;2.87]	[-1.52;2.23]
LEVERAGE	-2.03			-2.54			-1.52		
	[-4.35;-0.23]	[-3.72;-0.80]	[-3.35;-1.05] ***	[-4.61;-0.80]	[-4.00;-1.29]	[-3.74;-1.56] ***	[-4.38;0.95]	[-3.80;0.04]	[-3.35;-0.22] *
PSIZE	2.65			2.71			-0.04		
	[-0.19;7.59]	[0.66;6.05]	[0.98;5.55] **	[-0.52;6.79]	[0.10;5.82]	[0.67;5.53] **	[-2.20;2.20]	[-1.70;1.55]	[-1.45;1.30]
CSPE30	0.03			0.12			-0.13		
	[-0.18;0.24]	[-0.13;0.18]	[-0.09;0.16]	[-0.11;0.33]	[-0.04;0.28]	[-0.01;0.24]	[-0.36;0.03]	[-0.30;-0.02]	[-0.28;-0.05] **

Model	12a				12b				12c		
Entity	Portfolio				Parent				Sub		
Dependent Variable	CSPE 0 36M				CSPE 0 36M				CSPE 0 36M		
Constant	0.71				1.38				0.69		
	[-1.23;2.71]	[-0.54;2.24]	[-0.27;1.87]		[-0.30;3.29]	[0.33;2.68]	[0.51;2.38]	**	[-1.73;3.47]	[-0.90;2.93]	[-0.62;2.58]
OVINV	6.53				3.06				0.00		
	[3.28;10.10]	[4.12;8.87]	[4.56;8.39]	***	[-0.45;6.44]	[0.36;5.71]	[0.89;5.40]	**	[-1.72;1.56]	[-1.29;1.03]	[-1.04;0.85]
TRANSP	-10.71				-9.51				-2.80		
	[-24.16;-0.10]	[-19.98;-3.68]	[-18.50;-4.56]	***	[-34.30;5.32]	[-22.89;2.63]	[-20.72;0.04]		[-12.07;9.22]	[-8.70;6.55]	[-7.08;4.55]
FLOAT	0.83				0.47				0.62		
	[-0.11;1.62]	[0.15;1.45]	[0.28;1.35]	**	[0.09;0.30]	[0.12;0.27]	[0.13;0.26]	***	[-0.24;0.14]	[-0.20;0.09]	[-0.17;0.07]
FLOAT*	18.11				8.22				0.37		
OVINV	[9.75;25.15]	[12.42;23.19]	[13.42;22.35]	***	[-0.31;1.15]	[-0.10;0.96]	[-0.02;0.88]		[-0.99;2.21]	[-0.57;1.74]	[-0.34;1.54]
INFL_AR	0.23				0.20				-0.05		
	[0.05;0.41]	[0.09;0.37]	[0.12;0.35]	***	[-0.55;15.52]	[2.11;13.57]	[3.63;12.50]	**	[-3.63;4.22]	[-2.59;3.23]	[-1.93;2.71]
LEVERAGE	-2.03				-2.90				-1.11		
	[-4.45;0.23]	[-3.74;-0.56]	[-3.41;-0.82]	**	[-5.57;-1.02]	[-4.66;-1.42]	[-4.22;-1.74]	***	[-4.34;1.69]	[-3.77;0.76]	[-3.37;0.32]
PSIZE	2.58				2.60				-0.02		
	[-0.39;7.10]	[0.32;5.84]	[0.76;5.47]	**	[-0.34;6.27]	[0.49;5.73]	[0.81;5.34]	**	[-2.12;2.51]	[-1.77;1.79]	[-1.49;1.53]
CSPE30											

Table 46: Long-term cross-sectional regression, BHARs as dependent variable

	Expected sign	Reduced model w/ CSPE30		
Model		11a: Portfolio	11b: Parent	11c: Sub
Dependent Variable		BHAR 0 36M	BHAR 0 36M	BHAR 0 36M
Constant		0.13	0.20	0.31
		(0.45)	(0.67)	(0.64)
FOCUS				
OVINV	-	2.63	1.58	0.23
		(4.16) ***	(1.67) *	(0.71)
DEBT_RED				
DIV_PAYOUT				
ASYM				
TRANSP	-	-5.62	-3.21	-4.16
		(-2.14) **	(-1.10)	(-1.63)
ALIGN				
FLOAT	+	0.39	0.06	0.51
		(1.93) *	(0.27)	(1.15)
FLOAT*OVINV	-	7.62	4.69	0.79
		(4.32) ***	(1.95) *	(0.99)
INFL_AR	+	0.10	0.18	-0.05
		(3.81)	(4.73) ***	(1.15)
LEVERAGE	+/-	-0.80	-0.98	-0.63
		(-2.47) **	(-2.76) ***	(-1.09)
PSIZE	+/-	1.13	1.40	-0.80
		(3.74) ***	(4.23) ***	(-1.61)
ROA	+/-			
CSPE30	+/-	0.02	0.05	-0.07
		(0.55)	(1.26)	(-1.46)
Adjusted R^2		27.12%	17.47%	-0.62%
F		3.42 ***	2.30 **	0.96
White statistic		0.45	1.03	1.25
Breusch-Godfrey statistic		0.34	0.01	1.94
Durbin-Watson statistic		2.15	2.01	2.62
Jarque-Bera statistic		26.89 ***	4.62 *	42.29 ***
Akaike information criterion		0.9230	1.3423	2.1328
Schwarz information criterion		1.2580	2.2962	2.4770
CUSUM test significant at 5% level		No	No	Yes
Maximum VIF		2.02	1.72	4.22
Average VIF		1.38	1.31	1.95

Table 46 (continued)

Reduced model		
12a: Portfolio	12b: Parent	12c: Sub
BHAR 0 36M	BHAR 0 36M	BHAR 0 36M
0.15	0.37	0.24
(0.52)	(1.57)	(0.60)
2.55	1.46	0.00
(4.10) ***	(1.65)	(0.00)
-5.12	-1.37	-1.53
(-2.44) **	(-0.59)	(-1.43)
0.38	0.03	0.26
(1.97) *	(0.16)	(0.65)
7.50	4.64	0.14
(4.37) ***	(1.85) *	(0.23)
0.10	0.17	-0.03
(3.95) ***	(5.40) ***	(-0.21)
-0.80	-1.13	-0.60
(-2.42) **	(-3.61) ***	(-1.01)
1.09	1.35	-0.02
(3.54) ***	(4.29) ***	(-1.61)
28.44%	16.69%	
3.95 ***	2.40 **	
0.47	0.66	
0.33	0.00	
2.16	1.99	
23.68 ***	5.61 *	
0.8895	1.3357	
1.1869	1.6417	
No	No	
1.91	1.70	
1.35	1.27	

Table 47: Long-term abnormal returns regressions, alternative specifications

	Expected sign	Model CDAXPRIOR		
Model		13a	13b	13c
Dependent Variable		CSPE 0 36M	CSPE 0 36M	CSPE 0 36M
Constant		1.09	1.43	1.04
		(1.97) *	(2.78) **	(1.12)
OVINV	-	7.21	3.16	-0.16
		(6.27) ***	(2.60) **	(-0.42)
ASYM		-12.39	-10.06	-0.76
		(-2.89) ***	(-1.77) *	(-0.21)
FLOAT	+	0.87	0.49	0.60
		(3.10) ***	(1.69) *	(1.18)
FLOAT*OVINV	-	19.70	8.56	-0.09
		(7.05) ***	(3.23) ***	(-0.09)
INFL_AR	+	0.24	0.20	-0.05
		(4.52) ***	(4.37) ***	(-0.83)
LEVERAGE	+/-	-2.29	-2.90	-1.39
		(-3.74) ***	(-4.14) ***	(-1.35)
PSIZE	+/-	2.95	2.66	3.28
		(3.97) ***	(2.87) ***	0.36
CDAXPRIOR	+/-	-0.95	-0.17	-0.66
		(-2.17) **	(-0.40)	(-0.97)
CDAXPOST	+/-			
IPOSPRIOR	+/-			
CDAXPRIOR-CDAXPOST	+/-			
CDAX_PE	+/-			
Adjusted R^2		42.09%	25.08%	-2.30%
F		5.73 ***	3.05 ***	0.86
White statistic		0.45	0.42	0.95
Breusch-Godfrey statistic		0.94	0.29	0.05
Durbin-Watson statistic		2.39	2.28	1.96
Jarque-Bera statistic		0.11	1.70	1.03
Akaike information criterion		2.241	2.3494	2.7127
Schwarz information criterion		2.756	2.6935	3.0569
CUSUM test significant at 5% level		No	No	No
Maximum VIF				
Average VIF				

Table 47 (continued)

	Expected sign	Model CDAXPOST		
Model		14a	14b	14c
Dependent Variable		CSPE 0 36M	CSPE 0 36M	CSPE 0 36M
Constant		0.68	1.61	0.52
		(1.25)	(3.30) ***	(0.59)
OVINV	-	6.54	3.15	0.09
		(6.06) ***	(2.89) ***	(0.18)
ASYM		-11.10	-8.04	-2.59
		(-2.72) ***	(-1.55)	(-0.72)
FLOAT	+	0.84	0.42	0.71
		(2.80) ***	(1.51)	(1.38)
FLOAT*OVINV	-	17.89	9.39	0.35
		(7.14) ***	(3.86)	(0.35)
INFL_AR	+	0.23	0.21	-0.06
		(3.92) ***	(4.50) ***	(-1.04)
LEVERAGE	+/-	-2.03	-3.03	-1.03
		(-3.17) ***	(-4.72) ***	(-1.05)
PSIZE	+/-	2.62	2.49	3.45
		(2.65) **	(3.60) ***	0.06
CDAXPRIOR	+/-			
CDAXPOST	+/-	0.15	-0.65	0.76
		(0.31)	(-1.49)	(1.23)
IPOSPRIOR	+/-			
CDAXPRIOR-CDAXPOST	+/-			
CDAX_PE	+/-			
Adjusted R^2		36.98%	27.85%	-1.51%
F		4.81 ***	3.36 ***	0.91
White statistic		0.78	0.38	1.01
Breusch-Godfrey statistic		0.84	0.79	0.23
Durbin-Watson statistic		2.39	2.49	2.15
Jarque-Bera statistic		0.92	1.13	1.06
Akaike information criterion		2.3257	2.3117	2.7049
Schwarz information criterion		2.6602	2.6559	3.0491
CUSUM test significant at 5% level		No	No	No
Maximum VIF				
Average VIF				

Table 47 (continued)

	Expected sign	Model IPOSPRIOR		
Model		15a	15b	15c
Dependent Variable		CSPE 0 36M	CSPE 0 36M	CSPE 0 36M
Constant		1.09	1.51	0.81
		(1.50)	(2.68) **	(0.55)
OVINV	-	6.76	3.12	-0.03
		(5.74) ***	(2.59) **	(-0.07)
ASYM		-10.38	-9.59	-0.69
		(-2.40) **	(-1.66)	(-0.17)
FLOAT	+	0.89	0.50	0.61
		(2.94) ***	(1.61)	(1.25)
FLOAT*OVINV	-	18.77	8.48	0.22
		(6.27) ***	(3.04) ***	(0.19)
INFL_AR	+	0.24	0.20	-0.05
		(4.02) ***	(4.27) ***	(-0.79)
LEVERAGE	+/-	-2.42	-3.02	-1.24
		(-2.93) ***	(-4.16) ***	(-0.76)
PSIZE	+/-	3.09	2.77	8.78
		(3.36) ***	(2.82) ***	(0.05)
CDAXPRIOR	+/-			
CDAXPOST	+/-			
IPOSPRIOR	+/-	0.00	0.00	0.00
		(-0.94)	(-0.30)	(-0.05)
CDAXPRIOR-CDAXPOST	+/-			
CDAX_PE	+/-			
Adjusted R^2		38.00%	25.02%	-5.14%
F		4.99 ***	3.04 ***	0.70
White statistic		1.11	0.29	1.54
Breusch-Godfrey statistic		1.05	0.34	0.17
Durbin-Watson statistic		2.44	2.31	2.08
Jarque-Bera statistic		0.62	1.44	0.64
Akaike information criterion		2.3092	2.3501	2.7400
Schwarz information criterion		2.6437	2.6942	3.0841
CUSUM test significant at 5% level		No	No	No
Maximum VIF				
Average VIF				

Table 47 (conitnued)

	Expected sign	Model CDAXPRIOR-CDAXPOST		
Model		16a	16b	16c
Dependent Variable		CSPE 0 36M	CSPE 0 36M	CSPE 0 36M
Constant		0.87	1.39	0.85
		(1.69) *	(2.76) ***	(1.13)
OVINV	-	7.05	2.93	-0.08
		(6.63) ***	(2.72) ***	(-0.21)
ASYM		-13.63	-7.80	-2.81
		(-3.25) ***	(-1.47)	(-0.75)
FLOAT	+	0.93	0.42	0.72
		(3.53) ***	(1.40)	(1.52)
FLOAT*OVINV	-	18.29	8.18	-0.09
		(8.27) ***	(3.64) ***	(-0.10)
INFL_AR	+	0.22	0.20	-0.06
		(4.74) ***	(4.61) ***	(-1.12)
LEVERAGE	+/-	-2.22	-2.89	-1.28
		(-3.75) ***	(-4.28) ***	(-1.41)
PSIZE	+/-	3.02	2.44	0.43
		(2.68) **	(2.80) ***	(0.67)
CDAXPRIOR	+/-			
CDAXPOST	+/-			
IPOSPRIOR	+/-			
CDAXPRIOR-CDAXPOST	+/-	-0.68	0.32	-0.88
		(-1.92) *	(0.88)	(-2.16) **
CDAX_PE	+/-			
Adjusted R^2		41.20%	25.97%	2.84%
F		5.55 ***	3.15 ***	1.18
White statistic		0.87	0.41	1.03
Breusch-Godfrey statistic		0.77	0.85	0.03
Durbin-Watson statistic		2.31	2.46	2.02
Jarque-Bera statistic		0.23	1.14	0.72
Akaike information criterion		2.2563	2.3373	2.6611
Schwarz information criterion		2.5909	2.6815	3.0053
CUSUM test significant at 5% level		No	No	No
Maximum VIF				
Average VIF				

Table 47 (conituned)

	Expected sign	Model CDAX_PE		
Model		17a	17b	17c
Dependent Variable		CSPE 0 36M	CSPE 0 36M	CSPE 0 36M
Constant		1.61	1.97	0.78
		(1.47)	(1.95) *	(0.48)
OVINV	-	6.56	3.17	-0.02
		(6.46) ***	(2.73) ***	(-0.06)
ASYM		-10.60	-9.81	-0.81
		(-2.48) **	(-1.68)	(-0.23)
FLOAT	+	0.95	0.57	0.60
		(3.17) ***	(1.79) *	(1.27)
FLOAT*OVINV	-	18.07	8.46	0.25
		(7.40) ***	(3.13) ***	(0.26)
INFL_AR	+	0.22	0.19	-0.05
		(3.72) ***	(4.58) ***	(-0.76)
LEVERAGE	+/-	-2.20	-2.93	-1.19
		(-3.45) ***	(-4.10) ***	(-1.26)
PSIZE	+/-	2.72	2.69	0.03
		(3.02) ***	(2.89) ***	(0.04)
CDAXPRIOR	+/-			
CDAXPOST	+/-			
IPOSPRIOR	+/-			
CDAXPRIOR-CDAXPOST	+/-			
CDAX_PE	+/-	-0.04	-0.02	0.00
		(-1.00)	(-0.66)	(-0.02)
Adjusted R^2		38.11%	25.59%	-5.14%
F		5.00 ***	3.11 ***	0.70
White statistic		0.60	0.27	1.34
Breusch-Godfrey statistic		0.92	0.38	0.18
Durbin-Watson statistic		2.36	2.27	2.08
Jarque-Bera statistic		1.02	1.59	0.61
Akaike information criterion		2.3075	2.3425	2.7401
Schwarz information criterion		2.6420	2.6866	3.0842
CUSUM test significant at 5% level		No	No	No
Maximum VIF				
Average VIF				

As far as the variable CDAXPRIOR-CDAXPOST is concerned, a negative and significant relationship exists concerning parent/subsidiary portfolio and subsidiary abnormal returns. Thus, some evidence exists that ECOs that are successfully timed to market peaks, lead to an inferior subsequent performance of the subsidiary. However, again, this relationship disappears when alternative specifications of the abnormal return, based on e.g. the matching firm benchmark, are used.

In conclusion, evidence for a potential influence of market timing on long-term abnormal returns after ECOs is at best vague. Most of the indicators fail to exhibit a significant relationship.

4.5 Discussion

4.5.1 The impact of ECOs on firm value

4.5.1.1 Short-term impact

On the basis of the efficiency criterion for the analysis of ECOs from an agency perspective, the results on short-term abnormal returns presented in Section 4.4.1.1 can be summarized and interpreted as follows:

- Over the 1984-2001 sample period, ECOs on German capital markets lead to highly statistically significant positive announcement abnormal returns in the order of 1.3% (day 0), and 10% (extended event periods of up to 30 days preceding the announcement). Results differ between the 1984-1997 sample period (cumulative abnormal return in the order of 5%), and the 1998-2001 sample period (cumulative abnormal return in the order of 15%), but both periods exhibit significant positive abnormal returns.

- These abnormal returns are not only statistically, but also economically highly significant. Assuming an average 10% cumulative abnormal return, the announcement of an ECO results in short-term value creation in the order of 25% of the subsidiary market value (based on the IPO day market capitalization of the subsidiary).

- Results are robust to the application of different statistical methodologies. Inferences remain essentially unchanged using various modifications of test statistics accounting for unequal residual variance and event-induced variance shifts, various adjustments for thin-trading, and more advanced methods accounting for cross-sectional dependence (SUR) and stochastic volatility (GARCH).

- Information processing can be interpreted only as moderately efficient: While the absence of short-term abnormal returns post-announcement suggests capital market efficiency, the positive cumulative abnormal returns over relatively long periods up to thirty days preceding the announcement point towards leakage of information over non-public channels preceding the public announcement, and a gradual incorporation of ECO information into stock prices.

These results confirm findings of the previous ECO literature, summarized in Table 48. Announcement abnormal returns reported in the German ECO literature are largely similar, while U.S. results are slightly more positive.

Table 48: Literature on short-term capital market reaction

Author (Year)	Sample Size	Sample period	Event period (days)	Abnormal return
Panel A: U.S. studies				
Schipper/Smith (1986)	76	1963-1983	-4 0	1.83%**
Klein/Rosenfeld/Beranek (1991)	52	1966-1983	-1 0	1.06%*
Slovin/Sushka/Ferraro (1995)	32	1980-1991	0 +1	1.23%**
Allen/McConnell (1998)	188	1978-1993	-1 +1	1.90%***
Vijh (2002)	336	1980-1997	-1 +1	1.94%***
Hulburt/Miles/Woolridge (2002)	185	1981-1994	-1 +1	1.92***
Panel B: German Studies				
Pellens (1993)	11	1984-1991	-6W +7W	2.30%**
Hasselmann (1997)	8	1992-1994	-5W 0	4.02% (no test)
Kaserer/Ahlers (2000)	23	1984-1997	-10 0	0.28%***
Langenbach (2001)	32	1984-1999	-1 0	1.42%**
Löffler (2001)	19	1984-1999	0	0.86%*
Elsas/Löffler (2003)	37	1984-2000	0	1.08%***
Brettel/Junker/Pinker (2004)	50	1984-2000	-1 0	1.35%**

Event period in days, if not otherwise indicated; W: weeks

In conclusion, the results on short-term abnormal returns consistently indicate that ECOs are interpreted as good news by market participants: The capital market revises upwards its expectations on the announcement of an ECO. This pattern is extremely robust to changes in methodology, geography, or sample selection.

The differences between the two subsamples are consistent with investor sentiment based market timing: During the 1998-2001 period, where investors were potentially overoptimistic, a stronger reaction to good news was exhibited, as testified by the significantly larger announcement return. However, the stronger announcement effect in the 1998-2001 period is also consistent with the agency-based explanations developed in the present study, e.g. the wider use of incentive compensation, as will be discussed below. Thus, the potential influence of market timing cannot be determined based on the comparison of the two subsamples alone, but needs to be more closely analyzed based on the cross-sectional regression results.

4.5.1.2 Long-term impact

On the basis of the efficiency criterion for the analysis of ECOs from an agency perspective, the results on long-term abnormal returns presented in Section 4.4.1.2 can be summarized and interpreted as follows:

- During the three years following the ECO, the weighted portfolio of parent and subsidiary has a negative and statistically significant abnormal return in the order of -20%, compared to a reference portfolio of similar firms not experiencing an ECO. With slight variation, this result applies to both the 1984-1997 and the 1998-2001 subperiods.

- The negative abnormal performance of the weighted portfolio is solely due to the parent, which exhibits a sample average negative abnormal return in the order of -25% during the three years following the ECO.

  While the subsidiary exhibits significantly positive abnormal returns in the post-ECO year, this pattern is reversed in years two and three after the ECO. No abnormal returns can be detected over the entire three year period following the ECO using both reference portfolios and matching firms as benchmarks. The subsidiaries on average do significantly underperform the market index over the entire three year period, however, the market index is a methodologically inferior benchmark, since no adjustment for company-specific risk factors is made (refer back to Section 4.3.3.3).

- Results differ somewhat depending on the choice of estimated return, return metric, and test statistic, but conclusions are robust to methodological variations.

Estimated abnormal returns differ markedly between the four alternative methods used in order to determine expected returns: Underperformance is most pronounced when benchmarked against the market index (CDAX), and least pronounced when benchmarked against matching firms. However, while different in magnitude, long-term abnormal returns for the weighted portfolio are significantly negative under all four alternative methods applied.

Results again differ in magnitude when applying Cumulative Abnormal Returns (CARs) instead of Buy-and-hold Abnormal Returns (BHARs). However, the three-year portfolio abnormal return is significantly negative using CARs as well.

Skewness-adjustment and bootstrapping of test statistics do not materially change significance levels. Test statistics adjusted for cross-sectional dependence, in contrast, exhibit materially lower significance levels. However, parent and portfolio abnormal returns remain significant, with the exception of matching-firm adjusted returns. This mirrors results from the methodological literature (e.g. Lyon/Barber/Tsai (1999)) where the matching-firm method has been found to have lower power compared to the reference portfolio method due to the higher variance of matching-firm adjusted abnormal returns.

- The presence of long-term abnormal returns after ECOs is not reconcilable with capital market efficiency: The capital market's expectations appear systematically misguided.

Table 49: Literature on long-term capital market reaction

Author (Year)	Sample Size	Sample period	Abnormal return	
			Parent	Subsidiary
Panel A: U.S. studies				
Miles/Woolridge (1999)	87	1981-1993	-10.4%	28.7%**
Vijh (1999)	236/532	1981-1995	-3.2%/0.0%	-0.5%/5.5%
Prezas/Tarimcilar/Vasudevan (2000)	237	1986-1995		-7.8%
Powers (2003)	162	1981-1996		2.1%/13.4%
Panel B: German studies				
Langenbach (2001)	32	1984-1999		-28.70**
Brettel/Junker/Pinker (2004)†	30	1984-1999	-7.3%/-7.1%	0.2%/5.3%

Event period: ECO +36 months
Ranges given where abnormal returns were calculated via different methodologies
†Event Period: ECO +24 months

The finding of significantly negative long-term abnormal returns contradicts previous findings in the ECO literature (summarized in Table 49). U.S. studies have not found significant long-term abnormal returns after ECOs (Vijh (1999), Powers (2003)). German studies have found negative long-term abnormal returns, but these results were insignificant due to small sample size (Brettel/Junker/Pinker (2004)). An exception is Langenbach (2001), who finds significant long-term underperformance of the subsidiaries. However, he uses the CDAX Composite index in order to estimate expected returns. Thus, his result mirrors similar results from the present study showing underperformance relative to the market. As discussed in the methodological section (Section 4.3), the market index should be used as a benchmark only for illustrative purposes, since it represents only a crude measure of expected return. In conclusion, Langenbach's (2001) results are driven by a lack of adjustment for firm-specific factors in the expected return estimation, and should therefore be appropriately discounted.

The patterns of long-term returns is not fully consistent with an influence of market timing based on investor sentiment: According to the sentiment argument, the 1998-2001 subsample should exhibit more negative abnormal returns in order to correct the stronger initial overreaction (announcement effect). This pattern is not borne out by the data.

4.5.1.3 Overall impact and implications

The overall impact of ECOs on firm value, understood as the sum of the short-term and long-term capital market reaction, is negative: A positive short-term +10% announcement abnormal return is overcompensated by a negative long-term -20% parent/subsidiary portfolio long-term abnormal return, leaving a net effect in the order of -10%.[196] While a positive announcement effect testifies optimistic capital market expectations, these expectations are thus apparently not met in the long-term.

---

[196] The short-term capital market reaction refers to pre-announcement returns, while the long-term capital market reaction refers to post-ECO returns. Thus, the period between announcement and ECO is disregarded. The period between announcement and ECO is not included in the analysis because it differs in length across sample firms. Since abnormal returns in this intermediate period have not been found to be significantly different from zero in previous work (Brettel/Junker/Pinker (2004)), and these results have been confirmed in (unreported) analysis in this study,, a material effect on results can be ruled out.

Two main implications emerge from the observed pattern of short-term positive and long-term negative abnormal returns: Fundamental doubts are cast on the attractiveness of ECOs for financing and reorganizing groups of companies from an investor perspective, and the efficiency of the German capital market is again put into question.

These implications are in stark contrast to the dominant assessment of ECOs in the academic literature and by practitioners. Under the assumption of efficient capital markets, the short-term capital market reaction is a rational assessment of the impact of ECOs on firm value. Given the positive short-term and insignificant long-term abnormal returns, ECOs have thus generally been believed to increase firm value (e.g. Schipper/Smith (1986), Vijh (2002)). Value creation has been mainly attributed to efficiency increases stemming from improved incentive alignment and reduced agency problems (e.g. Allen/McConnell (1998), Vijh (2002)). Given that other transactions involving equity financing have long been shown to be associated with negative announcement effects (SEOs, e.g. Masulis/Korwar (1986)), or with long-term underperformance (IPOs: e.g. Ritter (1991), SEOs: e.g. Loughran/Ritter (1995)) in the academic literature, ECOs have enjoyed a special popularity. This popularity is shared among practitioners, as exemplified in case studies of ECOs published in academic journals (e.g. Hornung/Wullenkord (2001) on the ECO strategy of Metallgesellschaft), and in practical guidelines for the structuring of ECOs equally published in academic journals (Arbeitskreis Finanzierung der Schmalenbach-Gesellschaft (2003)).

Using the long-term change in equity value as a measure of value creation, the results of the present study fundamentally contradict the dominant assessment discussed above: In the present study, ECOs on German capital markets have been found to be associated with significant negative long-term abnormal returns. Taking together the short-term and long-term effects, ECOs have been found to destroy value on average. Thus, the attractiveness of ECOs as a means of financing and reorganization cannot be confirmed from an investor perspective.

Equally, the assumption of capital market efficiency can hardly be maintained based on the pattern of capital market reaction observed in the present study. On an efficient capital market, long-term abnormal returns must not be systematically different from zero. Fama (1998), however, maintains that significant long-term abnormal returns following a certain class of transactions (such as ECOs) are reconcilable with capital market efficiency when they are a pure chance result, i.e. when some classes of transaction are followed by positive, and others by negative long-term abnormal returns, so that long-term abnormal returns over all classes of transactions are zero. Following this argument, the negative long-term abnormal returns found in the present study are not sufficient in order to reject capital market efficiency. However, the pattern of short-term positive and long-term negative capital market reaction to ECOs directly contradicts capital market efficiency: On an efficient capital market, expectations are formed rationally. A repeated pattern of positive short-term followed by negative long-term abnormal returns should therefore induce negative short-term announcement effects over time.

The persistence of return reversal found throughout the sample period instead points towards a potential influence of investor sentiment, which will be further discussed below.

4.5.2 The determinants of the impact of ECOs on firm value

4.5.2.1 Agency costs and the capital market reaction

The efficiency criterion developed in Section 2.5.1 states that ECOs are an efficient method of restructuring when they are associated with a decrease in agency costs, as proxied by the change in equity value. Consequently, in order to examine the impact of ECOs on agency costs, the observed capital market reaction has been related to various agency cost measures via cross-sectional regression in Section 4.4.2. This approach is consistent with the dominant perspective in the empirical ECO literature, as reviewed in Section 1.4, where the capital market reaction to ECOs is also used as a proxy for the associated change in agency costs in cross-sectional regressions (e.g. Allen/McConnell (1998), Vijh (2002), Elsas/Löffler (2003), Wagner (2004)).

Adopting this paradigm, the the goodness-of-fit of the regressions indicates that the capital market reaction to ECOs on the German capital market is well-explained by the development of agency costs. In the short-term, up to 75% of the variation in announcement abnormal returns is explained by the variation of various agency cost measures. In the long-term, explained variation declines, but still up to 40% of the variation in portfolio abnormal returns is explained by the variation of agency cost measures. Goodness-of-fit for parent long-term abnormal returns is up to 30%. In contrast, the variation in subsidiary long-term abnormal returns cannot be explained by the variation of agency costs. A robust and significant relationship cannot be detected for any of the hypotheses.

The results on the four groups of hypotheses on the impact of ECOs on agency costs are reiterated in Table 50. In more detail, results for the short term and long term can be summarized and interpreted as follows. The discussion of long-term results focuses exclusively on portfolio abnormal returns, since the returns on the weighted parent/subsidiary portfolio are the ultimate measure of value creation (refer back to Section 4.3.1.1):

- *Focus and investment efficiency*: Short-term abnormal returns are strongly driven by capital market expectations of improvements in investment efficiency. As explained, investment efficiency is expected to improve since the size of the internal capital market is reduced due to the ECO under certain conditions, and inefficient cross-subsidization of weak businesses is made less likely, due to a decrease in diversification. In terms of the two-dimensional framework for the analysis of ECOs, interest divergence in the shareholder/parent management and parent management/subsidiary management principal-agent-relationships is expected to decline.

  Empirical evidence is supportive: A reduction of the heterogeneity of investment opportunities in the group of companies is positively related to the announcement effect (H1A). Thus, the capital market assesses those ECOs more positively, where parent and subsidiary are from different industries, and where the ECO reduces the degree of diversification of the group of companies. Consistent with theory, no relationship can be detected to long-term abnormal returns, since no new information is revealed.

  The relationship between abnormal returns and overinvestment is not as clear (H1B). Pre-ECO overinvestment is negatively related to short-term abnormal returns, as expected: The proceeds from the ECO represent a cash inflow, which purportedly leads to the exacerbation of empire-building overinvestment, where the group of companies already overinvests pre-ECO. Post-ECO overinvestment, however, is *positively* related to long-term abnormal returns, contrary to the hypothesis. A closer inspection of sample descriptive statistics, however, provides a potential explanation for this apparent contradiction: In the three fiscal years post-ECO, sample companies

Table 50: Summary of hypotheses and results

Value driver	Hypotheses	Short-term	Long-term
Focus and investment efficiency	H1A: The effect of ECOs on firm value is positively related to a reduction in divisional investment opportunities post-ECO	✓	-
	H1B: The effect of ECOs on firm value is negatively related to the presence of overinvestment	✓	✗
	H1C: The effect of ECOs on firm value is positively related to a payout to shareholders/debtholders of the proceeds from the ECO	✓	-
	H1D: The effect of ECOs on firm value is positively related to the creation of effective impediments against continued inefficient reallocations post-ECO via a separation of parent and subsidiary	✓	✓
Information asymmetries and disclosure	H2A: The effect of ECOs on firm value is positively related to the extent of information asymmetries among investors and between investors and management prior to the transaction	✗	-
	H2B: The effect of ECOs on firm value is positively related to the reduction in information asymmetries among investors and between investors and management after the transaction	✗	✓
Incentive compensation	H3A: The effect of ECOs on firm value is positively related to the introduction of a stock options program or managerial equity ownership	✓	-
	H3B: The effect of ECOs on firm value is negatively related to managerial influence over the pay setting process in the subsidiary	✓	✓
Ownership concentration	H4A: The effect of ECOs on firm value is positively related to the fraction of ownership retained by the parent company in the subsidiary immediately post-ECO	✓	
	H4B: The effect of ECOs on firm value is positively related to a subsequent relinquishment of parent control		✓

✓: supported; ✗: rejected; -: no relationship

invest on average less than their industry counterparts (median industry-adjusted capital expenditures/sales ratio -1.0%). Thus, it is not observed that post-ECO overinvestment is positively related to long-term abnormal returns, but in fact *less severe underinvestment*. While the variable OVINV is defined in such a way that true underinvestment cannot be distinguished from below-average investment due to inferior investment opportunities, the negative industry-adjusted capital expenditures/sales ratio could be due to underinvestment. In Section 3.3.3, theoretical arguments have been developed why underinvestment is less likely in companies with an internal capital market: financing constraints are relaxed (e.g. Stein (1997)), and self-financing is feasible (e.g. Inderst/Müller (2003)). Thus, apart from inefficient cross-subsidization, overinvestment has been identified as the central potential source of investment inefficiency. However, underinvestment can be a source of inefficiency, as exemplified in theoretical models on capital structure, which determine optimal leverage as the level of debt that balances the perils of overinvestment and underinvestment (e.g. Stulz (1990)). In conclusion, the empirical data do not indicate that long-term abnormal returns are positively related to overinvestment, which would run counter to the hypothesis, but that long-term abnormal returns are negatively related to investment levels significantly below industry averages, which potentially signify underinvestment. This pattern does not represent a reversal of the short-term capital market reaction, and can thus be more easily reconciled with theoretical arguments.

A payout of ECO proceeds is overall positively related to the short-term capital market reaction (H1C). However, ECO proceeds are in fact mostly not paid out: sample descriptive statistics indicate that absolute debt levels increase on average by 18%, i.e. ECO proceeds are on average *not* used for debt paydown. Also, dividend payout ratios on average decrease by 31%, i.e. ECO proceeds are on average *not* used for a payout to shareholders.

While a differentiation between payouts to shareholders and to debtholders was not made in the initial hypothesis, the effect of the retainment of funds differs between debt and equity. The use of ECO proceeds for a reduction in absolute debt is unequivocally positively related to the announcement effect, and the interaction with the level of overinvestment is positive. This is consistent with theory: A payout of proceeds would reduce the volume of the internal capital market, and thus effectively stifle empire-building activities, which is all the more necessary the more severe the overinvestment problem pre-ECO. The payout of ECO proceeds to shareholders in the form of an increased dividend payout ratio, in contrast, is negatively related to short-term abnormal returns. While this effect is highly significant when the short-term capital market reaction is measured as CSPE, it disappears when using CARs instead. Thus, the negative relation is not fully robust. Also, similar to debt reduction, the interaction between dividend payout and overinvestment is positive.

Given the contradictory signs for debt and equity, the magnitude of regression coefficients needs to be examined in order to estimate the direction of the overall effect of a payout of ECO proceeds and come to a definitive assessment of H1C. An inspection of the relative magnitude of the two coefficients on DEBT_RED and DIV_PAYOUT shows that the impact of debt reduction narrowly dominates on average: Based on Model (2), the mean effect of debt paydown on the CSPE (the product of the regression coefficient on DEBT_RED and the sample mean of the variable DEBT_RED) is -0.185, while the mean effect of dividend payout on the CSPE is 0.174, resulting in a net effect of -0.011. In conclusion, the hypothesis on the effects of a payout of ECO proceeds (H1C) is supported: On average, sample companies do not pay out ECO proceeds, but increase debt and decrease dividend payout ratios. Consistent with theory, this pattern is negatively associated to short-term abnormal returns. Also consistent with theory, a relationship with long-term abnormal returns cannot be detected, since no new information is revealed post-ECO.

Finally, the capital market rewards the creation of effective impediments against continued cross-subsidization both in the short-term and the long-term (H1D). The effect of overinvestment is particularly negative when the parent retains control in the subsidiary, and effective barriers against inefficient capital reallocations are thus not created. In the short term, this shows in the negative interaction term between overinvestment and parent ownership, and in the long term a similar effect is indicated by the positive interaction term between overinvestment and free-float: A relinquishment of parent control is especially beneficial when investment efficiency is low.

In conclusion, taking together the four hypotheses discussed above, it has been shown that short-term positive abnormal returns are clearly related the expectation of improvements in investment efficiency. In the long term, however, such expectations do not appear to fully materialize: Effective barriers against cross-subsidization are not created since most parents retain control of the subsidiaries over the three year post-ECO period under consideration. Contrary to theoretical arguments on financing constraints, a persistent overinvestment problem cannot be identified, but below industry-average investment negatively affects long-term abnormal returns.

- *Information asymmetries and disclosure*: The importance of information asymmetries and disclosure for short-term and long-term abnormal returns is very limited. This results runs counter to the hypotheses developed in the theoretical part, and widespread and well-established arguments concerning the role of information for potential value creation from ECOs (e.g. Schipper/Smith (1986)): In terms of the two-dimensional agency framework for the analysis of ECOs, theory predicts that agency costs decrease thanks to increased disclosure on the subsidiary, and thus reducing information asymmetries. The extent of pre-ECO information asymmetries is expected to be positively related to short-term abnormal returns, since severe ex ante asymmetries signify greater opportunities for improvement thanks to increased mandatory disclosure post-ECO.

  Empirical evidence does not support theoretical arguments: Information asymmetries decrease as a result from the ECO, as measured by the standard deviation of market model residuals. *In the short term*, however, pre-ECO information asymmetries are negatively related to short-term abnormal returns, contrary to the hypothesis (H2A), and the reduction in information asymmetries itself is also negatively related to short-term abnormal returns, contrary to the hypothesis (H2B). Thus, empirical evidence indicates that the short-term capital market reaction is most positive for those ECOs where there is little pre-ECO information asymmetry, and information asymmetry increases as a consequence of the ECO. While the first element of the result could be rationalized, e.g. assuming complementarity between private and public information (Kim/Verrecchia (1994)), implying that increased disclosure can actually exacerbate information asymmetries in an a priori opaque environment, the second element of the result is irreconcilable with standard theory: Standard theory unequivocally predicts that decreases in information asymmetry are positively related to stock returns, and improvements in disclosure have been documented to be associated with decreases in the cost of capital in empirical work (e.g. Healy/Hutton/Palepu (1999)).

In the long-term, the capital market reaction reverses: The reduction in information asymmetries is positively related to long-term abnormal portfolio returns (H1B), which is consistent with theory. The extent of pre-ECO information asymmetries is unrelated to long-term returns, which is also consistent with theory, since no new information on pre-ECO information asymmetries is revealed.

In order to reach a definitive verdict on the role of information asymmetries, the contradictory short-term and long-term reactions have to be analyzed in more detail. Four aspects emerge: First, the extent of pre-ECO information asymmetries and the reduction of information asymmetries are strongly negatively correlated, as already discussed in Section 4.4.2.1. This suggests that a separate test of the two hypotheses H2A and H2B is potentially infeasible. In the specification of the regression models, this was taken account of by including the two variables separately. Second, results are not robust under all circumstances. For example, the negative relation between pre-ECO information asymmetries and the short-term capital market reaction becomes insignificant when CARs are used instead of CSPEs as the dependent variable. This suggests a limited role of pre-ECO information asymmetries. The same pattern applies to the relationship between the reduction in information asymmetries and long-term abnormal returns. Third, the chosen operationalization of information asymmetries, while successfully applied in e.g. Krishnaswami/Subramaniam (2001) may not be effective at capturing true information asymmetries. However, the alternative specification based on analyst coverage was shown to lead to insignificant results as well. Fourth, coefficients are generally small in magnitude: The mean short-term effect of a reduction in information asymmetries on CSPEs (product of the coefficient on TRANSP and the sample average value of TRANSP) is only -0.01. The mean long-term effect is a mere 0.01. Taking together the four arguments, conclusive evidence for a material influence of information asymmetries on either short-term or long-term abnormal returns cannot be found. This result eases the contradiction between the short-term and long-term reaction: neither reaction is robust nor material.

In conclusion, the short-term and long-term capital market reaction to ECOs can be interpreted as unrelated to issues of information asymmetries and disclosure. Potential reductions in agency costs from an improvement in disclosure are minimal and not robustly related to stock returns.

- *Incentive compensation*: The capital market reaction to ECOs strongly depends on the introduction of incentive compensation for subsidiary managers, and the effective prevention of managerial influence on their own pay levels. In terms of the two-dimensional framework for the analysis of ECOs, theory predicts that agency costs can be decreased by reducing interest divergence in the parent/subsidiary management relationship.

  Empirical evidence is supportive of theoretical arguments. The short-term capital market reaction is significantly more positive to those ECOs where a stock options program or direct stock ownership by subsidiary management is introduced (H3A). Also, the magnitude of the coefficient is high: Depending on model specification, the difference in CSPE -30 0 between ECOs with and without incentive compensation is around 0.8. Consistent with theory, long-term abnormal returns are unrelated to the introduction of incentive compensation, since no new information is revealed post-ECO.

  The effective prevention of managerial influence on their own pay via parent supervisory board mandates is also positively related to short-term abnormal returns (H3B). However, results are not robust to the use of CARs instead of CSPEs as the dependent variable in all model specifications. In the long-term, the same relationship applies. However, parents on average are underrepresented on the subsidiary board relative to its ownership stake.

  In conclusion, the capital market reaction to ECOs is related to incentive compensation in the expected way. The observed pattern is both consistent with classic agency theory and the managerial power approach: The introduction of incentive compensation is positively related to returns since it decreases agency costs by reducing interest divergence. However, insufficient prevention of managerial influence on own pay levels is negatively related to returns since it potentially introduces excessive pay levels unrelated to managerial performance.

- *Ownership concentration*: Short-term and long-term abnormal returns are strongly related to ownership concentration. In terms of the two-dimensional framework for the analysis of ECOs, concentrated ownership represents a potentially superior monitoring technology and thus potentially reduces agency costs. The two hypotheses (H4A, H4B) relating to ownership concentration differentiate between costs and benefits of blockholders. In the short term, benefits from stronger monitoring incentives are expected to dominate since alternative control structures have not yet developed. In the long term, costs from expropriation of minority shareholders are expected to outweigh benefits.

  Empirical evidence supports these arguments: The short-term capital market reaction is positively related to parent ownership, while long-term portfolio abnormal returns are positively related to a relinquishment of parent control, measured by the free-float. From the magnitude of the coefficient estimates, it can be inferred that ownership concentration is a core driver of abnormal returns: In the short-term, a 10% reduction in parent ownership reduces the CAR -30 0 by around 3%, depending on model specification. In the long term, a 10% increase in free float increases the 36-month portfolio BHAR by around 4%, depending on model specification.

  In conclusion, the short-term capital market reaction shows that benefits from blockholder control by the parent are expected to dominate immediately post-ECO. In the long-term, however, costs of blockholder control dominate and ownership concentration becomes negatively related portfolio abnormal returns.

Summarizing the above discussion, hypotheses concerning incentive compensation and ownership concentration are supported by empirical evidence. Hypotheses concerning focus and investment efficiency are mostly supported. No robust relationship can be detected as far as information asymmetries and disclosure are concerned.

Thus, the short-term capital market reaction to ECOs is to a large part driven by the expectation of a decrease in agency costs. In the long-term, abnormal returns are negative, but agency-related variables are still related to abnormal returns in the expected (positive) direction. However, agency-related variables explain less than 40% of the variation of long-term portfolio abnormal returns. Thus, the negativity of long-term abnormal returns cannot be explained on the basis of agency-related variables. The control variables included in the regression give some indication on potential other factors influencing long-term abnormal returns: The main such factor is pre-ECO leverage, which is significantly negatively related to long-term abnormal returns.

Tentative evidence points towards a potential role of market timing as a driver of the short-term capital market reaction: A positive relationship exists between prior-year market performance and the announcement effect. However, the alternative indicators tested (subsequent market performance, prior frequency of IPOs, the difference between prior and subsequent year returns, and the market price-earnings ratio) are insignificant or only marginally significant, and none of the indicators is significant under all model specifications. In addition, no evidence of a relationship between market timing and long-term abnormal returns can be detected. While a behavioral explanation, in the sense that firms exploit investor overoptimism in their ECO decision cannot be ruled out, a strong influence of the timing of the transaction on abnormal returns therefore cannot be found.

4.5.2.2 Comparison to previous ECO literature

In the introduction (Section 1.4.3) the lack of an integrated theoretical framework for the analysis of the capital market reaction in the existing ECO literature was criticized. Accordingly, existing empirical ECO research on the determinants of the capital market reaction commonly focuses on individual drivers. These drivers are then usually analyzed via cross-sectional regression, similar to the present study. The literature review in Section 1.4.1 has concluded that U.S. empirical evidence largely supports the efficiency gains hypothesis: Positive short-term abnormal returns are related to the divestment of non-core businesses, and improved disclosure on the subsidiary. The efficiency gains hypothesis, while not derived from agency theory in a strictly rigorous manner, substantially borrows from it: For example, improved disclosure reduces agency costs originating from information asymmetries between principal (shareholders) and agents (management). Thus, the choice of agency theory as underlying theoretical framework fits naturally into the current stage of development of the ECO literature.

A more detailed summary of the findings of the existing literature with respect to the agency-related hypotheses of the present study is provided in Table 51. Three authors analyze the determinants of the short-term capital market reaction (U.S.: Allen/McConnell (1998), Vijh (2002), Germany: Elsas/Löffler (2003)), and one author focuses on long-term abnormal returns (U.S.: Vijh (1999)). The previous evidence on the four levers analyzed in the present study is discussed in the following:

- *Focus and investment efficiency*: As far as focus is concerned, Vijh (2002) and Elsas/Löffler (2003) find that ECOs where parent and subsidiary are from the same industry have inferior short-term abnormal returns, while Allen/McConnell (1998) cannot detect such a relationship. Vijh (1999) does not find a relationship between degree of diversification of the group of companies and subsequent subsidiary long-term abnormal returns. The evidence in Vijh (2002) and Elsas/Löffler (2003) is consistent with H1A of the present study: When parent and subsidiary are from the same industry, a material reduction in the heterogeneity of investment opportunities is not to be expected, and a less positive capital market reaction ensues.

  With reference potential overinvestment issues, Allen/McConnell (1998) find that a payout of ECO proceeds is positively related to short-term abnormal returns, consistent with H1B. Elsas/Löffler (2003), however, do not detect a difference in abnormal returns between ECOs where the parent receives (part) of the proceeds, and those where it does not. Equally, Allen/McConnell (1998) do not detect an influence of the fraction of ECO proceeds accruing to the parent on short-term abnormal returns. Vijh (2002) finds that mixed placements, i.e. placements where both primary and secondary shares are offered and the parent receives part of the ECO proceeds, have superior abnormal returns compared to pure primary or secondary placements. This evidence is difficult to interpret, since Vijh (2002) in his variable definition does not differentiate between pure primary and pure secondary placements. Vijh (2002) also finds that the capital market reacts positively to the mention of investment motives for the ECO in the announcement. Overall, previous evidence on ECOs and overinvestment is thus at best mixed.

Table 51: Literature on determinants of capital market reaction

Author (Year)	Sample period	Sample size	Perspective	Variable	Relationship to abnormal return
Allen/ McConnell (1998)	1978-1993	183	Short-term, [-1; +1]	Parent and subsidiary in same industry (dummy)	n.s.
				Payout of proceeds announced (dummy)	+
				Parent ownership in subsidiary post-ECO	n.s.
				Fraction of ECO proceeds to parent	n.s.
				Subsequent outside acquisition of subsidiary	n.s.
				Relative size of subsidiary (asset ratio)	+
				Leverage	n.s.
				Interest coverage	n.s.
				Profitability	n.s.
Vijh (1999)	1981-1995	94	Long-term [+36M] Subsidiary	Parent with four or more segments pre-ECO (dummy)	n.s.
				Above-median parent ownership post-ECO (dummy)	n.s.
				Above-median institutional holdings (dummy)	+
				Above-median offering value/parent market value (dummy)	n.s.
				Above-median subsidiary market value (dummy)	n.s.
				Above-median parent book-to-market ratio pre-ECO (dummy)	n.s.
				Above-median parent earnings-to-price ratio pre-ECO (dummy)	n.s.
Vijh (2002)	1980-1997	277	Short-term, [-1; +1]	Parent and subsidiary in same industry (dummy)	-
				Mixed placement (dummy)	+
				Financing motives announced (dummy)	n.s.
				Investment motives announced (dummy)	+
				Transparency motives announced (dummy)	+
				Subsequent spinoff (dummy)	+
				Relative size of subsidiary (market value ratio)	+
Elsas/ Löffler (2003)	1984-2000	37	Short-term, [-5; +5]	Parent and subsidiary in same industry (dummy)	-
				Parent does not receive capital inflow (dummy)	n.s.
				Information asymmetries (std. dev. of market model residuals)	-
				Relative size of subsidiary (sales ratio)	n.s.
				Ownership concentration in parent (Herfindahl index)	-
				Parent has ultimate owner (dummy)	-
				Bank debt/total assets	n.s.
				Bank ownership (dummy)	n.s.
				Bank proxy votes/total votes	n.s.

- *Information asymmetries and disclosure*: Previous evidence on information asymmetries is very thin. Vijh (2002) finds that the capital market positively rewards the mention of an increase in transparency as a motive for the transaction in the ECO announcement. However, the mention of such a motive does not guarantee that transparency is actually improved. Elsas/Löffler (2003), using a similar definition of information asymmetries as the present study, find that pre-ECO information asymmetries are negatively related to short-term abnormal returns.

  Thus, their result is consistent with results from the present study, but equally contradicts standard theory. Elsas/Löffler (2003) rationalize their result based on differential effects of information asymmetries for same-industry and cross-industry ECOs.

- *Incentive compensation*: In the literature surveyed, the introduction of incentive compensation has been repeatedly discussed as potential determinant of the capital market reaction since Schipper/Smith (1986), but to the knowledge of the author, no previous empirical evidence exists.

- *Ownership concentration*: While Allen/McConnell (1998) find that a subsequent outside acquisition of the subsidiary is unrelated to the short-term capital market reaction, Vijh (2002) finds that a subsequent full spin-off is positively related to short-term abnormal returns. This evidence is consistent with evidence on H4B in the present study, which states that a subsequent relinquishment of parent control is positively related to long-term abnormal returns.

In further analyses, Allen/McConnell (1998) and Vijh (2002) find that the relative size of the subsidiary is positively related to short-term abnormal returns, while Elsas/Löffler (2003), based on a German sample, do not detect such a relationship, consistent with results of the present study. Furthermore, Elsas/Löffler (2003) indicate a negative impact of ownership concentration *in the parent* on announcement returns, but do not find evidence for a special monitoring role of banks.

As far as market timing is concerned, evidence from the present study confirms concurrent evidence on the absent or at best limited role of market timing in German ECOs (Wagner (2004), Fucks (2004)).

Overall, the previous ECO literature thus contains some indications on the relationship between the short-term capital market reaction and variables related to agency costs. While no fundamental contradictions to results from the present study are found, none of the existing studies contains a complete analysis of the effect of ECOs on agency costs.

4.5.2.3 Relative importance of the four value levers

In the above discussion, focus and investment efficiency, incentive alignment, and ownership concentration have been shown to be significantly related to the capital market reaction, and some indications have been given on the relative magnitude of estimated coefficients. Also, results of the present study have been shown to be largely consistent with previous results, if such exist. In order to arrive at a more precise picture of the relevance of the four levers, their relative importance has to be assessed.

In order to arrive at an assessment of the relative importance of the four levers, the following highly simplified approach is applied: Each regression coefficient is multiplied by the sample mean of the variable it refers to (e.g. the coefficient on FOCUS is multiplied by the sample average value of FOCUS). Then, coefficients referring to the same group of hypotheses (H1, H2, H3, H4) are summed. The sum over all four hypothesis groups is then scaled to 100% in order to represent the relative weight of each value lever in explaining agency-cost related short-term and long-term abnormal returns (Figure 30). The short-term analysis is based on Model (3), and the long-term analysis is based on Model (11a), the long-term portfolio abnormal returns.

As can be immediately seen from Figure 30, ownership concentration is the most important determinant of abnormal returns in the short term as well as in the long term. Incentive compensation is the second most important component. As already discussed, the role of information asymmetries and disclosure is minimal. Focus and investment efficiency play a considerable role in explaining the short-term capital market reaction, but work in the opposite direction in the long-term, as discussed above. This results underlines the crucial importance of ownership concentration for the practical structuring of ECO transactions.

Figure 30: Relative importance of the four value levers

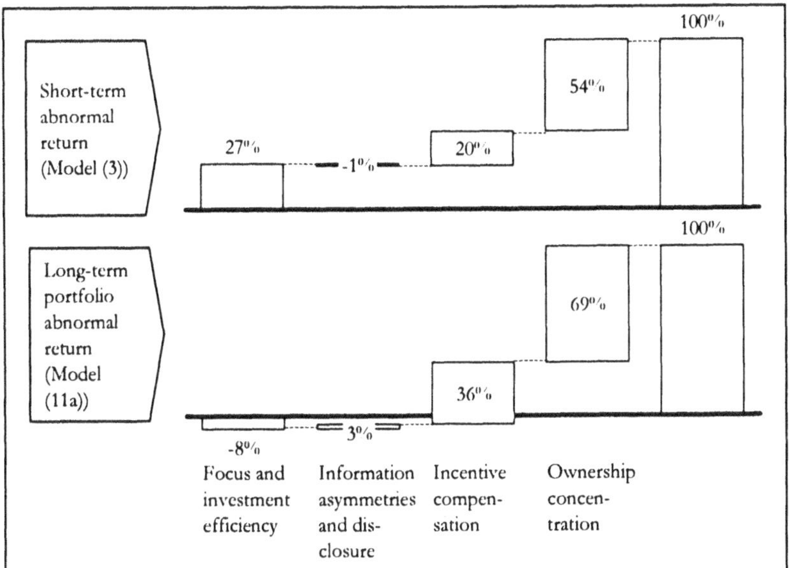

Calculation: Each regression coefficient is multiplied with the sample average value of the corresponding variable; products referring to each of the four hypothesis groups are summed; and the overall sum is scaled to 100%

4.5.3 Implications for research and practice

4.5.3.1 Research implications

The present study has found that ECOs are, on average, not an efficient instrument of restructuring from an investor perspective: Negative long-term abnormal returns overcompensate the positive short-term capital market reaction. This finding leaves open three research questions:

- *Why does the capital market overreact?* If ECOs consistently lead to negative long-term abnormal returns over a 20-year period, rational arbitrageurs should short-sell the parent stock at the ECO announcement, according to the assumptions of classical capital market theory. This should lead to a negative, not a positive announcement effect. Furthermore, the announcement effect should not be followed by non-zero long-term abnormal returns.

Instead, we consistently observe positive short-term abnormal returns, followed by negative long-term abnormal returns. The findings of the present study can thus be interpreted as evidence of overreaction. Since the pioneering study by DeBondt/Thaler (1985) on stock market overreaction, such reversals have also been found for other types of transactions: For example, Mitchell/Stafford (2000) find positive abnormal returns preceding SEOs, but negative long-term abnormal returns afterwards. In their interpretation, the capital market first overreacts to strong earnings growth, which explains the pre-SEO positive abnormal returns. Firms then take advantage of this reaction by announcing an SEO, and the overreaction is corrected via negative long-term abnormal returns post-SEO when earnings mean-revert. Rajan/Servaes (1997), in another example, document initial overoptimism among analysts on IPO announcements, which is corrected over the long term. Graham/Harvey (2001) find that (perceived) overvaluation is an important motivation behind the decision to issue equity. [197]

As the empirical analyses in the present study have shown, the influence of market timing, understood as the timing of issues to favorable capital market conditions, plays at best a limited role. However, the question remains if firms have the ability, based on their assessment of investor sentiment, to deliberately time ECOs to periods where *firm-specific* issuance conditions are particularly favorable. Also, while the present study has controlled for potential market timing related to general capital market conditions by analyzing two subsamples, one of which relates to a "hot issue market" (1998-2001), and by including various control variables as market timing indicators, a more detailed analysis of the issue could potentially shed more light into the investor reaction.

While attempts exist to reconcile such patterns with capital market efficiency (most prominently Fama (1998)), or to explain findings of long-term abnormal

[197] On the motivation to issue equity (vs. alternative forms of external finance), also see Aggarwal/Rivoli (1990), Korajczyk/Lucas/McDonald (1990, 1991), Ljungqvist (1996), Jung/Kim/Stulz (1996), Pagano/Panetta/Zingales (1998), Hovakimian/Opler/Titman (2001),

returns with methodological biases towards detecting abnormal performance (e.g. Eckbo/Masulis/Norli (2000)), patterns of over- or underreaction have come to be an accepted empirical fact by most researchers. The attempts of some researchers to uphold the efficient market hypothesis notwithstanding, findings of calendar anomalies (summarized in Fama (1991)), the predictability of stock returns (e.g. Lakonishok/Shleifer/Vishny (1994), Jegadeesh/Titman (1993)), and excess stock market variance (e.g. Shiller (1981), West (1988)) have led others to follow approaches that explicitly incorporate irrational investor behavior.[198] Under the noise-trader approach, popularized by DeLong et al. (1990) and Shleifer/Summers (1990), irrational investor behavior is assumed to have a potential influence on stock prices, since rational arbitrage does not always function.[199]

Asset pricing models are therefore needed which explicitly incorporate biases in investor behavior, and which can thus better explain observed patterns in capital market returns. Pioneering work in this area includes Daniel/Hirshleifer/Subrahmanyam (1998) and Barberis/Shleifer/Vishny (1998), with further contributions reviewed in Barberis/Thaler (2003).[200] However, despite the empirical evidence to the contrary, and the lively discussion on the issue partially reviewed above, the paradigm of capital market efficiency is still firmly established as a foundation in a major part of empirical corporate finance research. A re-evaluation of the effect of corporate finance transactions, such as ECOs, based on behavioral models would certainly contribute an interesting perspective.

- *Why does post-ECO long-term underperformance materialize at the parent?* ECO subsidiaries perform normally post-ECO, but ECO parents have negative long-term abnormal returns of -25%. In cross-sectional regressions, agency-related variables explain up to 30% of the variance of parent long-term ab-

[198] Early German research on capital market efficiency includes May (1984), Möller (1985)

[199] Noise traders act irrationally by falsely assuming that they possess information ("pseudo-signal"), and by trading on that information. The term "noise trader" is due to Kyle (1985) and further developed in Black (1986). Empirical examples for irrational behavior are contained in e.g. Shiller (1990), and in Oehler (1991, 1992, 1994). The effect of noise traders on stock market equilibrium is also discussed in LaPorta (1996) and Chen/Hong/Stein (1999).

[200] A practical introduction to the topic is provided in Goldberg/von Nitzsch (2004)

normal returns. Furthermore, most variables related to agency costs can be shown to have a positive influence on long-term abnormal performance at ECO parents. While opportunities to improve long-term performance of the parent, by e.g. fully relinquishing control of the subsidiary, are not taken, agency costs alone cannot explain long-term underperformance. In other words, it is unclear what drives the remaining 70% of unexplained variance.

A potential factor is selection bias: Technically, the findings of the present study cannot say that ECOs are related long-term underperformance *in general*, but only that ECOs are related to long-term underperformance *for those groups of companies that undertake ECOs*. However, it is possible that those groups of companies are especially likely to announce ECOs that expect long-term underperformance. This argument builds on a similar discussion in the current literature on diversification (reviewed in Section 3.3.2): Poor performance of diversified firms does not mean that diversification causes poor performance, it can also mean that a priori poorly performing firms have a higher likelihood to diversify (e.g. Campa/Kedia (2002), Villalonga (2003a)).

A promising avenue for further research would thus consist in the application of two-stage least squares or instrumental variables approaches, which explicitly incorporate the likelihood of undertaking an ECO, depending on certain firm characteristics, and which could thus neutralize potential selection bias.

- *Can the results be generalized to other geographies?* Results of the present study are based on a sample of 55 German ECOs. Results have been shown to be robust to methodological variations, and the results of CUSUM tests indicate that observed patterns are structurally stable across the entire sample period. However, sample size is small compared to benchmarks of U.S. empirical corporate finance research (e.g. Vijh (2002): sample size of 277 ECOs). Thus, it is open to question to what extent results can be generalized to other geographies, in particular the U.S., and to what extent results are explained by e.g. the special characteristics of the German governance system.

  Thus, it would certainly be interesting to test the hypotheses derived based on the unifying two-dimensional framework for the analysis of ECOs on a U.S. dataset. Implications would be especially interesting as far as ownership concentration is concerned, since ownership concentration has been shown to be a core driver of abnormal returns in the present study, and the relative benefits and costs of blockholders have been shown to differ between Anglo-Saxon and German governance systems.

4.5.3.2 *Practical implications*

At the most basic level, the finding of significant negative long-term portfolio abnormal returns, and the consequent verdict that ECOs do not represent an efficient instrument of restructuring, suggests a simple practical implication: Groups of companies should not undertake ECOs on the German capital market in the future. However, such a recommendation is oversimplified: Obviously, the initial enthusiasm of Schipper/Smith (1986, p. 153), who stated that ECOs are the only type of equity financing positively assessed by the capital market, must be rejected. However, long-term underperformance has been shown for other types of equity financing on the German capital market as well (e.g. Stehle/Ehrhardt/Przyborowski (2001) on IPOs and SEOs, Ljungqvist (1997) on IPOs), although underperformance is less pronounced than on the U.S. capital market. Empirical evidence on alternative types of reorganization transactions such as spin-offs or sell-offs on the German capital market is scarce, since e.g. spin-offs have not taken place in sufficient number in order to allow statistical analysis of long-term abnormal returns (Schultze (1998)). Thus, when deriving practical implications of the results of the present study, ECOs must not only be evaluated on absolute terms, but also be benchmarked against available alternative transactions. Under these conditions, it is still worthwhile to develop a set of structuring criteria that helps to achieve the best possible long-term performance post-ECO.

Based on the relative weight of the four levers, ***ownership concentration*** is by far the most important structuring criterion. Results suggest that ownership concentration must be systematically managed: ECOs should be understood as a staged exist strategy, where the parent retains control in the immediate post-ECO phase, but relinquishes control over the three years following the ECO. Such a strategy is consistent with indicative empirical evidence on the significance of second events after ECOs in Klein/Rosenfeld/Beranek (1991), and with theoretical models of IPOs as two-stage procedures (Zingales (1995b)). If, on the other hand, a full divestiture is not planned, e.g. because of operational synergies between the parent and subsidiary businesses, an

ECO should not be undertaken in the first place, due to the significant negative impact of persistent parent control in the subsidiary on long-term returns.

In addition, *incentive compensation* for the subsidiary management, either in the form of direct stock ownership or a stock options program, should be introduced. Well-founded skepticism towards stock options programs, particularly prevalent in the German academic literature (e.g. Wenger/Knoll (1999)), and in the recent U.S. literature (e.g. Bebchuk/Fried (2003)), must be countered with effective institutional arrangements preventing managerial influence on own pay, and thus preventing excessive pay levels at the subsidiary.

Concerning *focus and investment efficiency*, results prescribe the choice of a non-core unit for the ECO (reducing the heterogeneity of investment opportunities), and the creation of effective barriers against cross-subsidization between parent and subsidiary once the ECO has taken place. Also, the use of ECO proceeds to reduce debt levels is generally welcomed by the capital market.

Finally, *information asymmetries and disclosure* could not be shown to be related to the capital market reaction, and thus does not constitute a central structuring criterion.

In summary, despite their inefficiency when assessed in absolute terms, ECOs can constitute a valid form of restructuring when benchmarked in relative terms against alternative types of transactions. Firms have the opportunity to positively influence long-term abnormal returns when following certain practical structuring criteria. The most important among these is the use of ECOs as a staged exit strategy, where control of the subsidiary is fully relinquished in the long-term.

5 Conclusion

The present study has analyzed the determinants of the short-term and long-term impact on firm value of ECOs on the German capital market. Hypotheses were based on principal-agent-theory as overriding theoretical framework, and empirical evidence was presented based on a sample of 55 ECOs from the 1984-2003 period.

Representing 30% of the total IPO volume during the sample period, ECOs are an important class of corporate finance transactions on the German capital market. Their special interest is constituted by their dual character as a means of financing and reorganization, which leaves their impact on the structure of incentives in groups of companies a priori open to question. In addition, the limited success of prominent ECO transactions has recently sparked a renewed public debate.

Previous ECO research has documented a positive short-term capital reaction to ECO announcements in an event study framework (Schipper/Smith (1986)), and explained this reaction with efficiency gains due to the divestment of non-core businesses and improved transparency thanks to increased disclosure on the subsidiary. In deriving the efficiency gains hypothesis, the ECO literature has mainly borrowed from agency theory.

The long-term effects of ECOs on firm value, in contrast, could not be unequivocally determined. Thus, the overall effect of ECOs on firm value, and its determinants, have remained largely open to question.

The present study has aimed at narrowing this gap. Principal-agent theory was chosen as theoretical paradigm to guide hypothesis development on the impact of ECOs on firm value. The choice of principal-agent theory as underlying framework fits naturally into the current stage of development of the ECO literature: While behavioral approaches have gained considerable ground in finance in general, they have not yet exerted much influence in the ECO literature. The central aim of the present study as far as theory is concerned has thus lied in synthesizing existing agency approaches into a coherent framework that allows for a more systematic derivation of hypotheses compared to the existing literature.

An intuitive efficiency criterion was defined: ECOs constitute an efficient form of restructuring if they are associated with a reduction in agency costs of the group of companies, proxied for by the change in equity value related to the transaction.

As a guide to hypothesis development, a two-dimensional agency framework for the analysis of ECOs was developed: The first dimension is given by the determinants of agency costs identified in previous literature, namely interest divergence, information environment, and monitoring/bonding technology. The second dimension is given by the principal-agent relationships affected by ECOs, where groups of companies are understood as cascades of principal-agent relationships. The three relationships affected by ECOs are the relationships between parent shareholders and parent management, parent management and subsidiary management, and subsidiary shareholders and subsidiary management. On the basis of the two-dimensional framework, four value levers have been identified: focus and investment efficiency, information asymmetries and disclosure, incentive compensation, and ownership concentration.

Focus and investment efficiency refers to a potential improvement in investment efficiency thanks to ECOs. This improvement is related to a reduction of potential overinvestment if the volume of the internal capital market is reduced via a payout of ECO proceeds, and a reduction of inefficient cross-subsidization if a reduction in the heterogeneity of investment opportunities makes such cross-subsidization less likely, or effective barriers are created via a separation of parent and subsidiary.

Information asymmetries and disclosure refers to a potential reduction in agency costs thanks to ECOs based on increased disclosure on the subsidiary. An increase in mandatory disclosure stems from the requirement to publish separate annual reports post-ECO.

Incentive compensation refers to the reduction in interest divergence thanks to the introduction of stock-based incentives for subsidiary managers, either in the form of stock options or of direct stock ownership. A potential countervailing effects consists in managerial influence on own pay, resulting in excessive pay levels.

Finally, ownership concentration refers to potential benefits and costs from blockholder (parent) control. It is hypothesized that parent control is beneficial in the short-term, when alternative control structures have not developed, but detrimental in the long-term, when potential expropriation of minority shareholders can negatively affect returns.

The analysis of the capital market reaction to ECOs is guided by the four levers. In the short-term, announcement date abnormal returns in the order of +10% are found, using an extended multiday event period. The application of recent methodological developments does not materially alter results. Findings of the existing literature are thus confirmed.

In the long-term, negative parent/subsidiary portfolio abnormal returns in the order of -20% in the three years following the ECO are found. Thus, the long-term effect of ECOs on firm value, ambiguous in the existing literature, is clarified. The underperformance is exclusively due to the parent, while the subsidiary does not exhibit an abnormal development. Again, this result is robust to methodological variation.

Summing up the short-term and long-term effects, ECOs lead to a deterioration in firm value, and therefore do not represent an efficient form of restructuring based on the efficiency criterion defined above. Furthermore, the pattern of overreaction observed is hardly reconcilable with capital market efficiency.

Within the chosen theory, the short-term capital market reaction is well explained by the capital market's expectation of a decrease in agency costs: Statistically, the magnitude of the announcement effect is significantly related to a set of operating and financial variables that proxy for the development of agency costs. Among the four levers, ownership concentration, focus and investment efficiency, and incentive compensation work in the expected direction. Thus, positive short-term abnormal returns are related to the benefits of an external blockholder as superior monitoring technology, the improvement in investment efficiency relating to decreased cross-subsidization and less overinvestment, and the reduction of interest divergence thanks to the introduction of incentive compensation. Contrary to the hypothesis, a reduction in information asymmetries is negatively related to short-term abnormal returns, but this effect is hardly material.

The long-term portfolio abnormal returns are affected by agency-related variables as well: Insufficient barriers against continued cross-subsidization negatively influence returns. Effective constraints on managerial influence on own pay, and the relinquishment of control by the parent are positively related to long-term returns. A reduction of information asymmetries is also positively related to returns in the long-term, in contrast to the contradictory short-term evidence, but the effect is equally immaterial. Contrary to expectations, overinvestment, or more precisely, above-average investment, is positively related to long-term returns.

Summarizing the evidence on the four levers, the short-term capital market reaction is strongly driven by expectations of a decrease in agency costs. In the long-term, negative abnormal returns are exhibited, but a positive relation between decreases in agency costs and returns persists.

Alternative explanations unrelated to agency theory of the pattern of returns observed could be thought of: Most importantly, the capital market reaction could be explained based on an investor sentiment argument – overoptimistic investors overreact to the news conveyed by the ECO announcement, leading to a positive announcement effect, and this overreaction is corrected in the long term, leading to negative long-term abnormal returns. Consistent with the current stage of development of the ECO literature however, the present study has exclusively focused on agency theory. Still, in subsample analyses, a material influence of market timing on the pattern of returns observed could be ruled out: While the capital market reaction differs in magnitude for ECOs from the 1998-2001 hot issue period, it does not differ in direction. Also, market timing indicators introduced into the regression analyses are generally not related significantly to either short- or long-term abnormal returns.

Abstracting from potential alternative explanations outside agency theory, ownership concentration has by far the most weight among the four value levers analyzed in determining both the short-term and long-term capital market reaction. Thus, in the short-term, the capital market appears to expect decreases in agency costs resulting from a restructuring of incentives, but these benefits do not materialize in the long term since the subsidiary does not gain full independence, but largely remains within the group of companies.

From this finding follows the practical implication to interpret ECOs as a staged exit strategy, where a phase during which the parent retains control post-ECO should subsequently be followed by a full exit. While the inefficiency of ECOs from an investor perspective in absolute terms could be interpreted as leading to a recommendation not to undertake ECOs in the future, such an interpretation is oversimplified. Similar financing transactions such as IPOs and SEOs have equally been shown to be followed by long-term underperformance, so that ECOs can still be efficient in relative terms. Results on the four levers can be used to derive structuring criteria for ECOs that allow to positively influence long-term returns. Given the dominant influence of ownership concentration in determining the capital market reaction, the most important amongst these criteria is the structuring as a staged exit, as explained above.

As far as research implications are concerned, three promising avenues for further research are identified. The first avenue consists in incorporating biases in investor behavior (such as e.g. overoptimism, as explained above) in the empirical analysis, in order to more directly explain the pattern of overreaction. The second avenue consists in further analysis of the negative long-term abnormal returns of the parent. While agency-related variables explain up to 30% of the variation of parent returns, 70% remain unexplained; and agency-related variables give only a partial indication as to why long-term abnormal returns are negative. Statistical methods correcting for selection bias, such as the instrumental variables approach, have potential to provide further insights. The third avenue consists in an application of the two-dimensional framework for the analysis of ECOs derived to other geographies, first and foremost the U.S. Such an application provides insights into the generalizability of results, and the impact of specific governance systems on ECO performance.

6 References

ABARBANELL, J. S., and V. L. BERNARD (1992): Test of Analysts' Overreaction/Underreaction to Earnings Information as an Explanation for Anomalous Stock Price Behavior, *Journal of Finance*, 47, 1181-1208.

ABHYANKAR, A., and K.-Y. HO (2001): *Is the Long-Horizon Abnormal Performance after Seasoned Equity Offerings Illusory? New Evidence from the UK*. Working Paper, University of Warwick.

ABOODY, D., and R. KASZNIK (2000): CEO stock options awards and the timing of corporate voluntary disclosures, *Journal of Accounting and Economics*, 29, 73-100.

ABOWD, J. M., and D. S. KAPLAN (1999): Executive Compensation: Six Questions That Need Answering, *Journal of Economic Perspectives*, 13, 145-168.

ACHARYA, S. (1988): A generalized econometric model and tests of a signaling hypothesis with two discrete signals, *Journal of Finance*, 43, 413-429.

ACHARYA, V., K. JOHN, and R. SUNDARAM (2000): On the optimality of resetting executive stock options, *Journal of Financial Economics*, 57, 65-101.

AGGARWAL, R., and P. RIVOLI (1990): Fads in the initial public offering market?, *Financial Management*, 19, 45-57.

AGGARWAL, R. K., and A. A. SAMWICK (1999): The Other Side of the Tradeoff: The Impact of Risk on Executive Compensation, *Journal of Political Economy*, 107, 65-105.

AGGARWAL, R. K., L. KRIGMAN, and K. WOMACK (2002): Strategic IPO underpricing, information momentum, and lockup expiration selling, *Journal of Financial Economics*, 66, 105-128.

AGGARWAL, R. K., and A. A. SAMWICK (2003a): Performance Incentives within Firms: The Effect of Managerial Responsibility, *Journal of Finance*, 58, 1613-1651.

— (2003b): Why Do Managers Diversify Their Firms? Agency Reconsidered, *Journal of Finance*, 58, 71-119.

— (2003c): *Empire-builders and Shirkers: Investment, Firm Performance, and Managerial Incentives.* Working Paper, University of Virginia and Dartmouth College.

AGRAWAL, A., and C. R. KNOEBER (1996): Firm Performance and Mechnanisms to Control Agency Problems between Managers and Shareholders, *Journal of Financial and Quantitative Analysis*, 31, 377-397.

AGRAWAL, A., and J. F. JAFFE (2002): Do Takeover Targets Underperform? Evidence from Operating and Stock Returns, *Journal of Financial and Quantitative Analysis*, 38, 721-747.

AHN, S., and D. J. DENIS (2003): Internal Capital Markets and Investment Policy: Evidence from Corporate Spinoffs, *Journal of Financial Economics*, 71, 489-517.

AKAIKE, H. (1973): Information Theory and an Extension of the Maximum Likelihood Principle, in *Second International Symposium on Information Theory*, ed. by B. N. Petrov, and F. Csáki. Budapest: Akadémiai Kiadó.

AKGIRAY, V. (1989): Conditional heteroskedasticity in time series of stock returns: Evidence and forecasts, *Journal of Business*, 62, 55-80.

AKTAS, N., E. DE BODT, and J.-G. COUSIN (2003): *Event Study under Noisy Estimation Period.* Working Paper, Université Catholique de Louvain and Université de Lille.

AKTAS, N., E. DE BODT, and R. ROLL (in press): Market Response to European Regulation of Business Combinations, *Journal of Financial and Quantitative Analysis.*

ALBACH, H. (2001a): *Konzernmanagement.* Wiesbaden.

— (2001b): Shareholder Value und Unternehmenswert: Theoretische Anmerkungen zu einem aktuellen Thema, *Zeitschrift für Betriebswirtschaft*, 71, 643-674.

ALCHIAN, A. A. (1950): Uncertainty, evolution, and economic theory, *Journal of Political Economy*, 58, 211-221.

— (1969): Corporate Management and Property Rights, in *Economic Policy and the Regulation of Corporate Securities*, ed. by H. G. Manne. Washington, D.C.: American Enterprise Institute, 337-360.

ALCHIAN, A. A., and H. DEMSETZ (1972): Production, Information Costs and Economic Organization, *American Economic Review*, 62, 777-795.

ALFORD, A. W., J. J. JONES, R. LEFTWICH, and M. E. ZMIJEWSKI (1993): The Relative Informativeness of Accounting Disclosures in Different Countries, *Journal of Accounting Research*, 31, 183-223.

ALI, A., and L.-S. HWANG (2000): Country-Specific Factors Related to Financial Reporting and the Value Relevance of Accounting Data, *Journal of Accounting Research*, 38, 1-23.

ALLEN, F., and G. R. FAULHABER (1989): Signaling by Underpricing in the IPO Market, *Journal of Financial Economics*, 23, 303-324.

ALLEN, F., and D. M. GALE (2000): *Comparing Financial Systems*. Cambridge: MIT Press.

ALLEN, J. W., S. L. LUMMER, J. J. MCCONNELL, and D. K. REED (1995): Can Takeover Losses Explain Spin-Off Gains?, *Journal of Financial and Quantitative Analysis*, 30, 465-485.

ALLEN, J. W. (1998): Capital markets and corporate structure: the equity carve-outs of Thermo Electron, *Journal of Financial Economics*, 48, 99-124.

ALLEN, J. W., and J. J. MCCONNELL (1998): Equity Carve-Outs and Managerial Discretion, *Journal of Finance*, 53, 163-186.

ALLEN, J. W., and G. M. PHILLIPS (2000): Corporate Equity Ownership, Strategic Alliances, and Product Market Relationships, *Journal of Finance*, 55, 2791-2816.

ALTI, A. (2003): How Sensitive is Investment to Cash Flow when Financing is Frictionless?, *Journal of Finance*, 58, 707-722.

— (2004): *How persistent is the impact of market timing on capital structure?* Working Paper, University of Texas at Austin.

ALVAREZ, M. (2002): Segmentberichterstattung nach DRS3: Vergleich zu IAS 14 und SFAS 131, *Der Betrieb*, 55, 2057-2063.

ALVAREZ, M., and C. FINK (2003): Qualität der Segmentberichterstattung in Deutschland: eine empirische Analyse der Unternehmen des DAX100 und NEMAX50, *Zeitschrift für kapitalmarktorientierte Rechnungslegung*, 3, 275-288.

ALVAREZ, S., and V. M. GONZALEZ (2002): *Long-Run Performance of Initial Public Offerings (IPOs) in the Spanish Capital Market.* Working Paper, University of Oviedo.

AMIHUD, Y., and B. LEV (1981): Risk reduction as a managerial motive for conglomerate mergers, *Bell Journal of Economics*, 12, 605-617.

AMIHUD, Y., and H. MENDELSON (1986): Asset Pricing and the Bid-Ask Spread, *Journal of Financial Economics*, 17, 223-249.

ANDREWS, D. W., and M. BUCHINSKY (2000): A Three-Step Method for Choosing the Number of Bootstrap Repetitions, *Econometrica*, 68, 23-51.

ANG, J. S., R. A. COLE, and J. W. LIN (2000): Agency Costs and Ownership Structure, *Journal of Finance*, 55, 81-106.

ANG, J. S., and S. ZHANG (2004): An Evaluation of Testing Procedures for Long Horizon Event Studies, *Review of Quantitative Finance and Accounting*, 23, 251-274.

ANNEMA, A., W. C. FALLON, and M. H. GOEDHART (2001): Do carve-outs make sense?, *McKinsey on Finance*, Autumn, 6-10.

— (2002): When carve-outs make sense, *McKinsey Quarterly*, 13-15.

ANSELIN, L. (1988): *Spatial Econometrics: Methods and Models.* Dordrecht: Kluwer.

ANSLINGER, P., D. CAREY, K. FINK, and C. GAGNON (1997): Equity carve-outs: A new spin on the corporate structure, *McKinsey Quarterly*, Iss. 1, 165-172.

ANSLINGER, P., S. J. KLEPPER, and S. SUBRAMANIAM (1999): Breaking up is good to do, *McKinsey Quarterly*, Iss. 1, 16-27.

ANSLINGER, P., S. BONINI, and M. PATSALOS-FOX (2000): Doing the spin-out, *McKinsey Quarterly*, Iss. 1, 98-105.

ANTLE, R., and A. J. SMITH (1986): An Empirical Investigation of the Relative Performance Evaluation of Corporate Executives, *Journal of Accounting Research*, 24, 1-39.

ANTLE, R., and J. S. DEMSKI (1988): The Controllability Principle in Responsibility Accounting, *Accounting Review*, 63, 700-718.

ARMITAGE, S. (1995): Event study methods and evidence on their performance, *Journal of Economic Surveys*, 8, 25-52.

ARON, D. J. (1991): Using the capital market as a monitor: corporate spinoffs in an agency framework, *RAND Journal of Economics*, 22, 505-518.

ASQUITH, P., and D. MULLINS (1986): Equity issues and offering dilution, *Journal of Financial Economics*, 15, 61-89.

ASQUITH, P., P. HEALY, and K. G. PALEPU (1989): Earnings and stock splits, *Accounting Review*, 64, 387-403.

BAETGE, J., H.-J. KIRSCH, and S. THIELE (2002): *Konzernbilanzen*. Düsseldorf: IDW.

BAIMAN, S., and R. E. VERRECCHIA (1996): The relation among capital markets, financial disclosure, production efficiency, and insider trading, *Journal of Accounting Research*, 34, 1-23.

BAKER, G., M. C. JENSEN, and K. J. MURPHY (1988): Compensation and Incentives: Practice vs. Theory, *Journal of Finance*, 43, 593-616.

BAKER, G. (1992): Incentive Contracts and Performance Measurement, *Journal of Political Economy*, 100, 598-614.

BAKER, G., R. GIBBONS, and K. J. MURPHY (1994): Subjective Performance Measures in Optimal Incentive Contracts, *Quarterly Journal of Economics*, 109, 1125-1156.

BAKER, G. (2000): The Use of Performance Measures in Incentive Contracting, *American Economic Review*, 90, 415-421.

BAKER, M. P., and J. WURGLER (2000): The equity share in new issues and aggregate stock returns, *Journal of Finance*, 55, 2219-2257.

BAKER, M. P., and J. WURGLER (2002): Market Timing and Capital Structure, *Journal of Finance*, 57, 1-33.

BALDWIN, B. A. (1984): Segment earnings disclosure and the ability of security analysts to forecast earnings per share, *Accounting Review*, 59, 376-389.

BALL, C. A., and W. N. TOROUS (1988): Investigating Security-Price Performance in the Presence of Event-Date Uncertainty, *Journal of Financial Economics*, 22, 123-157.

BALL, R., and P. BROWN (1968): An Evaluation of Accounting Income Numbers, *Journal of Accounting Research*, 6, 159-178.

BALL, R., S. P. KOTHARI, and A. ROBIN (2000): The effect of international institutional factors on properties of accounting earnings, *Journal of Accounting and Economics*, 29, 1-52.

BALL, R., A. ROBIN, and J. S. WU (2003): Incentives versus standards: properties of accounting income in four East Asian countries, *Journal of Accounting and Economics*, 36, 235-271.

BANKER, R., and S. DATAR (1989): Sensitivity, Precision and Linear Aggregation of Accounting Signals, *Journal of Accounting Research*, 27, 21-39.

BANKER, R., S.-Y. LEE, and G. POTTER (1996): A Field Study of the Impact of a Performance-Based Incentive Plan, *Journal of Accounting and Economics*, 21, 195-226.

BARBER, B. M., and J. D. LYON (1996): Detecting abnormal operating performance: The empirical power and specification of test statistics, *Journal of Financial Economics*, 41, 359-399.

BARBER, B. M., and J. D. LYON (1997): Detecting long-run abnormal stock returns: The empirical power and specification of test statistics, *Journal of Financial Economics*, 43, 341-372.

BARBER, B. M. (2001): Can investors profit from the prophets? Security analyst recommendations and stock returns, *Journal of Finance*, 56, 531-563.

BARBERIS, N., A. SHLEIFER, and R. VISHNY (1998): A model of investor sentiment, *Journal of Financial Economics*, 49, 307-343.

BARBERIS, N., and R. H. THALER (2003): A survey of behavioral finance, in *Handbook of the Economics of Finance*, ed. by G. Constantinides, M. Harris, and R. M. Stulz. Amsterdam et al.: Elsevier, 1051-1121.

BARCLAY, M. J., and C. G. HOLDERNESS (1989): Private Benefits from Control of Public Corporations, *Journal of Financial Economics*, 25, 371-395.

— (1991): Negotiated Block Trades and Corporate Control, *Journal of Finance*, 46, 861-878.

BARKEMA, H. G., and L. R. GOMEZ-MEJIA (1998): Managerial Compensation and Firm Performance: A General Research Framework, *Academy of Management Journal*, 41, 135-145.

BARKEMA, H. G., and J. M. PENNINGS (1998): Top Management Pay: Impact of Overt and Covert Power, *Organization Studies*, 19, 975-1003.

BARRY, C. B., and S. J. BROWN (1985): Differential information and security market equilibrium, *Journal of Financial and Quantitative Analysis*, 20, 407-423.

BAYLESS, M., and S. CHAPLINSKY (1996): Is there a Window of Opportunity for Seasoned Equity Issuance?, *Journal of Finance*, 51, 253-278.

BEAVER, W. H. (1968): The Information Content of Annual Earnings Announcements, *Journal of Accounting Research*, 6, 67-93.

BEBCHUK, L. A., and L. A. STOLE (1993): Do Short-Term Objectives Lead to Under- or Overinvestment in Long-Term Projects, *Journal of Finance*, 48, 719-730.

BEBCHUK, L. A., R. KRAAKMAN, and G. TRIANTIS (2000): Stock Pyramids, Cross-Ownership and Dual-Class Equity: The Mechanisms and Agency Costs of Separating Control From Cash-Flow Rights, in *Concentrated Corporate Ownership*, ed. by R. Morck. Chicago: University of Chicago Press, 445-460.

BEBCHUK, L. A., J. M. FRIED, and D. I. WALKER (2002): Managerial Power and Rent Extraction in the Design of Executive Compensation, *University of Chicago Law Review*, 69, 751-846.

BEBCHUK, L. A., and J. M. FRIED (2003): Executive Compensation as an Agency Problem, *Journal of Economic Perspectives*, 17, 71-92.

BECHT, M., and E. BOEHMER (1999): Transparency of Ownership and Control in Germany, in *The separation of ownership and control: A survey of 7 European countries. Preliminary Report to the European Commission*, ed. by E. C. G. Network. Brussels: European Corporate Governance Network.

— (2003): Voting control in German corporations, *International Review of Law and Economics*, 23, 1-29.

BECHT, M., P. BOLTON, and A. RÖELL (2003): Corporate Governance and Control, in *Handbook of the Economics of Finance*, ed. by G. Constantinides, M. Harris, and R. M. Stulz.

BEHRENS, P. (1985): The Firm as a Complex Institution, *Journal of Institutional and Theoretical Economics*, 141, 62-75.

BENS, D. A., and S. J. MONAHAN (2004): Disclosure Quality and the Excess Value of Diversification, *Journal of Accounting Research*, 42, 691-731.

BENVENISTE, L. M., and P. A. SPINDT (1989): How investment bankers determine the offer price and allocation of new issues, *Journal of Financial Economics*, 24, 343-361.

BERA, A. K., and C. M. JARQUE (1981): *An Efficient Large-Sample Test for Normality of Observations and Regression Residuals*. Australian National University Working Papers in Econometrics 40.

BERA, A. K., and M. L. HIGGINS (1993): ARCH Models: Properties, Estimation and Testing, *Journal of Economic Surveys*, 7, 305-362.

BERGER, P. G., and E. OFEK (1995): Diversification's effect on firm value, *Journal of Financial Economics*, 37, 39-65.

— (1999): Causes and Effects of Corporate Refocusing Programs, *Review of Financial Studies*, 12, 311-345.

BERGER, P. G., and R. HANN (2003): The impact of SFAS No. 131 on information and monitoring, *Journal of Accounting Research*, 41, 163.

BERGLÖF, E. (1997): A note on the typology of financial systems, in *Essays and materials in comparative corporate governance*, ed. by K. J. Hopt, and E. Wymeersch. Berlin: Gruyter, 151-164.

BERLE, A. A., and G. C. MEANS (1932): *The Modern Corporation and Private Property*. New York: Macmillan.

BERNARD, V. L. (1987): Cross-sectional dependence and problems in inference in market-based accounting research, *Journal of Accounting Research*, 25, 1-48.

BERNARDO, A. E., and B. CHOWDRY (2002): Resources, real options, and corporate strategy, *Journal of Financial Economics*, 63, 211-234.

BERNARDS, O. (1995): Segmentberichterstattung in den Geschäftsberichten deutscher Unternehmen - theoretische und empirische Ergebnisse, *Deutsches Steuerrecht*, 35/1995, 1363-1368.

BERNDT, E. K., B. H. HALL, and J. A. HAUSMAN (1974): Estimation inference in nonlinear structural models, *Annals of Economic and Social Measurement*, 4, 653-665.

BERNHARDT, W., and P. WITT (1997): Stock Options und Shareholder Value, *Zeitschrift für Betriebswirtschaft*, 67, 85-101.

BERNHEIM, B. D., and M. D. WHINSTON (1990): Multimarket Contact and Collusive Behavior, *RAND Journal of Economics*, 21, 1-26.

BERRY, M. A., G. W. GALLINGER, and G. V. HENDERSON (1990): Using Daily Stock Returns in Event Studies and the Choice of Parametric versus Non-Parametric Test Statistics, *Quarterly Journal of Business and Economics*, 29, 70-85.

BERTRAND, M., and S. MULLAINATHAN (2000): Agents with and without principals, *American Economic Review*, 90, 203-208.

— (2001): Are CEOs Rewarded for Luck? The Ones Without Principals Are., *Quarterly Journal of Economics*, 116, 901-932.

BERTRAND, M., P. MEHTA, and S. MULLAINATHAN (2002): Ferreting out Tunneling: An Application to Indian Business Groups, *Quarterly Journal of Economics*, 117, 121-148.

BERTRAND, M., and S. MULLAINATHAN (2003): Enjoying the Quiet Life? Corporate Governance and Managerial Preferences, *Journal of Political Economy*, 111.

BETHEL, J. E., J. PORTER LIEBESKIND, and T. OPLER (1998): Block Share Purchases and Corporate Performance, *Journal of Finance*, 53, 605-634.

BHAGAT, S. (1983): The Effect of Pre-Emptive Right Amendments on Shareholder Wealth, *Journal of Financial Economics*, 12, 129-156.

BHAGAT, S., M. W. MARR, and G. R. THOMPSON (1985): The Rule 415 Experiment: Equity Markets, *Journal of Finance*, 40, 1385-1401.

BHATTACHARYA, S. (1979): Imperfect information, dividend policy and the 'bird in the hand' fallacy, *Bell Journal of Economics*, 10, 259-270.

BHATTACHARYA, S., H. DAOUK, and M. WELKER (2003): The World Price of Earnings Opacity, *Accounting Review*, 78, 641-678.

BHOJRAJ, S., C. M. C. LEE, and D. K. OLER (2003): What's My Line? A Comparison of Industry Classification Schemes for Capital Market Research, *Journal of Accounting Research*, 41, 745-775.

BHUSHAN, R. (1989): Firm characteristics and analyst following, *Journal of Accounting and Economics*, 11, 255-274.

— (1993): Cross-Sectional Dependence and the Use of Generalized Least Squares, *Contemporary Accounting Research*, 9, 450-462.

BICKEL, P. J., F. GÖTZE, and W. R. VAN ZWET (1997): Resampling fewer than n observations: Gains, losses, and remedies for losses, *Statistica Sinica*, 7, 1-31.

BILLETT, M. T., M. J. FLANNERY, and J. A. GARFINKEL (2001): *The Long-Run Performance of Firms Following Loan Announcements*. Working Paper, University of Iowa and University of Florida.

BILLETT, M. T., and D. MAUER (2003): Cross Subsidies, External Financing Constraints, and the Contribution of Internal Capital Markets to Firm Value, *Review of Financial Studies*, 16, 1167-1202.

BINDER, J. B. (1985): On the Use of the Multivariate Regression Model in Event Studies, *Journal of Accounting Research*, 23, 370-383.

— (1998): The Event Study Methodology Since 1969, *Review of Quantitative Finance and Accounting*, 11, 111-137.

BLACK, F., and M. SCHOLES (1973): The Pricing of Options and Corporate Liabilities, *Journal of Political Economy*, 81, 637-655.

BLACK, F. (1986): Noise, *Journal of Finance*, 41, 529-543.

BLACKWELL, D., M. W. MARR, and M. SPIVEY (1990): Shelf registration and the reduced due diligence argument: Implicatoins of the underwriter certification and the implicit insurance hypotheses, *Journal of Financial and Quantitative Analysis*, 25, 245-259.

BLANCHARD, O. J., F. LOPEZ DE SILANES, and A. SHLEIFER (1994): What Do Firms Do With Cash Windfalls?, *Journal of Financial Economics*, 36, 337-360.

BLOOM, M., and G. T. MILKOVICH (1998): Relationships Among Risk, Incentive Pay, and Organizational Performance, *Academy of Management Journal*, 41, 283-297.

BLOOMFIELD, R. J., and T. J. WILKS (2000): Disclosure Effects in the Laboratory: Liquidity, Depth, and the Cost of Capital, *Accounting Review*, 75, 13-42.

BLUME, M. E., and R. F. STAMBAUGH (1983): Biases in Computed Returns: An Application to the Size Effect, *Journal of Financial Economics*, 12, 387-405.

BÖCKING, H.-J., and B. BENECKE (1999): Der Entwurf des DRSC zur Segmentberichterstattung "E-DRS 3", *Die Wirtschaftsprüfung*, 21/1999, 839-845.

BOEHME, R. D., and S. M. SORESCU (2002): The Long-Run Performance Following Dividend Initiations and Resumptions: Underreaction or Product of Chance, *Journal of Finance*, 57, 871-900.

BOEHMER, E., J. MUSUMECI, and A. B. POULSEN (1991): Event study methodology under condition of event induced variance, *Journal of Financial Economics*, 30, 253-272.

BOHNEL, U. (1999): Die Mitwirkungskompetenz der Hauptversammlung von Holding-Gesellschaften bei der Veräußerung von Unternehmensbeteiligungen - insbesondere nach den Grundsätzen der Holzmüller-Entscheidung, *Der Betrieb*, 52, 2617-2622.

BOLLERSLEV, T. (1986): Generalized Autoregressive Conditional Heteroskedasticity, *Journal of Econometrics*, 31.

BOLLERSLEV, T., R. Y. CHOU, and K. F. KRONER (1992): ARCH modeling in finance: A review of theory and empirical evidence, *Journal of Econometrics*, 52, 5-59.

BOLLERSLEV, T., R. F. ENGLE, and D. B. NELSON (1994): ARCH Models, in *Handbook of Econometrics, Vol. IV*, ed. by R. F. Engle, and D. L. McFadden. Amsterdam et al.: Elsevier, 2959-3038.

BOLTON, P., and D. S. SCHARFSTEIN (1990): A theory of predation based on agency problems in financial contracting, *American Economic Review*, 80, 94-106.

— (1998): Corporate Finance, the Theory of the Firm, and Organizations, *Journal of Economic Perspectives*, 12, 95-114.

BOLTON, P., and E.-L. VON THADDEN (1998): Blocks, Liquidity, and Corporate Control, *Journal of Finance*, 53, 1-25.

BOONE, A., D. HAUSHALTER, and W. MIKKELSON (2003): An Investigation of the Gains from Specialized Equity Claims, *Financial Management*, 32, 67-83.

BÖRSCH-SUPAN, A., and J. KÖKE (2002): An Applied Econometrician's View of Empirical Corporate Governance Studies, *German Economic Review*, 3, 295-326.

BOTOSAN, C. (1997): Disclosure Level and the Cost of Equity Capital, *Accounting Review*, 72, 323-349.

— (2000): Evidence that greater disclosure lowers the cost of equity capital, *Journal of Applied Corporate Finance*, 12/4, 60-69.

BRAV, A., C. GECZY, and P. A. GOMPERS (2000): Is the Abnormal Return Following Equity Issuances Anomalous?, *Journal of Financial Economics*, 56, 209-250.

BRAV, A. (2000): Inference in Long-Horizon Event Studies: A Bayesian Approach with Application to Initial Public Offerings, *Journal of Finance*, 55, 1979-2016.

BRENNER, M. (1979): The Sensitivity of the Efficient Market Hypothesis on Alternative Specifications of the Market Model, *Journal of Finance*, 34, 915-929.

BRENNER, M., R. SUNDARAM, and D. YERMACK (2000): Altering the terms of executive stock options, *Journal of Financial Economics*, 57, 103-128.

BRENNER, S., and J. SCHWALBACH (2001): Management Quality, Firm Size, and Managerial Compensation: An International Comparison, *Schmalenbach Business Review*, 55, 280-293.

BRETTEL, M., L. JUNKER, and J. PINKER (2004): Wertsteigerung durch Equity Carveouts, *Zeitschrift für Betriebswirtschaft*, 74, 273-306.

BREUSCH, T. S. (1978): Testing for Autocorrelation in Dynamic Linear Models, *Australian Economic Papers*, 17, 334-356.

BREUSCH, T. S., and A. R. PAGAN (1979): A Simple Test for Heteroskedasticity and Random Coefficient Variation, *Econometrica*, 47.

— (1980): The Lagrange Multiplier Test and its Application to Model Specification in Economics, *Review of Economic Studies*, 47, 239-253.

BREUSCH, T. S., and L. G. GODFREY (1981): A Review of Recent Work on Testing for Autocorrelation in Dynamic Simultaneous Models, in *Macroeconomic Analysis: Essays in Macroeconomics and Econometrics*, ed. by D. Currie, R. Nobay, and D. Peel. London: Croon Helm, 63-105.

BROCK, W., J. LAKONISHOK, and B. LEBARON (1992): Simple Technical Trading Rules and the Stochastic Properties of Stock Returns, *Journal of Finance*, 47, 1731-1764.

BROCKETT, P. L., H.-M. CHEN, and J. R. GARVEN (1999): A new stochastically flexible event methodology with application to Proposition 103, *Insurance: Mathematics and Economics*, 25, 197-217.

BROWN, R. L., J. DURBIN, and J. M. EVANS (1975): Techniques for Testing the Constancy of Regression Relationship over Time, *Journal of the Royal Statistical Society, Series B*, 37, 149-192.

BROWN, L. D., and M. S. ROZEFF (1978): The Superiority of Analysts' Forecasts as Measures of Expectations: Evidence from Earnings, *Journal of Finance*, 33, 1-16.

BROWN, S., and J. WARNER (1980): Measuring security price performance, *Journal of Financial Economics*, 8, 205-258.

BROWN, S., and J. WARNER (1985): Using Daily Returns: The Case of Event Studies, *Journal of Financial Economics*, 14, 3-31.

BROWN, S. J., and M. I. WEINSTEIN (1985): Derived Factors in Event Studies, *Journal of Financial Economics*, 14, 491-495.

BÜHNER, R. (1998): Unternehmensspaltung - Motive und Aktienmarktreaktionen, *Zeitschrift für betriebswirtschaftliche Forschung*, 50, 809-840.

BÜHNER, R., and J. DIGMAYER (2003): Aktienmarktreaktionen auf die Ankündigungen von Spin-offs und Sell-offs, *Zeitschrift für betriebswirtschaftliche Forschung*, 55, 657-677.

BURCH, T., V. NANDA, and P. M. NARAYANAN (2002): *Industry structure and value-motivated conglomeration*. Working Paper, University of Michigan Business School.

BURCH, T. R., and V. NANDA (2003): Divisional diversity and the conglomerate discount: evidence from spin-offs, *Journal of Financial Economics*, 70, 69-99.

BURKART, M., D. GROMB, and F. PANUNZI (1997): Large Shareholders, Monitoring, and Fiduciary Duty, *Quarterly Journal of Economics*, 112, 693-728.

BURKART, M., and F. PANUNZI (2004): *Agency Conflicts, Ownership Concentration and Legal Shareholder Protection*. Working Paper DP 378, London School of Economics Financial Markets Group.

BUSCH, T., and W. GROß (2000): Vorerwerbsrechte der Aktionäre beim Verkauf von Tochtergesellschaften über die Börse?, *Die Aktiengesellschaft*, 45, 503-510.

BUSHEE, B. J., and C. F. NOE (2000): Disclosure Quality, Institutional Investors, and Stock Return Volatility, *Journal of Accounting Research*, 38, 171-202.

BUSHMAN, R. M., R. INDJEJIKIAN, and A. J. SMITH (1996): CEO Compensation: The Role of Individual Performance Evaluation, *Journal of Accounting and Economics*, 21, 161-193.

BUSHMAN, R. M., and A. J. SMITH (2001): Financial accounting information and corporate governance, *Journal of Accounting and Economics*, 32, 237-334.

BUSSE VON COLBE, W., D. ORDELHEIDE, G. GEBHARDT, and B. PELLENS (2003): *Konzernabschlüsse*. Wiesbaden: Gabler.

BUTLER, K. C., and L. H. P. LANG (1991): The Forecast Accuracy of Individual Analysts: Evidence of Systematic Optimism and Pessimism, *Journal of Accounting Research*, 29, 286-304.

BYUN, J., and M. S. ROZEFF (2003): Long-Run Performance after Stock Splits: 1927 to 1996, *Journal of Finance*, 58, 1063-1085.

CABLE, J., and K. HOLLAND (1999): Modelling normal returns in event studies: a model-selection approach and pilot study, *European Journal of Finance*, 5, 331-341.

CALVO, G., and S. WELLISZ (1978): Supervision, loss of control, and the optimal size of the firm, *Journal of Political Economy*, 86, 943-952.

CAMPA, J. M., and S. KEDIA (2002): Explaining the Diversification Discount, *Journal of Finance*, 57.

CAMPBELL, C. J., and C. E. WASLEY (1993): Measuring security price performance using daily NASDAQ returns, *Journal of Financial Economics*, 33, 73-92.

CANINA, L., R. MICHAELY, R. H. THALER, and K. WOMACK (1998): Caveat Compounder: A Warning about Using the Daily CRSP Equal-Weighted Index to Compute Long-Run Excess Returns, *Journal of Finance*, 53, 403-416.

CHANCE, D., R. KUMAR, and R. TODD (2000): The 'repricing' of executive stock options, *Journal of Financial Economics*, 57, 129-154.

CHANDLER, A. (1966): *Strategy and Structure.* Garden City, N.Y.: Anchor Books.

CHO, M.-H. (1998): Ownership Structure, Investment, and Corporate Value: An Empirical Analysis, *Journal of Financial Economics*, 47, 103-121.

CHOE, H., R. W. MASULIS, and V. NANDA (1993): Common stock offerings across the business cycle, *Journal of Empirical Finance*, 1.

CHOI, F. D. S. (1973): Financial Disclosure in Relation to a Firm's Capital Cost, *Accounting & Business Research*, 3, 282-292.

CHOW, C. (1960): Tests for Equality between Sets of Coefficients in Two Linear Regressions, *Econometrica*, 38, 591-605.

CLAESSENS, S., S. DJANKOV, J. P. H. FAN, and L. H. P. LANG (2002): Disentangling the Incentive and Entrenchment Effects of Large Shareholdings, *Journal of Finance*, 57, 81-112.

CLARKE, J., C. DUNBAR, and K. M. KAHLE (2001): Long-Run Performance and Insider Trading in Completed and Canceled Seasoned Equity Offerings, *Journal of Financial and Quantitative Analysis*, 36, 415-430.

— (2002): *The Long-Run Performance of Secondary Equity Issues: A Test of the Windows of Opportunity Hypothesis*. Working Paper.

CLARKE, J. E., E. C. FEE, and S. THOMAS (2004): Corporate diversification and asymmetric information: evidence from stock market trading characteristics, *Journal of Corporate Finance*, 10, 105-130.

CLARKSON, P., J. GUEDES, and R. THOMPSON (1996): On the Diversification, Observability and Measurement of Estimation Risk, *Journal of Financial and Quantitative Analysis*, 31, 69-84.

CLAUSSEN, C. (1999): Kapitalflußrechnung und Segmentberichterstattung, *Zeitschrift für Unternehmens- und Gesellschaftsrecht*, 28, 499-532.

COASE, R. H. (1937): The Nature of the Firm, *Economica*, 4, 386-405.

— (1960): The Problem of Social Cost, *Journal of Law and Economics*, 3, 1-44.

COENENBERG, A. G. (2003): Shareholder Value - Betriebswirtschaftliche Sicht und öffentliche Wahrnehmung, Augsburg.

COLES, J. L., U. LOEWENSTEIN, and J. SUAY (1995): On Equilibrium Pricing under Parameter Uncertainty, *Journal of Financial and Quantitative Analysis*, 30, 347-364.

COLLINS, W. A., and W. S. HOPWOOD (1980): A Multivariate Analysis of Annual Earnings Forecasts Generated from Quarterly Forecasts of Financial Analysts and Univariate Time-Series Models, *Journal of Accounting Research*, 18, 390-406.

COLLINS, D. W., and W. T. DENT (1984): A Comparison of Alternative Testing Methodologies Used in Capital Market Research, *Journal of Accounting Research*, 22, 48-84.

COLLINS, D. W., E. L. MAYDEW, and I. S. WEISS (1997): Changes in the value-relevance of earnings and book values over the past forty years, *Journal of Accounting and Economics*, 24, 39-67.

COMMENT, R., and G. A. JARRELL (1995): Corporate focus and stock returns, *Journal of Financial Economics*, 37, 67-87.

CONRAD, J., and G. KAUL (1993): Long-Term Market Overreaction or Biases in Computed Returns?, *Journal of Finance*, 48, 39-63.

CONYON, M. J., and K. J. MURPHY (2000): The Prince and the Pauper? CEO Pay in the United States and the United Kingdom, *Economic Journal*, 110, 640-671.

COPELAND, T. E., and D. GALAI (1983): Information effects and the bid-ask spread, *Journal of Finance*, 38, 1457-1469.

COPELAND, T. E., E. F. LEMGRUBER, and D. MAYERS (1987): Corporate Spinoffs: Multiple Announcement and Ex-Date Abnormal Performance, in *Modern Finance and Industrial Economics - Papers in Honor of J. Fred Weston.*, ed. by T. E. Copeland. New York.

COPELAND, T. E., and J. F. WESTON (1992): *Financial Theory and Corporate Policy.* Reading et al.

CORE, J. E., and W. GUAY (1999): The Use of Equity Grants to Manage Optimal Equity Incentive Levels, *Journal of Accounting and Economics*, 28, 151-184.

CORE, J. E., R. W. HOLTHAUSEN, and D. F. LARCKER (1999): Corporate Governance, Chief Executive Compensation, and Firm Performance, *Journal of Financial Economics*, 51, 371-406.

CORE, J. E., W. GUAY, and D. F. LARCKER (2003): Executive Equity Compensation and Incentives: A Survey, *Federal Reserve Bank of New York Economic Policy Review*, 9, 27-50.

CORE, J. E., W. GUAY, and R. E. VERRECCHIA (2003): Price vs. Non-Price Performance Measures in Optimal CEO Compensation Contracts, *Accounting Review*, 78, 957-983.

CORNELL, B., and Q. LIU (2001): The Parent Company Puzzle: Why is the Whole Worth Less Than One of the Parts?, *Journal of Corporate Finance*, 7, 341-366.

CORRADO, C. J. (1989): A nonparametric test for abnormal security-price performance in event studies, *Journal of Financial Economics*, Vol. 23, 385-395.

CORRADO, C. J., and T. L. ZIVNEY (1992): The Specification and Power of the Sign Test in Event Study Hypothesis Tests Using Daily Stock Returns, *Journal of Financial and Quantitative Analysis*, 27, 465-478.

COUGHLAN, A. T., and R. M. SCHMIDT (1985): Executive Compensation, Management Turnover, and Firm Performance: An Empirical Investigation, *Journal of Accounting and Economics*, 14, 43-66.

COUTTS, J. A., T. C. MILLS, and J. ROBERTS (1997): Time series and cross-section parameter stability in the market model: the implications for event studies, *European Journal of Finance*, 3, 243-259.

COWAN, A. R. (1992): Nonparametric Event Study Tests, *Review of Quantitative Finance and Accounting*, 2, 343-358.

COWAN, A. R., and A. M. SERGEANT (1996): Trading Frequency and Event Study Test Specification, *Journal of Banking and Finance*, 20, 1731-1757.

— (2001): Interacting biases, non-normal return distributions and the performance of tests for long-horizon event studies, *Journal of Banking and Finance*, 25, 741-765.

CRAWFORD, V. P., and J. SOBEL (1982): Strategic Information Transmission, *Econometrica*, 50, 1431-1453.

CRICHFIELD, T., T. DYCKMAN, and J. LAKONISHOK (1978): An Evaluation of Security Analysts' Forecasts, *Accounting Review*, 53, 651-668.

CUSATIS, P. J., J. A. MILES, and J. R. WOOLRIDGE (1993): Restructuring through spinoffs - The stock market evidence, *Journal of Financial Economics*, 33, 293-311.

CYERT, R., S.-H. KANG, and P. KUMAR (2002): Corporate Governance, Takeovers, and Top-Management Compensation: Theory and Evidence, *Management Science*, 48, 453-469.

CYREE, K. B., and R. P. DEGENNARO (2002): A Generalized Method for Detecting Abnormal Returns and Changes in Systematic Risk, *Review of Quantitative Finance and Accounting*, 19, 399-417.

DALEY, L., V. MEHROTRA, and R. SIVAKUMAR (1997): Corporate focus and value creation - Evidence from spinoffs, *Journal of Financial Economics*, 45, 257-281.

DANIEL, K., and S. TITMAN (1997): Evidence on the characteristics of cross sectional variation in stock returns, *Journal of Finance*, 52.

DANIEL, K., D. HIRSHLEIFER, and A. SUBRAHMANYAM (1998): Investor Psychology and Security Market Under- and Overreaction, *Journal of Finance*, 53, 1839-1885.

DANN, L. (1981): Common stock repurchases: An analysis of returns to bondholders and stockholders, *Journal of Financial Economics*, 9, 113-138.

DANN, L., and W. MIKKELSON (1984): Convertible debt issuance, capital structure change and financing-related information: Some new evidence, *Journal of Financial Economics*, 13, 157-186.

DANN, L., R. W. MASULIS, and D. MAYERS (1991): Repurchase tender offers and earnings information, *Journal of Accounting and Economics*, 14, 217-252.

DAVID, P., R. KOCHAR, and E. LEVITAS (1998): The Effect of Institutional Investors on the Level and Mix of CEO Compensation, *Academy of Management Journal*, 41, 200-208.

DAVISON, A., and D. HINKLEY (1997): *Bootstrap Methods and Their Application.* New York: Cambridge University Press.

DAYTON, C. M. (2003): Model Comparisons using Information Measures, *Journal of Modern Applied Statistical Methods*, 2, 281-292.

DE ANGELO, H., and L. DE ANGELO (1985): Managerial ownership of voting rights, *Journal of Financial Economics*, 14, 33-69.

DE MOTTA, A. (2002): Managerial Incentives and Capital Markets, *Journal of Finance*, 57, 1193-1220.

DEBONDT, W. F. M., and R. H. THALER (1985): Does the stock market overreact?, *Journal of Finance*, 50, 793-803.

DECHOW, P., and R. SLOAN (1997): Returns to contrarian investment strategies: tests of naive expectations hypothesis, *Journal of Financial Economics*, 43, 3-27.

DEGEORGE, F., and R. ZECKHAUSER (1993): The reverse LBO decision and firm performance: Theory and evidence, *Journal of Finance*, 48, 1323-1348.

DELONG, J. B., A. SHLEIFER, L. H. SUMMERS, and R. J. WALDMANN (1990): Noise Trader Risk in Financial Markets, *Journal of Political Economy*, 98, 703-738.

DEMERS, E., and K. LEWELLEN (2003): The marketing role of IPOs: Evidence from internet stocks, *Journal of Financial Economics*, 68, 413-438.

DEMOUGIN, D., and C. FLUET (2001): Monitoring versus incentives, *European Economic Review*, 45, 1741-1764.

DEMSETZ, H., and K. LEHN (1985): The Structure of Corporate Ownership: Causes and Consequences, *Journal of Political Economy*, 93, 1155-1177.

DEMSETZ, H. (1988): The Theory of the Firm Revisited, *Journal of Law, Economics and Organization*, 4, 141-162.

— (1997): The firm in economic theory: a quiet revolution, *American Economic Review*, 87, 426-430.

DEMSETZ, H., and B. VILLALONGA (2001): Ownership structure and corporate performance, *Journal of Corporate Finance*, 7, 209-233.

DENIS, D. J., and D. K. DENIS (1993): Managerial discretion, organization structure and corporate performance: A study of leveraged recapitalizations, *Journal of Accounting and Economics*, 16, 209-236.

DENIS, D., D. DENIS, and A. SARIN (1997): Agency Problems, Equity Ownership, and Corporate Diversification, *Journal of Finance*, 52, 135-160.

DENIS, D. L., and A. SARIN (2001): Is the Market Surprised by Poor Earnings Realizations following Seasoned Equity Offerings?, *Journal of Financial and Quantitative Analysis*, 36, 169-194.

DENIS, D. K., and J. J. MCCONNELL (2003): International Corporate Governance, *Journal of Financial and Quantitative Analysis*, 38, 1-36.

DESAI, H., and P. C. JAIN (1997): Long-run stock returns following stock splits and reverse splits, *Journal of Business*, 70, 409-434.

— (1999): Firm performance and focus: long-run stock market performance following spinoffs, *Journal of Financial Economics*, 54, 75-101.

DEWATRIPONT, M., and E. MASKIN (1995): Credit Efficiency in Centralized and Decentralized Economies, *Review of Economic Studies*, 62, 541-555.

DHERMENT-FERERE, I., J. KÖKE, and L. RENNEBOOG (2001): *Corporate monitoring by blockholders in Europe - empirical evidence of managerial disciplining in Belgium, France, Germany and the UK.* ZEW Mannheim Discussion Paper 01-24.

DIAMOND, D. W. (1985): Optimal release of information by firms, *Journal of Finance*, 40, 1071-1094.

— (1989): Reputation acquisition in debt markets, *Journal of Political Economy*, 97, 828-862.

DIAMOND, D. W., and R. E. VERRECCHIA (1991): Disclosure, Liquidity and the Cost of Capital, *Journal of Finance*, 46, 1325-1359.

DILTZ, J. D., and D. C. HYLAND (2002): *The Post-Announcement Performance of Diversifying Firms.* Working Paper, University of Texas at Arlington.

DIMSON, E. (1979): Risk measurement when shares are subject to thin trading, *Journal of Financial Economics*, 7, 197-226.

DIMSON, E., and P. MARSH (1986): Event study methodologies and the size effect: the case of U.K. press recommendations, *Journal of Financial Economics*, 17, 113-142.

DITTMANN, I., and E. MAUG (2003): *Lower Salaries and No Options: The Optimal Structure of Executive Pay.* Working Paper, Humboldt University at Berlin.

DITTMAR, A., and A. SHIVDASANI (2003): Divestitures and Divisional Investment Policies, *Journal of Finance*, 58, 2711-2745.

DODD, P., and J. WARNER (1983): On Corporate Governance: A Study of Proxy Contests, *Journal of Financial Economics*, 11, 401-438.

DOUKAS, J. A., C. KIM, and C. PANTZALIS (2000): Security Analysis, Agency Costs and Company Characteristics, *Financial Analysts Journal*, 54-63.

DROBETZ, W., M. KAMMERMANN, and U. WAELCHLI (2003): *Performance of Initial Public Offerings: The Evidence for Switzerland.* Working Paper, University of Basle.

DUNN, K., and S. NATHAN (1998): *The Effect of Industry Diversification on Consensus and Individual Analysts' Earnings Forecasts.* Working Paper.

DURBIN, J., and G. S. WATSON (1951): Testing for Serial Correlation in Least Squares Regression, *Biometrika*, 38.

DYBVIG, P. H., and J. F. ZENDER (1991): Capital Structure and Dividend Irrelevance with Asymmetric Information, *Review of Financial Studies*, 4, 201-219.

DYCK, A., and L. ZINGALES (2004): Private Benefits of Control: An International Comparison, *Journal of Finance*, 59, 537-600.

DYCKMAN, T., D. R. PHILBRICK, and J. STEPHAN (1984): A comparison of event study methodologies using daily stock returns: a simulation approach, *Journal of Accounting Research*, 22, Supplement, 1-30.

DYE, R. A. (1986): Proprietary and nonproprietary disclosures, *Journal of Business*, 331-336.

EASTERWOOD, J. C., and S. R. NUTT (1999): Inefficiency in Analysts' Earnings Forecasts: Systematic Misreaction or Systematic Optimism?, *Journal of Finance*, 54, 1777-1798.

EBERHART, A. C., W. F. MAXWELL, and A. R. SIDDIQUE (2004): An Examination of Long-Term Abnormal Stock Returns and Operating Performance Following R&D Increases, *Journal of Finance*, 59, 623-651.

EBERS, M., and W. GOTSCH (2001): Institutionenökonomische Theorien der Organisation, in *Organisationstheorien*, ed. by A. Kieser. Stuttgart, Berlin, Köln, 199-251.

ECKBO, B. E. (1985): Mergers and the Market Concentration Doctrine: Evidence from the Capital Market, *Journal of Business*, 58, 325-349.

ECKBO, B. E., V. MAKSIMOVIC, and J. WILLIAMS (1990): Consistent Estimation of Cross-Sectional Models in Event Studies, *Review of Financial Studies*, 3, 343-365.

ECKBO, B. E., R. W. MASULIS, and O. NORLI (2000): Seasoned public offerings: Resolution of the 'new issues puzzle', *Journal of Financial Economics*, 56, 251-292.

EDWARDS, J., and M. NIBLER (2000): Corporate governance in Germany: the role of banks and ownership concentration, *Economic Policy*, 239-267.

EDWARDS, J. S., and A. J. WEICHENRIEDER (2004): Ownership Concentration and Share Valuation, *German Economic Review*, 5, 143-171.

EFRON, B. (1979): Bootstrap Methods: Another Look at the Jackknife, *Annals of Statistics*, 7, 1-26.

EFRON, B., and R. TIBSHIRANI (1993): *An Introduction to the Bootstrap*. New York: Chapman and Hall.

EFRON, B. (2000): The bootstrap and modern statistics, *Journal of the American Statistical Association*, 95, 1293-1296.

EHRHARDT, O., and R. KOERSTEIN (2001): Der Einfluß der Benchmarkwahl auf das Ergebnis langfristiger Ereignisstudien, *OR Spektrum*, 23, 445-475.

EISENHARDT, K. M. (1989): Agency Theory: An Assessment and Review, *Academy of Management Review*, 14, 57-75.

ELSAS, R., and Y. LÖFFLER (2003): *Universal Banks, Corporate Control and Equity Carve-Outs and in Germany*. Working Paper, Universität Frankfurt.

ELSTON, J. A., and L. G. GOLDBERG (2003): Executive compensation and agency costs in Germany, *Journal of Banking and Finance*, 27, 1391-1410.

ELTON, E. J., M. J. GRUBER, and M. N. GULTEKIN (1985): Professional expectations: Accuracy and diagnosis of errors, *Journal of Financial and Quantitative Analysis*, 19, 351-363.

ELTON, E. J. (1999): Expected return, realized return and asset pricing tests, *Journal of Finance*, 54, 1199-1220.

EMMERICH, V., and M. HABERSACK (2003): *Aktien- und GmbH-Konzernrecht*. München: Beck.

ENGLE, R. F. (1982): Autoregressive Conditional Heteroskedasticity with Estimates of the Variance of United Kingdom Inflation, *Econometrica*, 50, 987-1007.

ENGLE, R. F., and D. KRAFT (1983): Multiperiod forecasts of error variances of inflation estimated from ARCH models, in *Applied time series analysis of economic data*, ed. by A. Zellner. Washington, D.C.: Bureau of the Census, 293-302.

ENGLE, R. F. (1984): Wald, Likelihood Ratio, and Lagrange Multiplier Tests in Econometrics, in *Handbook of Econometrics, Vol. II*, ed. by Z. Griliches, and M. D. Intriligator. Amsterdam et al.: Elsevier, 775-826.

— (2001): GARCH101: The use of ARCH/GARCH models in applied econometrics, *Journal of Economic Perspectives*, 15, 157-169.

ERWIN, G. R., and S. E. PERRY (2000): The effect of foreign diversification on analysts' prediction errors, *International Review of Financial Analysis*, 9.

ESPENLAUB, S., A. GREGORY, and I. TONKS (2000): Re-assessing the long-term underperformance of UK Initial Public Offerings, *European Financial Management*, 6, 319-342.

EVANS III, J. H., and S. S. SRIDHAR (1996): Multiple Control Systems, Accrual Accounting, and Earnings Management, *Journal of Accounting Research*, 34, 45-65.

FACCIO, M., L. H. P. LANG, and L. YOUNG (2001): Dividends and Expropriation, *American Economic Review*, 91, 54-78.

FACCIO, M., and L. H. P. LANG (2002): The ultimate ownership of Western European corporations, *Journal of Financial Economics*, 65, 365-396.

FAMA, E. F. (1965): The Behavior of Stock Market Prices, *Journal of Business*, 38, 34-105.

FAMA, E. F., L. FISHER, M. C. JENSEN, and R. ROLL (1969): The adjustment of stock prices to new information, *International Economic Review*, 10, 1-21.

FAMA, E. F. (1970): Efficient Capital Markets: A Review of Theory and Empirical Work, *Journal of Finance*, 33, 383-417.

— (1978): The effect of a firm's investment and financing decisions on the welfare of its security holders, *American Economic Review*, 68, 272-284.

— (1980): Agency Problems and the Theory of the Firm, *Journal of Political Economy*, 88, 288-307.

FAMA, E. F., and M. C. JENSEN (1983a): Separation of Ownership and Control, *Journal of Law and Economics*, 26, 301-326.

— (1983b): Agency Problems and Residual Claims, *Journal of Law and Economics*, 26, 327-349.

— (1985): Organizational Forms and Investment Decisions, *Journal of Financial Economics*, 14, 101-119.

FAMA, E. F. (1991): Efficient Capital Markets II, *Journal of Finance*, 46, 1574-1614.

FAMA, E. F., and K. R. FRENCH (1992): The cross-section of expected stock returns, *Journal of Finance*, 47, 427-465.

— (1995): Size and book-to-market factors in earnings and returns, *Journal of Finance*, 50, 131-155.

— (1996a): Multifactor explanations of asset pricing anomalies, *Journal of Finance*, 51, 55-84.

— (1996b): The CAPM is Wanted, Dead or Alive, *Journal of Finance*, 51, 1947-1958.

FAMA, E. F. (1998): Market efficiency, long-term returns and behavioral finance, *Journal of Financial Economics*, 49, 283-306.

FAN, J. P. H., and L. H. P. LANG (2000): The Measurement of Relatedness: An Application to Corporate Diversification, *Journal of Business*, 73, 629-660.

FAUVER, L., J. HOUSTON, and A. NARANJO (2003): Capital Market Development, International Integration, Legal Systems, and the Value of Corporate Diversification: A Cross-Country Analysis, *Journal of Financial and Quantitative Analysis*, 38, 135-158.

FAZZARI, S. R., R. G. HUBBARD, and B. PETERSEN (1988): Financing Constraints and Corporate Investment, *Brookings Papers on Economic Activity*, 141-195.

— (2000): Investment-cash flow sensitivities are useful: A comment on Kaplan and Zingales, *Quarterly Journal of Economics*, 115, 695-705.

FELDKÄMPER, U. (2003): Empirische Untersuchung der Segmentberichterstattung am deutschen Kapitalmarkt, *Der Betrieb*, 56, 1453-1457.

FERNIE, S., and D. METCALF (1999): It's not what you pay, it's the way you pay it and that's what gets results: Jockey's pay and performance, *Labour*, 13, 385-411.

FERRALL, C., and B. SHEARER (1999): Incentives and Transaction Costs within the Firm: Estimating an Agency Model Using Payroll Records, *Review of Economic Studies*, 66, 309-338.

FIELDS, T. D., T. LYS, and L. VINCENT (2001): Empirical Research on Accounting Choice, *Journal of Accounting and Economics*, 31, 255-307.

FINKELSTEIN, S., and D. C. HAMBRICK (1988): Chief executive compensation: a synthesis and reconciliation, *Strategic Management Journal*, 9, 543-558.

— (1989): Chief Executive Compensation: A Study of the Intersection of Markets and Political Processes, *Strategic Management Journal*, 10, 121-134.

FINKELSTEIN, S. (1992): Power in Top Management Teams: Dimensions, Measurement, and Validation, *Academy of Management Journal*, 35, 505-538.

FINKELSTEIN, S., and B. K. BOYD (1998): How Much Does the CEO Matter? The Role of Managerial Discretion in the Setting of CEO Compensation, *Academy of Management Journal*, 41, 179-199.

FISHER, J., and V. GOVINDARAJAN (1992): Profit Center Manager Compensation: An Examination of Market, Political and Human Capital Factors, *Strategic Management Journal*, 13, 205-217.

FISS, P. C., and E. J. ZAJAC (2004): *The Diffusion of Ideas Over Contested Terrain: The (Non-)Adoption of Shareholder Value Among German Firms.* Working Paper, Queen's University and Northwestern University.

FLANNERY, M. J., and K. P. RANGAN (2004): *Partial adjustment and target capital structures.* Working Paper, University of Florida.

FLEISCHER, H. (2001): Börseneinführung von Tochtergesellschaften, *Zeitschrift für das gesamte Handelsrecht und Wirtschaftsrecht*, 165, 513-549.

FOSTER, A., and M. ROSENZWEIG (1994): A Test for Moral hazard in the Labor Market: Contractual Arrangements, Effort and Health, *Review of Economics and Statistics*, 76, 213-227.

FOWLER, D. J., and C. H. RORKE (1983): Risk measurement when shares are subject to infrequent trading: comment, *Journal of Financial Economics*, 12, 279-283.

FRANK, K. E., and J. W. HARDEN (2001): Corporate Restructurings: A Comparison of Equity Carve-outs and Spin-offs, *Journal of Business Finance and Accounting*, 28, 503-529.

FRANK, K. E. (2001): Making Sense of Spin-Offs, Tracking Stock, and Equity Carve-Outs, *Strategic Finance*, 39-43.

FRANKS, J. R., and C. MAYER (2001): Ownership and Control of German Corporations, *Review of Financial Studies*, 14, 943-977.

FRECKA, T. J., and C. F. LEE (1983): Generalized Financial Ratio Adjustment Processes and Their Implications, *Journal of Accounting Research*, 21, 308-316.

FREEDMAN, D. A. (1981): Bootstrapping Regression Models, *The Annals of Statistics*, 9, 1218-1228.

FRENCH, K. R., G. W. SCHWERT, and R. STAMBAUGH (1987): Expected Stock Returns and Volatility, *Journal of Financial Economics*, 19, 3-29.

FU, H. (2002): *Information Asymmetry and the Market Reaction to Equity Carve-Outs.* Working Paper.

FUCKS, D. (2004): The Motivation Behind the Equity Carve-Out Decision - Evidence from German Equity Carve-Outs, *Working Paper, University of Bonn.*

FUNK, J. (1999): Wie schaffen diversifizierte Unternehmen Wert, *Zeitschrift für betriebswirtschaftliche Forschung*, 51, 759-772.

FURUBOTN, E. G., and R. RICHTER (1997): *Institutions and Economic Theory: The Contributions of the New Institutional Economics.* Ann Arbor: University of Michigan Press.

GAGNÉ, P., and C. M. DAYTON (2002): Best Regression Model Using Information Criteria, *Journal of Modern Applied Statistical Methods*, 1, 479-488.

GAREN, J. E. (1994): Executive Compensation and Principal-Agent Theory, *Journal of Political Economy*, 102, 1175-1199.

GAUTIER, A., and F. HEIDER (2002): *The Benefit and Cost of Winner Picking: Redistribution vs. Incentives.* Working Paper 31/2002, Bonn Graduate School of Economics.

GEBHARDT, W. R., C. M. C. LEE, and B. SWAMINATHAN (2000): Toward an Implied Cost of Capital, *Journal of Accounting Research*, 39, 135-176.

GEDAJLOVIC, E. R., and D. M. SHAPIRO (1998): Management and ownership effects: Evidence from five countries, *Strategic Management Journal*, 19, 533-554.

GEDENK, K., and S. ALBERS (1994): Empirische Ergebnisse zur Steuerung von Geschäftsführern, *Die Betriebswirtschaft*, 54, 327-345.

GEDENK, K. (1998): Agency-Theorie und die Steuerung von Geschäftsführern - Paradebeispiel oder Problemfall, *Die Betriebswirtschaft*, 58, 22-37.

GELB, D. S., and P. ZAROWIN (2002): Corporate Disclosure Policy and the Informativeness of Stock Prices, *Review of Accounting Studies*, 7, 33-52.

GERHART, B., and G. T. MILKOVICH (1990): Organizational Differences in Managerial Compensation and Financial Performance, *Academy of Management Journal*, 33, 663-691.

GERKE, W., and M. OERKE (1998): Marktbeeinflussung durch Analystenempfehlungen: Eine empirische Studie, *Zeitschrift für Betriebswirtschaft*, 68, Ergänzungsheft 2/98, 187-200.

GERKE, W., and J. FLEISCHER (2001): Die Performance der Börsengänge am Neuen Markt, *Zeitschrift für betriebswirtschaftliche Forschung*, 53, 827-839.

GERTNER, R. H., D. S. SCHARFSTEIN, and J. C. STEIN (1994): Internal versus external capital markets, *Quarterly Journal of Economics*, 109, 1211-1231.

GERTNER, R. H., E. A. POWERS, and D. S. SCHARFSTEIN (2002): Learning about Internal Capital Markets from Corporate Spinoffs, *Journal of Finance*, 57, 2479-2506.

GIBBONS, R., and K. J. MURPHY (1990): Relative Performance Evaluation for Chief Executive Officers, *Industrial and Labor Relations Review*, 43, 30-52.

— (1992): Optimal incentive contracts in the presence of career concerns: Theory and evidence, *Journal of Political Economy*, 100, 468-505.

GIBBONS, R. (1998): Incentives in Organizations, *Journal of Economic Perspectives*, 12, 115-132.

GIBSON, S., A. SAFIEDDINE, and R. SONTI (2003): Smart investments by smart money: evidence from seasoned equity offerings, *Journal of Financial Economics*.

GILSON, S. C., P. M. HEALY, C. F. NOE, and K. G. PALEPU (2001): Analyst Specialization and Conglomerate Stock Breakups, *Journal of Accounting Research*, 39, 565-582.

GIVOLY, D., and J. LAKONISHOK (1984): Properties of Analysts' Forecasts of Earnings: A Review and Analysis of the Research, *Journal of Accoutning Literature*, 3, 117-152.

GJESDAL, F. (1982): Information and incentives: The agency information problem, *Review of Economic Studies*, 49, 373-390.

GLOSTEN, L. R., and P. R. MILGROM (1985): Bid, Ask and Transaction Prices in a Market with Heterogeneously Informed Traders, *Journal of Financial Economics*, 14, 71-100.

GODE, D., and P. MOHANRAM (2003): Inferring the Cost of Capital Using the Ohlson-Juettner Model, *Review of Accounting Studies*, 8, 399-431.

GODFREY, L. G. (1978): Testing Against General Autoregressive and Moving Average Error Models when the Regressors Include Lagged Dependent Variables, *Econometrica*, 46, 1293-1302.

GOEL, A. M., V. NANDA, and P. M. NARAYANAN (2004): Career Concerns and Resource Allocation in Conglomerates, *Review of Financial Studies*, 17, 99-128.

GOERGEN, M., and L. RENNEBOOG (2003): Why are the levels of control (so) different in German and UK companies? Evidence from initial public offerings, *Journal of Law, Economics and Organization*, 19, 141-175.

GOLDBERG, J., and R. VON NITZSCH (2004): *Behavioral Finance*. FinanzBuch Verlag.

GOLDFELD, S. M., and R. E. QUANDT (1965): Some Tests for Homoskedasticity, *Journal of the American Statistical Association*, 60, 539-559.

GOMES, J., and D. LIVDAN (2004): Optimal Diversification: Reconciling Theory and Evidence, *Journal of Finance*, 59, 507-536.

GOMEZ-MEJIA, L. R., and R. M. WISEMAN (1997): Reframing Executive Compensation: An Assessment and Outlook, *Journal of Management*, 23, 291-374.

GOMPERS, P. A., and J. LERNER (2003): The Really-Long Run Performance of Initial Public Offerings: The Pre-NASDAQ Evidence, *Journal of Finance*, 58, 1355-1393.

GONEDES, N., and N. DOPUCH (1974): Capital Market Equilibrium, Information Production and Selecting Accounting Techniques: Theoretical Framework and Review of Empirical Work, *Journal of Accounting Research*, 12, supplement, 48-129.

GORECKI, P. K. (1974): The measurement of enterprise diversification, *Review of Economics and Statistics*, 56, 399-402.

GÖRLING, H. (1993): Die Verbreitung zwei- und mehrstufiger Unternehmensverbindungen, *Die Aktiengesellschaft*, 538-547.

GORTON, G., and F. A. SCHMID (2000): Universal banking and the performance of German firms, *Journal of Financial Economics*, 58, 29-80.

— (in press): Capital, Labor, and the Firm: A Study of German Codetermination, *Journal of the European Economic Association*.

GRAHAM, J. R., and C. R. HARVEY (1996): Market timing ability and volatility implied in investment newsletters' asset allocation recommendations, *Journal of Financial Economics*, 42, 397-421.

— (2001): The theory and practice of corporate finance: Evidence from the field, *Journal of Financial Economics*, 60, 187-243.

GRAHAM, J. R., M. L. LEMMON, and J. G. WOLF (2002): Does Corporate Diversification Destroy Value?, *Journal of Finance*, 52, 695-720.

GRAHAM JR, R. C., and C. E. LEFANOWICZ (1999): Majority and Minority Ownership of Publicly-Traded Firms: A Test of the Value of Control Using Market Multiples, *Journal of Business Finance and Accounting*, 26, 171-198.

GRASSHOFF, U., and J. SCHWALBACH (1999): Agency-Theorie, Informationskosten und Managervergütung, *Zeitschrift für betriebswirtschaftliche Forschung*, 51, 437-453.

GREENWALD, B. C., J. E. STIGLITZ, and A. WEISS (1984): Informational Imperfections in the Capital Market and Macroeconomic Fluctuations, *American Economic Review*, 74, 194-200.

GRINBLATT, M., and C.-Y. HWANG (1989): Signalling and the pricing of new issues, *Journal of Finance*, 44, 393-420.

GROSSMAN, S. J. (1976): On the efficiency of competitive stock markets where traders have diverse information, *Journal of Finance*, 31, 573-585.

— (1978): Further results on the information efficiency of competitive stock markets, *Journal of Economic Theory*, 18, 81-101.

GROSSMAN, S. J., and J. E. STIGLITZ (1980): On the impossibility of informationally efficient markets, *American Economic Review*, 70, 393-408.

GROSSMAN, S. J., and O. D. HART (1980a): Disclosure Laws and Takeover Bids, *Journal of Finance*, 35, 323-334.

— (1980b): Takeover bids, the free-rider problem, and the theory of the corporation, *Bell Journal of Economics*, 11, 42-64.

— (1981): The allocational role of takeover bids in situations of asymmetric information, *Journal of Finance*, 36, 253-270.

— (1983): An Analysis of the Principal-Agent Problem, *Econometrica*, 51, 7-45.

— (1986): The Costs and Benefits of Ownership: A Theory of Vertical and Lateral Integration, *Journal of Political Economy*, 94, 691-719.

— (1988): One share-one vote and the market for corporate control, *Journal of Financial Economics*, 20, 175-202.

GRUBB, D., and L. MAGEE (1988): A Variance Comparison of OLS and Feasible GLS Estimators, *Econometric Theory*, 4, 329-335.

GUGLER, H., D. C. MUELLER, and B. B. YURTOGLU (2003): The impact of corporate governance on investment returns in developed and developing countries, *Economic Journal*, 113, 511-539.

GUGLER, K., and B. B. YURTOGLU (2003): Corporate governance and dividend payout policy in Germany, *European Economic Review*, 47, 731-758.

GUGLER, H., D. C. MUELLER, and B. B. YURTOGLU (2004): Corporate Governance and Globalization, *Oxford Review of Economic Policy*, 20, 129-157.

HABBEL, M. (2001): *Kerngeschäftsstrategien und Divestments aus Kapitalmarksicht.* Wiesbaden.

HABIB, M. A., D. B. JOHNSEN, and N. Y. NAIK (1997): Spinoffs and Information, *Journal of Financial Intermediation*, 6, 153-176.

HABIB, M. A., and A. P. LJUNGQVIST (In Press): Firm Value and Managerial Incentives: A Stochastic Frontier Approach, *Journal of Business.*

HACKER, B. (2002): *Segmentberichterstattung: eine ökonomische Analyse.* Frankfurt am Main: Lang.

— (2003): Segmentberichterstattung im internationalen Vergleich, *Betrieb und Wirtschaft*, 2/2003, 50-55.

HADLOCK, C., M. RYNGAERT, and S. THOMAS (2001): Corporate structure and equity offerings: Are there benefits to diversification?, *Journal of Business*, 74, 613-635.

HAHN, K. (2000): Ausgestaltung und Aussage der Segmentberichterstattung nach §297 Abs. 1 HGB: vergleichende Analyse der Normen nach SFAS 131, IAS 14 und DRS 3 zur Schließung der Regelungslücke in §297 Abs. 1 HGB, in *Investororientierte Unternehmenspublizität*, ed. by L. Lachnit, and C.-C. Freidank. Wiesbaden: Gabler.

HAIL, L. (2002): The impact of voluntary corporate disclosures on the ex-ante cost of capital of Swiss firms, *European Accounting Review*, 11, 741-774.

HALL, B. J., and J. B. LIEBMAN (1998): Are CEOs Really Paid Like Bureaucrats?, *Quarterly Journal of Economics*, 13, 653-691.

HALL, B. J., and K. J. MURPHY (2002): Stock Options for Undiversified Executives, *Journal of Accounting and Economics*, 33, 3-42.

— (2003): The Trouble With Stock Options, *Journal of Economic Perspectives*, 17, 49-71.

HALL, P., and S. R. WILSON (1991): Two Guidelines for Bootstrap Hypothesis Testing, *Biometrics*, 47, 757-762.

HALL, P. (1994): Methodology and Theory for the Bootstrap, in *Handbook of Econometrics, Vol. IV*, ed. by R. F. Engle, and D. L. McFadden. Amsterdam et al.: Elsevier.

HALLER, A., and P. PARK (1994a): Grundsätze ordnungsgemäßer Segmentberichterstattung, *Zeitschrift für betriebswirtschaftliche Forschung*, 46, 499-521.

— (1994b): Regulation and Practice of Segmental Reporting in Germany, *European Accounting Review*, 3, 563-580.

HALLER, A., and D. PERMANSCHLAGER (2002): Anspruch und Wirklichkeit der Segmentberichterstattung nach US-GAAP, *Betriebs-Berater*, 57, 1411-1417.

HAND, J. R. M., and T. R. SKANTZ (1998): *The Market Timing Characteristics of Equity Carveouts*. Working Paper.

HANSEN, R. S., and C. CRUTCHLEY (1990): Corporate earnings and financing : An empirical analysis, *Journal of Business*, 63, 347-371.

HARRIS, M., and A. RAVIV (1988): Corporate governance: Voting rights and majority rules, *Journal of Financial Economics*, 20, 203-235.

— (1990): Capital structure and the informational role of debt, *Journal of Finance*, 45, 321-350.

— (1991): The Theory of Capital Structure, *Journal of Finance*, 46, 297-355.

HARRIS, M. S. (1998): The association between competition and managers' business segment reporting decisions, *Journal of Accounting Research*, 36, 111-128.

HARRIS, T. S., M. LANG, and H. P. MÖLLER (1994): The Value Relevance of German Accounting Measures: An Empirical Analysis, *Journal of Accounting Research*, 32, 187-209.

HART, O. D. (1983): The market mechanism as an incentive scheme, *Bell Journal of Economics*, 14, 366-382.

HART, O. D., and J. MOORE (1995): Debt and Seniority: An Analysis of the Role of Hard Claims in Constraining Management, *American Economic Review*, 85, 567-585.

HART, O. D. (2001): Financial Contracting, *Journal of Economic Literature*, 39, 1079-1101.

HASBROUCK, J. (1985): The characteristics of takeover targets and other measures, *Journal of Banking and Finance*, 9, 351-362.

HASSELMANN, H. (1997): *Going public von Tochtergesellschaften: Unternehmensfinanzierung und Unternehmenswertsteigerung*. Sternenfels.

HAUBRICH, J. (1994): Risk Aversion, Performance Pay, and the Principal-Agent-Problem, *Journal of Political Economy*, 102, 258-276.

HAYASHI, F. (2000): *Econometrics*. Princeton/Oxford: Princeton University Press.

HAYES, R., and R. J. LUNDHOLM (1996): Segment Reporting to the Capital Market in the Presence of a Competitor, *Journal of Accounting Research*, 34, 261-279.

HEALY, P. M. (1985): The Effect of Bonus Schemes on Accounting Decisions, *Journal of Accounting and Economics*, 7, 85-107.

HEALY, P. M., and K. G. PALEPU (1988): Earnings information conveyed by dividend initiations and omissions, *Journal of Financial Economics*, 21, 149-176.

— (1990): Earnings and risk changes surrounding primary stock offers, *Journal of Accounting Research*, 28, 25-48.

HEALY, P. M., K. G. PALEPU, and R. S. RUBACK (1992): Does corporate performance improve after mergers?, *Journal of Financial Economics*, 31, 135-175.

HEALY, P. M., A. P. HUTTON, and K. G. PALEPU (1999): Stock Performance and Intermediation Changes Surrounding Sustained Increases in Disclosure, *Contemporary Accounting Research*, 16, 485-520.

HEALY, P. M., and K. G. PALEPU (2001): Information Asymmetry, Corporate Disclosure, and the Capital Markets: A Review of the Empirical Disclosure Literature, *Journal of Accounting and Economics*, 31, 405-440.

HEATON, J. B. (2002): Managerial Optimism and Corporate Finance, *Financial Management*, 31, 33-45.

HEIN, S. E., and P. WESTFALL (2001): Improving Tests of Abnormal Returns by Bootstrapping the Multivariate Regression Model, *Journal of Financial Econometrics*, 2, 451-471.

HEINKEL, R., and A. KRAUS (1988): Measuring Event Impact in Thinly Traded Stocks, *Journal of Financial and Quantitative Analysis*, 23, 71-88.

HELMIS, S. (2002): *Corporate Governance in Deutschland: Eigentums- und Kontrollstrukturen und rechtliche Rahmenbedingungen in der "Deutschland AG"*. Institute for Mergers & Acquisitions, University of Witten-Herdecke, Working Paper 03/02.

HEMMER, T., O. KIM, and R. E. VERRECCHIA (1999): Introducing Convexity into Optimal Compensation Contracts, *Journal of Accounting and Economics*, 28, 307-327.

HENDERSON, G. V. (1990): Problems and Solutions in Conducting Event Studies, *Journal of Risk and Insurance*, 57, 282-307.

HENDRY, D. F. (1993): *Econometrics. Alchemy or Science?* Oxford: Basil Blackwell.

HENNIGS, R. (1995): *Die Börseneinführung von Tochtergesellschaften: Entscheidungsproblem im Konzern*. Wiesbaden.

HERMALIN, B. E., and M. KATZ (2001): Corporate Diversification and Agency, in *Incentives, Organization, and Public Economics: Papers in Honour of Sir James Mirrlees*, ed. by P. J. Hammond, and G. D. Myles. Oxford: Oxford University Press.

HERTZEL, M., M. LEMMON, J. S. LINCK, and L. REES (2002): Long-Run Performance Following Private Placements of Equity, *Journal of Finance*, 57, 2595-2617.

HILLIARD, J. E., and R. SAVICKAS (2002): On the Statistical Significance of Event Effects on Unsystematic Volatility, *Journal of Financial Research*, 25, 447-462.

HIMMELBERG, C. P., G. HUBBARD, and D. PALIA (1999): Understanding the Determinants of Managerial Ownership and the Link between Ownership and Performance, *Journal of Financial Economics*, 53, 353-384.

HINKLEY, D. V. (1988): Bootstrap Methods, *Journal of the Royal Statistical Society, Series B*, 50, 321-337.

HINTERHUBER, H. H., S. A. FRIEDRICH, K. MATZLER, and H. PECHLANER (2000): Die strategische Führung der diversifizierten Unternehmung - Wie schafft die Zentrale Werte, *Zeitschrift für Betriebswirtschaft*, 70, 1351-1370.

HIRSHLEIFER, D. (2001): Investor psychology and asset pricing, *Journal of Finance*, 56, 1533-1597.

HIRSHLEIFER, D., and S. H. TEOH (2003): Limited attention, information disclosure, and financial reporting, *Journal of Accounting and Economics*, 36, 337-387.

HITE, G. L., and J. E. OWERS (1983): Security price reactions around corporate spin-off announcements, *Journal of Financial Economics*, 12, 409-436.

HO, M. J., and R. S. HARRIS (2000): Brokerage Analysts' Rationale for Investment Recommendations: Market Responses to Different Types of Information, *Journal of Financial Research*, 23, 449-468.

HOFMANN, C. (2002): Gestaltung von Erfolgsrechnungen zur Steuerung von Verantwortungsbereichen, *Zeitschrift für Betriebswirtschaft*, 72, 1177-1205.

HOLDERNESS, C. G., and D. P. SHEEHAN (1988): The Role of Majority Shareholders in Publicly-Held Corporations, *Journal of Financial Economics*, 20, 317-346.

HOLDERNESS, C. G. (2003): A Survey of Blockholders and Corporate Control, *Federal Reserve Bank of New York Economic Policy Review*, 9, 51-63.

HOLMSTRÖM, B. (1979): Moral Hazard and Observability, *Bell Journal of Economics*, 10, 4-29.

— (1982): Moral Hazard in Teams, *Bell Journal of Economics*, 13, 324-340.

HOLMSTRÖM, B., and P. MILGROM (1987): Aggregation and Linearity in the Provision of Intertemporal Incentives, *Econometrica*, 55, 303-328.

HOLMSTRÖM, B., and J. TIROLE (1989): The Theory of the Firm, in *Handbook of Industrial Organization*, ed. by R. Schmalensee, and R. D. Willig. North Holland: Elsevier Science.

HOLMSTRÖM, B., and P. MILGROM (1990): Regulating trade among agents, *Journal of Institutional and Theoretical Economics*, 146, 85-105.

— (1991): Multitask Principal-Agent Analyses: Incentive Contracts, Asset Ownership, and Job Design, *Journal of Law, Economics and Organization*, 7, 24-52.

HOLMSTRÖM, B., and J. TIROLE (1993): Market Liquidity and Performance Monitoring, *Journal of Political Economy*, 101, 678-710.

HOLMSTRÖM, B., and J. ROBERTS (1998): The Boundaries of the Firm Revisited, *Journal of Economic Perspectives*, 12, 73-94.

HOLTHAUSEN, R. W., R. LEFTWICH, and D. MAYERS (1987): The effect of large block transactions on security prices: A cross-sectional analysis, *Journal of Financial Economics*, 19, 237-268.

HOLTHAUSEN, R. W., and R. E. VERRECCHIA (1990): The Effect of Informedness and Consensus Price and Volume Behavior, *Accounting Review*, 65, 191-208.

HOLTHAUSEN, R. W., and R. L. WATTS (2001): The Relevance of the Value Relevance Literature for Financial Accounting Standard Setting, *Journal of Accounting and Economics*, 32, 3-76.

HONG, H., and J. STEIN (1999): A unified theory of underreaction, momentum trading, and overreaction in asset markets, *Journal of Finance*, 54, 2143-2184.

HORNUNG, K., and A. WULLENKORD (2001): Equity Carve-outs von Tochterunternehmen, *Zeitschrift für betriebswirtschaftliche Forschung*, 53, 57-76.

HOUSTON, J., C. JAMES, and D. MARCUS (1997): Capital Market Frictions and the Role of Internal Capital Markets in Banking, *Journal of Financial Economics*, 46, 135-164.

HOVAKIMIAN, A., T. OPLER, and S. TITMAN (2001): The debt-equity choice, *Journal of Financial and Quantitative Analysis*, 36, 1-24.

HOVAKIMIAN, A. (2004): *Are observed capital structures determined by equity market timing?* Working Paper, Baruch College.

HUANG, R., and J. R. RITTER (2004): *Testing the Market Timing Theory of Capital Structure*. Working Paper, Kennesaw State University and University of Florida.

HUBBARD, R. G. (1998): Capital-Market Imperfections and Investment, *Journal of Economic Literature*, 36, 193-225.

HUBBARD, R. G., and D. PALIA (1999): A Reeximination of the Conglomerate Merger Wave in the 1960s, *Journal of Finance*, 54, 1131-1152.

HUGHES, P., and A. THAKOR (1992): Litigation risk, intermediation, and the underpricing of initial public offerings, *Review of Financial Studies*, 5, 709-742.

HULBURT, H. M., J. A. MILES, and J. R. WOOLRIDGE (2002): Value Creation from Equity Carve-Outs, *Financial Management*, 83-100.

HULL, J., and A. WHITE (1987): The pricing of options on assets with stochastic volatilities, *Journal of Finance*, 42, 281-299.

HUNT, H. G. (1986): The separation of ownership and control: Theory, evidence and implications, *Journal of Accounting Literature*, 5, 85-124.

HUPE, M., and G. RITTER (1997): Der Einsatz risikoadjustierter Kalkulationszinsfüße bei Investitionsentscheidungen - theoretische Grundlagen und empirische Untersuchung, *Betriebswirtschaftliche Forschung und Praxis*, 5/1997, 593-612.

HUTCHISON, T. W. (1984): Institutionalist Economics Old and New, *Journal of Institutional and Theoretical Economics*, 140, 20-29.

IBBOTSON, R. G., and J. F. JAFFE (1975): Hot Issue Markets, *Journal of Finance*, 30, 1027-1042.

IKENBERRY, D., J. LAKONISHOK, and T. VERMAELEN (1995): Market underreaction to open market share repurchases, *Journal of Financial Economics*, 39, 181-208.

INDERST, R., and H. M. MÜLLER (2003): Internal versus external financing: An optimal contracting approach, *Journal of Finance*, 58, 1033-1063.

INGRAM, M. A., and V. A. INGRAM (1993): Consistent Estimation of Residual Variance in Regulatory Event Studies, *Journal of Financial Research*, 16, 151-160.

ITTNER, C., D. F. LARCKER, and M. RAJAN (1997): The Choice of Performance Measures in Annual Bonus Contracts, *Accounting Review*, 72, 231-255.

JAFFE, J. F. (1974): Special Information and Insider Trading, *Journal of Business*, 47, 410-428.

JAIN, B. A., and O. KINI (1994): The post-issue operating performance of IPO firms, *Journal of Finance*, 49, 1699-1726.

JAIN, P. C. (1986): Analyses of the Distribution of Security Market Model Prediction Errors for Daily Returns Data, *Journal of Accounting Research*, 24, 76-96.

JAKOBSEN, J. B., and T. VOETMANN (1999): *Post-Acquisition Performance in the Short and Long Run*. Working Paper, Copenhagen Business School.

— (1999): *Volatility-Adjusted Performance - An Alternative Approach to Interpret Long-Run Returns*. Working Paper.

JAKOBSEN, J. B., and O. SORENSEN (2001): Decomposing and Testing Long-term Returns: an Application on Danish IPOs, *European Financial Management*, 7, 393-417.

JANAKIMARAN, S. N., R. A. LAMBERT, and D. F. LARCKER (1992): An Empirical Investigation of the Relative Performance Evaluation Hypothesis, *Journal of Accounting Research*, 30, 53-69.

JEANNERET, P. (2000): *Use of the Proceeds and Performance of French SEO Firms*. Working Paper, University of Neuchatel.

JEGADEESH, N., and S. TITMAN (1993): Returns to buying winners and selling losers: Implications for stock market efficiency, *Journal of Finance*, 48, 65-91.

JENSEN, M. C., and W. MECKLING (1976): Theory of the firm: Managerial Behavior, Agency Costs and Ownership Structure, *Journal of Financial Economics*, 3, 305-360.

JENSEN, M. C. (1978): Some anomalous evidence regarding market efficiency, *Journal of Financial Economics*, 6, 95-101.

JENSEN, M. C., and R. S. RUBACK (1983): The market for corporate control: The scientific evidence, *Journal of Financial Economics*, 11, 5-50.

JENSEN, M. C. (1983): Organization Theory and Methodology, *The Accounting Review*, 58, 319-339.

JENSEN, M. C., and C. W. SMITH JR (1984): The Theory of Corporate Finance: A Historical Overview, in *The Modern Theory of Corporate Finance*, ed. by M. C. Jensen, and C. W. Smith, Jr. New York, 2-20.

JENSEN, M. C. (1986): Agency costs of free cash flow, corporate finance and takeovers, *American Economic Review*, 76, 323-329.

JENSEN, M. C., and J. B. WARNER (1988): The distribution of power among corporate managers, shareholders, and directors, *Journal of Financial Economics*, 20, 3-24.

JENSEN, M. C., and K. J. MURPHY (1990a): Performance pay and top management incentives, *Journal of Political Economy*, 98, 225-264.

— (1990b): CEO Incentives: It's not How Much, but How, *Harvard Business Review*, May/June.

JENSEN, M. C. (1993): The modern industrial revolution, exit and the failure of internal control systems, *Journal of Finance*, 48, 831-880.

JIN, L. (2002): CEO Compensation, Diversification and Incentives, *Journal of Financial Economics*, 66, 29-63.

JOHN, K., and E. OFEK (1995): Asset sales and increase in focus, *Journal of Financial Economics*, 37, 105-126.

JOHN, T. A., and K. JOHN (1993): Top-Management Compensation and Capital Structure, *Journal of Finance*, 48, 949-974.

JOHNSON, N. J. (1978): Modified t-tests and confidence intervals for asymmetrical populations, *Journal of the American Statistical Association*, 73, 536-544.

JOHNSON, S., R. LAPORTA, F. LOPEZ DE SILANES, and A. SHLEIFER (2000): Tunneling, *American Economic Review*, 90, 22-27.

JOHNSTON, K., and P. HAMILL (2000): Dividend Initiation Announcement Effects in Initial Public Offerings, *Applied Financial Economics*, 10, 533-542.

JONES, J. J. (1991): Earnings Management During Important Relief Investigations, *Journal of Accounting Research*, 29, 193-228.

JOOS, P., and M. LANG (1994): The Effects of Accounting Diversity: Evidence from the European Union, *Journal of Accounting Research*, 32, 141-168.

JUNG, K., Y.-C. KIM, and R. M. STULZ (1996): Timing, investment opportunities, managerial discretion and the security issue decision, *Journal of Financial Economics*, 42, 159-185.

JÜRGENS, U., K. NAUMANN, and J. RUPP (2000): Shareholder value in an adverse environment: the German case, *Economy and Society*, 29, 54-79.

JÜRGENS, U., and J. RUPP (2002): *The German System of Corporate Governance: Characteristics and Changes*. Working Paper, Wissenschaftszentrum Berlin für Sozialforschung, FS II 02-203.

KADIYALA, P., and P. R. RAU (2004): Investor Reaction to Corporate Event Announcements: Under-Reaction or Over-Reaction?, *Journal of Business*, 77, 357-387.

KAHLE, K. M., and R. A. WALKLING (1996): The impact of industry classifications on financial research, *Journal of Financial and Quantitative Analysis*, 31, 309-336.

KAHN, C., and A. WINTON (1998): Ownership Structure, Speculation, and Shareholder Intervention, *Journal of Finance*, 53, 99-130.

KALAY, A., and A. SHIMRAT (1987): Firm value and seasoned equity offerings: An empirical investigation, *Journal of Financial Economics*, 19, 109-126.

KANODIA, C., and D. LEE (1998): Investment and Disclosure: The Disciplinary Role of Periodic Performance Reports, *Journal of Accounting Research*, 36, 33-55.

KAPLAN, S. N. (1989): The effects of management buyouts on operating performance and value, *Journal of Financial Economics*, 24, 217-254.

— (1994): Top Executives, Turnover, and Firm Performance in Germany, *Journal of Law, Economics and Organization*, 10, 142-159.

KAPLAN, S. N., and L. ZINGALES (1997): Do financing constraints explain why investment is correlated with cash flow?, *Quarterly Journal of Economics*, 112, 169-215.

KAPLAN, S. N., and L. ZINGALES (2001): Investment-cash flow sensitivities are not valid measures of financial constraints, *Quarterly Journal of Economics*, 116, 707-712.

KARAFIATH, I. (1994): On the Efficiency of Least Squares Regression with Security Returns as the Dependent Variable, *Journal of Financial and Quantitative Analysis*, 29, 279-300.

— (2004): *Is There a Viable Alternative to Ordinary Least Squares Regression when Security Abnormal Returns are the Dependent Variable?* Working Paper, University of North Texas.

KASERER, C., and M. AHLERS (2000): Kursreaktionen anläßlich der Börseneinführung von Tochterunternehmen - Signaling oder verbesserte Unternehmenskontrolle in Konzernen?, *Zeitschrift für betriebswirtschaftliche Forschung*, 52, 537-570.

KAYHAN, A., and S. TITMAN (2004): *Firms' histories and their capital structure.* Working Paper, University of Texas at Austin.

KEATING, A. S. (1997): Determinants of divisional performance evaluation practices, *Journal of Accounting and Economics*, 24, 243-273.

KENNEDY, P. (2000): *A Guide to Econometrics.* Cambridge: MIT Press.

KERR, K., and R. A. BETTIS (1987): Boards of directors, top management compensation, and shareholder returns, *Academy of Management Journal*, 30, 645-664.

KHANNA, N., and S. TICE (2001): The Bright Side of Internal Capital Markets, *Journal of Finance*, 56, 1489-1528.

KIANIFARD, F., and W. H. SWALLOW (1996): A Review of the Development and Application of Recursive Residuals in Linear Models, *Journal of the American Statistical Association*, 91.

KIM, O., and R. E. VERRECCHIA (1994): Market liquidity and volume around earnings announcements, *Journal of Accounting and Economics*, 17, 41-68.

KIM, S. K. (1995): Efficiency of an information system in an agency model, *Econometrica*, 63, 89-102.

KISS, I., and R. STEHLE (2002): *Underpricing and Long-Term Performance of Initial Public Offerings at Germany's Neuer Markt, 1997-2001*. Working Paper, Humboldt University Berlin.

KLEIN, A., J. ROSENFELD, and W. BERANEK (1991): The Two Stages of an Equity Carve-out and the Price Response of Parent and Subsidiary Stock, *Managerial and Decision Economics*, 12, 449-460.

KLEIN, B., R. CRAWFORD, and A. ALCHIAN (1978): Vertical Integration, Appropriable Rents, and the Competitive Contracting Process, *Journal of Law and Economics*, 21, 297-326.

KLEIN, P. G. (2000): New Institutional Economics, in *Encyclopedia of Law and Economics*, ed. by B. Bouckeart, and G. De Geest. Gent: Edward Elgar, 456-489.

KLEINBAUM, D. G., L. L. KUPPER, K. E. MULLER, and A. NIZAM (1998): *Applied Regression Analysis and other Multivariable Methods*. Pacific Grove et al.: Duxbury Press.

KLEMM, M. (1990): *Die Nutzung synergetischer Potentiale als Ziel strategischen Konzernmanagements*. Bergisch-Gladbach/Köln.

KNOLL, L. (1998): Anreizkompatible Entlohnung: Pro und Contra Stock Options, in *Quantitative und qualitative Personalanpassungsstrategien: Personalökonomische Analysen ihrer institutionellen Bedingtheit und ihrer Konsequenzen*, ed. by U. Backes-Gellner, M. Kräkel, and L. Geil. München, 95-117.

KNORR, L., and A. WITTICH (2002): Kapitalflussrechnung, Segmentberichterstattung und Zwischenberichterstattung, *Datenverarbeitung, Steuer, Wirtschaft, Recht*, 12/2002, 375-377.

KÖKE, J. (2001): New evidence on ownership structures in Germany, *Kredit und Kapital*, 34, 257-292.

KOOLI, M., J.-F. L'HER, and J.-M. SURET (2004): The aftermarket performance of initial public offerings in Canada, *Journal of Multinational Financial Management*, 14, 47-67.

KORAJCZYK, R., D. LUCAS, and R. MCDONALD (1990): Understanding stock price behavior around the time of equity issues, in *Asymmetric Information, Corporate Finance, and Investment*, ed. by G. Hubbard. Chicago, 257-277.

— (1991): The effects of information releases on the pricing and timing of equity issues, *Review of Financial Studies*, 4, 685-708.

KORAJCZYK, R., and A. LEVY (2003): Capital structure choice: Macroeconomic conditions and financial constraints, *Journal of Financial Economics*, 68, 75-109.

KOTHARI, S. P., and J. B. WARNER (1997): Measuring long-horizon security price performance, *Journal of Financial Economics*, 43, 301-339.

KOTHARI, S. P. (2001): Capital Markets Research in Accounting, *Journal of Accounting and Economics*, 31, 105-231.

KRÄMER, W., and H. SONNBERGER (1986): *The linear regression model under test.* Heidelberg/Vienna: Physica.

KRAWITZ, N. (1997): Zur Erweiterung der deutschen Segmentberichterstattung unter Berücksichtigung internationaler Entwicklungen, in *Jahresabschluß und Jahresabschlußprüfung: Probleme, Perspektiven, internationale Einflüsse*, ed. by T. R. Fischer, and R. Hömberg. Düsseldorf, 551-599.

KRISHNAN, J., and E. PRESS (2003): The North American Industry Classification System and its Implications for Accounting Research, *Contemporary Accounting Research*, 20, 685-718.

KRISHNASWAMI, S., and V. SUBRAMANIAM (1999): Information asymmetry, valuation and the corporate spin-off decision, *Journal of Financial Economics*, 53, 72-112.

KRISHNASWAMI, S., P. A. SPINDT, and V. SUBRAMANIAM (1999): Information asymmetry, monitoring, and the placement structure of corporate debt, *Journal of Financial Economics*, 51, 407-434.

KRITZMAN, M. P. (1994): What Practitioners Need to Know About Event Studies, *Financial Analysts Journal*, 17-20.

KUNKEL, G. (1982): Sufficient conditions for public information to have social value in a production and exchange economy, *Journal of Finance*, 37, 1005-1013.

KÜRSTEN, W. (2000): "Shareholder Value": Grundelemente und Schieflagen einer polit-ökonomischen Diskussion aus finanzierungstheoretischer Sicht, *Zeitschrift für Betriebswirtschaft*, 70, 359-381.

KYLE, A. S. (1985): Continuous Auctions and Insider Trading, *Econometrica*, 53, 1315-1335.

LAKONISHOK, J., A. SHLEIFER, and R. W. VISHNY (1994): Contrarian investment, extrapolation and risk, *Journal of Finance*, 49, 1541-1578.

LAMBERT, R. A. (1986): Executive Effort and Selection of Risky Projects, *RAND Journal of Economics*, 17, 77-88.

LAMBERT, R. A., and D. F. LARCKER (1987): An Analysis of the Use of Accounting and Market Measures of Performance in Executive Compensation Contracts, *Journal of Accounting Research*, 25, 85-125.

LAMBERT, R. A., D. F. LARCKER, and R. E. VERRECCHIA (1991): Portfolio Considerations in Valuing Executive Compensation, *Journal of Accounting Research*, 29.

LAMBERT, R. A., D. F. LARCKER, and K. WEIGELT (1993): The Structure of Organizational Incentives, *Administrative Science Quarterly*, 38, 438-461.

LAMBERT, R. A. (2001): Contracting theory and accounting, *Journal of Accounting and Economics*, 32, 3-87.

LAMONT, O. A. (1997): Cash Flow and Investment: Evidence from Internal Capital Markets, *Journal of Finance*, 52, 83-109.

LAMONT, O. A., and C. POLK (2001): The Diversification Discount: Cash Flow vs. Returns, *Journal of Finance*, 56, 1693-1721.

— (2002): Does diversification destroy value? Evidence from industry shocks, *Journal of Financial Economics*, 63, 51-78.

LAMONT, O. A., and R. H. THALER (2003): Can the Market Add and Subtract? Mispricing in Tech-Stock Carve-outs, *Journal of Political Economy*, 111, 227-268.

LANG, L. H. P., and R. M. STULZ (1994): Tobin's q, corporate diversification and firm performance, *Journal of Political Economy*, 102, 1248-1280.

LANG, L. H. P., A. POULSEN, and R. M. STULZ (1995): Asset sales, firm performance and the agency costs of managerial discretion, *Journal of Financial Economics*, 37, 3-37.

LANG, L. H. P., E. OFEK, and R. M. STULZ (1996): Leverage, Investment. and Firm Growth, *Journal of Financial Economics*, 40, 3-30.

LANG, M., and R. J. LUNDHOLM (1993): Cross-sectional determinants of analysts of corporate disclosures, *Journal of Accounting Research*, 31, 246-271.

— (1996): Corporate Disclosure Policy and Analysts, *Accounting Review*, 71, 467-492.

LANGENBACH, W. (2001): *Börseneinführungen von Tochtergesellschaften - Eine konzeptionelle und empirische Analyse zur Optimierung der Rationalitätssicherung durch Märkte.* Wiesbaden: Gabler.

LAPORTA, R. (1996): Expectations and the cross-section of stock returns, *Journal of Finance*, 51, 1715-1742.

LAPORTA, R., F. LOPEZ DE SILANES, A. SHLEIFER, and R. W. VISHNY (1997): Legal Determinants of External Finance, *Journal of Finance*, 52, 1131-1150.

— (1998): Law and Finance, *Journal of Political Economy*, 106, 1113-1155.

LAPORTA, R., F. LOPEZ DE SILANES, and A. SHLEIFER (1999): Corporate Ownership around the World, *Journal of Finance*, 54, 471-517.

LAPORTA, R., F. LOPEZ DE SILANES, A. SHLEIFER, and R. W. VISHNY (2000a): Investor Protection and Corporate Governance, *Journal of Financial Economics*, 58, 3-27.

— (2000b): Agency Problems and Dividend Policies around the World, *Journal of Finance*, 55, 1-33.

— (2002): Investor Protection and Corporate Valuation, *Journal of Finance*, 57, 1147-1171.

LAPORTA, R., F. LOPEZ DE SILANES, and A. SHLEIFER (In Press): What Works in Securities Laws?, *Journal of Finance*.

LAZEAR, E., and S. ROSEN (1981): Rank-Order Tournaments as Optimum Labor Contracts, *Journal of Political Economy*, 97, 561-580.

LEAMER, E., and H. LEONARD (1983): Reporting the Fragility of Regression Estimates, *Review of Economics and Statistics*, 65, 306-317.

LEAMER, E. (1983): Model Choice and Specification Analysis, in *Handbook of Econometrics, Vol I*, ed. by Z. Griliches, and M. D. Intriligator. Amsterdam et al.: North-Holland, 285-330.

LEASE, R., J. J. MCCONNELL, and W. MIKKELSON (1983): The market value of control in publicly traded corporations, *Journal of Financial Economics*, 11, 439-471.

LEHMANN, E., and J. WEIGAND (2001): Does the Governed Corporation Perform Better? Governance Structures and Corporate Performance in Germany, *European Finance Review*, 4, 157-195.

LELAND, H., and D. PYLE (1977): Information asymmetrics, financial structure, and financial intermediation, *Journal of Finance*, 32, 371-388.

LEUZ, C., and R. E. VERRECCHIA (2000): The Economic Consequences of Increased Disclosure, *Journal of Accounting Research*, 38, 91-124.

LEUZ, C. (2003): IAS versus US-GAAP: Information-Asymmetry Based Evidency from Germany's New Market, *Journal of Accounting Research*, 41, 445-472.

LEUZ, C., D. NANDA, and P. D. WYSOCKI (2003): Earnings management and investor protection, *Journal of Financial Economics*, 69, 505-528.

LEUZ, C., and J. WÜSTEMANN (2004): The Role of Accounting in the German Financial System, in *The German Financial System*, ed. by J. P. Krahnen, and R. H. Schmidt. Oxford: Oxford University Press.

LEVINTHAL, D. (1988): A Survey of Agency Models of Organizations, *Journal of Economic Behavior and Organization*, 9, 153-185.

LEWELLEN, W. G. (1971): A pure financial rationale for the conglomerate merger, *Journal of Finance*, 521-537.

LEWELLEN, W. G., and S. G. BALDRINATH (1997): On the measurement of Tobin's Q, *Journal of Financial Economics*, 44, 77-122.

LI, D., and S. LI (1996): A Theory of Corporate Scope and Financial Structure, *Journal of Finance*, 51, 691-709.

LIE, E. (2001): Detecting Abnormal Operating Performance: Revisited, *Financial Management*, 77-91.

LIM, T. (2001): Rationality and Analysts' Forecast Bias, *Journal of Finance*, 56, 369-386.

LINDENBERG, E., and S. ROSS (1981): Tobin's q and industrial organization, *Journal of Business*, 54, 1-32.

LINS, K. V., and H. SERVAES (1999): International evidence on the value of corporate diversification, *Journal of Finance*, 54, 2215-2239.

LINS, K. V., and H. SERVAES (2002): Is corporate diversification beneficial in emerging markets?, *Financial Management*, 31, 5-31.

LINTNER, J. (1965): The valuation of risk assets and the selection of risky investments in stock portfolios and capital budgets, *Review of Economics and Statistics*, 47, 13-37.

— (1969): The Aggregation of Investors' Diverse Judgements and Preferences in Purely Competitive Security Markets, *Journal of Financial and Quantitative Analysis*, 4, 347-400.

LITTKEMANN, J. (2001): Beteiligungscontrolling: Organisation und Effizienz - eine empirische Analyse aus zentraler und lokaler Controllingperspektive, *Zeitschrift für Betriebswirtschaft*, 71, 1283-1304.

LJUNGQVIST, A. P. (1996): Can Firms Outwit the Market? Timing Ability and the Long-Run Performance of IPOs, in *Empirical Issues in Raising Equity Capital*, ed. by M. Levis, 215-244.

— (1997): Pricing Initial Public Offerings: Further Evidence From Germany, *European Economic Review*, 41, 1309-1320.

LJUNGQVIST, A. P., and W. J. J. WILHELM (2003): IPO Pricing in the Dot Com Bubble, *Journal of Finance*, 58, 723-752.

LODERER, C., and K. MARTIN (1997): Executive stock ownership and performance: tracking faint traces, *Journal of Financial Economics*, 45, 223-255.

LÖFFLER, Y. (2001): *Desinvestitionen durch Verkäufe und Börseneinführungen von Tochtergesellschaften. Eine empirische Untersuchung der Bewertung am deutschen Kapitalmarkt.* Lohmar: Josef Eul Verlag.

LONG, J. S., and P. TRIVEDI (1992): Some Specification Tests for the Linear Regression Model, *Sociological Methods and Research*, 21, 161-204.

LONG, J. S., and L. H. ERVIN (2000): Using Heteroscedasticity Consistent Standard Errors in the Linear Regression Model, *The American Statistician*, 54, 217-224.

LOUGHRAN, T., J. R. RITTER, and K. RYDQVIST (1994): Initial public offerings: international insights, *Pacific Basin Finance Journal*, 2, 165-199.

LOUGHRAN, T., and J. R. RITTER (1995): The new issues puzzle, *Journal of Finance*, 50, 23-51.

— (1997): The operating performance of firms conducting seasoned equity offerings, *Journal of Finance*, 52, 1823-1850.

— (2000): Uniformly Least Powerful Tests of Market Efficiency, *Journal of Financial Economics*, 55, 361-390.

— (2002): Why Don't Issuers Get Upset About Leaving Money on the Table in IPOs?, *Review of Financial Studies*, 15, 413-443.

LOVELL, M. C. (1983): Data Mining, *Review of Economics and Statistics*, 55, 1-12.

LOWRY, M., and G. W. SCHWERT (2002): IPO market cycles: Bubbles or sequential learning?, *Journal of Finance*, 57, 1171-1200.

LOWRY, M. (2003): Why does IPO volume fluctuate so much?, *Journal of Financial Economics*, 67, 3-41.

LUCAS, D. J., and R. L. MCDONALD (1990): Equity issues and stock price dynamics, *Journal of Finance*, 45, 1019-1043.

LUCAS, R. E., and E. PRESCOTT (1971): Investment under uncertainty, *Econometrica*, 39, 659-681.

LUNDHOLM, R. J., and L. A. MYERS (2002): Bringing the Future Forward: The Effect of Disclosure on the Return-Earnings-Relation, *Journal of Accounting Research*, 40, 809-839.

LUTTER, M. (1997): Aktienoptionen für Führungskräfte - de lege lata und de lege ferenda, *ZIP Zeitschrift für Wirtschaftsrecht*, 18, 1-9.

— (2001): Noch einmal: Zum Vorerwerbsrecht der Aktionäre beim Verkauf von Tochtergesellschaften über die Börse, *Die Aktiengesellschaft*, 46, 349-353.

LYON, J. D., B. M. BARBER, and C.-L. TSAI (1999): Improved Methods for Tests of Long-Run Abnormal Stock Returns, *Journal of Finance*, 54, 165-201.

MACKINLAY, A. C. (1997): Event Studies in Economics and Finance, *Journal of Economic Literature*, 35, 13-39.

MACKINNON, J. G., and H. WHITE (1985): Some Heteroskedasticity-Consistent Covariance Matrix Estimators With Improved Finite Sample Properties, *Journal of Econometrics*, 29, 305-325.

MACKINNON, J. G. (1992): Model Specification Tests and Artificial Regressions, *Journal of Economic Literature*, 30, 102-146.

MADDALA, G. S., and H. LI (1996): Bootstrap based tests in financial models, in *Handbook of Statistics Vol. XIV: Statistical Methods in Finance*, ed. by G. S. Maddala, and C. R. Rao. Amsterdam et al.: Elsevier.

MAIS, E. L., W. T. MOORE, and R. C. ROGERS (1991): A Reexamination of Shareholder Wealth Effects of Calls on Convertible Preferred Stock, *Journal of Finance*, 44, 1401-1410.

MAKSIMOVIC, V., and G. M. PHILLIPS (2002): Do Conglomerate Firms Allocate Resources Efficiently Across Industries?, *Journal of Finance*, 57, 721-768.

MALATESTA, P. H., and R. THOMPSON (1985): Partially anticipated events: A model of stock price reaction with an application to corporate acquisitions, *Journal of Financial Economics*, 14, 237-250.

MALATESTA, P. H. (1986): Measuring Abnormal Performance: The Event Parameter Approach Using Joint Generalized Least Squares, *Journal of Financial and Quantitative Analysis*, 21, 27-38.

MALKIEL, B. G. (2003): The Efficient Market Hypothesis and Its Critics, *Journal of Economic Perspectives*, 17, 59-82.

MANDELBROT, B. (1963): The variation of certain speculative prices, *Journal of Business*, 36.

MANDELKER, G. (1974): Risk and Return: The Case of Merging Firms, *Journal of Financial Economics*, 1, 303-336.

MANSI, S. A., and D. M. REEB (2002): Corporate diversification: what gets discounted?, *Journal of Finance*, 57, 2167-2183.

MARKIDES, C. C. (1995): Diversification, restructuring and economic performance, *Strategic Management Journal*, 16, 101-118.

MARSH, T. A., and R. C. MERTON (1986): Dividend Variability and Variance Bounds Tests for the Rationality of Stock Market Prices, *American Economic Review*, 76, 1429-1445.

MARSHALL, A. (1928): *Principles of Economics*. London.

MARTIN, J. D., and A. SAYRAK (2003): Corporate diversification and shareholder value, *Journal of Corporate Finance*, 9, 37-57.

MAS-COLLEL, A., M. D. WHINSTON, and J. R. GREEN (1995): *Microeconomic Theory*. New York/Oxford.

MASULIS, R., and A. KORWAR (1986): Seasoned equity offerings: An empirical investigation, *Journal of Financial Economics*, 15, 91-118.

MATSUSAKA, J. G. (1993): Takeover motives during the conglomerate merger wave, *RAND Journal of Economics*, 24, 357-379.

— (2001): Corporate diversification, value maximization, and organizational capabilities, *Journal of Business*, 74, 409-431.

MATSUSAKA, J. G., and V. NANDA (2002): Internal Capital Markets and Corporate Refocusing, *Journal of Financial Intermediation*, 11, 176-212.

MAUG, E. (1998): Large shareholders as monitors: Is there a trade-off between liquidity and control?, *Journal of Finance*, 53, 65-99.

— (2001): Ownership Structure and the Life-Cycle of the Firm: A Theory of the Decision to Go Public, *European Finance Review*, 5, 167-200.

MAY, A. (1984): Zum Stand der empirischen Forschung über Informationsverarbeitung am Kapitalmarkt - Ein Überblick, *Zeitschrift für betriebswirtschaftliche Forschung*, 43, 313-335.

MAY, D. (1995): Do Managerial Motives Influence Firm Risk Reduction Strategies?, *Journal of Finance*, 50, 1291-1308.

MAYERS, C. (1998): Financial Systems and Corporate Governance: A Review of the International Evidence, *Journal of Institutional and Theoretical Economics*, 154, 144-166.

MAYSHAR, J. (1983): On Divergence of Opinion and Imperfections in Capital Markets, *American Economic Review*, 73, 114-128.

MCAFEE, R. P., and J. MCMILLAN (1995): Organizational diseconomies of scale, *Journal of Economis and Management Strategy*, 4, 399-426.

MCCONNELL, J. J., and H. SERVAES (1990): Additional Evidence on Equity Ownership and Corporate Value, *Journal of Financial Economics*, 27, 595-612.

MCDONALD, B. (1987): Event Studies and Systems Methods: Some Additional Evidence, *Journal of Financial and Quantitative Analysis*, 22, 495-504.

MCEACHERN, W. (1975): *Managerial control and performance*. Lexington: Lexington Books.

MCINISH, T. H., and R. A. WOOD (1986): Adjusting for beta bias: an assessment of alternative techniques - a note, *Journal of Finance*, 41, 277-286.

MCLAUGHLIN, R., A. SAFIEDDINE, and G. K. VASUDEVAN (1996): The operating performance of seasoned equity issuers: Free cash flow and post-issue performance, *Financial Management*, 25, Iss. 4, 41-53.

— (1998): The information content of corporate offerings of seasoned securities: An empirical analysis, *Financial Management*, 27, Iss. 2, 31-45.

MCWILLIAMS, A., and D. SIEGEL (1997): Event studies in management research: theoretical and empirical issues, *Academy of Management Journal*, 40, 626-657.

MCWILLIAMS, T. P., and V. B. WILLIAMS (2000): Another Look at Theoretical and Empirical Issues in Event Study Methodology, *Journal of Applied Business Research*, 16, Iss. 3, 1-11.

MEHRAN, H. (1995): Executive Compensation Structure, Ownership, and Firm Performance, *Journal of Financial Economics*, 38.

MELLEWIGT, T. (1995): *Konzernorganisation und Konzernführung. Eine empirische Untersuchung*. Frankfurt am Main.

MELLEWIGT, T., and W. MATIASKE (2000): Strategische Konzernführung: Stand der empirischen betriebswirtschaftlichen Forschung, *Zeitschrift für Betriebswirtschaft*, 70, 611-631.

MENNE, M. (2000): *Der Einfluss von Organisationsstrukturen auf Investitionsentscheidungen*. Dissertation, Universität Dortmund.

MERTON, R. (1987): A simple model of capital market equilibrium with incomplete information, *Journal of Finance*, 42, 483-510.

MEYER, M., P. MILGROM, and J. ROBERTS (1992): Organizational Prospects, Influence Costs, and Ownership Changes, *Journal of Economics and Management Strategy*, 1, 9-35.

MEZNAR, M., D. NIGH, and C. KWOK (1994): Effect of announcements of withdrawal from South Africa on stockholder wealth, *Academy of Management Journal*, 37, 1648-1663.

MICHAELY, R., and W. H. SHAW (1994): The pricing of initial public offerings: Tests of adverse-selection and signalling theories, *Review of Financial Studies*, 12, 653-686.

MIKKELSON, W. H. (1981): Convertible security calls and security returns, *Journal of Financial Economics*, 9, 237-264.

MIKKELSON, W. H., and M. M. PARTCH (1986): Valuation effects of security offerings and the issuance process, *Journal of Financial Economics*, 15, 31-60.

— (1988): Withdrawn Security Offerings, *Journal of Financial and Quantitative Analysis*, 23, 119-133.

— (1994): Consequences of unbundling managers' voting rights and equity claims, *Journal of Corporate Finance*, 1, 175-200.

MILES, J. A., and J. D. ROSENFELD (1983): The Effect of Voluntary Spin-Off Announcements on Shareholder Wealth, *Journal of Finance*, 38, 1597-1605.

MILES, J. A., and J. R. WOOLRIDGE (1999): Spin-offs and Equity Carveouts - Achieving Faster Growth and Better Performance, Harristown: Financial Executives Research Foundation.

MILGROM, P. (1988): Employment Contracts, Influence Activities and Efficient Organization Design, *Journal of Political Economy*, 96, 42-60.

MILGROM, P., and J. ROBERTS (1988a): An Economic Approach to Influence Activities in Organizations, *American Journal of Sociology*, 94, 154-179.

— (1988b): Economic theories of the firm: past, present, and future, *Canadian Journal of Economics*, 21, 444-459.

MILLER, J. S., R. M. WISEMAN, and L. R. GOMEZ-MEJIA (2002): The Fit Between CEO Compensation and Firm Risk, *Academy of Management Journal*, 45, 745-756.

MILLER, M. H. (1999): The History of Finance, *The Journal of Portfolio Management*, Summer, 95-101.

MIRRLEES, J. (1974): Notes on welfare economics, information, and uncertainty, in *Essays on economic behavior under uncertainty*, ed. by M. Balsch, D. McFadden, and S. Wu. Amsterdam: North-Holland.

— (1976): The Optimal Structure of Incentives and Authority within an Organization, *Bell Journal of Economics*, 7, 105-131.

MITCHELL, M. L., and K. LEHN (1990): Do Bad Bidders Become Good Targets, *Journal of Political Economy*, 98, 372-398.

MITCHELL, M. L., and E. STAFFORD (2000): Managerial Decisions and Long-Term Stock Price Performance, *Journal of Business*, 73, 287-329.

MODIGLIANI, F., and M. H. MILLER (1958): The Cost of Capital, Corporation Finance and the Theory of Investment, *American Economic Review*, 48, 261-297.

MÖLLER, H. P. (1985): Die Informationseffizienz des deutschen Aktienmarkts- eine Zusammenfassung und Analyse empirischer Untersuchungen, *Zeitschrift für betriebswirtschaftliche Forschung*, 37, 500-518.

MONTGOMERY, C. A., A. R. THOMAS, and R. KAMATH (1984): Divestiture, Market Valuation and Strategy, *Academy of Management Journal*, 27, 830-840.

MONTGOMERY, C. A. (1994): Corporate diversification, *Journal of Economic Perspectives*, 8, 163-178.

MOORE, N. H., D. R. PETERSON, and P. P. PETERSON (1986): Shelf Registrations and Shareholder Wealth: A Comparison of Shelf and Traditional Equity Offerings, *Journal of Finance*, 41, 451-464.

MORCK, R., A. SHLEIFER, and R. W. VISHNY (1988): Management Ownership and Market Valuation: An Empirical Analysis, *Journal of Financial Economics*, 20, 293-315.

— (1989): Alternative Mechanisms for Corporate Control, *American Economic Review*, 79, 842-852.

— (1990): Do Managerial Objectives Drive Bad Acquisitions, *Journal of Finance*, 46, 31-48.

MORGAN, A., and I. MORGAN (1987): Measurment of abnormal returns from small firms, *Journal of Business and Economic Statistics*, 5, 121-129.

MOSSIN, J. C. (1966): Equilibrium in a Capital Asset Market, *Econometrica*, 34, 768-783.

MUJKANOVIC, R. (2000): Die Vorschläge des Deutschen Standardisierungsrats (DSR) zur Segmentberichterstattung, *Die Aktiengesellschaft*, 3/2000, 122-127.

MURALI, R., and J. B. WELCH (1989): Agents, owners, control and performance, *Journal of Business Finance and Accounting*, 16, 385-398.

MURPHY, K. J. (1985): Corporate Performance and Managerial Remuneration, *Journal of Accounting and Economics*, 7, 11-42.

— (1995): Executive Compensation and the Modern Industrial Revolution, *International Journal of Industrial Organization*, 15, 417-426.

— (1999): Executive Compensation, in *Handbook of Labor Economics*, ed. by O. Ashenfelter, and D. Card.

— (2002): Explaining Executive Compensation: Managerial Power vs. the Perceived Cost of Stock Options, *University of Chicago Law Review*, 69, 847-869.

MYERS, S. C. (1977): The determinants of corporate borrowing, *Journal of Financial Economics*, 5, 147-175.

MYERS, S. C., and N. MAJLUF (1984): Corporate financing and investment decisions when firms have information that investors do not have, *Journal of Financial Economics*, 13, 187-221.

MYERS, S. C. (1984): The Capital Structure Puzzle, *Journal of Finance*, 38, 575-592.

— (2000): Outside Equity, *Journal of Finance*, 55, 1005-1037.

— (2001): Capital Structure, *Journal of Economic Perspectives*, 15, 81-102.

MYERSON, R. B. (1979): Incentive Compatibility and the Bargaining Problem, *Econometrica*, 47, 61-75.

NAKAMURA, A. O., M. NAKAMURA, and H. O. DULEEP (1990): Alternative Approaches to Model Choice, *Journal of Economic Behavior and Organization*, 14, 97-125.

NANDA, V. (1991): On the Good News in Equity Carve-Outs, *Journal of Finance*, 46, 1717-1737.

NANDA, V., and P. M. NARAYANAN (1999): Disentangling Value: Financing Needs, Firm Scope and Divestitures, *Journal of Financial Intermediation*, 8, 174-204.

NARAYANAN, P. M. (1985): Managerial incentives for short-term results, *Journal of Finance*, 40, 1469-1484.

NARDMANN, H. (2002): *Die Segmentberichterstattung: Anforderungen nach DRS 3 im internationalen Vergleich.* Herne: Verlag Neue Wirtschafts-Briefe.

NELSON, D. B., and C. Q. CAO (1992): Inequality constraints in univariate GARCH models, *Journal of Business Economics and Statistics*, 10, 229-235.

NEWEY, W. K., and K. D. WEST (1987): A Simple, Positive Semi-Definite, Heteroskedasticity and Autocorrelation Consistent Covariance Matrix, *Econometrica*, 55.

NICK, A. (1994): *Börseneinführung von Tochtergesellschaften - Instrument der Konzernfinanzierung und -gestaltung.* Wiesbaden.

O'BRIEN, P. (1990): Forecast Accuracy of Individual Analysts in Nine Industries, *Journal of Accounting Research*, 28, 286-305.

O'BRIEN, P., and R. BHUSHAN (1990): Analyst Following and Institutional Ownership, *Journal of Accounting Research*, 28, Supplement, 55-76.

OEHLER, A. (1991): "Anomalien" im Anlegerverhalten, *Die Bank*, 11/91, 600-607.

— (1992): "Anomalien", "Irrationalitäten" oder "Biases" der Erwartungsnutzentheorie und ihre Relevanz für die Finanzmärkte, *Zeitschrift für Bankrecht und Bankwirtschaft*, 11, Iss. 2, 97-120.

— (1994): Verhaltensmuster individueller Anleger - eine experimentelle Studie, *Zeitschrift für betriebswirtschaftliche Forschung*, 46, 939-958.

OFEK, E., and D. YERMACK (2000): Taking Stock: Equity-Based Compensation and the Evolution of Managerial Ownership, *Journal of Finance*, 55, 1367-1384.

OHLSON, J. A. (1995): Earnings, book values, and dividends in equity valuation, *Contemporary Accounting Research*, 11, 661-687.

— (2001): Earnings, Book Values and Dividends in Equity Valuation: An Empirical Perspective, *Contemporary Accounting Research*, 18, 107-120.

ORDELHEIDE, D., and M. STUBENRATH (1998): Segmentberichterstattung: US-GAAP im Vergleich mit HGB/DRS, in, ed. by W. Ballwieser. Stuttgart: Schäffer-Poeschel, 273-298.

PADBERG, S. (1996): *Der Einfluß von Kapitalerhöhungen auf den Marktwert deutscher Aktiengesellschaften*. Wiesbaden.

PAGANO, M., F. PANETTA, and L. ZINGALES (1998): Why do companies go public? An empirical analysis, *Journal of Finance*, 53, 27-64.

PAGANO, M., and A. RÖELL (1998): The choice of stock ownership structure: agency costs, monitoring, and the decision to go public, *Quarterly Journal of Economics*, 113, 187-226.

PALM, F. C. (1996): GARCH Models of Volatility, in *Handbook of Statistics, Vol. XIV: Statistical Methods in Finance*, ed. by G. S. Maddala, and C. R. Rao. Amsterdam et al.: Elsevier, 209-240.

PANZAR, J. C., and R. D. WILLIG (1981): Economies of Scope, *American Economic Review*, 71, 268-272.

PARRINO, R., and M. S. WEISBACH (1999): Measuring investment distortions arising from stockholder-bondholder conflicts, *Journal of Financial Economics*, 53, 3-42.

PATELL, J. (1976): Corporate Forecasts of Earnings per Share and Stock Price behavior: Empirical Tests, *Journal of Accounting Research*, 14, 246-276.

PELLENS, B. (1993): Börseneinführung von Tochterunternehmen - Aktienmarktreaktionen auf die Performance des Mutterunternehmens, *Zeitschrift für betriebswirtschaftliche Forschung*, 45, 852-872.

— (1994): *Aktionärsschutz im Konzern. Empirische und theoretische Analyse der Reformvorschläge der Konzernverfassung.* Wiesbaden.

PELLENS, B., and C. TOMASZEWSKI (1999): Kapitalmarktreaktionen auf den Rechnungslegungswechsel zu IAS bzw. U.S. GAAP, *Zeitschrift für betriebswirtschaftliche Forschung*, 199-228.

PENMAN, S. (1982): Insider Trading and the Dissemination of Firms' Forecast Information, *Journal of Business*, 55, 479-503.

PERFECT, S., and K. WILES (1994): Alternative Constructions of Tobin's Q: An Empirical Comparison, *Journal of Empirical Finance*, 1, 313-341.

PERSONS, J. (1994): Renegotiation and the Impossibility of Optimal Investment, *Review of Financial Studies*, 7, 419-449.

PETERSON, P. P. (1989): Event Studies. A Review of Issues and Methodology, *Quarterly Journal of Business and Economics*, 28, 36-66.

PETTENGILL, G. N., and J. M. CLARK (1999): Estimating Expected Returns in an Event-Study Framework: Evidence from the Dartboard Column, *Quarterly Journal of Business and Economics*, 40, 3-21.

PHILBRICK, D. R., and W. E. RICKS (1991): Using Value Line and IBES Analyst Forecasts in Accounting Research, *Journal of Accounting Research*, 29, 397-417.

POHMER, D. (1964): Das Verhältnis der Wirtschaftswissenschaft zur Rechtswissenschaft dargestellet am Beispiel der Konzerngestaltungen, in *Das Verhältnis der Wirtschaftswissenschaft zur Rechtswissenschaft, Soziologie und Statistik*, ed. by L. Raiser, H. Sauermann, and E. Schneider. Berlin, 57-66.

POON, S.-H., and C. W. GRANGER (2003): Forecasting Volatility in Financial Markets, *Journal of Economic Literature*, 41, 478-539.

POWERS, E. A. (2001): *Spinoffs, Selloffs and Equity Carveouts: An Analysis of Divestiture Method Choice.* Working Paper, University of South Carolina.

— (2003): Deciphering the Motives for Equity Carve-Outs, *Journal of Financial Research*, 26, 31-50.

PRABHALA, N. R. (1997): Conditional methods in event studies and an equilibrium justification for standard procedures, *Review of Financial Studies*, 10, 1-38.

PRAHALAD, C. K., and R. A. BETTIS (1986): The Dominant Logic: a New Linkage Between Diversity and Performance, *Strategic Management Journal*, 7, 485-501.

PRAHALAD, C. K., and G. HAMEL (1990): The core competence of the corporation, *Harvard Business Review*, 68, 79-91.

PRENDERGAST, C. (1999): The Provision of Incentives in Firms, *Journal of Economic Literature*, 37, 7-63.

— (2000): What Trade-off of Risk and Incentives?, *American Economic Review*, 90, 421-425.

— (2002): The Tenuous Trade-off between Risk and Incentives, *Journal of Political Economy*, 110, 1071-1102.

PREZAS, A. P., M. TARIMCILAR, and G. K. VASUDEVAN (2000): The Pricing of Equity Carve-Outs, *Financial Review*, 35, 123-138.

PRIGGE, S. (1998): A Survey of German Corporate Governance, in *Comparative Corporate Governance: The State of the Art and Emerging Research*, ed. by K. J. Hopt, H. Kanda, M. J. Roe, E. Wymeersch, and S. Prigge. Oxford: Clarendon.

RAJAN, R., and H. SERVAES (1997): Analyst Following of Initial Public Offerings, *Journal of Finance*, 52, 507-529.

RAJAN, R., and L. ZINGALES (1999): Power in a theory of the firm, *Quarterly Journal of Economics*, 113, 387-433.

RAJAN, R., H. SERVAES, and L. ZINGALES (2000): The cost of diversity: The diversification discount and inefficient investment, *Journal of Finance*, 55, 35-80.

RAU-BREDOW, H. (1999): *Finanzierungsverträge und Konzernbildung*. Habilitation: Universität Würzburg.

— (2001): Konzernbildung, Eigner/Gläubiger-Konflikte und Unterinvestitionsproblematik, *Kredit und Kapital*, 34, 106-129.

RAY, S., B. RAVIKUMAR, and E. SAVIN (2000): Robust Wald Tests in SUR Systems with Adding-Up Restrictions, *Econometrica*, 68, 715-720.

RICH, R. W., J. RAYMOND, and J. S. BUTLER (1991): Generalized instrumental variables estimation of autoregressive conditional heteroskedastic models, *Economics Letters*, 35, 179-185.

RITTER, J. R. (1984): The "hot issue" market of 1980, *Journal of Business*, 57.

— (1991): The long run performance of initial public offerings, *Journal of Finance*, 46, 3-27.

RITTER, J. R., and I. WELCH (2002): A review of IPO activity, pricing, and allocations, *Journal of Finance*, 57, 1795-1828.

RITTER, J. R. (2003a): Investment Banking and Securities Issuance, in *Handbook of the Economics of Finance*, ed. by G. Constantinides, M. Harris, and R. M. Stulz.

— (2003b): Differences between European and American IPO markets, *European Financial Management*, 9, 421-434.

ROBERTS, D. R. (1959): A general theory of executive compensation based on statistically tested propositions, *Quarterly Journal of Economics*, 74, 270-294.

ROCK, K. (1986): Why new issues are underpriced, *Journal of Financial Economics*, 15, 187-212.

ROLL, R. (1977): A critique of the asset pricing theory's tests Part I: On past and potential testability of the theory, *Journal of Financial Economics*, 4, 129-176.

— (1983): On Computing Mean Returns and the Small Firm Premium, *Journal of Financial Economics*, 12, 371-386.

— (1986): The Hubris Hypothesis of Corporate Takeovers, *Journal of Business*, 59, 197-216.

ROSS, S. A. (1973): The Economic Theory of Agency: The Principal's Problem, *American Economic Review*, 63, 134-139.

— (1976): The arbitrage theory of capital asset pricing, *Journal of Economic Theory*, 13, 341-360.

— (1977): The determination of financial structure: The incentive-signalling approach, *Bell Journal of Economics*, 8, 23-40.

— (1987): The Interrelations of Finance and Economics: Theoretical Perspectives, *American Economic Review*, 77, 29-34.

SALY, P. J. (1994): Repricing executive stock options in a down market, *Journal of Accounting and Economics*, 18, 325-356.

SAMBHARYA, R. B. (2000): Assessing the Construct Validity of Strategic and SIC-based measures of Corporate Diversification, *British Journal of Management*, 11, 163-174.

SAPPINGTON, D. E. M. (1991): Incentives in principal-agent relationships, *Journal of Economic Perspectives*, 5, 45-67.

SAPUSEK, A. (2000): Benchmark-Sensitivity of IPO Long-Run Performance: An Empirical Study for Germany, *Schmalenbach Business Review*, 52, 374-405.

SAVICKAS, R. (2003): Event-induced volatility and tests for abnormal performance, *Journal of Financial Research*, 26, 165-178.

SAWYER, K. R., and A. GYGAX (2001): *How Eventful are Event Studies?* Working Paper, University of Melbourne.

SCHALL, L. D. (1972): Asset Valuation, Firm Investment and Firm Diversification, *Journal of Business*, 45, 11-28.

SCHARFSTEIN, D. S. (1990): Herd Behavior and Investment, *American Economic Review*, 80, 465-479.

SCHARFSTEIN, D. S., and J. STEIN (2000): The Dark Side of Internal Capital Markets: Divisional Rent-Seeking and Inefficient Investment, *Journal of Finance*, 55, 2537-2564.

SCHEFFLER, E. (1999): Der Deutsche Standardisierungsrat - Struktur, Aufgaben und Kompetenzen, *Betriebswirtschaftliche Forschung und Praxis*, 407-417.

SCHENK, G. (1997a): *Konzernbildung, Interessenkonflikte und ökonomische Effizienz - Ansätze zur Theorie des Konzerns und ihre Relevanz für rechtspolitische Schlußfolgerungen.* Frankfurt: Peter Lang.

— (1997b): Corporate Spin-Offs - Schlanke Unternehmen durch eine alternative Form des Outsourcings, *Zeitschrift Führung und Organisation*, 1997, 213-217.

SCHILDBACH, T. (1999): Das private Rechnungslegungsgremium gemäß §342 HGB und die Zukunft der Rechnungslegung in Deutschland, *Der Betrieb*, 13/1999, 645-652.

— (2001): *Der Konzernabschluss nach HGB, IAS und US-GAAP.* Oldenbourg.

SCHILL, M. J., and C. ZHOU (2001): Pricing an Emerging Industry: Evidence from Internet Subsidiary Carve-outs, *Financial Management*, 12175.

SCHIPPER, K., and A. J. SMITH (1983): Effects of recontracting on shareholder wealth: The case of voluntary spinoffs, *Journal of Financial Economics*, 12, 439-468.

SCHIPPER, K., and R. THOMPSON (1983): The Impact of Merger-Related Regulations on the Shareholders of Acquiring Firms, *Journal of Accounting Research*, 21, 184-221.

— (1985): The Impact of Merger-Related Regulations Using Exact Distributions of Test Statistics, *Journal of Accounting Research*, 23, 408-415.

SCHIPPER, K., and A. J. SMITH (1986): A comparison of equity carve-outs and seasoned equity offerings: Share price effects and corporate restructuring, *Journal of Financial Economics*, 15, 153-186.

SCHMALENBACH-GESELLSCHAFT FÜR BETRIEBSWIRTSCHAFT, ARBEITSKREIS FINANZIERUNG (2003): Börsengänge von Konzerneinheiten - Handlungsempfehlungen des Arbeitskreises "Finanzierung" auf Basis einer empirischen Untersuchung deutscher Equity Carve-Outs und Spin-Offs (1997-2000), *Zeitschrift für betriebswirtschaftliche Forschung*, 55, 515-542.

SCHMID, F. A. (1997): Vorstandsbezüge, Aufsichtsratsvergütung und Aktionärsstruktur, *Zeitschrift für Betriebswirtschaft*, 67, 67-83.

SCHMIDT, R. H., and M. TYRELL (1997): Financial systems, corporate finance and corporate governance, *European Financial Management*, 3, 333-361.

SCHMIDT, R. H. (2003): *Corporate Governance in Germany: An Economic Perspective.* Center for Financial Studies Working Paper 2003/36, Universität Frankfurt.

SCHMIDT, R. H., and M. TYRELL (2004): What Constitutes a Financial System in General and the German Financial System in Particular?, in *The German Financial System*, ed. by J. P. Krahnen, and R. H. Schmidt. Oxford: Oxford University Press, 19-67.

SCHMITZ, R. H. (1993): Going Public von Tochtergesellschaften deutscher Konzerne, *Zeitschrift für das gesamte Kreditwesen*, 18, 842-844.

SCHOAR, A. S. (2002): Effects of corporate diversification on productivity, *Journal of Finance*, 57, 2379-2403.

SCHOLES, M., and J. WILLIAMS (1977): Estimating betas from non-synchronous data, *Journal of Financial Economics*, 5, 309-328.

SCHULTZ, P. (2003): Pseudo Market Timing and the Long-Run Underperformance of IPOs, *Journal of Finance*, 58, 483-519.

SCHULTZE, G. (1998): *Der spin-off als Konzernspaltungsform.* Wiesbaden.

SCHWALBACH, J., and U. GRASSHOFF (1997): Managervergütung und Unternehmenserfolg, *Zeitschrift für Betriebswirtschaft*, 67, 203-217.

SCHWALBACH, J. (1999): Entwicklung der Managervergütung, *Betriebswirtschaftliche Forschung und Praxis*, 6/1999, 592-602.

SCHWARZ, G. (1978): Estimating the Dimension of a Model, *Annals of Statistics*, 6, 461-464.

SCHWETZLER, B. (1999): Shareholder Value Konzept, Managementanreize und Stock Option Plans, *Die Betriebswirtschaft*, 59, 332-350.

SCOTT, J. T. (1982): Multi-market contact and economic performance, *Review of Economis and Statistics*, 64, 368-375.

SEFCIK, S. E., and R. THOMPSON (1990): An Approach to Statistical Inference in Cross-Sectional Models with Security Abnormal Returns as Dependent Variables, *Journal of Accounting Research*, 24, 316-334.

SEILER, M. J., and R. CHAKORNPIPAT (1997): Biases in Computing Long Term Returns in Event Studies, *American Business Review*, January, 106-112.

SEILER, M. J. (2000): The efficacy of event study methodologies: measuring EREIT abnormal performance under conditions of induced variance, *Journal of Financial and Strategic Decisions*, 13, 101-112.

SENGUPTA, P. (1998): Corporate Disclosure Quality and the Cost of Debt, *Accounting Review*, 73, 459-474.

SERRA, A. P. (2002): *Event Study Tests - a Brief Survey*. FEP Working Paper No. 117.

SERVAES, H. (1996): The value of diversification during the conglomerate merger wave, *Journal of Finance*, 51, 1201-1225.

SEWARD, J. K., and J. P. WALSH (1996): The Governance and Control of Voluntary Corporate Spin-Offs, *Strategic Management Journal*, 17, 25-39.

SHAO, J. (1996): Bootstrap model selection, *Journal of the American Statistical Association*, 88, 802-808.

SHAPIRO, C., and J. E. STIGLITZ (1984): Equilibrium unemployment as a worker discipline device, *American Economic Review*, 74, 433-444.

SHARPE, W. F. (1964): Capital Asset Prices: A Theory of Market Equilibrium under Conditions of Risk, *Journal of Finance*, 19, 425-442.

SHAVELL, S. (1979): Risk sharing and incentives in the principal and agent relationship, *Bell Journal of Economics*, 10, 55-73.

SHILLER, R. J. (1981): Do Stock Prices Move Too Much to be Justified by Subsequent Changes in Dividends?, *American Economic Review*, 71, 421-436.

— (1990): Speculative Prices and Popular Models, *Journal of Economic Perspectives*, 4, 55-65.

— (2003): From Efficient Markets Theory to Behavioral Finance, *Journal of Economic Perspectives*, 17, 83-104.

SHIN, H.-H., and R. M. STULZ (1998): Are Internal Capital Markets Efficient?, *Quarterly Journal of Economics*, 113, 531-552.

SHLEIFER, A., and R. W. VISHNY (1986): Large Shareholders and Corporate Control, *Journal of Political Economy*, 94, 461-488.

SHLEIFER, A., and R. VISHNY (1989): Management Entrenchment: The Case of Manager-Specific Investments, *Journal of Financial Economics*, 25, 123-139.

SHLEIFER, A., and L. H. SUMMERS (1990): The Noise Trader Approach to Finance, *Journal of Economic Perspectives*, 4, 19-33.

SHLEIFER, A., and R. VISHNY (1997): A survey of corporate governance, *Journal of Finance*, 52, 737-787.

SHLEIFER, A., and D. WOLFENZON (2002): Investor protection and equity markets, *Journal of Financial Economics*, 66, 3-28.

SHORT, H. (1994): Ownership, Control, Financial Structure and the Performance of Firms, *Journal of Economic Surveys*, 8, 203-249.

SHUMWAY, T. (1997): The delisting bias in CRSP data, *Journal of Finance*, 52, 327-340.

SINGH, M., and W. N. DAVIDSON III (2003): Agency costs, ownership structure and corporate governance mechanisms, *Journal of Banking and Finance*, 27, 793-816.

SINHA, P., L. D. BROWN, and S. DAS (1997): A Re-Examination of Financial Analysts' Differential Forecasting Accuracy, *Contemporary Accounting Research*, 14, 1-42.

SLOAN, R. (1993): Accounting Earnings and Top Executive Compensation, *Journal of Accounting and Economics*, 16, 55-100.

SLOVIN, M. B., M. E. SUSHKA, and S. B. FERRARO (1995): A comparison of the information conveyed by equity carve-outs, spin-offs and asset sell-offs, *Journal of Financial Economics*, 37, 89-104.

SMITH, A. J. (1990): Corporate ownership structure and performance - The case of management buyouts, *Journal of Financial Economics*, 27, 143-164.

SMITH JR, C. W., and J. B. WARNER (1979): On financial contracting: An analysis of bond covenants, *Journal of Financial Economics*, 7, 117-161.

SMITH JR, C. W., and R. M. STULZ (1985): The Determinants of Firms' Hedging Policies, *Journal of Financial and Quantitative Analysis*, 20, 391-405.

SMITH JR, C. W., and R. L. WATTS (1992): The Investment Opportunity Set and Corporate Financing, Dividends, and Compensation Policies, *Journal of Financial Economics*, 32, 263-292.

SPENCE, M., and R. ZECKHAUSER (1971): Insurance, Information and Individual Action, *American Economic Review*, 61, 380-387.

SPIESS, D. K., and J. AFFLECK-GRAVES (1995): Underperformance in long run stock returns following seasoned equity offerings, *Journal of Financial Economics*, 38, 243-267.

— (1999): The long-run performance of stock returns following debt offerings, *Journal of Financial Economics*, 54, 45-73.

SPREMANN, K. (1987): Agent and Principal, in *Agency Theory, Information, and Incentives*, ed. by Bamberg, and K. Spremann, 3-37.

STEHLE, R., and O. EHRHARDT (1999): Renditen bei Börseneinführung am deutschen Kapitalmarkt, *Zeitschrift für Betriebswirtschaft*, 69, 1395-1422.

STEHLE, R., O. EHRHARDT, and R. PRZYBOROWSKI (2000): Long-run stock performance of German initial public offerings and seasoned equity issues, *European Financial Management*, 6, 173-196.

STEIN, J. C. (1988): Takeover threats and managerial myopia, *Journal of Political Economy*, 96, 61-80.

— (1989): Efficient Capital Markets, Inefficient Firms: A Model of Myopic Corporate Behavior, *Quarterly Journal of Economics*, 104, 655-669.

— (1997): Internal Capital Markets and the Competition for Corporate Resources, *Journal of Finance*, 52, 111-134.

— (2002): Information Production and Capital Allocation: Decentralized vs. Hierarchical Firms, *Journal of Finance*, 57, 1891-1921.

— (2003): Agency, Information, and Corporate Investment, in *Handbook of the Economics of Finance*, ed. by G. Constantinides, M. Harris, and R. M. Stulz.

STEINITZER, E. (1908): *Ökonomische Theorie der Aktiengesellschaft*. Leipzig.

STICKEL, S. E. (1992): Reputation and Performance Among Security Analysts, *Journal of Finance*, 47, 1811-1836.

STIGLITZ, J. E. (1985): Credit Market and the Control of Capital, *Journal of Money, Credit, and Banking*, 17, 131-152.

— (2000): The contributions of the economics of information to twentieth century economics, *Quarterly Journal of Economics*, 115, 1441-1478.

STROBEL, W. (1999): Deutsches Rechnungslegungs Standards Committee: Der Standardentwurf E-DRS 3 zur Segmentberichterstattung, *Der Betrieb*, 52, Iss. 40, 2017-2020.

STROH, L. K., J. M. BRETT, J. P. BAUMANN, and A. H. REILLY (1996): Agency Theory and Variable Pay Compensation Strategies, *Academy of Management Journal*, 39, 751-767.

STRONG, N. (1992): Modelling Abnormal Returns: A Review Article, *Journal of Business Finance & Accounting*, 19, 544-553.

STULZ, R. M. (1988): Managerial Control of Voting Rights: Financing Policies and the Market for Corporate Control, *Journal of Financial Economics*, 20, 25-44.

— (1990): Managerial discretion and optimal financing policies, *Journal of Financial Economics*, 26, 3-27.

SUTTON, C. D. (1993): Computer-intensive methods for tests about the mean of an asymmetrical distribution, *Journal of the American Statistical Association*, 88, 802-808.

SWAMINATHAN, S. (1991): The impact of SEC mandated segment data on price variability and divergence of beliefs, *Accounting Review*, 0, 23-41.

TAUSSIG, F. W., and W. S. BARKER (1925): American corporations and their executives: a statistical inquiry, *Quarterly Journal of Economics*, 40, 1-51.

TEECE, D. (1980): Economies of scope and the scope of the enterprise, *Journal of Economic Behavior and Organization*, 1, 223-247.

— (1982): Towards an economic theory of the multiproduct firm, *Journal of Economic Behavior and Organization*, 3, 39-63.

TEETS, W., and R. PARKS (1992): *A Simulation Investigation of Seemingly Unrelated Regression as Used in Accounting Information Event Studies*. Working Paper, University of Illinois at Urbana-Champaign and Washington University.

TEOH, S. H., I. WELCH, and T. J. WONG (1998a): Earnings management and the underperformance of seasoned equity offerings, *Journal of Financial Economics*, 50, 63-99.

— (1998b): Earnings management and the long run market performance of initial public offerigs, *Journal of Finance*, 53, 1935-1974.

THEISEN, M. R. (2000): *Der Konzern: Betriebswirtschaftliche und rechtliche Grundlagen der Konzernunternehmung*. Stuttgart: Schaeffer-Pöschel.

THOMAS, S. (2002): Firm diversification and asymmetric information: Evidence from analysts' forecasts and earnings announcements, *Journal of Financial Economics*, 64, 373-396.

THOMPSON, J. E. (1988): More Methods that Make Little Difference in Event Studies, *Journal of Business Finance and Accounting*, 15, 77-86.

THOMPSON, R. (1985): Conditioning the Return-Generationg Process on Firm-Specific Event: A Discussion of Event Study Methods, *Journal of Financial and Quantitative Analysis*, 20, 151-168.

THOMPSON, R. (1996): Empirical Methods of Event Studies in Corporate Finance, in *Handbooks in Operations Research and Finance: Vol. 9 - Finance*, ed. by R. Jarrow: Elsevier, 963-992.

THONET, P. J., and O. H. POENSGEN (1979): Managerial Control and Economic Performance in Western Germany, *Journal of Industrial Economics*, 28, 23-37.

TIROLE, J. (1986): Hierarchies and Bureaucracies: On the Role of Collusion in Organizations, *Journal of Law, Economics and Organization*, 2, 181-215.

— (1995): *The Theory of Industrial Organization*. Cambridge: MIT Press.

TOSI JR, H. L., and L. R. GOMEZ-MEJIA (1989): The Decoupling of CEO Pay and Performance: An Agency Theory Perspective, *Administrative Science Quarterly*, 34, 169-189.

— (1994): CEO Compensation Monitoring and Firm Performance, *Academy of Management Journal*, 37, 1002-1016.

TOSI JR, H. L., J. P. KATZ, and L. R. GOMEZ-MEJIA (1997): Disaggregating the Agency Contract: The Effects of Monitoring, Incentive Alignment, and Term in Office on Agent Decision Making, *Academy of Management Journal*, 40, 584-602.

TOSI JR, H. L., S. WERNER, J. P. KATZ, and L. R. GOMEZ-MEJIA (2000): How Much Does Performance Matter? A Meta-Analysis of CEO Pay Studies, *Journal of Management*, 26, 301-339.

TRAPP, C., and W. SCHICK (2001): Die Rechtsstellung des Aktionärs der Obergesellschaft beim Börsengang von Tochtergesellschaften, *Die Aktiengesellschaft*, 46, 381-391.

VERMAELEN, T. (1984): Repurchase Tender Offers, Signaling, and Managerial Incentives, *Journal of Financial and Quantitative Analysis*, 19, 163-181.

VERRECCHIA, R. E. (1982): Information acquisition in a noisy rational expectations economy, *Econometrica*, 50, 1415-1430.

— (1983): Discretionay disclosure, *Journal of Accounting and Economics*, 5, 365-380.

— (1999): Disclosure and the cost of capital: A discussion, *Journal of Accounting and Economics*, 26, 271-284.

— (2001): Essays on disclosure, *Journal of Accounting and Economics*, 32, 97-180.

VIJH, A. M. (1999): Long-term returns from equity carveouts, *Journal of Financial Economics*, 51, 273-308.

— (2002): The Positive Announcement-Period Return of Equity Carveouts: Asymmetric Information or Divestiture Gains?, *Journal of Business*, 75, 153-190.

VILLALONGA, B. (2003): *Research Roundtable Discussion: The Diversification Discount.* Working Paper, Harvard Business School.

— (2004a): Does Diversification cause the "Diversification Discount"?, *Financial Management*, 33, 5-27.

— (2004b): Diversification Discount or Premium? New Evidence from Business Information Tracking Series Establishment-Level Data, *Journal of Finance*, 59, 475-502.

VINCENT, F., S. D. HARRIS, and P. BURNS (2003): When minority shareholders attack transfer prices, *International Tax Review*, 14, 34-36.

VOLK, G. (2000): Shareholder Value und die Börseneinführung von Tochtergesellschaften, in *Going Public - Der Gang an die Börse: Beratung, Erfahrung, Begleitung, Neuer Markt*, ed. by G. Volk. Stuttgart, 123-140.

WACKERBARTH, U. (2002): Aktionärsrechte beim Börsengang einer Tochter - obey the law, if not the spirit, *Die Aktiengesellschaft*, 47, 14-24.

WAGENHOFER, A. (1990): Voluntary Disclosure with a Strategic Opponent, *Journal of Accounting and Economics*, 12, 341-365.

WAGENHOFER, A., and R. EWERT (1993): Linearität und Optimalität in ökonomischen Agency-Modellen, *Zeitschrift für Betriebswirtschaft*, 63, 373-391.

WAGNER, H. (2004): *The Equity Carve-out Decision*. Working Paper, Said Business School, University of Oxford.

WALDMANN, R. J. (1984): Job assignments, signalling, and efficiency, *RAND Journal of Economics*, 15, 255-270.

WALSH, J. P., and J. K. SEWARD (1990): On the efficiency of internal and external corporate control mechanisms, *Academy of Management Review*, 15, 421-458.

WANG, P. (2003): *Financial Econometrics: Methods and Models*. London/New York: Routledge.

WARFIELD, T. D., J. J. WILD, and K. L. WILD (1995): Managerial Ownership, Accounting Choices and Informativeness of Earnings, *Journal of Accounting and Economics*, 20, 61-91.

WARNER, J. B. (1985): Stock market reaction to management incentive plan adoption: an overview, *Journal of Accounting and Economics*, 7, 145-149.

WASSSERFALLEN, W., and C. WITTLEDER (1994): Pricing Initial Public Offerings, *European Economic Review*, 38.

WATTS, R. L., and J. L. ZIMMERMAN (1978): Towards a positive theory of the determination of accounting standards, *Accounting Review*, 53, 112-134.

— (1990): Positive Accounting Theory: A Ten Year Perspective, *Accounting Review*, 65, 131-156.

WEINSTEIN, N. (1980): Unrealistic Optimism About Future Life Events, *Journal of Personality and Social Psychology*, 39, 806-820.

WEIR, C., D. LAING, and P. J. MCKNIGHT (2002): Internal and External Governance Mechanisms: Their Impact on the Performance of Large UK Public Companies, *Journal of Business Finance & Accounting*, 29, 579-611.

WELCH, I. (1992): Sequential sales, learning, and cascades, *Journal of Finance*, 47, 695-732.

WELKER, M. (1995): Disclosure Policy, Information Asymmetry, and Liquidity in Equity Markets, *Contemporary Accounting Research*, 11, 801-827.

WENGER, E., and L. KNOLL (1999): Aktienkursgebundene Management-Anreize: Erkenntnisse der Theorie und Defizite der Praxis, *Betriebswirtschaftliche Forschung und Praxis*, 6, 565-591.

WENGER, E., C. KASERER, and L. KNOLL (1999): Stock Options: Manageranreize zwischen Anspruch und Realität, in *Managementinstrumente und -konzepte*, ed. by A. Egger, O. Grün, and R. Moser. Stuttgart, 481-509.

WERNER, S., and H. L. TOSI (1995): Other People's Money: The Effects of Ownership on Compensation Strategy and Managerial Pay, *Academy of Management Journal*, 38, 1672-1691.

WERNERFELT, B. (1984): A Resource-based view of the firm, *Strategic Management Journal*, 5, 171-180.

WERNERFELT, B., and C. A. MONTGOMERY (1988): Tobin's q and the importance of focus in firm performance, *American Economic Review*, 78, 246-250.

WEST, K. D. (1988): Bubbles, Fads and Stock Price Volatility Tests: A Partial Evaluation, *Journal of Finance*, 43, 639-656.

WHITE, H. (1980): A Heteroskedasticity-Consistent Covariance Matrix Estimator and a Direct Test for Heteroskedasticity, *Econometrica*, 48.

WHITED, T. M. (2001): Is it Inefficient Investment that Causes the Diversification Discount?, *Journal of Finance*, 56, 1667-1691.

WILLIAMSON, O. E. (1975): *Markets and Hierarchies: Analysis and Antitrust Implications*. New York.

— (1985): Reflections on the New Institutional Economics, *Journal of Institutional and Theoretical Economics*, 141.

— (1988): Corporate finance and corporate governance, *Journal of Finance*, 43, 567-591.

— (1990): A Comparison of Alternative Approaches to Economic Organization, *Journal of Institutional and Theoretical Economics*, 146, 61-71.

— (1999): Strategy research: Governance and competence perspectives, *Strategic Management Journal*, 20, 1087-1108.

WÓJCIK, D. (2003): Change in the German model of corporate governance: evidence from blockholdings 1997-2001, *Environmental and Planning A*, 35, 1431-1458.

WOLFENZON, D. (1999): *A Theory of Pyramidal Ownership*. Working Paper, New York University Stern School of Business.

WOMACK, K. L. (1996): Do Brokerage Analysts' Recommendations Have Investment Value?, *Journal of Finance*, 51, 137-167.

WOO, C. Y., G. E. WILLARD, and U. S. DAELLENBACH (1992): Spin-off performance: a case of overstated expectations?, *Strategic Management Journal*, 13, 433-447.

WOOLDRIDGE, J. M. (2003): *Introductory Econometrics*. Mason: South-Western.

WULF, J. (2002): Internal Capital Markets and Firm-Level Compensation for Division Managers, *Journal of Labor Economics*, 20, 219-263.

YAU, J., M. G. FERRI, and T. F. SUGRUE (1994): An Analysis of the Wall Street Journal's Coverage of Corporate News and the Research Design of Event Studies, *Journal of Financial Research*, 27, 161-173.

YEH, Y.-H., C.-E. KO, and Y.-H. SU (2003): Ultimate Control and Expropriation of Minority Shareholders: New Evidence from Taiwan, *Academia Economic Papers*, 31, 263-299.

YERMACK, D. (1997): Good Timing: CEO Stock Option Awards and Company News Announcements, *Journal of Finance*, 52, 449-476.

YI, J.-H. (2001): Pre-Offering Earnings and the Long-Run Performance of IPOs, *International Review of Financial Analysis*, 10, 53-67.

YURTOGLU, B. B. (2003): Corporate Governance and Implications for Minority Shareholders in Turkey, *Corporate Ownership and Control*, 1, 72-86.

ZEILEIS, A. (2004): Alternative Boundaries for CUSUM Tests, *Statistical Papers*, 45, 123-132.

ZELLNER, A. (1962): An Efficient Method of Estimating Seemingly Unrelated Regressions and Tests for Aggregation Bias, *Journal of the American Statistical Association*, 5, 348-368.

ZIEGLER, A., E. EBERTS, M. SCHRÖDER, A. SCHULZ, and R. STEHLE (2003): *Multifaktormodelle zur Erklärung deutscher Aktienrenditen: Eine empirische Analyse*. Discussion Paper 03-45, ZEW Mannheim.

ZINGALES, L. (1994): The value of the voting right: A study of the Milan stock exchange, *Review of Financial Studies*, 7, 125-148.

— (1995a): Insider Ownership and the Decision to Go Public, *Review of Economic Studies*, 62, 425-448.

— (1995b): What determines the value of corporate votes?, *Quarterly Journal of Economics*, 110, 1075-1110.

— (2000): In Search of New Foundations, *Journal of Finance*, 55, 1623-1654.

ZUCKERMAN, E. W. (2000): Focusing the Corporate Product: Securities Analysts and De-diversification, *Administrative Science Quarterly*, 45, 591-619.

ZWIEBEL, J. (1995): Block Investment and Partial Benefits of Corporate Control, *Review of Economic Studies*, 62, 161-185.

— (1996): Dynamic Capital Structure under Management Entrechment, *American Economic Review*, 86, 1197-1215.